Simply Simpático

from the
Junior League of Albuquerque
New Mexico

Copyright © 1981
The Junior League of Albuquerque, Inc.
Albuquerque, New Mexico

First Printing May 1981 20,000 copies
Second Printing October 1982 20,000 copies
Third Printing August 1984 20,000 copies
Fourth Printing March 1987 20,000 copies

ISBN 0-9609278-0-8
Library of Congress Catalog Card Number: 80-51756

To order additional copies of SIMPLY SIMPÁTICO,
send check for $12.00 (includes postage and handling) to

SIMPLY SIMPÁTICO
2920 Yale Boulevard SE
Albuquerque, New Mexico 87106

For your convenience, order blanks are included in the back of the book.

The purpose of the Junior League is exclusively educational and charitable and is to promote voluntarism; to develop the potential of its members for voluntary participation in community affairs; and to demonstrate the effectiveness of trained volunteers.

The proceeds realized from the sale of SIMPLY SIMPÁTICO will be returned to the community through the projects of the Junior League of Albuquerque, Inc.

ACKNOWLEDGEMENTS

The Junior League of Albuquerque wishes to thank its families and friends, whose names are too numerous to list, for their contributions and support during the creation of Simply Simpático.

The Cookbook Committees wish to thank all of the Junior League of Albuquerque Actives and Sustainers for submitting, soliciting and testing recipes and for proofing and promoting Simply Simpático.

Printed by Hart Graphics
Austin, Texas

TABLE OF CONTENTS

COOKBOOK COMMITTEE

PHASE I

Chairman	Susan McCreary
Assistant Chairman	Charlotte Kanter
Editor	Lynn Villella

Recipe Chairmen	Jane Armayor
	Nancy Ruggles
Native Dishes	Lynn Villella
Appetizers	Charlene Knipfing
Beverages	Julie Binford
	Susan McCreary
Soups	Barbara David
Sandwiches	Carolyn Sedberry
Breads	Julie Binford
Salads and Salad Dressings	Nancy Ruggles
Accompaniments	Carolyn Sedberry
	Kate Moody
Eggs and Cheese	Kathi Tate
Vegetables	Charlotte Kanter
Fish and Shellfish	Susan McCreary
Meats	Judy Harris
	Ginny Gibbs
Poultry and Game	Jane Armayor
Cakes	Connie Johnson
Pies, Cookies and Candies	Patti Kuswa
Desserts	Stephanie Tartaglia

Publisher Liaison	Lyn Rodeman
Marketing	Patti Kuswa
Secretary	Patti Kuswa
Sustainer Advisor	Julie Binford
Executive Liaison	Harlene Geer

Typists	Jane Dick
	Harlene Geer
	Nancy Ruggles

4

INTRODUCTION

Embossed into every license plate issued in the state of New Mexico is a proud slogan: "Land of Enchantment." It is a motto that succinctly captures the mystery and the mystique of this vast land of space and sun.

In its totality New Mexico wears the vestments of a long and colorful history. It is a land of astonishing contrasts and contradictions, of bone-white desert dunes and snow-white mountain summits, of picturesque villages and sunlit plains, of quiet riverbanks and of small arroyos that widen into the hypnotically beautiful canyons that encompass all known eras of geologic time.

It also is a land of serenity, orderly progress and quiet achievement. Here the silent ruins of ancient dwellings stand beside solar-powered homes; the oldest towns in the nation now include the most starkly modern subdivisions; native artists exhibit the most abstract canvases near locations of prehistoric rock etchings.

New Mexico is vibrant with the artistic expression of four centuries and four cultures — Indian, Spanish, Mexican and Anglo — blended into a harmonious whole. It is a citadel of tradition where these cultures guard their individual histories and creative minds and hands preserve and perpetuate them in ceremonies, handicrafts, methods of worship and cuisine.

Simply Simpático is dedicated to New Mexico's heritage and to the congenial style of living that has emerged from its unique cultural matrix. It spotlights the aspects of "enchantment" that continue to enthrall natives and newcomers alike. And, of course, it focuses on the cornucopia of foods which so vividly reflect the lifestyles and culinary habits of modern-day New Mexicans — foods that have roots in New Mexico's past but which still are a contemporary expression of today's gracious, casual, simpático living.

Recipes in *Simply Simpático* were gathered over a two-year period from members and friends of the Junior League of Albuquerque and also from outstanding hostesses and chefs from all parts of the state who generously shared with us treasured family recipes and the best of their personal collections.

An important feature of our book is the introductory chapter which we call "Comida Simpática." Here our focus is on tradition and on the native vegetables and spices which, through the centuries, have formed the basis of New Mexican cooking.

And it is a distinctive aspect of *Simply Simpático* that while time-honored native dishes are presented in pure and authentic form, there also are scores of elegant dishes which reflect innovative and intriguing variations on traditional themes and put to use most effectively our robust native ingredients. Throughout the book modern-day adaptations of native dishes are designated by a special symbol: 🦅

We have stressed authentic tastes — be they traditional or entirely updated — throughout our book in the hope of fostering the increasingly widespread appeal of New Mexican foods and Southwestern cuisine.

The Junior League of Albuquerque hopes that each page of *Simply Simpático* will be an invitation to pause and to experience the varied delights of true "New Mexican enchantment."

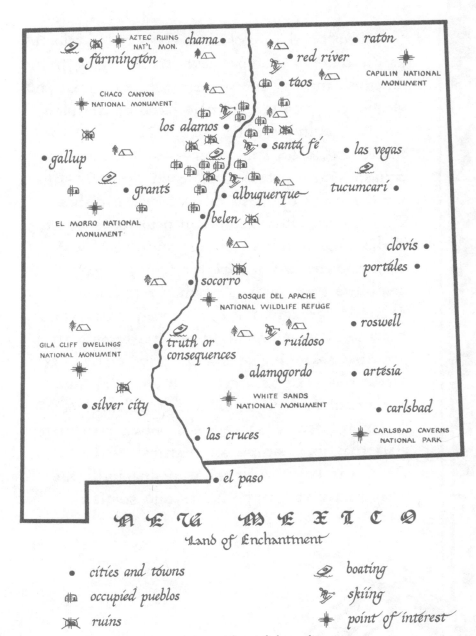

NEW MEXICO
Land of Enchantment

- cities and towns
- occupied pueblos
- ruins
- mountains, camping, fishing, hiking, hunting
- boating
- skiing
- point of interest

The Making of a Cuisine.....

New Mexican cooking is every bit as colorful as the country that produces it. Emerging from an ethnic mix of Indian, Spanish, Mexican and Anglo, the food is a splendid blend of complementary cultures. The early Indians used the native vegetables and spices -- vanilla, cinnamon, squash, beans, potatoes and corn -- which still are the basis of native New Mexican dishes. The Spanish introduced many new foods -- rice, garlic, onions, wheat, citrus fruits, beef and pork and the use of lard for frying -- and combined them with what they found here. They also brought the chili pepper, that versatile and piquant product which has become the principal seasoning of many native dishes. It serves the locals as vegetable, herb, spice and condiment as well as a lavishly colorful decoration for serene adobe walls. Given raw materials that were simple and natural, New Mexicans have developed a cuisine with an imaginative range of flavors and scents ·

Comida Simpática

PIÑATA

Comida Simpática

The unique flavor and distinctive character of New Mexican cookery are the result of a blending of four cultures — Indian, Spanish, Mexican and Anglo. Each culture has made its own imprint on the state's culinary heritage.

To cook and to eat native New Mexican food is to celebrate the centuries through which local cooks took materials that were simple and natural and developed a cuisine that is unlike any other.

But when we speak of New Mexican cuisine we are speaking of more than just the food. Dining well, New Mexico-style implies bright colors, a fiesta atmosphere, distinctive aromas, a casualness that can best be described as "comida simpática."

This special section of *Simply Simpático* is designed to introduce the novice cook and the newcomer to the basics of New Mexican cookery. In the pages that follow, readers will discover many of the "building blocks" upon which our culinary heritage is based. In simple, step-by-step fashion, the roots of our regional cuisine are presented along with a treasury of authentic traditional recipes.

Seasoned cooks will welcome this collection of traditional "old family favorite" recipes and use this introductory chapter to help enhance further exploration of *Simply Simpático* and its scores of updated innovations on time-honored themes.

Panza lleno — corazon contento!

New Mexican Menus

(See Index for Recipes)

HOLIDAY BUFFET
Sangria
Albondigas (use appetizer variation)
Posole
Red Chili Sauce
Tamales
Pastelitos
Empanaditas
Bizcochitos
Cafe' Mexicano

FIESTA PARTY
Margaritas or Mexican Beer
Chili con Queso
Harlequin Dip
Tostados
Guacamole
Tacos (Chicken and
   Beef Filling)
Assorted Toppings
Frijoles Refritos
Pastelitos

COMPANY COMBINATION PLATE
Chilies Rellenos
Enchiladas
Tacos
Pinto Beans
Spanish Rice
Sopaipillas or Flour Tortillas
Natillas or Capirotada

Glossary

Albondigas (al-bon´-de-gahs) Meat balls of various sizes served as appetizers and in stews and soups.

Arroz con pollo (ar-ros´ cone po'yo) Classic chicken and rice dish.

Bizcochitos (biz-co-chee'tos) Anise seed cookies.

Burritos (boor-ree´-tos) Rolled white flour tortillas, filled with pinto beans and/or meat mixture and topped with a chili sauce.

Calabacitas (cah-lah-bah-see´-tahs) Summer squash. It is usually combined with corn and green chili.

Calabaza (Cah-lah-bah'sah) Baked pumpkin.

Caldillo - (cal-dee'yo) Stew made of meat, onions, potatoes and green chili.

Capirotada (cah-pe-ro-tah'dah) See sopa.

Carne Adovada (car´-nay ah-do-bah'dah) Strips of pork marinated in red chili sauce.

Chalupas (chah-loo'pahs) Tostadas shaped into little cups and filled with pinto beans, chicken, lettuce, tomatoes, etc.

Chili con queso (chee´-lay cone kay´-so) Dip made of melted cheese and green chili served with tostados.

Chili (green) (chee'lay) Harvested from late July until October; roasted and peeled. It is used for sauces, relishes and dips.

Chili (red) (chee´-lay) Harvested before the first frost, in early fall, dried for later use and crushed into powder. Green chili ripens into red pods.

Chili rellenos (chee´-lay ray-yen'nos) Peeled and whole green chili stuffed with cheese, dipped in an egg batter and deep fried.

Cilantro (ci-lahn´-tro) Fresh coriander. It is commonly used as a flavoring and garnish. You can grow your own. Buy the seeds (coriander) from the spice department and plant during warm weather. It can be found in supermarkets and sometimes is called Chinese parsley.

Comino (co-mee´-no) Cumin.

Empanadas (em-pah-nah´-dahs) Turnovers stuffed with meat, chicken or fruits. They can be served as an appetizer, dessert or entree.

Enchiladas (en-chee-lah´-dahs) White or blue corn meal tortillas that are stacked or rolled and made with any combination of meat, cheese, onion, tomato, lettuce, sour cream and chili sauce.

Ensalada (en-sah-lah´-dah) Salad.

Flan (flahn) Light custard served in carmelized cups.

Guacamole (goo-ah-cah-mo´-lay) Dip of mashed avocados and seasonings served with tostados. This can be used as a salad on lettuce or as a garnish on enchiladas, tacos, etc.

Huevos (oo-ay´-vos) Eggs.

Huevos rancheros (oo-ay'-vos ran-chay-ros) Fried or poached eggs usually served on warm tortillas with chili sauce and various garnishes.

Indian Fry Bread - A deep-fried puffed bread often served with honey.

Jalapenos (hah-lah'-pay'-nyos) Small, green hot peppers excellent pickled or in sauces.

Jicama (hee'-cah'mah) A crisp, sweet, white root vegetable shaped somewhat like a turnip and covered with a brown skin. They are often eaten raw in salads with a flavor between that of a crisp apple and Chinese water chestnuts.

Masa (mah'-sah) Corn-based dough used to make tortillas and tamales.

Masa harina (mah'-sah ah-ree'-nah) Commercial mix of corn treated with lime water and specially ground corn flour used to make tortillas.

Masa trigo (mah'-sah tree'-go) Commercial mix composed of blended flour, shortening, salt and leavening used for tortillas and tamales.

Nachos (nah'-chos) Corn chips topped with cheese and jalapeno strips, broiled and served as an appetizer.

Natillas (nah-tee'-yas) Boiled egg custard pudding.

Posole (po-so'-lay) Stew made with hominy and pork and traditionally served at Christmas.

Quelites (kay-lee'-tays) Spinach with pinto beans and dried red chile.

Refried beans - Cooked pinto beans which are mashed and refried in oil.

Ristra (rees'trah) A string of red chilies tied together for drying purposes. They are often seen hanging on front porches as decorations.

Salsa (sahl'-sah) Chili sauce, green or red.

Sopa - (so'-pah) Bread pudding with raisins, cinnamon and cheese. Also referred to as Capirotada.

Sopaipillas (so-pah'-ee-pee-yahs) Puffy, deep fried bread traditionally served with honey.

Tacos (tah'-cos) Fried crisp tortillas which are folded and stuffed with meat, chicken or pinto beans, lettuce, tomato, onion, etc., and topped with a taco or chili sauce.

Tamales (tah-mah'-lays) A mixture of pork and red chile enclosed in masa, wrapped in cornhusks and steamed.

Tortillas (tor-tee'-yahs) A flat bread made of corn flour or white flour. The tortilla is the basis of many New Mexican recipes.

Tostadas (tos-tah'-dahs) Crisp tortillas served open-faced with any combination of meat, chicken, pinto beans, lettuce, tomato, onion, sour cream, etc.

Tostados (tos-tah'-dos) Crisp tortillas cut into wedges and used for dips.

BASIC PREPARATIONS

CHILI

The most basic ingredient in New Mexican cuisine is chili. Fresh, dried, canned, frozen, mild or hot, chili appears in a multitude of dishes. Red or green chili can be a dish in itself. Fresh chili yields the most memorable flavor but if you are in a region where it is unobtainable you will have to use whatever form is available.

GREEN CHILI

Green chili is easy to prepare . . . when you know how. Rinse and dry fresh green chilies. Pierce with a fork to prevent popping. Place on a cookie sheet and broil 4 to 6 inches below heated broiler unit. (An outdoor barbeque may also be used and is probably faster.) Roast the chilies (turning often) until they are blistered on all sides. Remove from oven and cover with a damp cloth for 10 to 15 minutes. Chilies may then be frozen unpeeled. To use in a recipe, thaw and prepare as follows: remove the skins by starting at stem end pulling downward. Then remove the stems and most of the seeds. At this point they are ready to use in a recipe. For use as a side dish or garnish, chop and add salt, garlic and chopped onion to taste.

GREEN CHILI SAUCE

2   **tablespoons oil or lard**
1   **clove garlic (optional)**
½   **cup minced onion (optional)**
1   **tablespoon flour**
1   **cup water**
1   **cup diced green chili**
     Salt to taste

In oil in a heavy saucepan, saute' garlic and onion. Blend in flour with wooden spoon. Add water and green chili. Bring to a boil and simmer, stirring frequently, for 5 minutes.

This sauce may be used as a topping for eggs, served with beans or meat, in tacos or made into green enchiladas. Refer to recipes calling for green chili.

RED CHILI SAUCE

16-18 dried red chili pods
Hot water
2 cloves garlic
Salt to taste

Open each dried red chili pod. Wash well inside and out and remove blemishes. Remove stems, some seeds and veins from 16-18 pods. For hotter chili leave some veins. Rinse with cold water and soak in hot water for one hour or until soft. Place the pods in an electric blender and add enough water to almost cover them, leaving about two inches headspace. Blend until smooth and skins disappear, about 2-3 minutes. If sauce seems to be too thick, add more water and blend for another 1 minute or until skins disappear. Add 2 cloves garlic and process until well blended. Salt to taste.

Serve with hamburgers, enchiladas, tamales, eggs or any dish that calls for zesty red chili.

SALSA

Salsa is a combination of ingredients using chili as a base. Salsa is basic to many recipes. It may be made from green or red chili, fresh, canned, frozen or dried. Purists won't add tomatoes to chili but doing so makes a superb cold salsa which is commonly used on eggs, beans, in tacos or on top of hamburgers. It can be stored in the refrigerator for up to a week and used with breakfast, lunch, dinner or as a dip in between meals. When making a salsa, remember that the flavor improves with age so make it a day ahead of time or at least several hours before it is needed.

SALSA SUPREME   1 pint

1 large tomato, chopped
1 medium onion, chopped
2 fresh green chilies, chopped (or 1 4-ounce can)
½ teaspoon garlic salt
½ teaspoon monosodium glutamate (optional)
Salt to taste

Combine all ingredients and chill, covered, in refrigerator at least one hour.

A New Mexico-style accompaniment for eggs, grilled steaks, hamburgers or guacamole dip!

MEXICAN SALSA

1 cup

1 **8-ounce can tomato sauce**
2 **tablespoons crushed red chili**
½ **teaspoon cumin powder**
½ **teaspoon oregano**
1 **teaspoon salt**
2 **garlic cloves, minced (or ¼ teaspoon garlic powder)**
2 **teaspoons vinegar**
   Juice of half a lemon

Combine all ingredients and mix well. Let stand for 3 hours. Excellent with tacos or as a dip for tortilla chips.

FIESTA RELISH

8 servings

2 **medium tomatoes, diced**
2 **medium avocados, diced**
1 **4-ounce can chopped green chilies, drained**
¼ **cup lemon juice**
1 **tablespoon salad oil**
1 **teaspoon sugar**
¾ **teaspoon salt**

Combine all ingredients; toss gently to coat well. Cover and refrigerate several hours to blend flavors, stirring occasionally.

This relish provides zesty accompaniment to almost any Southwestern menu. Don't forget to try it with pinto beans or with beef burritos.

TORTILLAS

The tortilla is as basic to New Mexico cooking as the chili itself. The tortilla is the bread of New Mexico, eaten alone or in a variety of fashions, as an accompaniment or as one of the ingredients in a main dish. The tortilla can be either flour or corn. Flour tortillas can be purchased in packages but the flavor cannot compare to those freshly grilled. The packaged ready-made corn tortillas are inexpensive, readily available and are quite good. In recipes calling for corn tortillas use the ready made variety or follow directions on instant masa mix.

FLOUR TORTILLAS   12 tortillas

4   cups all purpose flour
1½   teaspoons salt
1½   teaspoons baking powder
4   tablespoons lard or shortening
1½   cups warm water

Combine dry ingredients in a mixing bowl. Cut in shortening. Make a well in the center and add water, a small amount at a time, to form a dough. Knead dough in bowl until it is smooth and feels elastic. Cover and set aside for ten minutes. Form dough into egg-sized balls and flatten between palms. With rolling pin, roll each ball into a 6 inch circle, about 1/8" thick. Cook on preheated ungreased skillet over medium high heat, approximately two minutes on each side, until tortilla looks slightly speckled. Cover with a clean towel to keep warm and soft until served. The tortillas may be cooled and stored in plastic bags in the freezer for later use.

TOSTADOS

Tortilla chips, which are a basic snack favorite, can easily be made from packaged tortillas. Simply cut each tortilla into eight wedges, leaving them attached at the center. Fry the tortilla until crisp. As you remove from the frying pan drain on paper towels and poke the center with your finger. The "chips" will then come apart in 8 even triangles.

TOSTADAS MUY SIMPÁTICAS   6 servings

2   avocados, mashed
1   tablespoon lime juice
1   tablespoon thinly sliced green onion
¼   cup sour cream
¼   cup mild bottled taco sauce
½   teaspoon salt
1   teaspoon cooking oil
1   16-ounce can refried beans
1   cup shredded Cheddar cheese
6   packaged tostada shells
3   cups shredded lettuce
1   cup chopped tomato
6   slices avocado for garnish

Combine avocado, lime juice, onion, sour cream, taco sauce and salt; chill. Heat refried beans in oil; stir in cheese until melted. On heated tostada shells spread beans, then lettuce and tomatoes. Spoon avocado dressing over each. Top with avocado slices.

INDIAN FRY BREAD

2 cups flour
⅓ cup powdered milk
2 teaspoons baking powder
1 teaspoon salt
2 tablespoons lard
¾ cup warm water
Oil

Mix dry ingredients. Cut in 1 tablespoon lard until crumbly. Add water and mix until a soft dough forms. Knead until dough is smooth and springy in texture. Make into 12 balls. Melt 1 tablespoon lard and brush on each ball of dough. Set aside for 30-45 minutes. On a lightly floured surface roll ball to a 4" circle. Then stretch to 7-8" in diameter. Poke hole in center. Fry in oil at 365° until lightly browned, turning once. Serve with butter or honey.

This bread, familiar to New Mexican travelers, has become popular in recent years. It is a big attraction at the New Mexico State Fair when the state's Indian tribes come in to prepare this delightful treat. It can replace rolls at dinner or can be served as a snack with butter or honey.

SOPAIPILLAS

4 cups flour
1 tablespoon baking powder
2 teaspoons sugar
1½ teaspoons salt
¼ cup lard
1¼ cups water or more, if needed
Honey

Sift dry ingredients together. Cut in lard until crumbly. Add water and mix until holds together. Knead 10-15 times until dough forms a smooth ball. Cover and let set for 20 minutes. Divide dough into two parts. Roll dough to 1/8" thickness on lightly floured board. Cut into 3" squares or triangles. Do not allow to dry; cover those waiting to be fried. When ready to fry, turn upside down so that surface on bottom while resting is on top when frying. Fry in 3" hot oil until golden brown, turning once. Add only a few at a time to maintain proper temperature. Drain on paper towels and serve immediately with honey.

COMIDA SIMPÁTICA

SOPAIPILLAS

1   **package active dry yeast**
¼   **cup warm water (110°)**
1½   **cups milk**
3   **tablespoons lard or shortening**
1½   **teaspoons salt**
2   **tablespoons sugar**
    About 4 cups all-purpose unsifted flour
1   **cup whole wheat flour**
    Salad oil

In a large mixing bowl, dissolve yeast in warm water. In another bowl combine milk, lard, salt and sugar. Heat to 110° and add to dissolved yeast. Beat in 3 cups of the all-purpose flour and all of the whole wheat flour. Add about ½ cup all-purpose flour and mix until a stiff sticky dough forms. Place dough on a floured board and knead, adding more flour as needed, until dough is smooth and non-sticky. Place dough in a greased bowl turning over to grease top. Cover and let stand at room temperature 1 hour. Punch dough down. The dough may be covered and chilled as long as overnight. Knead dough on a lightly floured board to expel air. Roll dough out, a portion at a time, to slightly less than 1/8″ thick. Cut in 2″ x 5″ rectangles or 3″ squares for appetizers. Place on lightly floured pans and lightly cover. If you work quickly you can let cut sopaipillas stay at room temperature up to 5 minutes; otherwise, refrigerate them until all are ready to fry. In a deep wide frying pan or kettle heat 1½-2 inches salad oil to 350° on a deep-fat frying thermometer. Fry 2 or 3 sopaipillas at a time. When the bread begins to puff, gently push the bread into the hot oil several times to help it puff more evenly. Turn several times and cook just until pale gold on both sides, 1-2 minutes total. Drain on paper towels. Serve immediately or place in a warm oven until all are fried. Or if made ahead, cool, cover and chill or freeze. To reheat, bake uncovered in a 300° oven, turning once, just until warm, 5-8 minutes. Do not overheat or they will become hard. Makes 2 dozen large sopaipillas or about 4 dozen small ones.

This is a New Mexican specialty and a southwest favorite. These pillows of golden fried bread are a must with New Mexican meals and while the recipe looks complicated, it is deceptively easy if you follow the step-by-step directions. Sopaipillas can be eaten as an accompaniment to a meal, usually served with honey, or as a main dish stuffed with meat or other fillings.

TACOS

Ready-made taco shells are available in some markets but they are easy enough to prepare starting with either homemade or store-bought tortillas. You can buy devices to hold tortillas in shape while being fried and racks to hold them while being stuffed but they are not necessary. For a different flavor, blue corn tortillas may be used. They too are available in some markets.

To make taco shells, heat ½" of lard or vegetable oil in a large skillet to 365°. Dip a flat corn tortilla in the hot lard or oil on both sides to soften it. Holding it with tongs fold the softened tortilla in half and fry to desired crispness. Some people prefer very crisp shells while others like a softer shell. Make certain that when you fold in half that they are not folded flat because the shell will crack when you open it a little to fill it. Drain taco shells on paper towels.

To fill a taco shell, gently pull it open without breaking it. Spoon in beef, pork, chicken, turkey, cheese or pinto beans. Imagination, likes or dislikes dictate what else goes in a taco. Some of the usual condiments include chopped lettuce, tomato, onion, grated cheese, guacamole and sour cream. Mini tacos make excellent appetizers as do many of the other main dishes within this book which can be adapted to fit the occasion. Keep filled tacos in the oven until serving time. At serving time individuals add to their tacos some of the condiments mentioned above. Arrange the garnishes in separate bowls or in a sectioned platter.

BEEF TACOS

6 servings

1	pound ground beef
1	chopped onion
	Salt to taste
1	clove minced garlic (optional)
12	taco shells
	Grated Cheddar cheese
1	cup green chili or taco sauce

Saute' the beef and onion until brown. Salt to taste. Add garlic if desired. Place a heaping tablespoon of meat mixture in each shell and stuff with lettuce, tomato and cheese. Serve with the chili or taco sauce and top with sour cream or guacamole for an added treat.

COMIDA SIMPÁTICA

CHICKEN TACOS

6 servings

¼ cup green onion, chopped
1 tablespoon shortening
2 cups cooked chicken, shredded
1 8-ounce can taco sauce or green chili salsa (Refer to index for recipe)
  Salt to taste
12 taco shells
1 cup grated Cheddar cheese
  Chopped lettuce
  Chopped tomato
  Sour cream
  Guacamole

Saute' the onion in the shortening until transparent. Add the chicken, green chili salsa or taco sauce and salt to taste. Heat to boiling. Prepare shells according to package directions. Put two tablespoons of the chicken mixture and one tablespoon of grated cheese in each shell. Serve with option of lettuce, tomato, sour cream or guacamole and extra chili sauce as desired.

ENCHILADAS (Red Chili)

6 servings

18 corn tortillas
1 quart red chili (See Index)
1 pound Cheddar cheese, grated
1 large onion, chopped
  Fried eggs (optional)

Fry corn tortillas in deep fat to soften. Immerse in chili sauce and place on a warm oven-proof plate. Spinkle with grated cheese and chopped onion. Cover with red chili sauce and place another tortilla on top. Repeat the process then pour enough chili sauce over them to cover tortillas. Three tortillas make one serving. A fried egg is traditional on top of each enchilada.

ENCHILADA VERDES (Green Enchiladas)

4 servings

12 blue corn tortillas (if not available, regular corn tortillas may be used)
4 tablespoons oil or lard
1 clove garlic
1 tablespoon flour
4 cups green chili sauce (See Index)
  Salt to taste
2 cups grated Cheddar or Monterey Jack cheese
¼ cup minced onion

Fry tortillas in deep fat to soften. Heat garlic in oil then discard garlic. Blend flour into oil. Stir in green chili sauce and heat thoroughly. If mixture is too thick, add water. Add salt to taste. Layer tortillas with sauce, minced onion and cheese on ovenproof plates. Sprinkle cheese on top. Use 3 tortillas for each serving. Place in oven to allow cheese to melt.

For a real New Mexican touch place a poached or fried egg on top. The egg seems to help "meld" all the flavors.

GREEN CHILIES RELLENOS (Stuffed Green Chili)

5 servings

10 green chilies, roasted and peeled (canned) chili may be used)
10 ounces Longhorn cheese or Monterey Jack cheese
Batter
Hot oil or lard

BATTER:

1 cup all-purpose flour
1 teaspoon baking powder
½ teaspoon salt
¾ cup cornmeal
1 cup milk
2 eggs, slightly beaten

Cut cheese into slices ½" thick and the length of the chili. Make a small slit in chili just big enough to insert cheese. Dip in batter and fry in hot oil or lard until golden brown. Drain and serve. May be garnished with green chili sauce if desired. To make batter, combine flour, baking powder, salt and cornmeal. Blend milk with egg; then combine milk and egg mixture with the dry ingredients. Add more milk if necessary for smooth batter. Using a spoon, dip stuffed chilies in batter.

SWEET CHILIES RELLENOS

20 croquettes

3 pounds cubed beef or ground beef
1 cup raisins
¾ cup sugar
2 teaspoons cinnamon
⅛ teaspoon black pepper
¼ teaspoon ground cloves
2 cups chopped green chili
1 cup nuts, chopped (pecans or pinon)
1 egg, beaten
¾ cup flour
3 eggs, separated
1 teaspoon flour
⅛ teaspoon salt

SYRUP:

1 cup sugar
½ cup brown sugar
½ cup water
¼ teaspoon cinnamon

Cover meat with water and simmer until tender, about 1 hour. Drain meat and shred by hand or grind coarsely. (If ground beef is used, brown and add 1 tablespoon flour to thicken). Combine beef with raisins, sugar, spices, chili, nuts and 1 beaten egg. Form into 2" oval croquettes; roll each croquette in the ¾ cup flour until lightly coated. Beat egg whites until stiff; fold in yolks beaten with 1 teaspoon flour and the 1/8 teaspoon salt. Dip each floured croquette into egg batter. Fry croquettes, one or two at a time, in 2 inches of hot (420°) oil until golden brown. Drain on paper towels and serve warm with the syrup poured on top. To make the syrup, caramelize white sugar in pan. Add brown sugar and water. Simmer. Add cinnamon.

TAMALES

MEAT FILLING:

8   pounds lean beef or pork, cubed
2   garlic cloves
3   garlic cloves, minced
6   tablespoons lard
6   tablespoons flour
4   cups red chili sauce (See Index)
4   cups reserved broth
    Salt

MASA:

2   pounds corn husks
1½ pounds lard
5   pounds masa harina or fresh masa
2   cups reserved red chili sauce
    Beef broth

Simmer beef or pork in a large pot with water to cover. Add 2 garlic cloves for flavor. When meat is tender, remove and shred, reserving all of the broth. Meat may be prepared the day before and refrigerated overnight. This is desirable since it is easier to spread when it is cool. Fry minced garlic in 6 tablespoons lard. Add flour and brown slightly. Add 6 cups red chili sauce and approximately 4 cups of the reserved broth; simmer for 10 minutes. Remove 2 cups and set aside. Add the shredded meat to the simmering chili sauce and simmer 20 minutes. Add salt to taste; cool. Soak separated corn husks in water at least 20 minutes. When ready to be used, open each husk, rinse and clean thoroughly; drain on newspaper. While meat is simmering, place lard in large electric mixer bowl and cream for approximately 20 minutes. Fresh masa can be purchased in several southwestern locales. If this is not available packaged masa harina can be found in most grocery stores. Combine masa harina or masa with creamed lard and 2 cups reserved red chili sauce. Mixing constantly with hands, gradually add beef broth until it is good spreading consistency. Add salt to taste. Using clean husks, spread a layer of masa over the bottom half of the husk just thick enough that you can't see through it — about 2 tablespoons. Top this with 1 generous tablespoon of meat mixture. Fold the sides of the husks toward the center, one side at a time. Fold the bottom of the husks up and the top down, tying if desired. Place on cookie sheet. When sheet is full of one layer of tamales place in freezer for 20-30 minutes or until slightly firm. Then place by the dozen in freezer bags or aluminum foil and freeze for future use. Continue with process until all ingredients are used up. If using tamales the same day they are made do not freeze. Place standing up in steamer or on tray in a large pot. Place small amount of water in bottom of pot. Cover tightly and steam until masa is firm — usually about an hour. Time may vary at different altitudes. Check water often to prevent burning. If desired, heated red chili sauce may be served on the side for those who wish to top their tamales with some added color, moisture and zest.

CARNE ADOVADA (Marinated Pork)   6 servings

4	pounds pork (spare-ribs, shoulder chops or other)
2	teaspoons salt
3	garlic cloves, crushed
2-3	teaspoons whole leaf oregano
1	quart blended red chili (See Index)

Sprinkle meat with salt. Add garlic and oregano to blended chili. Pour over meat and marinate in refrigerator 6-8 hours or overnight. Cook slowly on top of stove or in 350° oven until meat is done, about 1 hour. Thick slices of potatoes may be marinated with the meat.

ALBÓNDIGAS (Meatballs)   8 servings

MEATBALLS:

1½	pounds ground beef
6	tablespoons corn meal or 1 cup bread crumbs
2	eggs, beaten
2	cloves garlic, crushed
2	teaspoons ground coriander seed
2	teaspoons salt
1	teaspoon pepper
½	onion, chopped fine

Combine meatball ingredients and mix well. Shape into balls of desired size. Melt fat and brown flour in it. Add water and seasonings. When it starts boiling, drop the meatballs and potatoes into it and cook until meat is cooked and potatoes are tender, about 30 minutes.

SOUP:

4	tablespoons fat
2	tablespoons flour
4	cups hot water
2	tablespoons fresh coriander (cilantro)
	Salt to taste
4	potatoes, cubed

BURRITOS

2 cups pinto beans (See Index)
Dash salt
1 clove garlic, minced
1 teaspoon bacon drippings
6 white flour tortillas (See Index)
2 green onions finely chopped
½ cup grated Monterey Jack or Cheddar cheese
Coarsely chopped Romaine lettuce
Red or Green Chili Sauce (See Index)

Mash the beans, season to taste with salt and garlic and refry in drippings. Cover tortillas with aluminum foil and keep warm in a 250° oven. Spoon the hot bean mixture down the center of each warm tortilla. Top with chopped green onions and cheese. Roll and heat in 350° oven until the cheese melts, about 15 minutes. Nestle chopped lettuce around the warm burritos. Serve with a generous portion of red or green chili sauce.

Burritos are usually served with pinto bean filling but beef, pork or chicken can be used. They are folded into neat packages, baked and served with a favorite sauce such as chili, tomato, taco or enchilada. Imagination is a basic ingredient.

CHALUPAS

Vegetable oil
6 large corn tortillas
1 cup refried beans
Salsa (See Index)
1 pound ground beef, browned
1 clove garlic, minced
½ cup minced onion
1 cup grated Cheddar cheese
1½ cups shredded lettuce
1 medium tomato
1½ cups guacamole (See Index)
½ cup sour cream
Ripe olives

Fry tortillas one at a time in hot oil. Hold down center of tortilla with wooden spoon so that the tortilla becomes cup-shaped. Drain on paper towels. Mix beans with salsa to taste. Spread each tortilla with bean mixture. Top with browned ground beef. Sprinkle with onions and cover with grated cheese. Place in 375° oven for about 10 minutes. (Use a cookie sheet or oven-proof plates.) To serve, top each tortilla with lettuce and tomatoes. Spoon guacamole on top. Decorate with a spoonful of sour cream and ripe olive slices. Serve immediately.

Try shredded chicken in place of the ground beef for an interesting change.

ARROZ CON POLLO

4 servings

1½ cups rice
4 tablespoons shortening
1 large frying chicken, cut in pieces
2 teaspoons salt
1 large garlic clove
1 cup canned whole tomatoes
½ cup onion, sliced
1 teaspoon ground black pepper
1 teaspoon ground cumin seed
2-3 cups warm water

Brown rice in shortening. In separate frying pan, brown pieces of chicken that have been sprinkled with salt. Add chicken to rice. Crush garlic, adding a little water to it, and pour over the mixture. Add the tomatoes, onion, ground spices, 2 cups of warm water, and salt. Cover and simmer over low heat until rice is tender and fluffy. If the mixture dries before the rice is cooked, add a little more cold water until fully cooked.

EMPANADITAS DE CARNE (Meat Turnovers)

36 turnovers

FILLING:

1 pound beef chuck, cooked in water to cover until tender (reserve broth)
1 pound lean pork, cooked in water to cover until tender (reserve broth)
1 cup raisins
2 cups applesauce or mincemeat or 1 cup of each
1 cup sugar
1 teaspoon cinnamon
½ teaspoon cloves
1 teaspoon salt
½ cup pinon nuts or chopped pecans

DOUGH:

3 cups flour
1 teaspoon baking powder
1 teaspoon salt
3 tablespoons shortening or lard
1 tablespoon sugar
1 egg, beaten
1 cup water
Salad oil

Grind meat. Add remaining ingredients and place in large pot. Add enough reserved meat stock to thoroughly moisten. Simmer for about 15 minutes. If mixture appears too dry after simmering, add more meat stock. Allow to cool thoroughly. Combine dough ingredients. Blend in shortening until coarse. Add beaten egg and slowly add water, mixing well until dough forms a ball. Roll dough out to about 1/8" thick and cut with biscuit cutter. Fill each round with meat filling, fold over and pinch, sealing well. Fry in deep hot oil until browned.

NEW MEXICAN GREEN CHILI STEW (Caldillo)

4 servings

2   pounds lean beef
      round or pork
2   tablespoons oil
3   medium potatoes,
      peeled and diced
½   cup onion, sliced
1   large garlic clove,
      minced
2   teaspoons salt
6-8   green chilies

Cube round steak, sprinkle with salt and fry until brown in oil. Add potatoes to browned meat together with onion, garlic, salt, chili and enough water to cover. Continue to add water if necessary. It should be of a soupy consistency.

POSOLE

12-14 servings

2   pounds pork roast, cut
      in chunks
½   pound pork rinds
      (skins)
2   pork shanks or pigs
      feet
1   tablespoon salt
2   cups posole (usually
      found in the meat sec-
      tion of your market)
1   teaspoon oregano
2   cloves mashed garlic
2   tablespoons chopped
      onion
4   red chili pods, seeds
      removed

Place meat and pork rinds and pork shanks in a large kettle and add about 5 quarts of water or enough to cover meat. Add approximately 1 tablespoon salt and bring to a boil. Cook over medium heat for about 1½ hours. Remove excess grease and set aside. Reserve liquid. Wash the posole very carefully until the water is clear so as to remove lime from kernels. Put in large kettle and cover with water. Boil until posole has popped. Mix meat, posole, rind and shanks or pig's feet. Add oregano, garlic, onion and chili pods. Let simmer for about ½ hour. Posole may be served as a main dish with hard rolls or crackers. Additional red chili sauce may be added at serving time for more spice. (Refer to Index for chili sauce recipe.)

This posole will lose its authenticity but none of its tastiness if pork rinds, pork shanks or pigs feet are omitted.

FRIJOLES
(Pinto Beans)

The pinto bean is so named because of its spotted appearance or dark splotches on a cream or buff background. Frijoles furnish at a low cost an excellent source of energy, iron and the vitamins of the important B complex. In addition, it is a source of protein and contains a significant amount of calcium.

Since beans are usually served with chili, cheese, tomatoes and/or small amounts of meat, the combination of these foods constitutes a balanced meal.

In high altitudes, such as New Mexico, the pinto bean requires a relatively long cooking period but there are several methods to shorten the process.

One of the simplest of these methods and one which would apply at all altitudes is the soaking process. The beans may be soaked overnight or until they have approximately doubled in size. This process is not recommended unless it is absolutely necessary to cut down on the cooking time because many valuable nutrients are thrown out with the soaking water.

A pressure cooker will also shorten cooking time significantly. Approximately 1 hour at 15 pounds pressure will make the beans tender. Continued cooking for a few minutes in an open pot will remove the pressure cooker flavor which some people find objectionable. It will also allow the juices to thicken.

In order to secure the best flavor in pinto beans, they should be cooked to the point when the skin is practically as tender as the inside of the bean. If they are to be served without mashing, the beans should not become broken or mushy.

If the beans are cooked in soft water, they will not only cook more quickly but the flavor will be improved. If it's necessary to cook in hard water, it's advisable to boil the water first to remove the calcium salts as it has been shown that calcium toughens the skin of the beans.

FRIJOLES REFRITOS (Refried Beans)

6 servings

2 cups cooked beans
3 tablespoons lard or bacon drippings
½ cup grated longhorn cheese

Heat lard or bacon drippings in frying pan or saucepan. Add beans, mash and simmer for 5 minutes. Top with cheese and serve when melted.

NEW MEXICO PINTO BEANS

8-12 servings

3 cups pinto beans (2⅓ cups equal 1 pound)
2½ quarts water
1 meaty ham bone (or ¼ pound salt pork or cubed bacon)
1 teaspoon salt (or more to taste)

Wash and pick over the beans, removing loose skins or shriveled beans. Put in a large covered pot and cover with hot water. Soak overnight if you want to cut down on cooking time. When beans start to simmer add ham bone, salt pork, or cubed bacon. Add more water as needed but add only hot or boiling water. Never add cold water or the beans will turn dark. If you cook without a lid the beans will also turn a dark color. When the skins are almost as tender as the inside of the beans, they are done. They should not be broken. Add salt and allow to stand before serving.

CHILI BEAN SOUP

5-6 servings

1 pound pinto beans
8 cups boiling water
1 teaspoon garlic salt
1 teaspoon onion salt
¼ teaspoon thyme
¼ teaspoon marjoram
1 10½ ounce can beef broth
1 16-ounce can stewed tomatoes
1 package (1-5/8 ounce) chili seasoning mix
1 cup hot water

Rinse, sort and soak beans overnight. Drain and empty them into a large pot; add boiling water, garlic and onion salts, thyme and marjoram. Cover and simmer until beans are tender, about 3 hours. (Don't let beans boil dry; add hot water as needed.) Spoon out 3 cups of cooked beans to use another day in another way. Mash remaining beans with their liquid. Add remaining ingredients. Heat 10 minutes to blend flavors.

Those spooned-out beans make great marinated bean salad additions or can be mashed and fried to use as burrito filling.

GUACAMOLE SALAD

4 servings

5   large avocados
1   medium garlic clove, minced
2½   tablespoons lemon juice
1   teaspoon salt

Peel and chop avocados into a bowl. Mash with remaining ingredients until mixture is smooth and creamy. To prepare individual salads, spoon guacamole mixture on shredded or whole lettuce leaves. Top with diced tomato for garnish and serve with tostados. If prepared ahead of time, cover with plastic wrap and press on top of mixture to prevent it from darkening.

SPANISH RICE

4-6 servings

3   tablespoons shortening
1½   cups rice
½   cup onion, sliced
½   cup bell pepper, sliced
1   14-ounce can whole tomatoes
1   medium clove garlic, minced or crushed
1   teaspoon black pepper
2   teaspoons salt
3   cups water

Melt shortening in large skillet. Add rice and brown. When rice is a golden brown, reduce heat and add onion, bell pepper, tomatoes, garlic and pepper. Mix well and add 1½ cups warm water or enough to just cover rice. Add salt. Cover and let simmer until almost dry. Add remaining water, cold, a little at a time, cooking over low heat until fluffy. This is the secret to fluffy rice.

MAMACITA'S SPANISH RICE

6-8 servings

1   cup uncooked long grain white rice
4   tablespoons cooking oil
2   tablespoons diced bell pepper
3   tablespoons diced onion
1   teaspoon dried parsley flakes
3   ounces tomato paste
2   cloves crushed garlic
2½   cups cold water
¾   teaspoon salt

Lightly brown rice in oil over medium heat, stirring constantly. Add bell pepper and onion and saute' five minutes more, stirring often. Remove from heat; add parsley, tomato paste and garlic. Stir well and then add water and salt. Heat mixture to boiling, cover tightly and simmer 20 to 30 minutes or until liquid is absorbed. Remove from heat and let steam 10 minutes before serving.

TRADITIONAL CALABACITAS CON LECHE

4-6 servings

4 medium summer squash, thinly sliced
¼ cup butter or margarine
1 15-ounce can whole kernel corn, drained
½ cup onion, thinly sliced
½ teaspoon salt
Dash pepper
1 4-ounce can chopped green chilies
1 cup milk
½ cup grated Cheddar cheese

Saute' squash in butter until soft. Reduce heat and add corn, onions, salt, pepper and green chili. Mix well and add milk. Simmer until well blended. Add cheese and cover until cheese is melted.

CALABACITAS

6 servings

3-4 zucchini or yellow squash, sliced
1 large onion, chopped
3 tablespoons oil
¼ teaspoon garlic salt or 2 cloves fresh garlic, minced
1 4-ounce can chopped green chilies
1 16-ounce can whole kernel corn
1 cup grated Cheddar cheese

Saute' squash and onion in oil until barely tender. Add garlic salt (or fresh garlic), chilies, corn and cheese; mix well. Put in buttered 1-quart casserole and bake at 400° for 20 minutes.

QUELITES (Spinach with Beans)

4-6 servings

3 tablespoons onion, chopped
1 tablespoon bacon drippings
1½ cups prepared pinto beans (See Index)
1 tablespoon chili seeds
¼ teaspoon salt
1½ pounds cooked fresh spinach (frozen or canned may be substituted)
1 boiled egg, sliced

Saute' onion in fat and add beans, chili, salt and spinach. Simmer for 10 minutes. Add egg slices as garnish and serve.

Quelites is the name for wild spinach but since this is sometimes difficult to find fresh spinach has been substituted.

BIZCOCHITOS

4 dozen

1   cup lard or shortening
½   cup sugar
1   egg
3   cups flour
1½ teaspoons baking powder
½   teaspoon salt
1   teaspoon anise seed
3   tablespoons sweet wine
¼   cup sugar
1   tablespoon cinnamon

Cream lard and sugar until quite creamy. Add egg and beat until very fluffy. Sift together flour, baking powder and salt; add to creamed mixture. Stir in wine and anise seed. Roll dough out on floured board to ¼" thick and cut in plain squares or fancy shapes. Combine ¼ cup sugar and 1 tablespoon cinnamon and sprinkle on top of each cookie. Bake in a preheated 350° oven for 15-20 minutes or until light brown. Freezes well.

This is a traditional New Mexican recipe revered by Albuquerque cooks since territorial days.

MEXICAN CHOCOLATE SAUCE

1½ cups

4   ounces unsweetened chocolate
2   tablespoons butter
¼   cup light corn syrup
¼   cup sugar
    Dash salt
¼   cup Kahlua
¼   cup cream

In top of double boiler combine all ingredients and cook, stirring constantly for 10 minutes. Serve over pound cake or ice cream. To store, pour into a jar and cover. Sauce keeps in refrigerator up to 3 months. To warm sauce, set jar in pan of hot water over low heat.

MEXICAN WEDDING COOKIES

36 cookies

1   cup butter, softened
1   cup powdered sugar
2   cups sifted flour
1   cup ground nuts
1   teaspoon vanilla

Combine all ingredients. Form into 1½" balls. Bake on cookie sheet at 350° for about 10-15 minutes or until set. Roll in powdered sugar while still warm.

COMIDA SIMPÁTICA

EMPANADAS DE FRUTA

7-8 dozen cookies

DOUGH:

6   cups flour
1   teaspoon salt
1   tablespoon sugar
¾   cup shortening
1   egg
1½   cups water

FRUIT FILLING

20   ounces mixed dried fruit
½   pound raisins
¾   cup sugar
½   teaspoon cloves
1   teaspoon cinnamon
½   teaspoon nutmeg
1   cup pinon nuts (other nuts may be used)

Mix flour, salt and sugar; add shortening and mix well. Add beaten egg to water and then to dry mixture. Dough should be soft but not sticky. Make small balls of dough. Roll out to 5 inches in diameter and 1/8″ thick. Place a heaping teaspoon of filling on half of rolled out dough turning other half of dough over and pressing edges together. Pinch edges between thumb and forefinger giving the dough a half-turn. Fry in deep fat until golden brown. Drain. To make fruit filling, add enough water to cover the dried fruit and raisins. Cook over low heat until tender. Add sugar, spices and nuts. Mix until well-blended. (A 21-ounce can of fruit pie filling can be substituted for the fruit filling.)

NATILLAS

6-8 servings

4   eggs, separated
¼   cup flour
1   quart milk
¾   cup sugar
⅛   teaspoon salt
    Nutmeg

Make a paste of egg yolks, flour and 1 cup of the milk. In a medium saucepan, add the sugar and salt to the remaining milk and scald at medium temperature. Add the egg yolk mixture to the scalded milk and continue to cook at medium temperature until it reaches the consistency of soft custard. Remove from heat and cool to room temperature. Beat the egg whites until stiff but not dry and fold into the custard. Chill before serving. Spoon custard into individual dishes. Sprinkle each with nutmeg before serving.

CLASSIC MEXICAN FLAN

8 servings

½ cup granulated sugar
1 14-ounce can sweetened condensed milk
1 cup milk
3 large eggs
   Yolks of 3 large eggs
½ teaspoon almond extract
1 teaspoon vanilla extract

In a small saucepan melt sugar over moderate heat, stirring frequently, until sugar is a dark, caramel-colored liquid. Remove from heat and pour into a 4-cup metal ring mold or 8 individual molds. Quickly turn mold to coat bottom and sides with the caramel. Let cool so caramel hardens. Heat oven to 325°. Put the condensed milk, milk, eggs, egg yolks and flavorings into an electric blender. Cover and blend to mix well. Pour mixture into mold; put mold in a larger pan filled with water to a depth of ½ inch. Bake for 1 hour. Remove from oven and remove mold from water. Cool and then refrigerate up to 2 days. Cover mold with an inverted serving platter. Hold mold and platter together and turn them over. Lift off mold. Caramel will fall as a liquid sauce over the custard.

This rich, caramel custard makes a delicious finale for any traditional Southwestern meal. It's do-ahead feature makes it great party fare too!

CAPIROTADA (Bread Pudding)

6-8 servings

8 slices toasted bread
2 cups water
1 cup sugar
1 teaspoon cinnamon
½ teaspoon nutmeg
½ teaspoon cloves
¼ teaspoon salt
1½ cups grated Cheddar cheese
1½ cups raisins
2 tablespoons butter
   Whipped cream (optional)

Toast the sliced bread, break into 2″ pieces. Make a syrup of water, sugar, spices and salt. Bring to a boil and simmer for 10 minutes. Butter an oblong baking pan. Layer bread, cheese, raisins and butter. Pour syrup over bread mixture and bake at 350° for 20 minutes or until syrup is absorbed. May be served warm or cold. If served warm, top with whipped cream.

COMIDA SIMPÁTICA

MOLLETES (ANISE SEED ROLLS)

yields 3 dozen

1   package dry yeast
2   tablespoons sugar
2   cups warm water
     (105-115°)
½   cup shortening
1½   cups sugar
2   eggs
1   teaspoon salt
1   teaspoon anise seed
6-7   cups all-purpose flour
⅓   cup margarine, melted

In a large mixing bowl, dissolve yeast and 2 tablespoons sugar in warm water. In another bowl, cream shortening with 1½ cups sugar. Beat in eggs and add salt and anise seed. Add egg mixture to yeast and mix thoroughly. Gradually add flour until moderately firm dough forms. Turn dough onto a lightly floured surface and knead until it is smooth and elastic. Place dough in a greased bowl, cover, and allow to rise until double in size. Punch down, knead 2 or 3 times, and allow to rise double in size again. Grease generously two baking sheets. Punch down and shape dough into egg-size balls. Place on baking sheet, cover, and allow to rise double in size again. Preheat oven to 375°. Lightly brush rolls with melted margarine and bake for 20-25 minutes. Serve warm for breakfast or brunch. Freezes well.

PASTELITOS

40 squares

FILLING:

½   pound dried apricots
     (other dried fruits may
     be used)
1½   cups water
1   cup sugar

PASTRY:

4   cups flour
1½   teaspoons salt
1½   cups shortening
½-¾ cup ice cold water

TOPPING:

1½   teaspoons sugar
½   teaspoon cinnamon

Cook dried fruit in water in a covered saucepan until tender, about 3 hours. Add more water if needed to prevent burning. Add 1 cup sugar to pulp and cook until thick, approximately 1 hour. Mash fruit so no large chunks of fruit remain. Allow fruit to cool while preparing pastry and before spreading. Preheat oven to 400°. Prepare pastry by sifting dry ingredients into bowl. Cut in shortening until mixture resembles coarse meal. Add ice water slowly until dough binds together. Divide dough in half and roll each half out, very thin, on floured surface to fit 15½" x 10½" cookie sheet. Spread fruit mixture evenly over pastry. Place second layer of pastry over fruit filling. Press edges together to seal. Sprinkle with mixture of sugar and cinnamon. Make several vent openings with knife. Bake 30 minutes. Cool and cut into 2" squares.

CAFÉ MEXICANO

1 serving

1   ounce coffee liqueur
½   ounce brandy
1   teaspoon chocolate
     syrup
     Dash ground cinnamon
     Hot coffee
     Sweetened whipped
     cream

Combine coffee liqueur, brandy, chocolate syrup and cinnamon in a coffee cup or mug. Fill to the top with hot coffee. Top with whipped cream.

MEXICAN EGGNOG

about 1 quart

2   cups milk
1   pint half-and-half
½   cup sugar
1¼   teaspoons vanilla
8   egg yolks
¼-½ cup light rum
     (optional)
     Cinnamon sticks

In a 3-quart pan over medium-high heat, bring the milk and half-and-half to a boil; remove from heat and let cool. With a spoon, lift off and discard scum. Add sugar and vanilla to the milk mixture, bring to a boil, and boil gently over medium heat for 20 minutes. Let cool, then skim. In a large mixer bowl, beat egg yolks at high speed for about 5 minutes until thick and lemon-colored. Reduce speed to low and gradually add the cool milk mixture and rum, if used. Pour into a pitcher, cover, and refrigerate as long as overnight. To serve, place a cinnamon swizzle stick in each glass and add the well-chilled milk mixture.

NEW MEXICAN HOT CHOCOLATE

6 servings

¼   cup unsweetened
     cocoa
¼   cup sugar
¾   teaspoon cinnamon
     Dash salt
1   quart milk
¼   cup light cream
¾   teaspoon vanilla

Combine the cocoa, sugar, cinnamon and salt and mix well. In medium saucepan, heat 1 cup milk until bubbling. Stir in cocoa mixture; beat with wire whisk until smooth. Over low heat, bring to boiling, stirring. Gradually stir in rest of milk. Return to boiling. Stir in cream and vanilla; heat gently. Before serving, beat with wire whisk until frothy.

In the Beginning.....

The history of New Mexico is inseparable from a great, meandering river known as the Rio Grande. Bisecting the state from north to south with grace and beauty, it has traveled through the area's misty past, its life-giving waters giving birth to the Indian pueblos, Spanish villages and cities of today and yesterday. New Mexico's earliest inhabitants, known as Anasazi, left their material remains and spiritual intimacy beside the waters. Along the river's upper course -- the Rio Arriba -- and upon the giant ledges slanting down from the neighboring mountains, through the basins drained by the San Juan and the Little Colorado, down in the Gila wilderness and over the valley plains the excavator's spade turns up reminders of these ancient ones. These community strongholds, where early Southwesterners were able to live and thrive, are the legacy of the Rio Grande ❖

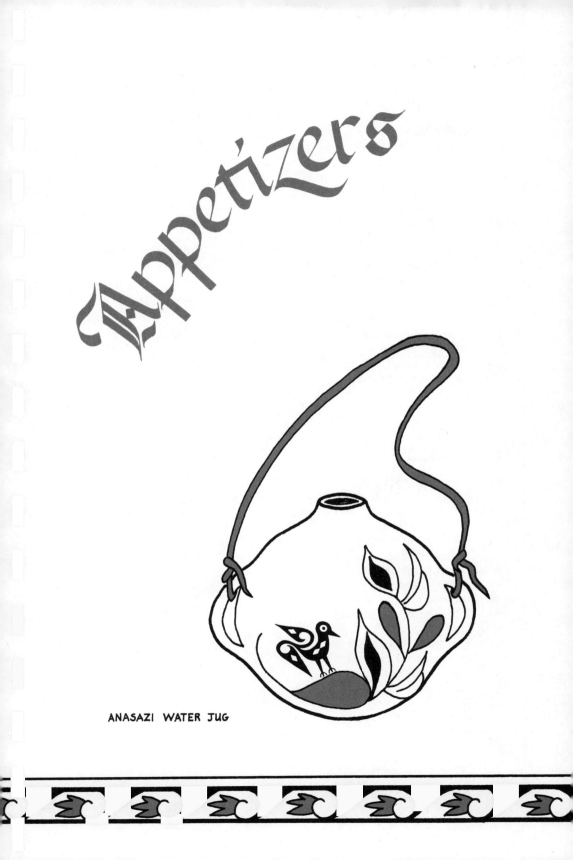

Appetizers

ANASAZI WATER JUG

🦃 GUACAMOLE DIP

2 cups

6-8 ripe avocados
½ cup chopped green chili
1 garlic clove
1 teaspoon lemon juice
Salt to taste

Peel and pit avocados. Mash avocados with a fork. Stir in remaining ingredients. Serve with tostados or other chips.

🦃 HARLEQUIN DIP

8-10 servings

2 4-ounce cans chopped green chilies
2 4½-ounce cans chopped black olives
3 tomatoes, chopped
4 green onions, chopped
2 tablespoons wine vinegar
1 tablespoon oil
Salt and pepper to taste

Combine all ingredients and mix well. Use as a dip with crisp tortilla chips.

SPINACH DIP

10-15 servings

1 10-ounce package frozen chopped spinach, thawed, drained and squeezed
1 tablespoon dried parsley flakes
1 tablespoon green onion, chopped
½ tablespoon dill weed
½ tablespoon seasoned salt
1 cup mayonnaise
8 ounces sour cream
4 ounces cream cheese
2 tablespoons lemon juice
Dash oregano, basil and pepper

Mix all ingredients together and refrigerate for 6 hours before serving. Serve with chips or vegetable dippers.

CHILI CON QUESO

1 tablespoon salad oil
¼ cup minced onion
1 4-ounce can chopped green chilies, drained
½ teaspoon garlic, crushed
⅓-½ cup light cream or milk
1 8-ounce package pasteurized process cheese spread, cut in cubes
1 cup grated Cheddar cheese
Tortilla chips or fresh vegetables for dipping

In a small saucepan heat oil over moderately high heat. Add onion, chilies and garlic and cook 5 to 7 minutes, stirring frequently, until onion is lightly browned. Reduce heat to low and add ⅓ cup of the cream; then add cheeses and stir until mixture is smooth. If necessary, thin sauce with additional cream. Serve in a small chafing dish with tortilla chips or fresh vegetable dippers.

FRIJOLE DIP

24-30 servings

1 16-ounce can refried beans, drained and mashed
½ pound cooked hot sausage, drained
1 onion, chopped
1 pound processed American cheese, cubed
1-3 tablespoons taco sauce
1 tablespoon chili powder
½ teaspoon garlic salt
Grated Cheddar cheese for garnish

In skillet, fry beans, sausage and onion until onions are done. Stir in cheese, taco sauce, chili powder and garlic salt. Serve in dish that can be held at a low temperature. Garnish with grated Cheddar cheese.

GREEN CHILI DIP

1½ cups

1 8-ounce package cream cheese, softened (or 1 cup sour cream)
6 fresh green chilies, chopped or 1 4-ounce can chopped green chilies
Garlic salt to taste

Mix cream cheese or sour cream with finely chopped green chili and garlic salt. Serve with tostados or other chips.

DELIGHTFUL BEEF DIP

8 servings

1   8-ounce package
    cream cheese
2   tablespoons milk
1   2½-ounce jar dried
    beef, diced
¼   cup chopped green
    pepper
¼   teaspoon garlic
    powder
¼   teaspoon pepper
1   tablespoon grated
    onion
½   cup sour cream

Combine first eight ingredients and mix until well blended. Put into 8" pie pan or ovenproof dish of same capacity. Saute' pecans and salt in butter until nuts are lightly browned. Sprinkle over cheese-beef mixture. Bake for 20 minutes at 350°. Serve hot with low-salt crackers or melba toast.

A company favorite!

TOPPING:

½   cup chopped pecans
¼   teaspoon salt
2   tablespoons butter

ALMOND CHEESE SPREAD

20-30 servings

½   pound soft butter
1   pound cream cheese
⅓   cup almond-flavored
    liqueur
4   green onions, chopped
1   pound Cheddar
    cheese, grated
1   pound cottage cheese
    Sliced almonds
    Chopped green onions

Cream butter and cream cheese. Add liqueur. Combine with onions, Cheddar cheese, cottage cheese. With a damp cheese cloth line a 6 cup mold. Press mixture firmly and evenly into mold. Cover with cheese cloth and chill. Unmold and remove cheese cloth. Garnish with almonds and green onions. Serve with crackers.

Leftovers are excellent mixed with hot noodles.

CAMEMBERT SPREAD

6 appetizer servings

1   ripe Camembert
1   egg yolk
1   tablespoon finely
    minced onion
1   clove garlic, crushed
    Dash of paprika
    Salt and freshly
    ground black pepper
    Onion rings, hard-
    cooked egg wedges
    and parsley for garnish
    Assorted crackers

Mash cheese with fork. Add yolk and blend well. Add onion, garlic, paprika, salt and pepper and mix thoroughly. Turn onto serving plate and shape into loaf. Garnish with onion rings, egg and parsley. Serve with crackers.

A hearty appetizer, Munich-style. Serve with chilled Bavarian beer.

BEEF-AND-CHEESE SPREAD

3 cups

½   pound very sharp Cheddar cheese, shredded (2 cups)
1   8-ounce package cream cheese, softened
1   2½-ounce jar or 1 3-ounce package dried beef, chopped
¼   cup beer
1   teaspoon Worcestershire sauce
1   teaspoon hot pepper sauce

In covered blender container at low speed or food processor blend all ingredients until well mixed. Increase speed to high and blend about 5 minutes longer or until mixture is smooth, occasionally stopping to scrape container with rubber spatula. Spoon mixture into small covered casserole or individual 1-cup containers; refrigerate. Use spread on unsalted crackers, celery sticks or thin cucumber slices for hor d'oeuvres. This may be made up to 2 weeks ahead.

CHEESE IN A BREAD BOWL

20-30 servings

2   pounds pasteurized process cheese
¼   pound blue cheese
2   8-ounce packages cream cheese
1   cup chopped onions
1   cup chopped parsley
1   cup chopped pecans
1   large oval or round rye bread, unsliced
   Paprika for garnish
   Party rye rounds

Soften cheeses to room temperature, cut into hunks and mix together well. Mix in onions, parsley and nuts. Hollow out bread, reserving as much as possible to slice thinly for the dip. "Sawtooth" the crust rim as you would a watermelon. Fill the bread bowl with the cheese mixture. Garnish with paprika and refrigerate. Serve with reserved rye and with party rye rounds.

AVOCADO CHEESE BALL

20-30 servings

2   8-ounce packages cream cheese
1   cup sharp Cheddar cheese, grated
1   medium ripe avocado, mashed
1   small onion, minced
½   cup finely chopped nuts
1   teaspoon garlic powder
1   4-ounce can chopped green chili, drained

Mash cream cheese and mix well with Cheddar. With a wooden spoon, stir in the avocado, onion, nuts, garlic powder and chili. Form into a ball and roll in parsley, chili powder or additional chopped nuts. Serve with crackers.

LIPTAUER CHEESE

30 servings

2 8-ounce packages cream cheese, softened
1 cup butter, softened
½ cup sour cream
1½ tablespoons caraway seed
1½ tablespoons capers
4 chopped anchovies (optional)
¼ cup chopped chives
1 clove crushed garlic
¾ teaspoon dry mustard
   Salt and pepper
   Paprika
   Pumpernickle bread

In mixer or food processor combine cheese, butter and sour cream. Add rest of ingredients except paprika and pack into a decorative mold. Chill thoroughly. Unmold and sprinkle with paprika. Serve with pumpernickle bread. Can make small sandwiches if preferred.

RICHARD'S HOMEMADE BOURSIN

2½ cups

2 8-ounce packages cream cheese
4 ounces butter
1 teaspoon oregano
¼ teaspoon dill
¼ teaspoon basil
¼ teaspoon thyme
¼ teaspoon marjoram
¼ teaspoon cracked pepper
2 cloves garlic

Process all ingredients until smooth in blender or food processor. Refrigerate at least four hours. Serve as a spread with crackers. (To make into a ball, omit pepper from the recipe and roll the ball in cracked pepper.)

JEZEBEL

about 4½ cups

1 12-ounce jar apple jelly
1 12-ounce jar pineapple jelly
1 12-ounce jar peach jelly
2½ ounces prepared horseradish
2 tablespoons dry mustard
1 tablespoon white pepper

Mix thoroughly and keep covered in refrigerator. Should stand for several days before serving. Pour over cream cheese and serve with crackers.

Also delicious with ham or beef.

MUSHROOM SPREAD

2½ cups spread

4 slices bacon
8 ounces fresh mush-
rooms, chopped (3
cups)
1 medium onion, finely
chopped
2 cloves garlic, crushed
2 tablespoons flour
¼ teaspoon salt
⅛ teaspoon pepper
1 8-ounce package
cream cheese, cubed
2 teaspoons Worcester-
shire sauce
1 teaspoon soy sauce
½ cup dairy sour cream

In skillet cook bacon till crisp; drain, reserv-ing 2 tablespoons drippings. Crumble bacon and set aside. Cook mushrooms, onion and garlic in reserved drippings until tender and most of the liquid has evaporated. Stir in flour, salt and pepper. Add cream cheese, Worcestershire sauce and soy sauce. Heat and stir till cheese is melted. Stir in sour cream and crumbled bacon. Heat through but do not boil. Serve warm with rye bread rounds, party crackers.

NACHOS

6-8 servings

1 8-ounce bag tortilla
chips
1 10-ounce can jalapeno
bean dip
1 4-ounce can chopped
green chilies
½ pound Cheddar
cheese, sliced thin

Place tortilla chips on cookie sheet. Put a dab of bean dip on each chip. Top with a dab of green chili, and end with a small slice of cheese. Heat in 350° oven for about 10-15 minutes. Serve hot.

Bite-size bits of Southwestern flavor!

PIÑATA CHEESE SNACKS

6 dozen appetizers

1 pound sharp Cheddar
cheese, coarsely
grated
3 tablespoons wine
vinegar
1 cup ripe olives,
chopped
¾ cup tomato sauce
2 medium onions,
chopped fine
2 garlic cloves, chopped
1 4-ounce can chopped
green chilies
Salt and pepper to
taste

Combine all ingredients and mix well. Spread on shredded wheat snack crackers or tostados and broil under heated broiler unit until cheese melts.

Spread may be frozen.

🐦 AZTEC CALENDAR APPETIZER PLATTER

10-12 servings

1	16-ounce can refried beans (with chili and onions if available)
1	1¼-ounce envelope taco seasoning mix
3	avocados, mashed
3	tablespoons sour cream
2	tablespoons lemon juice
¼	teaspoon garlic salt
1	4-ounce can chopped green chilies, drained
4	green onions, chopped; greens only
½	pound Cheddar cheese, shredded
½	pound Monterey Jack cheese, shredded
12	pitted ripe olives, sliced
1	large tomato, seeded and cubed
	Chili powder
	Fresh parsley
1	7-ounce bag round tortilla chips

Use 10" to 12" glass pie plate or similar shallow round plate. For layer 1 mix refried beans and taco seasoning. Spread onto plate, not quite to edge. Layer 2: Mash avocados with sour cream, lemon juice, and garlic salt. Spread on top of bean mixture. Layer 3: Sprinkle green chili and green onions over avocado mixture. Layer 4: Combine cheeses and sprinkle over chili and onions, to completely cover. Layer 5: Decorate top of dip with sliced olives in a wedge shape design and dot with tomato pieces. Sprinkle with chili powder and decorate with fresh parsley sprigs around outside edge. Serve with spreaders and large round tortilla chips.

Pleases the eye as well as the palate.

PATÉ WITH CREAM CHEESE AND CAVIAR

6-8 servings

1	4½-ounce can deviled ham
1	4½-ounce can liverwurst
1	teaspoon onion juice
2	teaspoons Worcestershire sauce
	Dash hot pepper sauce
4	ounces cream cheese
2	tablespoons mayonnaise
1	4-ounce jar caviar
	Water cress or parsley for garnish

Combine ham, liverwurst, onion juice, Worcestershire sauce and hot pepper sauce; mix well. On a serving plate shape the mixture into a round mold 1" thick. Refrigerate at least 1 hour. Make next layer by mixing cream cheese with enough mayonnaise to make the consistency of cake icing. Spread over pate' as you would frost a cake. Top with caviar and surround with water cress or parsley. Serve with melba toast rounds or crackers.

TUNA AND PISTACHIO PATÉ

1½ cups

1	7-ounce can tuna in oil
2-3	tablespoons Cognac
2	hard-cooked eggs
2	3-ounce packages cream cheese, room temperature
	White pepper
3	tablespoons pistachio nuts, coarsely chopped
	Consomme, refrigerated until almost jellied
	Horseradish sauce (optional)

Break tuna into small pieces. Blend a small amount at a time with tuna oil and cognac. Add eggs. Add the cream cheese and pepper. Blend until very smooth. Place in a bowl. Taste for seasoning. Stir in pistachio nuts. Spoon into a 1½-2 cup mold. Cover with consomme and refrigerate until firm. Serve with unflavored crackers or warm French bread. Serve with horseradish sauce for more zip.

An easy and inexpensive pate'.

SALMON PARTY BALL

10-12 servings

1	16-ounce can salmon
1	8-ounce package cream cheese, softened
1	tablespoon lemon juice
¼	cup chopped onion
1	teaspoon horseradish
¼	teaspoon liquid smoke
½	cup chopped pecans
3	tablespoons chopped parsley

Drain and flake salmon, removing bones and skin. Combine salmon, cheese, lemon juice, onion, horseradish, salt, and liquid smoke; mix thoroughly. Chill several hours. Shape salmon into a ball and roll in nuts and parsley combined.

SALMON MOUSSE

5 cups

1½ tablespoons plain gelatin
¼ cup cold water
1 10½ ounce can condensed cream of mushroom soup
⅔ cup mayonnaise
1 tablespoon Worcestershire sauce
1 tablespoon minced onion
½ teaspoon salt
1 8 ounce package cream cheese, softened
1 7¾ ounce can salmon, drained and flaked
1 cup finely chopped celery

Soften gelatin in cold water. Combine soup, mayonnaise, Worcestershire, minced onion and salt in top of double boiler and heat. Mash cream cheese and add to soup mixture and stir until smooth. Add gelatin and stir until dissolved. Refrigerate until slightly thickened. Fold in salmon and celery. Turn into mold. Chill until set. Serve as spread with cocktail rye bread. May also serve as a salad.

CRABMEAT CANAPE

6-8 servings

8 ounces softened cream cheese
1 tablespoon milk
2 tablespoons chopped onion
½ teaspoon creamed horseradish
1 6½-ounce can crabmeat
¼ teaspoon salt
Dash of pepper
⅓ cup sliced toasted almonds

Cream the cheese. Add the milk, onion, horseradish, crabmeat, salt and pepper. Blend well. Place in a 9″ pie plate. Top with the almonds. Bake at 375° for 15 minutes. Serve with crackers.

HOT CRABMEAT SPREAD

1   **8-ounce package cream cheese, softened**
½   **teaspoon horseradish (or more, to taste)**
2   **tablespoons grated onion**
1   **tablespoon milk**
½   **cup or one 7½-ounce can crabmeat**
    Salt and pepper to taste
    Paprika

Combine all ingredients except paprika. Put into 8" or 9" pie pan and heat in 375° oven for 15 minutes. Sprinkle with paprika and serve as a spread with crackers or rye rounds. Serve warm.

CRAB-CLAM SPREAD

40-50 servings

1   **7-ounce can crab meat, drained**
1   **7-ounce can minced clams, drained**
4   **tablespoons butter, softened**
⅓   **cup mayonnaise**
6   **ounces cream cheese, softened**
¼   **teaspoon Tabasco**
¼   **teaspoon Worcestershire sauce**
1   **tablespoon chopped parsley, optional for color**
    Party Rye

Mix butter, mayonnaise, cream cheese, Tabasco, Worcestershire and parsley, with a wooden spoon until smooth. Stir in crab and clams. Spread on party rye and place six inches under broiler until bubbly and brown. (May be flash frozen and removed as needed. Broil as above.)

APPETIZERS

SHRIMP OR CRAB MOLD

4 cups

1   package unflavored
    gelatin
¼   cup water
1   8-ounce package
    cream cheese
1   can condensed cream
    of mushroom soup
1   teaspoon Worcester-
    shire sauce
1   tablespoon grated
    onion
1   cup diced celery
3   tablespoons mayon-
    naise
1   6½-7 ounce can crab
    meat
    or
    6-ounces frozen
    shrimp

Dissolve gelatin in cold water while you heat mushroom soup and cream cheese until cheese is melted. Stir gelatin into soup mixture to dissolve completely. Add Worcestershire, onion, celery, mayonnaise and crab or shrimp. Mix well. Pour into 4-cup mold (or bowl). Chill until set. Serve as a spread with a variety of crackers.

POTTED SHRIMP

8-10 servings

1   4½-ounce can broken
    shrimp
¼   cup lemon juice
¼   cup butter at room
    temperature
1   8-ounce package
    cream cheese at room
    temperature
1   tablespoon dill
½   teaspoon salt
    Dash of cayenne
    Few sprigs of parsley
2   green onions with tops
1   tablespoon coarsely
    ground black pepper

Drain and soak shrimp in lemon juice for 1 hour. Drain again. Process butter and cream cheese until light and creamy. Add and process dill, salt, cayenne, and parsley. Add green onion and drained shrimp and process with 4 to 5 on-off pulses. Put in a serving dish. Top with pepper. Refrigerate for 5 hours or overnight. Bring to room temperature and serve on crackers.

SHRIMP COCKTAIL MOLD

4-8 servings

1   5-ounce can shrimp
½   cup chili sauce
¼   cup ketchup
1   tablespoon grated
     onion
½   teaspoon Worcester-
     shire sauce
½   teaspoon horseradish
1½   tablespoon lemon
     juice
     Dash hot pepper sauce
½   teaspoon sugar
1   tablespoon unflavored
     gelatin

Combine all the ingredients in the top of a double boiler. Heat through, stirring constantly. Pour into a greased 1-cup mold. Refrigerate until firm. Serve with crackers.

SHRIMP MOUSSE

3 cups

3   4½-ounce cans small
     shrimp
1½   envelopes unflavored
     gelatin
¼   cup water
1   10-ounce can tomato
     soup
3   3-ounce packages
     cream cheese, soften-
     ed
1   cup mayonnaise
¾   cup finely chopped
     green onion
¾   cup finely chopped
     celery

Rinse shrimp in water, drain and crumble. Dissolve gelatin in ¼ cup water. Heat soup and stir in gelatin and softened cream cheese. Beat with mixer on low speed until blended. Add mayonnaise, onion and celery and blend well. Pour into a 3-cup mold. Chill overnight. When ready to serve, invert mold onto serving tray and surround with crackers or rye rounds.

IMPERIAL ARTICHOKE APPETIZER

40 appetizers

2   6½-ounce jars
    marinated artichoke
    hearts
1   small onion, chopped
4   eggs
2   cups sharp Cheddar
    cheese, grated
2   tablespoons chopped
    parsley or parsley
    flakes
¼   cup seasoned dry
    bread crumbs
¼   teaspoon salt
¼   teaspoon pepper
    Few drops Tabasco
    sauce

Drain and reserve oil from one jar of artichokes. Cook chopped onion in the reserved oil. Coarsely chop the artichoke hearts and add to onion mixture. Beat the eggs and mix with onions and artichokes. Add remaining ingredients and mix well. Pour into a greased 9" x 13" pan and bake at 325° for 30 minutes. Cut into bite-sized squares and serve hot.

MARINATED ARTICHOKE HEARTS

4-6 servings

2   tablespoons water
2   tablespoons lemon
    juice
2   tablespoons salad oil
¼   teaspoon dried tar-
    ragon, crushed
    Dash of garlic salt
1   tablespoon sugar
¼   teaspoon oregano
1   14-ounce can artichoke
    hearts, drained
    Paprika

Combine all ingredients except artichoke hearts. Place artichoke hearts in a bowl and pour mixture over them. Cover. Chill several hours or overnight. Drain and sprinkle with paprika.

EMBASSY MUSHROOMS

20 servings

2   pounds large mushrooms (about 60)
4   strips bacon
6   tablespoons butter
2   tablespoons minced onion
2   eggs
1   cup heavy cream
½   cup Swiss cheese, shredded
½   teaspoon salt

Preheat oven to 350°. Rinse, pat dry and remove stems from mushrooms. Chop stems and set aside. In a large skillet, saute' bacon until crisp. Crumble and set aside. Pour off bacon fat. In same skillet melt butter. Use about 4 tablespoons of the melted butter to brush the outsides of the mushroom caps. Place caps in a large shallow baking pan or cookie sheet. To remaining butter in skillet, add onion. Saute' for 2 minutes. Add chopped mushroom stems and saute' two minutes longer. Remove skillet from heat. In a mixing bowl, lightly beat eggs, stir in cream, Swiss cheese and salt. Add bacon and mushroom/onion mixture. Fill each mushroom cap to top. Bake for 30 minutes or until filling is set.

ONION OLÉ

36 servings

1   13¾-ounce package hot roll mix
1   tablespoon chopped chives or instant minced onions
1   cup mayonnaise
4   cups grated Cheddar cheese
½   cup sliced green onions or chopped onions
¼   cup stuffed green olives, drained and chopped
1   teaspoon capers
2   tablespoons grated Parmesan cheese

Prepare hot roll mix as directed on package, adding chives. Cover and let rise in warm place until doubled in size, 30-45 minutes. Roll out or pat dough to fit a greased 10" x 15" jelly roll pan. Combine mayonnaise, grated cheese, onions, olives and capers. Spread mayonnaise mixture over dough in pan to within 1" from edges. Sprinkle top with Parmesan cheese. Bake at 375° 30-45 minutes, until bubbling and golden brown. Cut in squares and serve at once. Dough may be divided in half and patted to fit 2 14" pizza pans. Spread half mayonnaise mixture over each and sprinkle with Parmesan cheese. Bake at 375° 15-20 minutes. Can be made ahead and assembled and cooked at the last minute.

CHEESE-STUFFED MUSHROOMS

8-10 servings

2	pounds large mushrooms
½	cup grated Parmesan cheese
¾	cup dry bread crumbs
½	cup onion, grated
2	cloves garlic, minced
3	tablespoons parsley, minced
1	teaspoon salt
½	teaspoon black pepper
½	teaspoon oregano
¾	cup olive oil

Preheat oven to 350°. Wash mushrooms; remove stems and chop. Mix chopped stems with cheese, bread crumbs, onion, garlic, parsley, salt, pepper and oregano. Stuff caps with mixture. Pour a little of the olive oil into a baking dish. Arrange mushrooms in the dish. Drizzle remaining oil over the mushrooms, being sure to cover each one. Bake for 25 minutes. Serve hot. These may be made early in the day and covered with plastic wrap until ready to bake.

MUSHROOM ROLL-UPS

7-8 dozen

1	pound mushrooms, chopped fine
½	cup butter
6	tablespoons flour
1½	teaspoon salt
2	cups light cream
2	teaspoons lemon juice
1	teaspoon onion salt
1½	loaves sandwich bread
½	cup butter, melted

Saute' mushrooms in ½ cup butter for 5 minutes. Cool. Add flour and blend well. Add salt. Stir in cream and cook until thick, stirring constantly. Add lemon juice and onion salt. Cool. Remove crusts from bread and roll slices flat. Spread mushroom mixture on the bread and roll up. Freeze slightly and cut into thirds. Dip into melted butter. The roll-ups may be frozen at this point. Bake at 375° for 15-20 minutes.

GARLIC OLIVES

10-12 servings

1	7-ounce can large pitted ripe olives
½	cup red wine vinegar
¼	cup salad oil
¼	teaspoon crushed red pepper
1	clove minced garlic
¼	cup finely chopped onion
1	teaspoon oregano

Place olives and their liquids into a screwtop quart jar. Add vinegar, oil, red pepper, garlic, onion, and oregano. Cover tightly. Shake well. Refrigerate several days, shaking jar occasionally. Drain before serving.

CRAB-STUFFED TOMATOES

20 appetizers

20 small cherry tomatoes
1   cup mayonnaise
¼   cup finely chopped
    shallots or scallions
2   tablespoons chopped
    chives
2   teaspoons tarragon
1   tablespoon chopped
    parsley
1   teaspoon thyme
2   tablespoons basil
1   tablespoon finely
    minced garlic
1   hard-cooked egg,
    sieved fine
½   pound crab meat
    Salt and black pepper
    to taste
    Parsley for garnish

Remove core of each tomato, leaving a cavity for the crab filling. Salt inside of tomatoes and turn them upside down to drain. Combine remaining ingredients and use to fill centers of tomatoes. Garnish with parsley sprigs and serve cold.

PESTO STUFFED CHERRY TOMATOES

24 appetizers

2   cups (1 pint) cherry
     tomatoes
1   3-ounce package
     cream cheese, soften-
     ed
2   tablespoons fresh
     lemon juice
¼   cup grated Parmesan
     cheese
¼   cup finely chopped
     pine nuts or sunflower
     seeds
¾   cup finely chopped
     fresh parsley
¼   cup finely chopped
     watercress (optional)
1½   teaspoons dried basil
     leaves
2   cloves garlic, crushed

Cut tops off cherry tomatoes; scoop out pulp. Drain tomatoes upside down on paper toweling while preparing filling. Beat cream cheese with lemon juice in medium bowl until smooth. Stir in remaining ingredients. Fill cherry tomatoes with cheese mixture; chill.

BAKED ZUCCHINI APPETIZERS

40 squares

3 cups sliced zucchini, uncooked
1 cup prepared biscuit mix
½ cup finely chopped onion
½ cup Parmesan cheese, grated
2 tablespoons snipped parsley or parsley flakes
½ teaspoon salt
½ teaspoon seasoned salt
½ teaspoon oregano or marjoram
   Dash pepper
1 clove garlic, crushed
½ cup vegetable oil
4 eggs, slightly beaten

Preheat oven to 350°. Grease a 9" X 13" ovenproof pan. Mix all ingredients together well. Spread in pan. Bake until golden brown, about 25 minutes. Cut into 2" X 1" squares. Serve hot.

CLUB CANAPES

5 dozen canapes

1 cup mayonnaise
1 cup Parmesan cheese
5 dozen 1" white bread rounds
3 green onions

Mix mayonnaise and cheese. Put on top of bread rounds. Top with slices of green onion. Broil for 2-3 minutes or until canapes are puffed and golden.

🐦 MEXICAN SOUFFLÉ APPETIZER

40 appetizers

2 4-ounce cans whole green chilies, drained, rinsed and seeded
½ pound sharp Cheddar cheese, shredded
¾ cup dry bread crumbs
3 eggs, beaten
1 teaspoon parsley flakes
½ teaspoon ground cumin
1 teaspoon salt
1 teaspoon oregano
½ cup light cream
½ cup milk

Grease 9" x 13" pan. Cover bottom with chilies. Sprinkle cheese over chilies. Spread bread crumbs over cheese. Beat eggs until light. Add remaining ingredients to eggs and beat again. Pour over cheese. Bake at 375° for 40 minutes. Cut into small squares for hors d'oeuvres or into larger portions for main course servings.

🐦 BOLITAS DE QUESO CALIENTE

2 cups grated Gruyere cheese
6 walnuts, very finely chopped
3 tablespoons flour
½ teaspoon paprika
2 egg whites
½ teaspoon hot sauce
1 tablespoon dry sherry
1 cup fine bread crumbs Cooking oil

Combine cheese, walnuts, flour and paprika. Beat egg whites until very stiff; add hot sauce and sherry. Fold into cheese mixture. Form mixture into tiny balls, roll in bread crumbs and fry in deep, hot cooking oil until golden. Remove to paper toweling; serve hot.

Guests love these hot tiny cheese ball appetizers.

CHEESE CANAPES

24 canapes

6 English muffins, halved
1 6-ounce can ripe olives, pitted and chopped
½ cup mayonnaise
¼ cup green onions, minced
½ teaspoon salt
½ teaspoon curry powder
½ teaspoon chili powder
2 cups sharp Cheddar cheese, grated

Preheat oven to 325°. Arrange muffin halves on baking sheet. Combine remaining ingredients and spread evenly on muffins. Bake for 15 minutes at 325°. Then broil under broiler unit until cheese is bubbling and lightly brown. Remove from oven and cut each muffin into quarters. Serve hot.

🐦 NIPPY CHILI-CHEESE CANAPES

4 dozen appetizers

1 8-ounce package pasteurized process cheese spread, shredded
1 4-ounce can chopped green chilies, drained
2 tablespoons mayonnaise
2 teaspoons grated onion
¼ teaspoon chili powder
12 slices white bread
1 7-ounce jar pimientos, drained

In a small bowl mix well cheese, chilies, mayonnaise, onion and chili powder. Preheat oven to 450°. Cut crusts from bread; cut each slice into 4 triangles. Place triangles on cookie sheets; bake until lightly browned on top, about 4 minutes. Remove cookie sheets from oven; turn triangles, untoasted side up. Spread 1 teaspoon cheese mixture evenly on untoasted side of each bread triangle; garnish with a piece of pimiento. Bake 3 minutes or until cheese is bubbly. Serve immediately.

SNAPPY CHEESE SNACKS

6 dozen

½   **pound butter, softened**
1   **pound New York —
style sharp Cheddar
cheese, grated**
½   **teaspoon baking
powder**
¼   **teaspoon cayenne
pepper**
1   **teaspoon salt**
2   **cups flour**

Cream butter; add grated cheese and mix. Sift baking powder, pepper and salt with flour. Add to cheese mixture to make stiff dough. Make dough into 2 rolls, wrap in foil and put in refrigerator or freezer to harden. (It takes about 1½ hours to chill in refrigerator, and 25 minutes in the freezer.) To serve, cut into ¼″ thick slices and bake at 350° 8-10 minutes on ungreased cookie sheet.

Cayenne pepper adds "bite" to these snacks. The dough can be made in advance and kept in the freezer for several months. To use after freezing, let soften enough to slice. Be sure to use New York sharp cheese, as other cheese may make the dough crumble.

🦆 BECKY'S ANTECOUCHOS

16-20 servings

4   **pounds sirloin**

MARINADE:

½   **cup salad oil**
⅓   **cup red cider vinegar**
1   **tablespoon ground
cumin**
6-8   **cloves crushed garlic**
2   **teaspoons salt**
2   **teaspoons cracked
pepper**
2-3   **tablespoons cracked
red chile peppers
moistened with 1
tablespoon oil**

SAUCE:

6   **green onions, chopped**
¼   **cup vinegar**
1   **teaspoon cumin**
1   **teaspoon cracked
pepper**

Cut sirloin into bite-size pieces. Mix marinade ingredients and pour over meat. Marinate at least 24 hours before cooking. Remove meat reserving marinade for sauce. Broil or saute' meat over hot flame. Should be served rare, hot and with sauce. To make sauce skim as much oil as possible from reserved marinade. Add sauce ingredients and heat to boiling. Use wooden picks or fondue forks for dipping meat into sauce.

🦃 CHILI-BEEF HORS D'OEUVRES

40-50 appetizers

1	3-4 pound chuck roast
	Water
1	cup chopped green chili (or more to taste)
1	teaspoon garlic powder
1½	teaspoons salt
3	eggs, lightly beaten
4	eggs, separated
	Pinch of salt
4	tablespoons flour
	Cooking oil

Place roast in a Dutch oven with a small amount of water and cook, tightly covered, until meat is tender and can be shredded. Reserve broth. Shred beef with a fork or in a food processor. Place shredded beef in a large bowl, add a small amount of reserved cooking broth, the chili, seasonings and 3 eggs. Mix well and set aside. Make a batter by beating 4 egg whites until stiff. While beating, gradually add the egg yolks, salt and flour, blending gently. Roll meat into bite-sized balls and dip in the batter. Fry balls in at least 3 inches of cooking oil heated to 375°. When lightly browned, remove from oil and drain well. Serve hot. These freeze well and may be reheated in a 350° oven for 20 minutes.

FESTIVE PARTY MEATBALLS

3-4 dozen appetizers

	Instant mashed-potato flakes
	Salad oil
1	large onion, minced
2	pounds ground beef
¾	cup dried bread crumbs
2	eggs
¼	teaspoon pepper
	Salt
1	20-ounce can pineapple chunks in natural juice
2	teaspoons cornstarch
1	8-ounce jar apple jelly

Prepare instant mashed potatoes for 2 servings (1 cup) as label directs but do not add salt. In a 12" skillet over medium-high heat, in 2 tablespoons hot salad oil, cook onion until tender. In large bowl, mix well onion, mashed potatoes, ground beef, bread crumbs, eggs, pepper and 2 teaspoons salt. Shape mixture into 1" balls. In same skillet, in 2 more tablespoons oil, cook meatballs until well browned. Remove meatballs to a large bowl as they brown and wipe skillet clean. Drain and reserve ½ cup juice from pineapple. In cup, stir reserved juice with cornstarch and ¾ teaspoon salt until smooth. In same skillet, over medium heat, melt apple jelly. Gradually stir pineapple-juice mixture into skillet and cook, stirring constantly, until sauce is thickened. Return meatballs to skillet, add pineapple chunks; heat through. Serve meatballs in chafing dish with cocktail picks.

🦆 CHILIES RELLENOS WON-TON

12 servings

2   **pounds lean ground beef**
2   **medium onions, chopped**
1   **clove garlic, crushed**
1½ **teaspoons salt**
½   **teaspoon oregano**
1   **teaspoon ground cumin**
4   **cups Cheddar cheese, shredded**
24 **fresh green chilies, roasted and peeled (or use canned)**
24 **egg roll wrappers**

Brown beef slowly over low heat; drain off excess grease. Add onions, garlic and seasonings; stir and cook until onions are golden. Remove from heat and add cheese. Blend well. Remove seeds from chilies, spread open and pat dry with paper towels. Fill each chili with 2 tablespoons of meat mixture. Roll up chilies like a jellyroll. Place each filled chili diagonally on individual egg roll wrapper. Wrap each chili as follows: lift lower triangle flap over chili and tuck the point under it. Bring left and right corners toward the center and roll, sealing edges with a few drops of water. Deep fry at 325° until golden brown. Drain on paper towels. Serve immediately.

Absolutely spectacular!

🦆 SWEET CHILIES RELLENOS APPETIZERS

20 appetizers

2   **pounds beef chuck, cut into 1″ chunks**
1   **cup raisins**
1   **cup brown sugar**
1   **teaspoon salt**
2   **teaspoons cinnamon**
⅛   **teaspoon black pepper**
¼   **teaspoon ground cloves**
1   **cup chopped green chili**
½   **cup nuts, chopped**
1   **egg, beaten**
¾   **cup flour**
3   **eggs, separated**
1   **teaspoon flour**
⅛   **teaspoon salt**

Barely cover beef with water and simmer until tender, about 1 hour. Drain meat and shred by hand or grind coarsely. Combine beef with raisins, sugar, salt, spices, chili, nuts and 1 beaten egg. Form into 2 inch oval croquettes; roll each croquette in the ¾ cup flour until lightly coated. Beat egg whites until stiff; fold in yolks beaten with 1 teaspoon flour and 1/8 teaspoon salt. Dip each floured croquette into egg batter. Fry croquettes, one or two at a time, in 2 inches of hot (420°) oil until golden brown. Drain on paper towels and serve warm.

🐦 TAQUITAS (Rolled Taco Appetizers)   24 appetizers

2   **pounds ground beef**
1   **medium onion, chopped finely**
2   **teaspoons salt**
1   **teaspoon black pepper**
    Dash hot pepper sauce
1   **cup tomato sauce**
1   **cup medium sharp Cheddar cheese, shredded**
12   **corn tortillas**
    Cooking oil

Brown beef and onion until onions are tender. Drain off excess grease. Mix in the salt, pepper, hot pepper sauce, tomato sauce, and cheese and blend until cheese is melted. Prepare tortillas by dipping briefly in hot oil (three seconds per side). They should remain soft. Drain well on paper towels before filling with two level tablespoons of meat mixture. Roll up and secure with toothpick. Deep fry at 350° for two minutes or until crisp. Drain well. Serve with Mexican salsa for dipping.

May be frozen and packaged for later use. Thaw before frying.

CAPONATA   10 servings

1   **eggplant**
½   **teaspoon salt**
¼   **teaspoon pepper**
2   **tablespoons olive oil**
2   **tablespoons lemon juice**
3   **green onions, chopped**
2   **tablespoons parsley, chopped**
1   **clove garlic, minced**
3   **tablespoons capers**
¼   **cup sliced, stuffed green olives**
¼   **teaspoon dried oregano leaves**

Bake unpeeled, whole eggplant in 450° oven until skin blisters. Peel. Place eggplant in a bowl. Chop or mash. Add remaining ingredients and mix well. Chill. This is a most pleasing accompaniment to roast meats or poultry. It may also be used as an antipasto, served on individual plates atop a Romaine leaf or may be spread on crackers.

CHICKEN NUT BITES

60-75 appetizers

1 cup chicken broth
½ cup butter or margarine
1 cup flour
1 tablespoon snipped parsley
2 teaspoons salt
2 teaspoons Worcestershire sauce
¾ teaspoons celery seed
½ teaspoon paprika
⅛ teaspoon cayenne
4 eggs
1 5-ounce can boned chicken, drained and chopped
¼ cup chopped toasted almonds

In saucepan combine broth and butter, bring to boiling. Stir in flour, parsley, salt, Worcestershire, celery seed, paprika and cayenne. Cook, beating rapidly, until mixture leaves sides of pan and forms a smooth, compact ball. Remove from heat. Add eggs one at a time, beating well after each addition, until mixture is shiny. Stir in chicken and almonds. Drop by scant rounded teaspoons onto lightly greased baking sheets. Bake at 400° 15-20 minutes or until browned. Serve hot. Can be frozen and warmed before serving.

SAVORY CHICKEN LIVERS

6-8 servings

1 pound chicken livers, rinsed well and patted dry
2 tablespoons salad oil
1 tablespoon minced parsley or parsley flakes
1 teaspoon tarragon leaves
1 small onion, diced
¼ teaspoon salt
⅛ teaspoon pepper
Flour
Butter or oil

Combine chicken livers, oil, parsley, tarragon, onion, salt and pepper and marinate 30 minutes. Dredge livers in flour and saute' in hot butter or oil in frying pan. Remove livers to pan and keep in 250° oven until ready to serve.

Also a savory main dish.

BAKED STUFFED CLAMS

½ cup butter
⅓ cup green onions, finely diced
⅔ cup celery, finely diced
2 6½-ounce cans minced clams
Salt to taste
Pepper to taste
1 teaspoon oregano
2 tablespoons Parmesan cheese
¾-1 cup bread crumbs
1 tablespoon clam juice
Paprika
Pastry shells
Parsley for garnish

Melt butter in fry pan. Saute' green onions and celery. Add clams. Heat gently and blend well; season with oregano, salt and pepper. Add Parmesan cheese and bread crumbs and stir until pasty. Add clam juice. Spoon into pastry shells and sprinkle with paprika. Slide under broiler until tops look crusty. Garnish with parsley.

SHRIMP DIJON

2 pounds cleaned shrimp
2 tablespoons shrimp spice
½ cup red wine vinegar
¼ cup salad oil
1½ teaspoons salt
2 tablespoons minced chives
2 tablespoons chopped dill pickle
2 tablespoons prepared mustard with horse-radish

Cook shrimp in boiling water with shrimp spice. Drain well. Mix remaining ingredients. Pour over warm shrimp. Cover and chill several hours, turning occasionally. Drain before serving.

Up, Up and Ole!

On many a cool, crisp New Mexico morning the windless sky is transformed into an outrageously colorful canvas by hot air balloons soundlessly hovering above city, village and desert. The color becomes a veritable riot each October when hundreds of balloonists from around the world participate in the International Balloon Fiesta, an annual event that lasts nine days and keeps area residents in a marathon session of sky-gazing! During the fiesta there are several mass ascensions that fill the sky with blazing color; there also are numerous competitions that test the skill of the balloonists and their crews. Tradition dictates that if a balloon lands in your yard, its occupants must present the resident with a bottle of champagne -- usually to be uncorked right on the spot! Many pioneers and record-holders in balloon travel and technology come from the Albuquerque area ❖

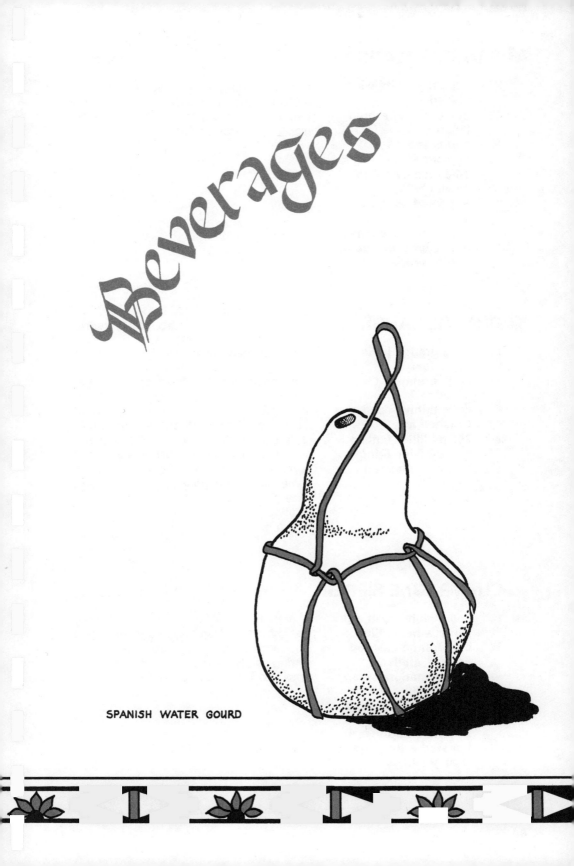

Beverages

SPANISH WATER GOURD

🦢 SANGRÍA BLANCA

5½ cups

3½	cups dry white wine, chilled
½	cup orange-flavored liqueur
¼	cup brandy
¼	cup sugar
1	10-ounce bottle club soda, chilled
1	unpeeled lemon, sliced
2	limes, cut in wedges
1	unpeeled green apple, cut in wedges

Combine wine, orange liqueur, brandy and sugar in a clear glass pitcher until well blended. To serve, stir in club soda. Garnish with pieces of fruit.

🦢 ORANGE SANGRÍA

about 2½ quarts

1¼	cups orange juice
1	cup sugar
2	large oranges, thinly sliced
1	lime, thinly sliced
	Crushed ice
2	750-milliliter bottles dry red wine (Pinot Noir or Zinfandel)

In a saucepan combine the orange juice and sugar and bring the mixture to a boil over moderately low heat, stirring occasionally until sugar is dissolved. Simmer the syrup, undisturbed, for 5 minutes and let it cool. Add fruits and let macerate, chilled, for at least 4 hours. Fill a large pitcher one third full with crushed ice, spoon in the fruit, mashing it slightly to release some juice, and pour in the syrup and wine. Stir well.

Wonderful!

CHAMPAGNE SIPPER

25 servings

1	750-milliliter bottle dry white wine, chilled
½	cup orange-flavored liqueur, chilled
¼	cup grenadine syrup
2	750-milliliter bottles dry pink champagne, chilled
1	28-ounce bottle carbonated water, chilled
	Orange slices

In a punch bowl combine wine, liqueur and grenadine. Carefully pour champagne and carbonated water down side of bowl, stirring gently. Garnish with orange slices. Pour into 4 ounce cups and serve.

✦MARGARITAS OLÉ

4 servings

3   ounces lime juice
3   ounces triple sec
6   ounces daiquiri mix
6   ounces tequila
1   egg white
1   tablespoon honey

Combine all ingredients in blender and mix well.

APPLE MIST

2 servings

½   cup vodka
6-8   ice cubes
1   cup apple cider
1   cup ginger ale

In each of 2 chilled 12-ounce glasses pour ¼ cup of the vodka over 3 or 4 ice cubes. Stir in ½ cup each of apple cider and ginger ale.

Inspired by native New Mexican apples!

BLOODY MARY PITCHER

8 servings

   Ice cubes
2   cups vodka
1   46-ounce can tomato juice, chilled
1   tablespoon lemon juice
⅛   teaspoon salt
⅛   teaspoon ground red pepper
1½   teaspoons Worcester-shire sauce
   Hot pepper sauce

In a large pitcher with ice cubes, combine vodka, tomato juice, lemon juice, salt, red pepper and Worcestershire sauce. For a spicier drink add a few drops of hot pepper sauce. Stir well. Makes about 2 quarts.

GRANDMA ANNA'S FIRE VODKA

6-8 servings

1   cup honey
½   cup water
1   teaspoon vanilla
¼   teaspoon nutmeg
1   tablespoon cinnamon
½   teaspoon ground cloves
1   teaspoon grated lemon rind
2½   cups vodka

Combine honey and water, vanilla, spices, lemon rind. Bring to boil, cover and simmer 5 minutes. Add vodka, heat through and serve immediately.

Chase away winter chills!

LIME APPEAL

4-6 servings

2½ cups cracked ice
1 6-ounce can frozen limeade concentrate, partially thawed
¼ cup lemon juice
1¼ cups vodka
1 10-ounce bottle club soda, chilled
Mint sprigs for garnish

Combine ice, limeade concentrate and lemon juice in blender and mix at medium speed 1 minute. Add vodka and blend well. Pour in soda and mix briefly on low speed. Serve in stemmed cocktail or wine glasses and garnish with mint.

STRAWBERRY REFRESHER

4 servings

1 cup whole frozen strawberries
Juice of ½ lemon
1 cup vodka
1 cup carbonated lemon-lime soda
6 ice cubes
1 egg white

Blend well strawberries, juice, vodka, carbonated beverage and ice in a blender. Add egg white and reblend. Pour into glasses and serve immediately.

HOPPEL POPPEL

6-8 servings

4 egg yolks
7 tablespoons sugar
1 teaspoon vanilla extract
1 quart hot milk
1 cup rum or cognac
Nutmeg

Beat egg yolks with sugar until frothy. Stir in vanilla and slowly pour in hot milk, beating constantly. Mix with rum or cognac and pour into heated mugs or punch cups. Dust with nutmeg.

In 17th century Holland, this was a "ladies' drink".

PIÑAS COLADAS

1 quart

½ cup cream of coconut (or coconut-milk cream)
1 cup unsweetened pineapple juice, chilled
⅔ cup light rum
2 cups crushed ice

Refrigerate 6 cocktail glasses to chill well. In blender, combine cream of coconut, pineapple juice, rum and ice; cover and blend at high speed ½ minute. Pour into chilled glasses. If desired, serve with a pineapple spear.

TEETOTALER'S REVENGE

8 cups

2 cups rum
⅔ cup sugar
1 cup orange juice
¼ cup lemon juice
¼ cup vodka
4 cups hot strong tea
Orange and lemon
slices for garnish

Combine rum and sugar in pan and bring to a boil over medium heat. Increase heat to reduce liquid by one-fourth. Stir in remaining liquids. Divide among eight 8-ounce mugs rinsed with boiling water. Garnish with slices of orange and lemon.

Great after a day of skiing!

RUM PUNCH

30 servings

1 12-ounce can frozen orange juice concentrate
1 12-ounce can frozen lemonade concentrate
1 46-ounce can pineapple juice
1 46-ounce can grapefruit juice
2 cups sugar
2 1-quart bottles carbonated lemon-lime soda
Rum to taste

Mix juices and sugar in a large container. Freeze for 24 hours in two half-gallon milk cartons. Take out of freezer 1 hour before serving. Mixture should have a slushy consistency. To serve, combine 1 quart carbonated beverage and 1 milk carton of juice mixture in a punch bowl. Pour in rum to taste. Pour into 6-ounce glasses.

RIPSNORTIN PUNCH

40-50 servings

1 750-milliliter bottle Southern Comfort
3 quarts ginger ale
1 6-ounce can frozen lemonade concentrate
1 6-ounce can frozen orange juice concentrate
6 ounces fresh lemon juice
4 ounces grenadine syrup
Orange and lemon slices to float

Combine all ingredients in a punch bowl and chill with an ice mold.

BOURBON SLUSH

10 servings

2 tea bags
1 cup boiling water
1 cup sugar
3½ cups water
1 6-ounce can frozen orange juice concentrate, thawed
½ cup bourbon
1 6-ounce can frozen lemonade concentrate, thawed

Steep tea bags in the boiling water for 3 minutes. Remove the bags, stir in sugar and add remaining ingredients. Mix until sugar is dissolved. Pour into freezer container and freeze until firm. Remove about 10 minutes before serving. Serve in punch cups.

APRICOT BRANDY SLUSH

8-10 servings

2 tea bags
1 cup boiling water
1 cup sugar
3½ cups cold water
1 6-ounce can frozen orange juice concentrate, undiluted
1 6-ounce can frozen lemonade concentrate, undiluted
1 cup apricot brandy
1 quart lemon lime soda

Place tea bags in boiling water and steep 5 minutes. While hot add sugar and stir until dissolved. Add water, orange juice, lemonade and brandy and stir. Place in covered container in freezer. When ready to serve, fill glass three-quarters full with slush mixture. Cover with lemon-lime soda.

BRANDY FIZZ

6-8 servings

1 6-ounce can unthawed frozen orange juice concentrate
1 6-ounce can unthawed frozen lemonade concentrate
2 cups ice cubes
1 teaspoon sugar
2 cups club soda
1 cup brandy

Spoon concentrates into the work bowl of a food processor fitted with a steel knife, distributing evenly. Process until smooth, about 1 minute. Add ice cubes, sugar and mix until ice is completely crushed and mixture is fluffy, about 2 to 3 minutes. Transfer to pitcher. Stir in club soda and brandy. Pour into chilled wine glasses.

SPICED CRANBERRY-CIDER DRINK

20-30 servings

8 cups apple cider
3 cups cranberry juice
1 teaspoon whole cloves
1 teaspoon whole allspice
6 cinammon sticks
1 orange, quartered
1-1½ cups brandy

Combine cider and cranberry juice in a saucepan. Place the cloves, allspice, and cinnamon sticks in a cheese cloth or tea ball and place in the liquid. Add the orange. Simmer for 30 minutes. Just before serving add the brandy.

A great holiday drink!

HOME-STYLE CREME DE MENTHE

2½ quarts

8 cups sugar
6 cups water
1 500-milliliter bottle grain alcohol (190 proof)
1 ounce peppermint extract
1 tablespoon green food coloring

In a saucepan combine sugar and water and bring to a boil; simmer for 15 minutes. Cool. Stir in remaining ingredients. Pour mixture into a gallon container; cover and let ripen for at least 1 month.

HOT TÍA MARIA AND COFFEE

1 drink

1 teaspoon sugar
   Hot coffee
1½ ounces Tia Maria
3 tablespoons heavy cream, lightly whipped
   Chocolate shavings

In an Irish coffee glass or mug combine the sugar and enough hot coffee to dissolve the sugar. Add the Tia Maria and fill the glass to within 1 inch of the rim with hot coffee. Float 3 tablespoons lightly whipped cream on the coffee and sprinkle it with chocolate shavings to taste.

HOT CHOCOLATE DELUXE

1 serving

1 cup chocolate milk
1 ounce almond-flavored liqueur
   Marshmallow creme
   Cinnamon

Heat chocolate milk. Remove from heat and add the liqueur. Pour into a mug. Top with the marshmallow creme and sprinkle with cinnamon.

Rich enough for dessert.

CHOCOLATE LIQUEUR

6 servings

5	egg yolks
¾	cup powdered sugar
1½	tablespoons chocolate syrup
1⅔	cups vodka
½	cup heavy cream

Beat egg yolks with sugar until thick and creamy. Add syrup. Add vodka and mix. Whip cream; fold into liqueur. Serve after dinner.

Rich as the richest dessert!

SPICED TEA

1 gallon

1	cup orange juice
1½	lemons, juiced
1"	stick cinnamon
1	teaspoon whole cloves
½	gallon apple juice
1	cup sugar
2½	tablespoons tea leaves
3	quarts water

Mix all ingredients except dry tea and water. Bring water to a boil, add tea and steep 5 minutes. Add remaining ingredients and steep 5 minutes more. Serve hot.

ORANGE FROTHY

about 3 cups

½	of 6-ounce can frozen orange juice concentrate
½	cup milk
½	cup water
¼	cup sugar
½	teaspoon vanilla
	5 or 6 ice cubes
	Rum or Vodka to taste (optional)

Combine all ingredients in blender container; cover and blend till smooth, about 30 seconds. Serve immediately.

ALMOND PUNCH

12-18 servings

1	6-ounce can frozen orange juice concentrate
1	6-ounce can frozen lemonade concentrate
¼	cup sugar
2	teaspoons almond extract
3	teaspoons vanilla
10	6-ounce cans water

Mix all ingredients well and serve hot or cold.

TROPICAL COCONUT COOLER

6 servings

3   **cups pear or apricot nectar**
1   **15-ounce can coconut cream**
1   **cup rum**
1   **cup club soda**
½   **cup lime juice**

Combine ingredients in blender. Place in pitcher with ice and stir.

Without the rum, this is a wonderful children's drink.

PATIO COOLER

6-8 servings

4   **bananas**
2   **cups crushed pineapple, undrained**
2   **cups orange juice**
10   **maraschino cherries**
¾   **cup sugar**
2   **tablespoons lemon juice**
     Pinch salt
     Lemon-lime carbonated beverage

Place half of the ingredients in blender and blend. Blend rest of ingredients and combine the two mixtures. Freeze in 3 ice cube trays with dividers in. To store, place cubes in plastic bags in freezer. To serve, place 3-4 cubes in a tall glass and fill with chilled lemon-lime carbonated beverage. (You may also add a jigger of vodka, if desired.)

CRANBERRY PUNCH

3 quarts

1½   **cups sugar**
6   **cups water**
2-3   **cinnamon sticks**
2   **cups cranberry juice**
1   **cup pineapple juice**
2   **cups orange juice**
1   **cup lemon juice**

In a saucepan, combine sugar and 2 cups water and boil for 10 minutes. Add remaining ingredients. Cover and simmer for at least 1 hour. Good served hot or cold.

AMBROSIA SHAKE

5 servings

4   **fully ripe bananas, sliced**
⅓   **cup orange juice**
6   **tablespoons honey**
     Pinch of salt
¼   **teaspoon almond extract**
1   **quart cold milk**
½   **cup whipping cream, whipped**
¼   **cup shredded coconut**

Combine bananas, juice, honey, salt and almond extract in a blender. Whip until smooth. Add milk and blend until well-mixed. To serve, pour into 8-ounce glasses and garnish with whipped cream and coconut.

The Melting Pot.....

Twentieth century New Mexico is a tapestry woven by four very different cultures: Indian, Spanish, Mexican and Anglo. Descendants of the original Indian settlers are today's Navajo, Apache and Pueblo Indians. Spanish and Mexican influence in the area began with the northern expedition of Spanish explorer Coronado in 1540 and is evidenced today in the state's distinctive cuisine, architecture, religions and arts. Spanish language, the first official language, is an integral part of New Mexican culture. The Anglo latecomers began arriving in New Mexico during the westward migration over the Santa Fé Trail and with the extension of the Santa Fé Railroad in 1880. This unique rectangular relationship has produced a rich cultural mixture that is manifested in the state's pageantry, handicrafts, cuisine and methods of worship ❖

Soups and Sandwiches

COPPER SOUP POT

BLACK BEAN SOUP

4-6 servings

1 cup dry black beans
6 cups stock, either chicken or beef
¼ cup oil
1 cup chopped celery
1 cup chopped onion
2 cloves garlic, crushed
⅓ cup uncooked brown rice
⅛ teaspoon cayenne
1 bay leaf
1 teaspoon salt
2-4 peppercorns
2 whole cloves
½ cup powdered milk

Soak beans overnight. Drain and cook with 6 cups stock until tender, about 2 hours. In large Dutch oven, heat oil; saute' celery, onion and garlic until soft. Add rice and saute' 2-3 minutes longer. Stir in 1 cup of stock from beans. Add beans and rest of liquid in which they were cooked. Add remaining ingredients except milk. Cook 1-2 hours. Blend milk with ½ cup soup broth; add mixture to soup. Serve garnished with chopped green onion and lime slices, if desired.

BROCCOLI-CAULIFLOWER SOUP

6-8 servings

1 10-ounce package frozen cauliflower
1 10-ounce package frozen chopped broccoli
1 13¾ ounce can condensed chicken broth
½ teaspoon dried dillweed
½ teaspoon ground mace
⅓ cup chopped onion
¼ cup margarine
2 tablespoons flour
Salt and pepper to taste
3½ cups milk
4 ounces shredded Swiss cheese

In a saucepan cook the cauliflower in half the chicken broth for 6 minutes. In a second saucepan cook the broccoli, dill and remaining broth for 6 minutes. Then, in a blender bowl blend the cauliflower (with liquid) and mace until smooth. In a Dutch oven saute' the onions in the margarine; stir in flour, salt and pepper. Add the milk and cook until bubbly. Stir in all other ingredients and heat until cheese is melted. Do not boil. Serve hot.

CREAM OF CAULIFLOWER SOUP

4 servings

½   small green pepper,
    cut in julienne strips
½   small red pepper, cut
    in julienne strips
    Water
    Large head cauliflower
1½ cups chicken stock
1   cup half-and-half
½   cup heavy cream
¾   teaspoon salt
¾   teaspoon white pepper
6   tablespoons butter,
    softened

Blanch peppers in boiling water to cover for 1 minute. Drain and refresh under cold water and set aside. Trim cauliflower and break into flowerettes. Boil in salted water 15 minutes; drain. Puree cauliflower in blender with chicken broth. Bring cauliflower mixture to a boil in a kettle. Stir in creams, salt and pepper; heat just to boiling point. Swirl in butter. Ladle the soup into heated bowls and garnish with pepper strips.

CREAM OF FRESH TOMATO SOUP

8 servings

4   cups fresh tomatoes,
    peeled and seeded
6   tablespoons butter
2   tablespoons flour
1   teaspoon salt
⅛   teaspoon pepper
⅛   teaspoon cloves
⅛   teaspoon cinnamon
½   teaspoon baking soda
4   cups milk
    Croutons for garnish

Chop tomatoes and cook in half the butter in 4-quart pan for 5 minutes. In another large saucepan melt remaining butter; add flour, salt, pepper, cloves and cinnamon. Cook mixture for 2 minutes stirring with wire whisk. Add baking soda to cooked tomatoes and mix well. Add tomato mixture to flour mixture. Cook 5 minutes. Add milk and bring just to boiling. Serve hot with croutons.

CREAMY ONION SOUP

10-12 servings

1½ cups butter (3 sticks)
4   cups white onions,
    sliced
1¾ cups flour
12 cups beef stock
½   teaspoon cayenne
1½ tablespoons salt
1   egg yolk
2   tablespoons cream

In a 6-quart soup kettle melt butter. Add onions and reduce heat to very low; cook until onions are translucent. (Be careful not to brown onions in the first stage of cooking.) Add flour and cook 5-10 minutes more, stirring occasionally. Blend in beef stock very slowly. Add salt and cayenne and bring to a boil. Reduce heat and simmer about 15 minutes. Remove kettle from heat. Beat together egg yolk and cream, add a little of the soup and mix quickly; then add to the soup kettle. Serve in soup cups topped with toasted rounds of bread sprinkled with grated Parmesan cheese. Brown quickly under broiler and serve immediately.

FRENCH ONION SOUP

6-8 servings

4 tablespoons butter
2 tablespoons oil
1 teaspoon salt
2 pounds onions, thinly sliced (approximately 7 cups)
3 tablespoons flour
4 cups beef broth
6-8 1″ slices French bread
¼ cup olive oil
½ cup Swiss cheese, grated
½ cup fresh Parmesan, grated

Melt butter and oil; add salt and onions. Cook over low heat for 20-30 minutes until onions are clear, stirring often. Sprinkle flour over onions and stir for 2-3 minutes; remove from heat. Heat stock until it simmers in a large pot. Add onions to stock and simmer for 30-40 minutes. Correct seasoning to taste. While soup simmers, prepare topping: brush bread slices with olive oil and brown on both sides. Then ladle some soup into a bowl, add a spoon of cheese, then a bread slice, then more cheese. Bake for 10-12 minutes at 375° or until cheese bubbles.

HOTCHPOT CHOWDER

6 servings

2 cups whole kernel corn
2 cups chopped celery
½ cup green pepper, cut in strips
1 onion, sliced thin
1 cup chopped tomatoes
1 tablespoon salt
⅛ teaspoon pepper
1 cup cold water
¼ cup butter or margarine
3 tablespoons flour
¼ teaspoon paprika
3½ cups milk, scalded
½ cup grated sharp Cheddar cheese
1 pimiento, sliced thin

In a saucepan combine corn, celery, green pepper, onion, tomatoes, salt and pepper and water. Bring to a boil; reduce heat and simmer covered for 15 minutes. Knead butter, flour and paprika together and stir into hot milk. Add milk mixture to vegetable mixture. Transfer to an ovenproof casserole, cover and bake in 300° oven for 15-20 minutes. Add cheese and pimiento and continue baking until cheese is melted, about 5 minutes longer.

MINESTRONE SOUP WITH PESTO

¼	cup olive oil
1	clove garlic, minced
1	onion, finely chopped
1	leek, washed and diced
1	tablespoon parsley
½	teaspoon dried thyme
1	tablespoon tomato paste
3	medium tomatoes, peeled, seeded and chopped
2	stalks celery, chopped
2	carrots, diced
2	potatoes, diced
1	10-ounce package frozen green beans
12	cups water
12	beef boullion cubes
1	cup elbow macaroni or detali
1½	cups kidney beans, cooked and drained
	Pesto (below)
	Parmesan cheese

Heat oil; add garlic, onion, leek, parsley and thyme. Add tomato paste, tomatoes, celery, carrots, potatoes, string beans, water and boullion cubes. Simmer, covered, about 1 hour. Bring to a boil, add macaroni and cook until tender, about 8-10 minutes. Add beans; heat. If more liquid is needed add 1 cup and 1 boullion cube per serving. Serve with pesto and Parmesan cheese.

PESTO:

1	10-ounce package frozen chopped spinach, thawed and well-drained
1	teaspoon dried basil
3	cloves, garlic, minced
1	tablespoon parsley flakes
4	tablespoons salad oil
2	tablespoons butter
¼	cup Parmesan cheese

Combine all ingredients in blender till smooth. Put 1-2 tablespoons in each bowl of minestrone.

Pesto is also delicious served over pasta.

CURRIED MUSHROOM SOUP

4 servings

1	pound fresh mushrooms
5	tablespoons butter
1	teaspoon curry powder
2	tablespoons all-purpose flour
1	10½ ounce can condensed beef broth, undiluted
¼	teaspoon salt
⅛	teaspoon white pepper
3	cups half-and-half

Rinse mushrooms and pat dry; cut in half. Melt 4 tablespoons butter in saucepan; add mushrooms and curry powder. Saute' until mushrooms are lightly browned, stirring constantly. Remove mushrooms from saucepan and set aside. Melt remaining butter in same saucepan and blend in flour; add broth, salt and pepper. Cook until thickened, stirring constantly. Add half-and-half and cook 8 additional minutes, stirring constantly. Do not boil. Return sauteed mushrooms to soup.

SPECIAL PUMPKIN SOUP

8-10 servings

1½	cups white bread crumbs
4-8	pound pumpkin with a flat bottom
7	tablespoons butter
1	teaspoon salt
⅔	cup minced onion
⅛	teaspoon pepper
⅛	teaspoon nutmeg
½	teaspoon sage
1	bay leaf
½	cup grated Swiss cheese
	Chicken broth, enough to fill within ½" of rim
1	cup heavy cream
	Parsley

Dry bread crumbs in oven at 300° for 15 minutes. Cut a lid in pumpkin, remove seeds and fibrous insides; discard. Rub inside of pumpkin with mixture of 1 tablespoon butter and ½ teaspoon salt. Cook onions in 6 tablespoons butter for 10 minutes. Stir in bread crumbs, continue stirring and cook 10 minutes longer. Stir in ½ teaspoon salt, other seasonings and cheese. Put crumbs and cheese in pumpkin. Fill pumpkin with enough chicken broth to fill with in ½" of top. Put pumpkin lid on. Place on a cookie sheet and bake at 400° for 1½ hours. Reduce heat to 350°. Remove lid and add enough cream to fill to rim. Put on lid and heat through. To serve, use the pumpkin as a soup tureen. Make sure to ladle out the soft inside of the pumpkin. Garnish with parsley.

It's fun to decorate a table around this eye-catching entree.

CALDO LARGO

4 servings

2 tablespoons salad oil
2 medium tomatoes, peeled and diced
1 medium green pepper, cut in strips
1 4-ounce can chopped green chilies
1 10-ounce can tomatoes and green chilies
1½ cup chicken broth
1 cup evaporated milk
Salt to taste
¼ pound Monterey Jack cheese, diced

Heat oil. Add the tomatoes and pepper and cook until soft. Combine cooked tomatoes and peppers, chili, tomatoes and green chilies and broth. Simmer 10 minutes. Stir in milk and salt. Do not boil. Mix in cheese and when it starts to melt ladle into soup bowls.

TORTILLA SOUP

6-8 servings

1 package (12) small corn tortillas
Peanut oil
1 medium onion, diced
3 14½ ounce cans chicken broth
2 8-ounce cans tomato sauce
1 16-ounce can tomatoes, diced
¼ teaspoon garlic powder
Dash hot pepper sauce
3 cups grated Cheddar cheese

Cut tortillas into chips. Deep fry chips in oil heated to 375°. Add chips in batches and fry until golden brown. Drain well. Heat small amount of oil in large saucepan. Add onions and saute until clear. Add broth, tomato sauce, tomatoes, garlic powder and hot pepper sauce; simmer 20 minutes. Place a few chips in individual soup bowls. Fill ¾ full with soup and top generously with cheese. Serve with remaining tortilla chips.

Too busy to cook? Try this soup — it's hearty but quick.

CHICKEN CHEESE CHOWDER

4 servings

4 tablespoons butter or margarine
1 cup shredded carrots
¼ cup chopped onion
¼ cup all-purpose flour
2 cups milk
1 13¾ ounce can chicken broth
1 cup diced cooked chicken
1 tablespoon dry white wine
½ teaspoon celery seed
½ teaspoon Worcester- shire sauce
1 cup shredded sharp process American cheese
   Snipped chives

In a large saucepan, melt butter or margarine and cook carrots and onions until tender but not brown. Blend in flour; add milk and chicken broth. Cook and stir until thickened and bubbly. Stir in chicken, wine, celery seed and Worcestershire sauce. Heat through. Add cheese and stir until melted. Garnish with snipped chives, if desired.

CHICKEN CREOLE GUMBO

6-8 servings

1 whole fryer, about 3 pounds
1 quart water
2 stalks celery, chopped
1 teaspoon salt
⅛ teaspoon pepper
1 large onion, chopped
2 chicken bouillon cubes
3 tablespoons margarine
1 green pepper, chopped
1 bay leaf
1 teaspoon gumbo file' powder
1 16-ounce can stewed tomatoes
1 cup sliced okra, fresh, canned or frozen
¼ cup converted rice, un- cooked
1 tablespoon chopped parsley

Cook chicken in a large kettle in the water with the celery, salt, pepper, onion and bouillon cubes for 1 hour. Lift chicken from broth, reserving broth for later. Bone, skin and cut up chicken into bite-sized pieces. Melt margarine in large skillet and saute' chicken and green pepper. Then add chicken, peppers, bay leaf, gumbo file', tomatoes, okra, rice and parsley to the reserved broth. Cook for 45 minutes. Add more water, if desired, and adjust seasoning.

CRAB AND PEA SOUP

4 servings

2 cups canned chicken broth
1 10½-ounce can condensed cream of pea soup
1 7-ounce can crabmeat, flaked
2 tablespoons white rum
¼ teaspoon salt
¼ teaspoon white pepper
⅛ teaspoon nutmeg
1 cup whipping cream, whipped

Bring two soups to boiling, stirring occasionally, then simmer. Add crab, rum and spices. Heat for 5 minutes or until crab is heated through. Fold in whipping cream, heat but do not boil. Serve with croutons.

CREAM OF SHRIMP SOUP

4 servings

1 pound shelled shrimp, cleaned
1 quart water
¼ cup butter
¼ cup flour
2 cups chicken broth
2 cups half-and-half
½ teaspoon salt
½ teaspoon white pepper
4 tablespoons tomato paste

Put shrimp into boiling water and cook for 3-4 minutes; drain. Melt butter in a large saucepan and stir in the flour to make a smooth paste; do not scorch. Add chicken broth slowly, stirring constantly until thickened. Stir in half-and-half, shrimp, salt, white pepper and tomato paste. Simmer until heated through, stirring frequently.

BEEF AND TOMATO SOUP

6-8 servings

½ pound flank steak
2 tablespoons soy sauce
1 tablespoon corn starch
2 tablespoons peanut oil
2 medium sized tomatoes, peeled and sliced into eighths
2 green onions, chopped
6 cups water
1 slice ginger root
¼ teaspoon salt
Dash of pepper
1 egg

Trim steak of all fat. Cut into strips about 1″ wide, cutting with the grain, then slice strips across grain on the diagonal about ¼″ thick. Marinate meat in mixture of cornstarch and one tablespoon soy sauce. Heat peanut oil in 3-quart saucepan; add tomatoes and chopped green onions. Cook over medium heat, stirring constantly, about 5 minutes. Add water and ginger root and bring to a boil. Stir in marinated meat; bring to a second boil and cook for five minutes. Add salt, pepper and remaining soy sauce. Beat egg lightly and stir gradually into soup mixture. Remove and serve when egg has formed threads.

A good soup for Saturday lunch. Serve with a thick grilled cheese sandwich.

BEEF 'N' VEGETABLE SOUP

8-10 servings

½ cup butter or margarine
1 cup flour
1 quart hot water
2 pounds ground chuck
1 cup onions, chopped
1 cup carrots, cut in 1" cubes
1 cup celery, sliced
1 10-ounce package frozen mixed vegetables
2 cups canned tomatoes, chopped
2 tablespoons beef flavor base paste (if liquid form is used, double the amount)
Black pepper to taste (the more the better)

Melt margarine or butter in a large Dutch oven. Blend in flour to make a smooth paste. Stir in hot water. Saute' ground beef in a large skillet and drain off drippings. Add meat to liquid. Add frozen and fresh vegetables, tomatoes and seasonings. Bring soup to a boil; then simmer until vegetables are cooked. Serve hot.

CHINESE NOODLE MEAT BALL SOUP

4-6 servings

½ pound ground beef round
1 teaspoon cornstarch
2 tablespoons finely minced green onions
¼ teaspoon salt
Pepper to taste
2 10½-ounce cans beef broth
3¾ cups water
2 tablespoons dry sherry
1 tablespoon soy sauce
1 teaspoon minced, peeled ginger root (optional)
1½ cups very fine egg noodles
1⅓ cups thinly sliced mushrooms
1⅓ cups small pieces of torn fresh spinach, tightly packed

In a small bowl combine beef, cornstarch, green onions, salt and pepper. Shape teaspoonfuls of meat mixture into balls and set aside. Place beef broth, water, sherry, soy sauce and ginger in a 3-quart saucepan and bring to a boil over moderately high heat. Gradually add noodles to broth, and when mixture returns to a boil, gradually add meat balls; continue cooking soup uncovered 6 minutes. Add sliced mushrooms to the soup and cook 5 minutes longer. Stir in the spinach and cook 1 minute.

GULASCHSUPPE

3 tablespoons cooking oil
6 pounds cubed stewing beef
1½ pounds onions, chopped
2 green peppers, diced
1 pound mushrooms, sliced
10 cups water
1 tablespoon salt
¼ teaspoon garlic powder
6 tablespoons paprika
1 teaspoon ground cumin
2 cups beef bouillon
1 8-ounce can tomato sauce
1 6-ounce can tomato paste
2 cups dry red wine

Heat oil in a large kettle, brown meat and then onions. Add green peppers, mushrooms, water and spices. Simmer until meat is tender, about 1-1½ hours. Add bouillon, tomato sauce and paste. Return to boiling and simmer for 1 hour. To serve, stir in wine and heat through. Add water if needed.

HUNGARIAN MEATBALL SOUP

6 servings

6 cups water
2 cups tomatoes
½ cup chopped bell pepper
6 chopped green onions
3 sliced carrots
2-3 sliced celery stalks
2 teaspoons salt
2 peppercorns

MEATBALLS:

1 pound ground beef
1 cup uncooked rice
2 teaspoons salt
1 teaspoon paprika
1 teaspoon dried parsley
½ teaspoon garlic powder
¼ cup flour
Salad oil

Combine the first 8 ingredients and simmer 30 minutes. During this time make the meatballs by combining the next 6 ingredients. Make meatballs about 1″ in diameter. Dredge meatballs in flour and brown lightly in hot oil. When browned, add meatballs to soup and simmer 20 minutes. Remove peppercorns and serve.

A soup with old country flavor!

🐦 NEW MEXICO MEATBALL SOUP
4-6 servings

2   hard-cooked eggs
½   cup cooked brown rice
¼   cup soft bread crumbs
¼   cup chopped green onion
¼   cup chopped pitted ripe olives
¼   teaspoon dried rosemary
     Dash ground cloves
     Dash cinnamon
½   pound lean ground beef
½   pound ground pork
     Raisins
2   cups water
1   10½ ounce can condensed tomato soup
1   tablespoon chili powder
1   teaspoon instant beef bouillon granules
½   cup shredded Monterey Jack cheese
     Sliced olives for garnish
     Chopped green onion for garnish

Separate egg yolks from egg whites. Chop each separately. In a bowl combine the egg yolks, rice, bread crumbs, green onion, olives, rosemary, cloves and cinnamon. Add meats; mix well. Using 1½ tablespoons of meat mixture for each meatball, wrap mixture around three or four raisins and shape into balls. In a large saucepan combine water, soup, chili powder, bouillon granules and meatballs. Bring to a boil. Reduce heat; simmer covered for 30 minutes. Stir in chopped egg whites. To serve ladle into soup bowls, top each serving with some of the cheese, additional olives and chopped green onion.

This hearty soup is a meal in itself and should always be offered with generous amounts of crispy corn chips.

SPLIT PEA AND SAUSAGE SOUP
8-10 servings

1   pound dry green split peas
2   quarts water
1   ham bone or ham hock
1   cup chopped onions
¼   teaspoon garlic salt
2   bay leaves
1   crushed red chili pepper (or ½ teaspoon crushed red pepper)
¼   teaspoon crushed marjoram
1   cup chopped celery
1   cup chopped carrots
¾   pound Polish sausage, cut in large chunks

Cover peas with water. Bring to boil for 2 minutes, remove from heat and soak for 1 hour. To soaked peas add ham, onion, garlic salt, marjoram and red chili pepper. Bring to boil and add bay leaves. Reduce heat and simmer covered for 2 hours, stirring occasionally. Remove ham bone and cut meat into bite-size pieces. Put meat, celery and carrots in soup. Add sausage chunks. Simmer over low heat 1 hour.

TIFFANY'S BEAN POT SOUP

2	cups dried pinto beans
1	pound ham, cubed
1	quart water
1	22-ounce can tomato juice
4	cups chicken stock
3	onions, chopped
3	cloves garlic, minced
3	tablespoons chopped parsley
¼	cup chopped green pepper
4	tablespoons brown sugar
1	tablespoon chili powder
1	teaspoon salt
1	teaspoon crushed bay leaves
1	teaspoon oregano
½	teaspoon cumin seeds, ground
½	teaspoon rosemary leaves, crushed
½	teaspoon celery seed
½	teaspoon ground thyme
½	teaspoon ground marjoram
½	teaspoon sweet basil
¼	teaspoon curry powder
4	whole cloves
1	cup sherry

Soak cleaned beans in water overnight in a large Dutch oven. Drain and add remaining ingredients except the sherry. Bring to a boil, cover and cook slowly until beans are tender, about 3 hours. Add sherry. Serve in generous soup bowls topped with chopped green onion, if desired.

This soup probably was the best known item served at Tiffany's Saloon in Cerrillos, N.M. This saloon, operating in the Territorial Period, was one block east of the hotel where Governor Lew Wallace completed the writing of his famous "Ben Hur." Tiffany's burned to the ground on March 15, 1977. This recipe was made public by the restaurant.

WHITE GAZPACHO

2	cups sour cream
2	cups chicken broth
2-3	cucumbers
1	teaspoon salt
	Chives
	Diced green pepper
	Diced tomatoes
	Toasted almonds

Blend first four ingredients well in a blender or food processor and chill overnight. Before serving, blend again. Serve topped with chives, diced green pepper, diced tomatoes and toasted almonds.

CURRIED BROCCOLI SOUP

6 servings

2	**pounds broccoli**
2	**14-ounce cans chicken broth, undiluted**
3	**tablespoons butter**
2	**medium onions, chopped**
1½	**teaspoons curry powder**

Trim ends from broccoli. Cut flowerettes into bite-sized pieces. Coarsely chop stems. Set aside. Bring 1 cup of broth to boil in 3-quart saucepan; add half the flowerettes and boil, uncovered, 3-4 minutes or until tender when pierced. Drain, saving broth; cool, cover and chill broccoli. In same pan melt butter over medium heat; add onion and curry powder and cook onion until limp. Stir in broccoli stems, remaining flowerettes and remaining broth. Cover and simmer 12 minutes or until tender when pierced. Cool and divide into parts in order to whirl smooth in blender. Cover and chill. To serve, ladle into small bowls and top with reserved cooked flowerettes. Sprinkle with sour cream and peanuts or grated cheese and sunflower seeds, if desired.

AVOCADO SOUP

3-4 servings

1	**13¾ ounce can chicken broth**
2	**medium avocados, seeded, peeled and cut into chunks**
2	**tablespoons dry sherry**
½	**teaspoon salt**
¼	**teaspoon onion powder**
⅛	**teaspoon dried dillweed**
¾	**cup half-and-half**

Put all ingredients except the half-and-half in a blender and blend until smooth. Stir in half-and-half and refrigerate. Chill well. To serve, top each bowl with a slice of avocado or a dollop of sour cream or both.

COLD CURRIED PEA SOUP

4 servings

1	**cup raw potatoes, coarsely chopped**
1	**cup frozen green peas**
¼	**cup scallions, sliced**
1½	**cups canned chicken bouillon**
1	**cup half-and-half**
¼	**teaspoon curry powder (or more to taste)**
¼	**teaspoon celery salt (or more to taste)**

Add potatoes, peas and scallions to bouillon in saucepan. Bring to boil, reduce heat and simmer, covered, until vegetables are tender. Put mixture into blender for 30 seconds until pureed. (May use food processor.) Mix half-and-half, curry powder and celery salt together and pour slowly into pea mixture. Stir well and chill. To serve, top with garlic croutons.

ICY SPICY NEW MEXICAN SOUP

6-8 servings

2   **pounds ripe tomatoes, cut up, or 1 35-ounce can Italian tomatoes, undrained**
2   **tablespoons olive oil**
½   **cup diced onion**
1   **teaspoon minced garlic**
1   **4-ounce can chopped green chilies, drained**
3   **tablespoons flour**
3   **cups chicken broth**
1   **chicken-flavor bouillon cube**
¼   **teaspoon ground cumin seed**
¼   **teaspoon ground coriander seed**
¼   **teaspoon salt**
¼   **teaspoon ground pepper**
1   **teaspoon granulated sugar**
½   **cup sour cream**

Put tomatoes in a blender and blend 30 seconds or until pureed. In a large saucepan heat oil over moderate heat. Add onions, garlic and chilies and cook 3 minutes, stirring frequently. Add flour and cook 1 minute longer, stirring constantly. Gradually stir in pureed tomatoes and chicken broth. Add bouillon cube, cumin, coriander, salt and pepper; reduce heat to low and simmer 20 minutes, stirring often. Remove from heat and add sugar. Cover and refrigerate soup at least 3 hours or until it is completely cooled. Stir in sour cream, cover and refrigerate 2 to 4 hours. Ladle soup into bowls, mugs or wineglasses.

Utterly delectable!

CREAMY ZUCCHINI SOUP

6-8 servings

½   **cup green onions, sliced**
3   **tablespoons butter**
1½   **pounds zucchini, sliced**
1   **carrot, diced**
6   **cups chicken broth**
1½   **teaspoons wine vinegar**
¾   **teaspoon dried dillweed**
4   **tablespoons quick-cooking cream of wheat**
1   **teaspoon salt**
½   **teaspoon pepper**
½   **cup sour cream**

Cook green onion in butter until tender. Add zucchini, carrot, chicken broth, vinegar and herbs. Bring to boil; add cream of wheat and simmer 25 minutes; puree and add salt and pepper. For cold soup add sour cream right away, stir until smooth and chill before serving. For hot soup add sour cream to heated soup just before serving.

SUMMER SUNSHINE SOUP

1 clove garlic
1 tablespoon sugar
1½ teaspoons salt
1 teaspoon Worcestershire sauce
2 tablespoons lemon juice
2 ounces salad oil
1 46-ounce can tomato juice
2 cups diced fresh tomatoes
1½ cups diced cucumbers
¾ cup diced green pepper
1 cup diced carrots
1 cup diced celery
¼ cup diced green onions

Mash the garlic and put it and the next 6 ingredients in the blender and blend well. Add remaining ingredients, stir and chill. Serve with croutons, if desired.

SHRIMP GAZPACHO

12 servings

1 clove garlic, split
6-8 ounces small shrimp, cooked
3 ounces lemon juice
½ green pepper, chopped
4 large tomatoes, chopped
2 cups tomato juice
½ onion, chopped
¼ cup parsley, minced
1 large cucumber, chopped
2 tablespoons chives, minced
2 teaspoons salt
⅓ cup olive oil
Dash Tabasco

Rub a large wooden bowl with one split garlic. Place shrimp in bowl and sprinkle with lemon juice. Add remaining ingredients and refrigerate overnight. Additional tomato juice can be added if thinner consistency is desired. Serve as an appetizer or luncheon main course.

RUSSIAN CHOLODNIK

6 serving

4	cups buttermilk
1	cup shrimp, boiled and diced
1	cup unpeeled cucumber, diced and seeded
1	garlic clove, crushed
1	tablespoon grated onion
1	teaspoon dried dill
1	teaspoon salt
½	teaspoon powdered fennel
¼	teaspoon white pepper

Combine all ingredients well and let stand at room temperature 45 minutes. Chill well before serving.

RASPBERRY SOUP

3-4 servings

1	cup fresh or frozen raspberries
½	cup rose' wine
½	cup brown sugar
½	cup sour cream
	Lime slices, cut paper thin

Blend all ingredients except lime slices until smooth. Add more wine if too thick. Pour into chilled bowl and garnish with lime slices.

FROSTY STRAWBERRY SOUP

4 servings

1	quart strawberries or 10 ounces frozen strawberries, thawed
1	teaspoon grated lemon peel
1	cup orange juice
1½	tablespoons instant tapioca
1	cup buttermilk
⅛	teaspoon allspice (or more to taste)
⅛	teaspoon cinnamon (or more to taste)
½	cup sugar
1	tablespoon lemon juice
2	lemon slices, halved
2	cantaloupes

Reserve some berries for a garnish and put the rest in the blender with the lemon peel and orange juice. Blend until smooth and strain into a saucepan. Mix tapioca with a little of the strawberry puree and then add to the remaining mixture in the saucepan. Heat stirring until mixture comes to a full boil, then allow to cook 1 minute or until it thickens. Remove from heat and add remaining ingredients except lemon slices and cantaloupes. Chill thoroughly. Cut cantaloupes in half making a decorative sawtooth edge. Scoop out seeds, turn upside down on paper towels and refrigerate until ready to serve. Pour well-chilled soup into cantaloupe halves and garnish with lemon slices and reserved berries.

Cool, refreshing and elegant.

FRUIT YOGURT SOUP

6 servings

2   cartons (8-ounces each) apricot-flavored yogurt
1   cup milk
½   cup orange juice
2   tablespoons orange liqueur (optional)
6   thin orange slices
6   sprigs fresh mint

In medium bowl combine yogurt, milk, orange juice and liqueur; stir to mix well. Refrigerate until well-chilled, at least 1 hour. Serve in sherbet glasses. Float a thin slice of orange and a sprig of mint on each serving.

A cool and refreshing first course.

BACON AND MUSHROOM SANDWICHES

4 servings

4   bagels or English muffins, split
2   tablespoons butter or margarine, softened
1½   cups fresh mushrooms, sliced
2   tablespoons chopped onion
1   tablespoon butter or margarine
8   ounces Canadian bacon, sliced 1/8" thick (12 slices)
4   slices American cheese
4   thin green pepper rings

Spread cut surfaces of bagels or English muffins with softened butter or margarine. In skillet, cook mushrooms and onion in the remaining 1 tablespoon butter or margarine until tender but not brown. Slash edges of Canadian bacon. Place 3 Canadian bacon slices atop each of 4 bagel or muffin halves. Top each with one-fourth of the mushroom-onion mixture. Place on a greased broiler pan. Broil 5" from heat 6-7 minutes. Place a cheese slice and green pepper ring atop each remaining bagel or English muffin half. Place on broiler pan with stacked halves and broil for 2 more minutes or until cheese melts. Place halves together and serve.

CURRIED BEEF PITA

4 servings

1   pound lean ground beef
1   medium onion, diced
1   clove garlic, crushed
1   tablespoon curry powder (or more to taste)
1   medium zucchini, diced
½   cup water
1¼   teaspoons salt
½   teaspoon sugar
¼   teaspoon pepper
1   medium tomato, diced
1   9-ounce package sandwich pockets (pita bread)

In 10-inch skillet over medium-high heat, cook ground beef, onion, garlic and curry powder until meat is browned and onion is tender, about 10 minutes, stirring frequently. Add zucchini, water, salt, sugar and pepper; heat to boiling. Reduce heat to low; cover and simmer 15 minutes or until zucchini is tender, stirring occasionally. Stir in tomato; heat through.

Meanwhile, cut each sandwich pocket in half; place on large cookie sheet. Heat sandwich pockets in 350° oven until warm, about 5 minutes. Spoon meat mixture into sandwich pockets. Arrange filled sandwich pockets on a large platter.

GREEK BEEF SANDWICHES

4 servings

¾   **pound lean ground beef**
1   **medium onion, diced**
¾   **cup water**
2   **tablespoons flour**
1   **teaspoon salt**
¾   **teaspoon oregano leaves**
¼   **teaspoon pepper**
1   **medium tomato, diced**
1   **3½ ounce can pitted ripe olives, drained and sliced**
2   **tablespoons red wine vinegar**
¼   **pound feta cheese, crumbled**
4   **pitas (sandwich pocket breads)**

In a large skillet over high heat, cook ground beef and onion until all pan juices evaporate and beef is well browned. Skim off excess fat. In a cup, stir water and flour until blended. Stir flour mixture into meat mixture with salt, oregano and pepper; heat to boiling. Reduce heat to medium and cook, stirring constantly, until mixture is thickened. Remove skillet from heat; stir in tomato, olives and vinegar; then stir in cheese. To serve, cut each pita crosswise in half. Spoon in some ground beef mixture.

Unusual and delicious!

TORTILLA BURGER

6 servings

6   **packaged corn tortillas, fried as label directs**
1   **pound lean ground beef**
1   **8-ounce jar mild taco sauce**
1   **16-ounce can refried beans**
1   **tablespoon salad oil**
6   **eggs**
   Salt and pepper to taste
1   **cup shredded iceberg lettuce**
⅓   **cup shredded Cheddar cheese**

Prepare tortillas and keep warm. In medium bowl, mix well ground beef and ⅓ cup taco sauce. Shape beef mixture into six 5-inch-round patties. In same skillet over high heat, cook patties 4 minutes or until desired doneness, turning once; keep warm. In a 1-quart saucepan over medium heat, heat refried beans; keep warm. In a 10-inch skillet over medium heat, in hot salad oil, fry eggs, 3 at a time, until yolks are of desired firmness; remove from skillet; sprinkle with salt and pepper to taste; keep warm. To serve, place a tortilla on a plate; spread with some refried beans; top with some of the shredded lettuce, then a beef patty. Pour some taco sauce over patty; top with an egg, then some shredded cheese. Repeat with remaining ingredients.

This is a real south-of-the-border-style hamburger with all the trimmings!

REUBEN SANDWICH CASSEROLE

6-8 servings

1   16-ounce can sauerkraut, drained
2   tomatoes, peeled and sliced
8   ounces corned beef, shredded
8   ounces Swiss cheese, grated
2   tablespoons bottled Thousand Island dressing
2   tablespoons butter
1   can of 6 refrigerated biscuits
2   rye crackers, crushed
¼   teaspoon caraway seeds

Layer in a 12" x 8" baking pan the sauerkraut, tomatoes, corned beef and Swiss cheese. Dot with dressing and butter. Bake at 425° for 15 minutes. Remove from oven. Separate biscuits and arrange on top, overlapping to form 3 rows. Sprinkle with cracker crumbs and caraway seeds. Bake at 425° for 15-20 minutes or until biscuits are brown.

SPICY SHEPHERD SANDWICH

8 servings

4   pita bread pockets or 8 flour tortillas
1   pound cooked roast beef, thinly sliced
1   4-ounce can chopped green chilies
½   pound Longhorn cheese, shredded

If using pita bread, use scissors to open and cut three-quarters of the way around. If using tortillas, lay flat. Fill pita with ¼ pound of beef, fill tortilla with 2 ounces of beef. Cover beef with green chilies and then cheese. Close pita bread and cut in half; roll tortillas. Wrap each in foil. Bake at 325° for 20 minutes, or until cheese melts.

ITALIAN STALLION

6 sandwiches

6   mild Italian sausages
2   tablespoons butter
2   cups sliced mushrooms
1   cup chopped green pepper
½   cup chopped onion
1   clove garlic, minced
6   large French rolls
2   8-ounce cans pizza sauce
6   slices mozzarella cheese
2   teaspoons dried oregano
½   teaspoon paprika

Simmer sausages in water until done. Melt butter in skillet; saute' mushrooms, green pepper, onion and garlic about 6 minutes. Split rolls in half. Divide vegetable mixture among them. Split cooked sausage and place on top of vegetables. Pour about ⅓ cup sauce over each sandwich and top each with a slice of cheese. Sprinkle with oregano and paprika. Heat under broiler until cheese melts and begins to brown, about 3-5 minutes.

🐦 MEXICAN SANDWICH SPREAD

4-6 servings

1 pound lean ground beef
1 onion, chopped
1 clove garlic, minced
1 tablespoon cooking oil
1 4-ounce can chopped green chilies, drained
1 cup tomatoes, chopped and drained
¼ cup cream
1 pound pasteurized process cheese, cubed
Salt, pepper and chili powder to taste

Brown beef, drain and set aside. Cook onion and garlic in oil until tender. Add chilies, tomatoes, and cream and simmer 10 minutes. Add cubed cheese and well-drained beef. Stir until cheese melts and serve on toast.

Freezes well.

GLAZED CRAB SANDWICHES

4 servings

1 cup fresh crabmeat (or 1 7½-ounce can)
2 tablespoons green onion, chopped
1 tablespoon lemon juice
2 tablespoons catsup or chili sauce
4 slices bread, toasted
1 large avocado, sliced
½ cup mayonnaise
¼ cup Cheddar cheese, grated

Combine crabmeat, onion, lemon juice, and catsup or chili sauce. Spread on toast. Top each with avocado slices. Mix mayonnaise and cheese and cover top of each sandwich. Place under broiler for a few minutes until cheese bubbles. Crab mixture can be assembled hours before use.

🐦 GREEN CHILI TUNA GRILL

8 servings

1 7-ounce can tuna, drained
½ cup green chilies, chopped
2 tablespoons onion, finely chopped
½ cup sour cream
½ cup Swiss cheese, shredded
Salt to taste
Pepper to taste
16 slices rye bread
Butter or margarine, softened

Combine first 7 ingredients and spread on 8 bread slices. Top with remaining slices. Spread outside of sandwich with butter or margarine. Cook on griddle over medium heat about 4 minutes on each side until filling is heated through and bread is golden

MEDITERRANEAN SALAD SANDWICH

8 servings

2 cups shredded lettuce
½ mild red onion, sliced
1 2¼-ounce can sliced black olives, drained
½ small cucumber, thinly sliced
1 6-ounce jar marinated artichoke hearts, drained and liquid reserved
1 6½-ounce can chunk-style tuna, drained
2 tablespoons lemon juice
¼ teaspoon basil
¼ teaspoon oregano
4 pita breads

In a salad bowl combine lettuce, onion, olives, cucumber, artichoke hearts and tuna. Cover and chill. Mix together artichoke marinade, lemon juice, basil and oregano. Let stand at room temperature. Pour dressing over salad mixture; stir gently. Cut pita breads in half. Fill each with salad.

Delicious served with soup.

SHRIMP PARTY SANDWICHES

36 canapes

1 pound cooked shrimp
1 tablespoon onion, minced
1 tablespoon celery, finely chopped
1 teaspoon green pepper, minced
2 teaspoons lemon juice
¼ teaspoon lemon rind, grated
¼ teaspoon salt
4 drops hot pepper sauce
Dash pepper
¾ cup mayonnaise
Parsley to garnish
36 bread rounds

Cut shrimp into very fine pieces or mince in a food processor. Mix together remaining ingredients and add more seasonings, if desired. Add shrimp and blend carefully. Chill well to blend flavors. On each bread round place a heaping teaspoon of shrimp mixture. Garnish with parsley.

BAKED CHICKEN SANDWICHES

6 servings

1   10½-ounce can con-
     densed cream of
     mushroom soup
1   tablespoon minced
     onion
1   2-ounce jar pimientos,
     chopped
1½   cups cooked chicken,
     diced
3   tablespoons flour
½   cup milk
12   slices bread, crusts
     removed
2   eggs, slightly beaten
3   tablespoons milk
3   cups potato chips,
     crushed

Mix soup, onion, pimiento and chicken in a saucepan. Blend flour and milk and add to soup mixture. Cook over medium heat, stirring constantly until thick. Chill. Place 6 slices of bread on a cookie sheet. Spread chicken mixture on top. Cover with remaining bread slices. Chill several hours. Mix eggs and milk. Cut chilled sandwiches into halves. Dip both sides in mixture and then in potato chips. Arrange on buttered cookie sheet. Bake at 350° for 25 minutes. You can make them several hours in advance, even the last step, and then keep in the refrigerator.

PARTY TURKEY SANDWICHES

4-6 servings

1   ripe avocado, mashed
1   tablespoon lemon or
     lime juice
1   cup sour cream
1   teaspoon salt
     Dash cayenne pepper
     Sourdough bread
     slices, lightly toasted
     Lettuce, shredded
     Tomatoes, peeled and
     sliced
     Breast of turkey, thinly
     sliced
     Salt and pepper to
     taste
     Monterey Jack cheese,
     grated

Combine avocado, lemon or lime juice, sour cream, salt and cayenne pepper. Spread avocado mixture on bread slices. Top with lettuce, tomatoes, a generous layer of turkey, salt and pepper and grated cheese. Top with a dollup of the avocado mixture.

The avocado mixture is also excellent on hamburgers topped with alfalfa sprouts.

SWEET TEA SANDWICHES

24 sandwiches

2   cups raisins, finely
     chopped or ground
½   cup chopped walnuts
½   cup evaporated milk
12   slices white sandwich
     bread

Combine raisins, nuts, and milk. Cover; chill till thickened, at least 1 hour. Trim crusts from bread, if desired. Spread raisin mixture on half the bread slices; top with remaining bread. Cut into quarters.

🦆MEXICAN EGG SALAD SANDWICH　　　　6 servings

⅓　cup sour cream
3　tablespoons chopped green chilies (or more to taste)
1　tablespoon lemon juice
1　teaspoon salt
2　teaspoons bottled taco sauce
9　hard-cooked eggs, chopped
6　slices tomato
6　slices wholewheat bread, toasted
1　cup shredded Cheddar cheese

Combine sour cream, chilies, lemon juice, salt and taco sauce. Fold in eggs and mix well. For each sandwich, place one tomato slice on each slice of toasted bread. Spread each with about ½ cup egg mixture; sprinkle with shredded cheese. Broil until cheese melts, about 3 minutes.

🦆GUACAMOLE POCKET SANDWICHES

4 servings

2　large pita breads
1　large avocado
1　tablespoon lemon juice
1　tomato, diced
1　teaspoon chopped chives
1　4-ounce can chopped green chilies
¼　teaspoon salt
4　slices Monterey Jack or Cheddar cheese
　　Sliced pastrami

Cut pita bread in half. Mash avocado and mix with lemon juice. Add tomato, chives, chili and salt and mix thoroughly. Spread inside pita bread. Add cheese and pastrami slices. Wrap in foil and heat at 350° for 10-15 minutes or until cheese melts.

AVOCADOWICHES

1   large firm-ripe avocado
1   tablespoon lemon juice
½   cup thinly sliced green onion
1   2¼-ounce can sliced ripe olives, drained
2   hard-cooked eggs, chopped
1   small tomato, peeled, seeded, and chopped
½   cup shredded Cheddar cheese
½   cup diced celery
    Garlic salt to taste
    Liquid hot pepper seasoning to taste
4-5   Arab pocket breads, halved
3   cups shredded iceberg lettuce

Peel, pit, and dice the avocado. With a fork, mash avocado with lemon juice until well blended. Then stir in the green onion, olives, eggs, tomato, cheese, and celery. Season to taste with garlic salt and hot pepper seasoning. If done ahead, cover and refrigerate as long as 2 hours. To serve, wrap bread in foil and heat in a 350° oven for 10 minutes or until hot. Or place in a plastic bag and heat in the microwave oven at half power for about 50 seconds or until hot. To serve, tuck a portion of lettuce, then avocado mixture into each bread half.

AVOCADO-CREAM CHEESE SANDWICHES

1   8-ounce package cream cheese, softened
3-4   slices stoneground bread
3   large avocados
1   pint sour cream
3   scallions, chopped
    Salt
    Freshly ground pepper

Spread a thick layer of softened cream cheese on 3 or 4 slices of bread. Peel and slice the avocados and cover the cream cheese with them. Spread sour cream over the avocados and sprinkle with chopped scallions. Season with salt and pepper. (May also add a little mayonnaise and bean sprouts.)

Pots and Pans of the Past.....

By 3,000 B.C. agriculture was established in the Southwest by emerging Indian cultures. To foster this way of life, the metate (flat milling stone) and the basket became the Indian's most important implements. The metate was used for grinding seeds, nuts and later corn. The basket, made of plant fiber, had many uses: gathering seeds, nuts and berries, storage and food preparation. As food production became more important, pottery was developed to store and cook foods more efficiently. Pots also were used in religious rituals for it was believed that they would serve the needs of the dead in the afterlife. Later, as populations grew and more food was needed, clay-lined ovens known as hornos were used to bake and roast foods before storing. Hornos still are being used today in many Indian communities and horno-baked Indian bread is considered to be one of life's treats ❖

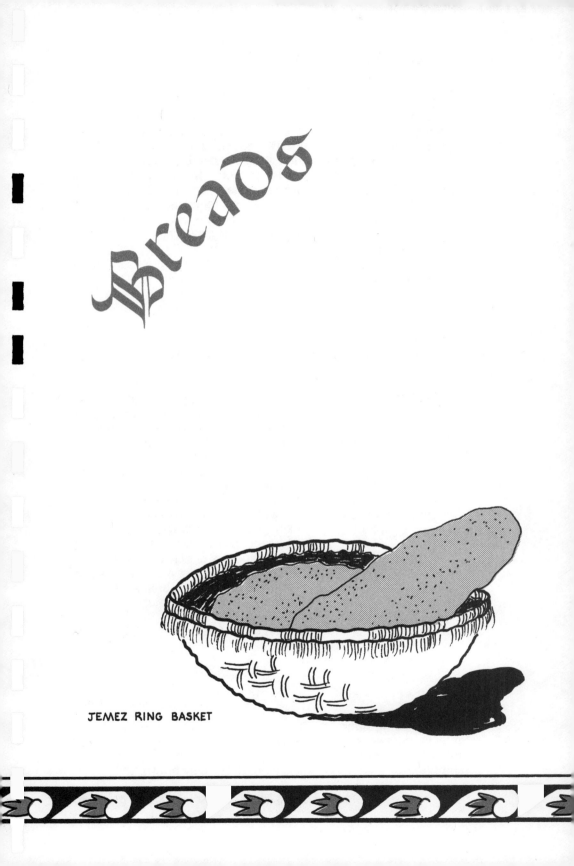

Breads

JEMEZ RING BASKET

AVOCADO BREAD

½	cup butter, softened
1	cup sugar
1	cup mashed avocado
2	teaspoons lemon juice
2	eggs, well beaten
2	cups all-purpose flour
½	teaspoon salt
1½	teaspoons baking powder
¼	teaspoon ground cloves
¼	teaspoon ground cinnamon
1	cup pecans, chopped

Preheat oven to 375°. Grease 9" x 5" loaf pan. Cream butter and sugar together. Mash avocado with the lemon juice. Add avocado and eggs to butter mixture and blend well. Combine flour, salt, baking powder, cloves and cinnamon and add to batter. Mix well and add nuts. Turn into loaf pan and bake for 15 minutes. Lower temperature to 350° and bake for 55 minutes or until done. Put on rack to cool before slicing.

BANANA WALNUT BUTTERMILK BREAD

1 loaf

1½	cups sugar
½	cup unsalted butter, softened
2	large eggs
4	very ripe bananas, mashed
1	teaspoon vanilla
1	teaspoon baking soda
⅓	cup buttermilk
1½	cups unbleached flour
1	cup finely chopped nuts

In a large bowl cream together the sugar and butter; add eggs one at a time, beating well after each addition. Beat in mashed bananas and vanilla and continue beating until mixture is smooth. In a measuring cup stir baking soda into the buttermilk and add it to the banana mixture along with the flour and chopped nuts. Stir the batter until it is just combined. Pour batter into a greased and floured 9" x 5" loaf pan and bake in a 350° oven for 1 hour or until a cake tester inserted in the center comes out clean. Transfer the bread to a rack and let it cool in the pan for 10 minutes. Turn the bread out onto a rack and let it cool completely.

This rich bread freezes beautifully.

BEER BREAD

1 loaf

3	cups self-rising flour
3	tablespoons sugar
12	ounces beer, room temperature

Preheat oven to 375°. Combine all ingredients and stir to mix. Place in greased 9½" x 5½" loaf pan. Bake about 45 minutes or until nicely brown.

Looks like a big biscuit and can be sliced and buttered for great toast.

CHOCOLATE ORANGE BREAD

1 loaf

3	cups sifted all purpose flour
1	cup sugar
4	teaspoons baking powder
1½	teaspoons salt
1	teaspoon cinnamon
1	teaspoon nutmeg
½	cup chopped nuts
3	tablespoons grated orange rind
1	cup semi-sweet chocolate chips
1	egg
1½	cups orange juice
2	tablespoons salad oil
1	cup powdered sugar
2	tablespoons orange juice

Preheat oven to 300°. Grease one 9" x 5" loaf pan. Sift together flour, sugar, baking powder, salt, cinnamon and nutmeg into a large bowl. Stir in nuts, orange rind and chocolate chips. In a small bowl, beat egg and stir in orange juice and oil. Add to flour mixture; mix well. Turn into loaf pan. Bake for 75 minutes or until cake tester comes out clean. Cool and remove from pan. Make an orange glaze by mixing powdered sugar and orange juice until smooth and glossy. Drizzle glaze over bread. (At high altitudes use 3 teaspoons baking powder and bake at 325°.)

COCONUT ZUCCHINI BREAD

2 loaves

3	eggs
2	cups sugar
1	cup vegetable oil
3	cups zucchini, grated
2	teaspoons vanilla extract
3	cups flour
1	teaspoon salt
1	teaspoon baking soda
1	teaspoon baking powder
1	teaspoon ground cinnamon
1	cup coconut, flaked
1	cup chopped nuts (optional)

Preheat oven to 375°. Grease two 9" x 5" loaf pans. In a large mixing bowl, beat together eggs, sugar and oil. Mix in zucchini and vanilla. Add to mixture flour, salt, soda, baking powder and cinnamon. Mix well. Stir in coconut and nuts. Pour batter evenly into loaf pans. Bake for 50-60 minutes or until done.

This freezes well.

CRANBERRY-ORANGE BREAD

1 loaf

2   cups sifted flour
½   teaspoon salt
1½   teaspoons baking
       powder
½   teaspoon soda
1   cup granulated sugar
1   egg, beaten slightly
2   tablespoons melted
       butter
½   cup orange juice
2   tablespoons hot water
½   cup chopped nuts
1   cup coarsely cut cran-
       berries
1   tablespoon grated
       orange rind

Preheat oven to 350°. Sift dry ingredients together; add egg, melted butter, orange juice and water. Mix only until dry ingredients are moistened. Fold in nuts, cranberries, and orange rind. Pour into a greased 9" x 5" loaf pan. Let stand 20 minutes, then bake for 50 minutes or until bread tests done. When cool, wrap in waxed paper. The bread improves in flavor and slices more easily if allowed to stand for 24 hours before cutting.

HARVEST LOAF

1 loaf

1¾   cups all purpose flour,
       sifted
1   teaspoon soda
½   teaspoon salt
1   teaspoon ground cin-
       namon
1   teaspoon nutmeg
¼   teaspoon ginger
¼   teaspoon ground
       cloves
½   cup butter
1   cup sugar
2   eggs
¾   cup canned pumpkin
¾   cup semi-sweet
       chocolate chips
¾   cup walnuts, chopped
½   cup sifted powdered
       sugar
⅛   teaspoon nutmeg
⅛   teaspoon ground cin-
       namon
1-2   teaspoons cream

Preheat oven to 375°. Grease bottom of a 9" x 5" loaf pan. Combine flour with soda, salt and spices. In a large bowl cream butter. Gradually add sugar and cream well. Blend in eggs; beat well. At a low speed, add dry ingredients alternately with pumpkin, beginning and ending with dry ingredients. Stir in chocolate chips and nuts. Pour mixture into loaf pan and bake for 60-75 minutes. Cool. Remove from pan and drizzle with glaze. To make glaze, combine remaining four ingredients and mix until mixture is of desired consistency. Let stand at least 6 hours before slicing.

MARZIPAN-CEREAL BREAD

3 loaves

1 cup crunchy cereal nuggets
3 cups milk
¼ cup melted margarine
1¼ cups sugar
2 eggs, beaten
3 cups all-purpose flour
½ teaspoon salt
2¼ teaspoons baking powder
1 teaspoon soda
1 cup crumbled marzipan

Combine cereal and milk; store in refrigerator overnight. Combine margarine and sugar; add eggs, mixing well. Combine flour, salt, baking powder, and soda. Add cereal mixture and dry ingredients alternately to sugar mixture, ending with cereal; beat well after each addition. Add marzipan and mix well. Preheat oven to 375°. Lightly grease three 8″ loaf pans and spoon batter evenly into the pans. Bake for 45 minutes or until bread tests done. (At altitudes below 3,000 feet, use 3 teaspoons baking powder and bake at 350° for 60 minutes or until bread tests done.)

ONION SHORTBREAD

10-12 servings

1 large onion chopped
¼ cup margarine
¼ teaspoon dill weed
1 cup sharp cheese, grated
½ teaspoon salt
1½ cups prepared corn muffin mix
1 egg, beaten
⅓ cup milk
1 cup cream-style corn
1 cup sour cream

Saute' onion in margarine. Cool. Stir in dill weed, cheese, and salt. Preheat oven to 425°. Grease an 8″ square dish. In a mixing bowl, combine muffin mix, egg, milk, corn and sour cream. Mix well and turn into baking dish. Spread onion-cheese mixture over batter. Bake for 25-30 minutes.

RAISIN OATMEAL BREAD

1 loaf

1 cup quick oats
1 cup buttermilk
½ cup dark brown sugar
1 egg
1 cup whole wheat flour
1 teaspoon baking powder
1 teaspoon salt
½ teaspoon baking soda
6 tablespoons butter, melted and cooled
½ cup raisins

Soak oats in buttermilk for 1-2 hours. Stir in sugar and egg; beat well. In another bowl combine flour, baking powder, salt and baking soda. Combine the two mixtures and add the melted butter and raisins. Spoon into a greased 8″ x 4″ loaf pan. Bake in 400° oven for 25-35 minutes.

This makes a hearty winter bread. Serve with a bacon omelet and applesauce.

PERSIAN CRACKLE POPPY BREAD

1 loaf

1¼ cups whole wheat flour
½ cup sesame seeds
2 tablespoons non-fat dry milk solids
2 teaspoons poppy seeds
1½ teaspoons baking powder
½ teaspoon salt
2 eggs
¼ cup honey
¼ cup orange juice
2 tablespoons butter, melted
2 tablespoons oil

Combine flour, sesame seeds, dry milk, poppy seeds, baking powder and salt in a bowl. Mix eggs, honey, orange juice, butter and oil in a small bowl. Stir egg mixture into flour mixture just until mixed. Spoon batter into greased 8" x 4" loaf pan. Bake on center rack in 350° oven 35-40 minutes. Cool in pan 10 minutes. Remove and cool on wire rack.

Good with orange flavored whipped cream cheese.

SALAMI LOAF

1 loaf

3 cups all-purpose flour
2 tablespoons sugar
1½ tablespoons baking powder
1 teaspoon salt
1 teaspoon fennel seeds
¼ teaspoon baking soda
3 tablespoons Parmesan cheese
11 ounces cream cheese, softened
1 cup milk
2 eggs, beaten
¼ cup vegetable oil
1 cup hard salami, thinly sliced and diced

Preheat oven to 375°. Grease a 9" x 5" x 3" loaf pan. Sift together flour, sugar, baking powder, salt and soda into a large mixing bowl. Stir in fennel seeds and Parmesan cheese. In a separate bowl beat cream cheese until smooth and gradually beat in the milk to make a smooth mixture. Add eggs, oil and salami. Add cream cheese mixture all at once to the dry mixture and stir only until it is moistened. Mixture will be lumpy. Turn batter into loaf pan and bake 50-60 minutes or until done. Cool in pan 5 minutes.

SESAME SEED LOAF

1 loaf

½ cup butter
¾ cup sugar
1 egg
1½ cups milk
3 cups flour
3 teaspoons baking powder
1 teaspoon salt
6 tablespoons toasted sesame seeds

Melt butter; add sugar and egg. Mix well. Beat in milk. Sift flour, baking powder and salt; add to mixture. Fold in sesame seeds. Pour into greased and floured 9" x 5" x 3" loaf pan. Bake 1 hour at 350°.

STRAWBERRY MONKEY BREAD

8-10 servings

2½ cups whole frozen strawberries
4 10-ounce cans refrigerated buttermilk biscuits
⅔ cup sugar
1 teaspoon grated lemon peel
10 tablespoons margarine
1½ teaspoons almond extract

Preheat oven to 350°. Grease a 10" tube pan. Thaw strawberries and cut into quarters. Cut biscuits in quarters and roll in ⅓ cup sugar. In tube pan arrange ¼ of the biscuits and 3 tablespoons of the berries in an even layer. Repeat process 3 more times. In a saucepan combine remaining berries, sugar, lemon peel, margarine and almond extract. Bring to a boil. Reduce heat. Cook, stirring frequently, until sugar has dissolved and the margarine has melted. Pour mixture over biscuits in pan. Bake for 60 minutes. Place foil loosely over top the last 10 minutes of baking time to keep from burning. Turn onto a cake plate and serve. Good reheated.

TOUCH-OF-LEMON LOAF

1 loaf

¾   cup margarine
1½   cups sugar
3   eggs
2¼   cups plus 2 table-
     spoons flour
¼   teaspoon salt
¼   teaspoon soda
¾   cup buttermilk
     Grated rind of one
     lemon
¾   cup chopped nuts

GLAZE:

     Juice of one lemon
½   cup sugar

Cream margarine and sugar and beat in eggs. Sift dry ingredients together and add to batter alternating with buttermilk. Mix well. Stir in grated lemon rind and nuts. Pour into greased and floured 9" x 5" loaf pan. Bake at 325° for 1 hour and 15 minutes if glass pan is used; otherwise, bake at 350° for one hour. While loaf is baking, prepare a glaze of lemon juice and sugar. Allow to stand until sugar dissolves. After removing loaf from pan, pierce top of loaf with a cake tester and spoon glaze over. Allow to cool before slicing.

Freezes well.

WALNUT LOAF

1 loaf

¼   cup butter
¾   cup sugar
2   eggs
1   teaspoon vanilla ex-
     tract
2   cups flour
1½   teaspoons baking
     powder
1   teaspoon salt
½   teaspoon baking soda
½   teaspoon ground
     cinnamon
¼   teaspoon ground
     nutmeg
1   cup sour cream
2   tablespoons soft butter
⅓   cup brown sugar
½   teaspoon ground cin-
     namon
1   cup walnuts, chopped

Preheat oven to 350°. Grease a 9" x 5" x 3" loaf pan. Cream butter with sugar, eggs and vanilla until fluffy. Sift together flour, baking powder, salt, soda, cinnamon and nutmeg and stir into batter alternately with sour cream. In a separate bowl, mix together soft butter, brown sugar and cinnamon. Stir in walnuts. Place ⅓ of the loaf mixture in the bottom of loaf pan. Sprinkle with half the nut mixture. Top with another ⅓ of loaf mixture. Sprinkle with remaining nut mixture. Spread remaining ⅓ loaf mixture evenly over the top. Bake 55-60 minutes or until loaf is done. Allow to cool in pan. Serve as a bread or coffeecake.

PRETZELS

1 package dry yeast
1½ cups warm water (105-115°)
1 teaspoon salt
1 teaspoon sugar
4 cups unbleached flour
1 egg, beaten
⅓ cup Kosher salt

In a large bowl, dissolve yeast in warm water. Stir in salt, sugar and 2 cups flour. Beat until smooth. Stir in enough of the remaining flour to make dough easy to handle. Turn dough onto lightly floured surface and knead until smooth and elastic, about 5 minutes. Place dough in a greased bowl and turn dough to coat top. In a warm place, let dough rise double in bulk. Preheat oven to 425°. Grease two baking sheets. Punch down dough; cut into 16 equal pieces; roll each piece into a 18" rope; twist each rope into a pretzel shape. Place on baking sheet; brush with egg; and sprinkle generously with Kosher salt. Bake until brown, about 15-20 minutes. Cool on wire rack. Variation: Cut dough into 1" balls; brush with egg and roll in salt; bake until brown, 7-10 minutes.

SANTA FE FLOUR TORTILLAS

5 cups all-purpose flour, unsifted
4 teaspoons baking powder
1 teaspoon salt
½ cup bacon drippings
2 cups buttermilk

In a bowl, combine flour, baking powder and salt. Cut in bacon drippings until fine, even crumbs form. Gradually add buttermilk, mixing with fork until soft, nonsticky dough forms. Knead in bowl 3-5 minutes. Divide into 12-18 equal pieces. Shape each piece into a smooth ball. To shape each tortilla, flatten a ball of dough to a 3-4" round. On a floured board, roll each to a 7" circle about ¼" thick. Grease heavy large frying pan with bacon drippings and place over a medium heat. Place dough round in pan and cook slowly until bubbly and brown, about 2-3 minutes on each side. Preheat oven to 250°. After tortillas are cooked, put them directly on the rack in the oven for 5 minutes. Remove and stack 5 or 6 at a time in foil and return to warm oven until serving time. They hold well up to 2 hours. Serve with butter and honey.

INDIAN BLUE CORNBREAD

6 servings

1 cup blue cornmeal
⅔ cup white flour
2 tablespoons sugar
1 teaspoon salt
1 teaspoon soda
1 teaspoon baking powder
2 eggs, lightly beaten
½ cup margarine, melted and cooled
1 cup buttermilk

Preheat oven to 400°. Combine cornmeal, flour, sugar, salt, soda, and baking powder. Add beaten eggs, cooled margarine and buttermilk. Mix with a fork. Pour into a well-greased 9" x 12" baking dish. Bake 15-20 minutes or until brown. Do not overcook.

Goes well with pinto beans or a hearty soup.

ZINGY CHILI CORN BREAD

12-18 servings

3 cups prepared corn bread mix
2½ cups milk
¼ cup salad oil
3 eggs, beaten
1 onion, grated
1 cup cream-style corn
1¼ cups Cheddar cheese, grated
1 4-ounce can chopped green chilies, drained
1 2-ounce jar pimientos, drained

Preheat oven to 400°. Grease a 9" x 13" baking pan. In a large mixing bowl, combine all ingredients and mix well by hand. Pour batter into baking pan and bake for 45 minutes. To serve, cut into squares. This makes a moist spoon bread.

POORI

2 dozen

3 cups whole wheat flour
1 cup lukewarm water
4 tablespoons vegetable oil
Vegetable oil for deep frying

Combine flour and water and knead for 7-8 minutes. Form into a ball and place in a bowl. Cover with a wet towel and let stand for 1 hour. Roll into a log about 3 inches in diameter. Cut into balls about ½" thick. Roll in 4 tablespoons oil. Roll out flat. Heat oil. Drop the poori in the hot oil. As it starts to rise, keep pushing the poori down until it starts to puff up. Turn it over with a slotted spoon and cook another 30 seconds. Remove from the oil, and drain on a paper towel. The puffs may be wrapped in foil to stay warm. (This will keep them soft.)

This is an East Indian bread. Delicious served with curry and other East Indian dishes.

COFFEE CAN BREAD

2 loaves

4 cups all-purpose flour
1 package dry yeast
½ cup butter
½ cup water
½ cup milk
¼ cup sugar
1 teaspoon salt
2 eggs, slightly beaten
½ cup chopped nuts (optional)
½ cup chopped raisins (optional)

Coat insides of two 1-pound coffee cans with small amounts of cooking oil. In a large, bowl mix 2 cups flour and yeast together. In a saucepan stir together butter, water, milk, sugar and salt over low heat until butter melts. Cool 5 minutes. Add to flour and yeast. Mix in 2 more cups flour, eggs, nuts and raisins. Dough will be stiff. Turn onto a floured board and knead until dough is smooth and elastic. Divide dough in half and place in prepared coffee cans. Cover with plastic lids and let rise in warm place until dough is 1″ from the top. Preheat oven to 375°. Remove plastic lids and bake 35 minutes. Remove from cans and cool.

Makes delicious toast.

COTTAGE DILL LOAVES

2 small loaves

¼ cup warm water
1 tablespoon dry yeast
1 tablespoon sugar
1 cup creamed cottage cheese
2 tablespoons onion, chopped
2 tablespoons butter, melted
1 egg
1 teaspoon salt
2¼ cups flour
¼ cup wheat germ
1 tablespoon dried dill weed

Put water in food processor. Stir in the yeast and sugar and let stand 5 minutes. Process 10 seconds. Add cottage cheese, onion, butter, egg, and salt. Mix 20 seconds. In mixing bowl combine flour, wheat germ, and dill. Add the cheese mixture and stir until mixture pulls away from the side of the bowl. Grease a bowl. Turn dough onto floured board and knead until smooth and elastic, adding flour to keep from sticking about 5 minutes. Put the dough into the greased bowl and turn to coat the dough with the grease. Cover and let stand in a warm area until it doubles in volume, about 1 hour. Punch the dough down and divide in half. Shape into 2 loaves and put in pans. Let the dough stand until it doubles in volume. Bake at 350° for 35-40 minutes.

CRUSTY FAT-FREE BREAD

2 loaves

1 envelope dry yeast
2 cups lukewarm water
1 tablespoon salt
1 tablespoon sugar
4½ cups unbleached flour
¼ cup cornmeal

In a large mixing bowl, dissolve yeast in warm water. Add salt and sugar and mix well. With a wooden spoon, beat in flour, one cup at a time, to form a smooth ball that clears sides of bowl. Cover and set in warm place until double in bulk, about 1½ hours. Stir down dough and turn out on lightly floured board. Knead a few turns, then cut in half. Shape each half in a 12" loaf. Put on baking sheet well sprinkled with cornmeal. Wait five minutes, then slash tops in five places with sharp knife. Brush with water and place in a cold oven with a pan of boiling water on bottom rack. Turn oven to 400° and bake 40 minutes or until crusty and brown.

Great accompaniment for Italian entrees!

MUSHROOM BREAD

3 loaves

¼ cup margarine
½ pound mushrooms, finely chopped
1 cup onion, finely chopped
2 cups milk
3 tablespoons molasses
5 teaspoons salt
½ teaspoon ground black pepper
½ cup very warm water
2 packages dry yeast
1 egg
1 cup wheat germ
8-9 cups unsifted all-purpose flour

Melt 2 tablespoons margarine in a large skillet over medium heat. Add mushrooms and onion and saute' until liquid has evaporated. Cool. Scald milk; stir in remaining margarine, molasses, salt and pepper. Cool. Into a large bowl pour water, sprinkle in yeast and stir until dissolved. Add milk mixture, mushroom mixture, egg, wheat germ and 2 cups flour. Beat hard until smooth. Stir in enough additional flour to make a stiff dough. Knead on floured board until smooth and elastic, about 8 minutes. Place dough in large greased bowl. Turn to grease top of dough. Let rise in warm place until doubled in bulk. Grease three 9" x 5" x 3" loaf pans. Punch down dough and divide into 3 balls. Roll out each ball into a 12" x 9" rectangle. Roll up each rectangle separately, starting with the narrow end. Place each roll seam down in loaf pan. Cover, let rise in warm place until double in bulk. Bake in preheated 400° oven 35-45 minutes or until done. Remove from pans and cool on wire racks.

SOURDOUGH STARTER

3 cups

1 package dry yeast
2 cups warm water
2 cups unbleached flour

In a bowl, dissolve yeast in water. Add flour and stir until well blended. Cover and let stand at room temperature for 2 days. The starter is ready when bubbly and a yellowish liquid forms on top. Store starter in a container with a loose fitting lid in the refrigerator. After using starter in a recipe, it must be replenished. Always reserve 1 cup of starter and mix with 1 cup of flour, 1 cup milk and 1 cup sugar. Store in refrigerator.

OATMEAL CINNAMON RAISIN BREAD

2 loaves

1 envelope active dry yeast
1 tablespoon salt
5-6 cups unbleached flour
2 cups very warm water
5 tablespoons melted butter
2 tablespoons molasses
1 cup sourdough starter (recipe in cookbook)
1½ cups rolled oats
1½ teaspoons baking soda
½ cup sugar
4 teaspoons cinnamon
1½ cups raisins
Vegetable oil

In large mixing bowl combine yeast, salt and 2½ cups flour. Pour in water and blend well; then beat at high speed with a mixer 2 minutes. Stir in 3 tablespoons butter, molasses, starter, oats and baking soda until blended. Stir in enough flour to make a stiff dough (about 2 cups). Turn dough out onto floured board; knead until smooth and elastic (about 8-10 minutes), using remaining flour as needed to prevent sticking. Place dough in oiled bowl; turn once to coat both sides. Cover bowl with a towel; place in warm place. Let rise until double in bulk. Punch dough down, knead 1-2 minutes, divide into halves. On floured board, roll out half of dough to a 9" x 12" rectangle; brush with 1 tablespoon of remaining butter. Combine sugar and cinnamon; sprinkle half over dough. Place half the raisins in a single layer over cinnamon-sugar. Starting at narrow end, roll dough tightly. Pinch seam together to seal; press ends down with sides of hands and tuck neatly under. Place loaf seam side down in a greased 9" x 5" x 3" loaf pan. Brush lightly with vegetable oil. Repeat with remaining dough and ingredients to make second loaf. Cover pans with towel. Allow to rise in warm place until double in bulk. Bake in preheated 400° oven 35-40 minutes or until tops are nicely browned and bottoms give a hollow sound when tapped. Remove loaves from pans and cool on wire racks.

SOURDOUGH WHOLE WHEAT BREAD

2 loaves

1 cup milk
1 cup boiling water
1 package dry yeast
3 cups whole wheat flour, unsifted
4½ cups unbleached flour
¾ cup sourdough starter (recipe in cookbook)
¼ cup molasses
1 tablespoon salt
3 tablespoons butter, softened
1 teaspoon baking soda

In a large bowl combine milk and water; cool to 110°, then add yeast and let stand 5 minutes to soften. Stir in wheat flour, 1 cup unbleached flour and starter. Beat until smooth and elastic, about 5 minutes. Cover bowl with plastic wrap and let stand in a warm place until very thick, bubbly and spongy looking, about 1½-2 hours. Stir in molasses, salt, butter and soda. Gradually mix in enough of the remaining flour to form a very stiff dough. Turn dough onto a floured surface and with well floured hands, knead until smooth, about 10 minutes. Add more flour if needed to prevent dough from sticking. Place dough in a greased bowl, turn over to grease top, cover and let rise in warm place until double in bulk. Grease two 9″ x 5″ x 3″ loaf pans. Punch down dough and divide in half. Form each piece into an oval. Fold over lengthwise, pinch seam together. Tuck ends under and pinch to seal. Place each loaf in a pan, cover and let rise until almost double in size. Preheat oven to 375°. Bake bread for 35 minutes or until nicely brown and it makes a hollow sound when tapped. Remove from pans and cool on racks.

MASA HARINA SHELLS

10 shells

1 cup masa harina (instant masa mix)
½ teaspoon salt
2 teaspoons chopped parsley or cilantro
1 scallion, very finely chopped
2 tablespoons Cheddar cheese, finely grated
2 tablespoons melted bacon drippings or oil
½ cup plus 1 tablespoon water
1 egg yolk
½ teaspoon milk

Preheat oven to 450°. Grease a Madeleine pan. Place masa, salt, parsley, scallion and cheese in a bowl and toss to mix. Stir in bacon drippings or oil and water until dough is moist. Divide dough evenly into 10 pieces. Roll each piece into a ball and press down with the finger tip to completely fill the shell. Smooth off the top flush with the pan. Combine egg yolk and milk and brush over surface of shells. Bake 15 minutes. Shells will be crisp on the outside and solid on the inside. They are not meant to be like a raised cornbread. Serve hot.

May be made earlier in the day and reheated later.

SESAME TOASTS

3　sticks (1½ cups) butter
2　garlic cloves, crushed
¼　teaspoon thyme
　　Salt and pepper to taste
2　12″ loaves Italian bread
1　cup sesame seeds

In a saucepan, melt the butter with garlic cloves, thyme, salt and pepper. Cut loaves of Italian bread into ¾″ slices and dip the slices into the butter mixture. Spread 1 cup sesame seeds on a sheet of wax paper, roll the bread crusts in the sesame seeds and sprinkle one side of each slice with sesame seed. Put the slices seeded sides up on a baking sheet and bake them in a preheated 400° oven for 20 to 25 minutes or until they are lightly toasted.

Ordinary bread made elegant!

BREADS

TORTILLA BREAD

2 loaves

2¾-3 cups all purpose flour
1　envelope dry yeast
2　cups warm water
1　tablespoon sugar
2　teaspoons salt
2　cups masa harina
1　tablespoon milk

In a large bowl, combine 2½ cups flour and the yeast. In a small bowl stir together water, sugar, and salt. Add to dry mixture and beat with electric mixer at low speed for 30 seconds, scraping sides of bowl constantly. Beat 3 minutes at high speed. By hand, stir in masa harina and enough of remaining flour to make a moderately stiff dough. Turn out on lightly floured board and knead gently 3 to 5 minutes. Shape into ball. Place dough in lightly greased bowl turning once. Cover and let rise in a warm place until double in size, 50-60 minutes. Grease two 1 quart souffle dishes. Punch down dough and divide in half. Let rest 10 minutes. Shape into two round loaves and place in greased dishes. Let rise in a warm place until double in size, 30-45 minutes. Brush tops with milk. Bake in a preheated 375° oven for 25-30 minutes. Remove from oven and cool.

This bread has a definite tortilla flavor; goes well with soups or chili and freezes well.

ORANGE YOGURT BRAID

2 braids

5-5½ cups unbleached flour
2 packages dry yeast
½ teaspoon ground cardamon
½ cup butter
1 cup plain yogurt
1 teaspoon salt
½ cup sugar
3 eggs, reserve 1 egg yolk
1 tablespoon freshly grated orange peel
⅓ cup orange juice
1 tablespoon milk

In large bowl, combine 2 cups flour, yeast and cardamon. Melt butter and stir in yogurt, salt and sugar. Add yogurt mixture to flour mixture. Add eggs (reserve 1 yolk), orange peel and juice to flour. Mix well and then beat for 2 minutes. Stir in remaining flour to make a soft dough. Turn onto floured surface and knead about 5 minutes. Place in greased bowl; turn to grease top, cover and let rise in warm place about 1 hour. Punch down. Divide in half and divide each half into 3 pieces. Roll each piece into a 16" rope. Braid loosely into two braids and place on greased baking sheet. Cover and let rise in a warm place about 35 minutes. Mix remaining egg yolk with milk and brush over braids. Bake in a preheated 350° oven for 25-30 minutes or until bread sounds hollow when tapped on bottom. Cover loosely with foil last 10 minutes to prevent top from over-browning.

Delicious as toast.

HOLIDAY MUFFINS

18 muffins

¾ cup packed brown sugar
¼ cup butter, melted
¾ cup mashed cooked sweet potatoes
3 eggs
⅓ cup orange juice
2½ cups sifted all-purpose flour
½ teaspoon salt
1½ teaspoons baking powder
½ teaspoon baking soda
1 teaspoon ground cinnamon
½ teaspoon ground nutmeg
1 cup fresh cranberries, coarsely chopped
½ cup sliced almonds

Preheat oven to 350°. Line 18 muffin cups with paper baking cup liners. In large bowl cream sugar and butter. Stir in potatoes, eggs and juice. In separate bowl sift dry ingredients together. Add to potato mixture and mix well. Fold in cranberries and almonds. Fill muffin cups ¾ full and bake 20 minutes.

DANISH ROLLS

4 dozen

4	packages yeast
1	tablespoon sugar
1	cup lukewarm water
1	cup milk, scalded and cooled
7	cups all purpose flour
½	cup margarine
½	cup sugar
3	eggs
1	tablespoon salt
½	teaspoon vanilla
½	teaspoon lemon extract (optional)
¾	cup margarine
2	cups powdered sugar
1	teaspoon maple flavoring
	Water
½	cup nuts (optional)

Dissolve yeast and sugar in water. Add milk and 3 cups flour. Beat until smooth. Cream shortening, sugar and eggs. Add salt and flavoring. Add this mixture to yeast mixture and beat well. Add remaining flour to make moderately stiff dough. Knead lightly on floured board about 3 minutes until smooth and elastic. Place in greased bowl, cover, and let rise for 45 minutes. Roll on floured board into oblong piece ½" thick. Using ¾ cups margarine, place in small pieces over center ⅓ of dough. Fold one side over to cover butter. Place remaining margarine on top then fold other ⅓ of dough to cover this layer of margarine. Press edges down well. Turn dough ¼ way around and roll out again ½" thick. Fold ¼ of dough at each end to center and fold again. Chill in refrigerator about ½ hour. Roll out again as above and chill again. Roll out into rectangles ½" thick. Roll as for jelly roll and make 1" slices. Let rise sntil double, about 30-40 minutes. Place on lightly greased baking sheet and bake at 350° until light brown, about 25-30 minutes. Combine powdered sugar, maple flavoring and enough water to make drizzling consistency. Drizzle over rolls. Top with nuts, if desired.

EASY DINNER ROLLS

45 rolls

½	cup shortening
¼	cup sugar
1	teaspoon salt
½	cup boiling water
1	egg, well beaten
1	tablespoon dry yeast
½	cup lukewarm water
3	cups sifted flour

Cream shortening, sugar and salt thoroughly. Add boiling water and let cool. Add the egg and the yeast which has been dissolved in lukewarm water. Mix thoroughly. Add flour and mix. Cover and put in refrigerator overnight. Make into rolls with 2" diameter. Let rise until doubled. Bake at 350° for 12-15 minutes or until lightly browned.

BLUEBERRY MUFFINS

24 muffins

3 eggs
8 tablespoons sugar
3 tablespoons butter
2 cups sour cream
2⅔ cups sifted all-purpose flour
2 teaspoons baking powder
½ teaspoon baking soda
¾ teaspoon salt
1½ cups frozen blueberries

Preheat oven to 400°. Generously grease 24 muffin cups. Beat eggs until light. Beat in sugar, butter and sour cream. Sift together flour, baking powder, soda and salt; add to egg mixture. Mix only until blended. Fold in frozen blueberries. Fill muffin cups ⅔ full and bake 20 minutes.

DAD'S CHEESE BISCUITS

20-24 biscuits

2 cups all-purpose flour
3 teaspoons baking powder
1 teaspoon salt
1½ teaspoons sugar
¼ cup plus 1 tablespoon margarine
1 cup sharp Cheddar cheese, grated
⅔ cup evaporated milk

Preheat oven to 450°. Grease a jelly roll pan. In a bowl combine flour, baking powder, salt and sugar. Cut in margarine. Stir in cheese. Stir in milk with a fork, using just enough to make soft but not sticky dough. On a floured surface knead the dough about 1 minute. With a lightly floured rolling pin roll dough ½″ thick. Cut into squares or rounds. Space biscuits evenly on pan and bake 12-15 minutes. Serve with butter, honey or jams.

MINCEMEAT DELIGHTS

30-36 muffins

2 cups sugar
1 cup butter
3 eggs, beaten
1 cup buttermilk
1 teaspoon soda
¼ teaspoon salt
1 9-ounce box dry mincemeat, crumbled
½ cup chopped pecans
2¾ cups flour
1 teaspoon vanilla extract

Preheat oven to 400°. Cream sugar and butter. Add remaining ingredients to make a soft batter. Line large muffin tins with paper baking cups. Fill baking cups ⅔ full. Bake for approximately 15 minutes.

SOURDOUGH COFFEECAKE

6-8 servings

1   **cup sourdough starter at room temperature (See Index)**
¾   **teaspoon baking soda**
½   **cup sugar**
⅓   **cup margarine, softened**
2   **cups all-purpose flour**
½   **teaspoon nutmeg**
½   **teaspoon salt**
1   **apple, pared and chopped (optional)**
½   **cup nuts, chopped (optional)**
½   **cup raisins (optional)**
1-2   **tablespoons milk**
¼   **cup sugar**
2   **teaspoons ground cinnamon**

Grease a 9" x 9" pan. In a bowl combine first 10 ingredients. Beat well. Spread in pan. Sprinkle top with milk. Use back of spoon to lightly "push" milk into batter. Combine ¼ cup sugar and cinnamon and sprinkle over coffeecake. Let rise 45 minutes. Bake in a preheated 375° oven for 35 minutes or until done.

WALNUT CROWN COFFEECAKE

12 servings

⅓   **cup ground walnuts**
3   **tablespoons light brown sugar**
2   **cups flour**
1¾   **cups sugar**
1   **teaspoon baking powder**
1   **teaspoon baking soda**
½   **teaspoon salt**
1   **egg**
1   **cup buttermilk**
⅔   **cup melted butter**
1   **teaspoon vanilla**

Combine ground walnuts and light brown sugar. Butter a 2½-quart Kugelhoph pan or tube pan well and coat it with the walnut mixture. Sift together flour, sugar, baking powder, baking soda and salt. In another bowl beat egg and add buttermilk, butter and vanilla. Beat in the flour mixture until the batter is smooth. Turn into the prepared pan and bake 375° for 50-60 minutes or until a cake tester inserted in the center comes out clean. Let the cake cool in the pan for 5 minutes, turn it out on a wire rack, and let it cool completely. Wrapped tightly in plastic wrap and foil, this cake will keep up to 7 days at room temperature. Because of the richness of this cake, it will fall slightly.

A moist product that keeps well.

CHEESE DANISH BRAID

1 loaf

1 loaf frozen white bread dough
1 cup ricotta cheese
¼ cup sugar
1 tablespoon flour
½ teaspoon salt
1 teaspoon vanilla
1 teaspoon grated orange peel
2 egg yolks
2 tablespoons white raisins
1 egg white
1 tablespoon water
2 tablespoons pinon nuts or pecans, chopped

Thaw dough according to package directions. In a sauce pan, combine cheese, sugar, flour, salt, vanilla, peel and egg yolks. Cook, stirring constantly, until quite thick. Cool and add raisins. Divide dough in half. On a lightly floured surface, roll each half into a 6" x 14" rectangle. Spread half the cheese filling down the center of each half. Fold dough over lengthwise, pinching the side and end seams to seal. Follow the same procedure on the second half. Grease a jelly roll pan. Tightly braid the two halves together, keeping the seam sides down. Tuck ends under. Mix egg white and water together and brush over top of braid. Sprinkle top with chopped nuts. Let rise in a warm place until half again as big. Preheat oven to 375°. Bake bread for 20-25 minutes or until golden brown. (Some of the filling may seep out.) Can be made by the day before it is to be served. Serve warm.

MICROWAVE APRICOT RING

6-8 servings

¼ cup margarine
½ cup brown sugar, packed
½ teaspoon ground cinnamon
1 8-ounce can apricot halves, drained
¼ cup nuts, coarsely chopped
1 7.5-ounce package refrigerated buttermilk biscuits

In an 8" round bowl microwave margarine at high for 1 minute or until melted. Combine sugar and cinnamon with margarine and mix well. Place an 8-ounce drinking glass in center of bowl. Cut apricot halves in half and layer evenly over sugar mixture. Sprinkle nuts over apricots. Arrange biscuits over mixture in petal shape, squeezing to fit. Microwave for 4 minutes at Medium. Turn dish ½ turn and microwave for 5½ minutes at Medium. Remove glass and invert onto serving plate. Let bowl stand over rolls a few minutes until most of the syrup has drizzled over rolls. Serve warm.

BAVARIAN BREAKFAST ROLL

2 rolls

2 cups all purpose flour
1 cup sour cream
1 cup margarine, softened
2 cups fruit preserves
1 cup coarsely chopped nuts
1 cup shredded coconut

In a bowl, combine flour, sour cream and margarine. Mix well. Place dough in plastic wrap and refrigerate overnight. Divide dough in half. On a floured cloth surface, roll each half into a 17″ x 9″ rectangle. Cover each rectangle with half of the preserves, nuts and coconut. Preheat oven to 350°. Tightly roll up each rectangle starting with the wide side. Place rolls seam side down on a jelly roll pan. Tuck the ends under. Bake for 45 minutes. Cool on the pan. Each roll yields 17 1″ slices.

PRIZE-WINNING COFFEE CAKE

8-12 servings

½ pound butter
¾ cup sugar
3 eggs
1 teaspoon vanilla
1 tablespoon lemon rind, grated
12 ounces sour cream
2 tablespoons cognac
2½ cups flour
1 scant teaspoon baking soda
1 teaspoon salt
2 teaspoons baking powder

STREUSEL:

½ cup brown sugar
2-3 teaspoons cinnamon
3-4 tablespoons chopped nuts
1 tablespoon melted butter

Combine butter and sugar and cream well. Add eggs, one at a time, beating well after each addition. Add vanilla, lemon rind, sour cream and cognac to egg mixture. Sift flour with soda, salt and baking powder; add to eggs. Combine streusel ingredients and mix well. Grease and flour a large fluted pan. Pour half the batter into pan, sprinkle with half the streusel. Repeat layers. Swirl slightly on top with a knife. Bake 50 minutes at 350°.

HOLIDAY APPLE STRUDEL

2 cups flour
1 teaspoon salt
½ cup butter
⅓ cup ice water
8 medium apples, peel-
ed and diced fine
¼ cup raisins
⅓ cup pecans, coarsely
chopped
¾ cup sugar
1 tablespoon cinnamon
3 tablespoons butter

Combine flour and salt; cut butter into flour and salt mixture until well blended. Add the water and knead in the bowl for 10 minutes. Divide dough into two balls; wrap in plastic wrap and store in refrigerator overnight. To make the strudel, roll out one ball of chilled dough on a well floured cloth. Roll dough into a large rectangle. The dough should be very thin and quite transparent. Spread half the apples, raisins and nuts over the dough leaving one long edge of the dough clean. Combine the sugar and cinnamon and spread half of the mixture over the filling. Dot filling with half the butter. Very carefully, tightly roll up the strudel using the cloth. If a tear should occur in the dough, patch it with a piece of dough and water. Place roll seamside down on a greased jellyroll pan. Fold ends of strudel under to keep juices from escaping during cooking. Repeat process with second ball of dough. The strudels may be frozen at this point. To bake, preheat oven to 375° and cook strudels for 50 minutes or until golden brown. Cool. Serve sliced for breakfast or for a dessert. Each strudel yields 6 to 10 servings.

COTTAGE CHEESE PANCAKES

32 small pancakes

4	eggs
1	cup cottage cheese
1	8-ounce carton sour cream
¾	cup all-purpose or wholewheat flour
1	tablespoon sugar
¼	teaspoon salt

Beat eggs in a small mixing bowl. Add cottage cheese and sour cream, mixing well. Stir in remaining ingredients and beat until thick. Drop batter by tablespoonfuls onto a hot, lightly oiled griddle. Turn pancakes when tops are covered with bubbles and edges look cooked. Serve hot with butter and syrup.

Light and airy, these pancakes melt in your mouth!

HAPPY DAY PANCAKES

14-16 pancakes

⅔	cup all-purpose flour
⅔	cup whole-wheat flour
¼	cup yellow corn meal or wheat germ
2	tablespoons sugar
2	teaspoons baking powder
1	teaspoon salt
½	teaspoon baking soda
2	cups buttermilk
2	eggs
2	tablespoons vegetable oil

Mix flours, corn meal or wheat germ, sugar, baking powder, salt and baking soda. In a medium-sized bowl beat milk, eggs and vegetable oil until well blended. Add flour mixture and stir just until ingredients are moistened. Heat a lightly oiled griddle or heavy skillet over low heat. Drop batter onto griddle, using about ¼ cup for each pancake. When several bubbles have burst on top of cakes, turn and cook second side, until steam stops rising from them and pancakes are browned.

Time saving tip: While you're measuring the dry ingredients, measure one or two more batches into plastic bags, label and store in a cool dry place ready for a fast, easy future breakfast!

KATE'S KROPSU (FINNISH PANCAKE)

4-6 servings

¼ cup butter
1 cup all-purpose flour, sifted
½ teaspoon salt
2 eggs
1 cup milk

Preheat oven to 400°. Put butter in an 8" x 12" pan and place pan in oven to melt butter. Sift flour and salt together. In a bowl, beat eggs slightly. Add milk and flour alternately. Add melted butter to mixture. Beat ingredients only enough to mix well. Pour batter into hot pan. Bake for 20 minutes. (Pancake will rise and puff and then fall). To serve, cut into squares. Serve with powdered sugar or syrup.

PANCAKES PLUS

25 pancakes

2 cups all-purpose flour
2 teaspoons baking powder
1 teaspoon salt
1 teaspoon ground cinnamon
1 teaspoon ginger
½ teaspoon ground allspice
½ teaspoon ground cloves
3 tablespoons sugar
2 eggs
2¼ cups milk
1 cup vegetable oil
½ cup raisins (optional)

Sift flour twice with baking powder, salt, the spices and sugar. In a mixing bowl, beat eggs with milk. Stir in oil, add flour mixture all at once and beat until smooth. For best results let mixture sit overnight. Grease griddle lightly. Pour out about ¼ cup batter for each pancake. Sprinkle raisins on batter as soon as it is poured. Cook until top side is full of air bubbles and underside is golden brown. Turn and cook until done on flip side. Serve at once with butter and syrup.

🐦PICACHILI PANCAKES

12-16 pancakes

3	eggs, separated
2	tablespoons all-purpose flour
1	teaspoon minced instant onions
¼	teaspoon Worcestershire sauce
1	4-ounce can diced green chili
¾-1	teaspoon salt

Beat egg yolks until thick. Stir in flour, onions, Worcestershire sauce, chili and salt. Mix well, cover and let mixture rest for at least 1 hour. In another mixing bowl, beat egg whites until stiff. Fold chili mixture into egg whites. With a large spoon, spoon pancake mixture onto a moderately hot greased griddle. Brown pancakes on both sides and serve.

A great change of pace from potatoes or rice to accompany pot roast. They will hold a short while in a warm oven.

OVEN FRENCH TOAST

4 servings

2	eggs
½	cup milk
1	teaspoon sugar
⅛	teaspoon salt
4	slices white bread
1	tablespoon butter
4	bananas
½	cup maple syrup
½	teaspoon ground cinnamon

Preheat oven to 500°. Beat eggs until foamy. Stir in milk, sugar and salt. Dip bread in egg mixture; let stand until all liquid is absorbed. Place bread into a well buttered shallow baking dish. Bake for 5 minutes then turn toast. Bake an additional 3-5 minutes or until golden brown. While toast is baking the first 5 minutes, peel bananas, slice them lengthwise and place in another shallow baking dish. Pour syrup over bananas, and sprinkle with cinnamon. Bake in oven with toast the last 5 minutes. To serve, cut each slice toast in half and place on platter. Top each slice with ½ a banana; spoon syrup over all.

A Feast of Culture.....

The region that comprises New Mexico today was explored in 1540 by Coronado and his army who came north from Mexico. Searching for the fabled Seven Golden Cities of Cibola, the Spaniards found instead a poor and relatively arid land dotted with small pueblos of Indians who were farming ribbons of fertile land along the few year-round waterways. But although the area did not have gold, it did have a hospitable climate and enough attractive land for a small colonizing force. The terrain in many ways resembled Spain and the invaders gradually gained control of the best land, by power or persuasion. La Villa Real de Santa Fé, the Royal City of the Holy Faith, was established in 1609 as the capital of New Mexico, thus making Santa Fé the oldest capital in the United States. Because of its spectacular mountain setting, its seclusion, its feasts of tradition and somewhat bohemian atmosphere, Santa Feans proudly refer to their home as the City Different ❖

Salads

MEXICAN GOURD BOWL

BAVARIAN SALAD

6-8 servings

1   27-ounce can
     sauerkraut
1   cup diced celery
1   large bell pepper,
     chopped
1   large red onion,
     chopped

DRESSING:

½   cup salad oil
⅓   cup white wine vinegar
⅓   cup white vinegar
1   cup sugar
2   teaspoons caraway
     seed (optional)

Drain sauerkraut in colander; add celery, bell pepper and red onion. Mix dressing of salad oil, white wine vinegar, white vinegar, sugar and caraway seed; blend well. Pour over sauerkraut and refrigerate several hours or overnight. Drain before serving.

Terrific for picnics.

CAULIFLOWER SALAD

6-8 servings

4   ounces Caesar salad
     dressing
2   tablespoons olive juice
6   ounces sour cream
1   head raw cauliflower,
     broken into flowerettes
1   2½-ounce jar pimien-
     tos, chopped
2   stalks chopped celery
1   2-ounce jar sliced
     green olives
1   bell pepper, chopped
4   ounces processed
     American cheese,
     cubed

Mix salad dressing, olive juice and sour cream to make dressing. Toss remaining ingredients with dressing.

CUCUMBER SALAD

6-8 servings

1   tablespoon white
     vinegar
1   garlic clove, chopped
1   cup sour cream
½   teaspoon salt
     Dash of pepper
2   tablespoons olive oil
1½   tablespoons fresh mint
     leaves, chopped
3   medium cucumbers

Pour vinegar over chopped garlic and let stand for 10 minutes. Drain vinegar into bowl and discard garlic. Add sour cream, salt, pepper, olive oil and mint. Mix thoroughly. Pare cucumber. Cut lengthwise into quarters. Cut quarters into strips about 1½ inches long. Add cucumbers to sour cream mixture and refrigerate covered several hours. Serve on lettuce leaves.

CASA GRANDE SALAD BOWL

6-8 servings

½ cup mayonnaise
¼ cup minced green onion
2 tablespoons chili sauce
2 teaspoons cider vinegar
1 teaspoon onion salt
½ teaspoon chili powder
4 drops hot pepper sauce
1 12-ounce can whole kernel corn, well-drained
1 8-ounce can red kidney beans, well-drained
1 7-ounce can pitted ripe olives, well-drained
2 cups shredded lettuce

Mix first 7 ingredients. Cover and chill. Combine corn, beans and olives; spoon into a lettuce-lined bowl. Before serving toss with dressing.

A CHINESE GARDEN SALAD

4 servings

3 cups cauliflower, cut into bite-sized flowerets
1 pound green beans, trimmed

SAUCE:

¼ cup peanut oil
1 clove minced garliic
3 tablespoons soy sauce
3 tablespoons white vinegar
2 tablespoons dry sherry or vermouth
1 tablespoon sugar
Salt
2 cups fresh or canned lotus root (available in oriental markets)
1 zucchini, sliced thinly
¼ cup toasted sesame seeds

Bring pot of salted water to boil. Add cauliflower and blanch 3-5 minutes. Remove and drain. Add beans to same water and blanch 2 minutes. Drain and cool. Heat oil in wok or pan. Add garlic and stir-fry. Remove from heat and add soy sauce, vinegar, sherry, sugar and dash of salt. Arrange cauliflower, lotus root and zucchini in center of large platter. Place beans along both sides. Drizzle with sauce and sprinkle with sesame seeds.

GAZPACHO SALAD

8 servings

2　medium cucumbers, peeled and sliced
2　teaspoons salt
⅔　cup olive oil
⅓　cup wine vinegar
1　clove garlic, minced
1　teaspoon dried basil
1　teaspoon dried tarragon
1　teaspoon salt
½　teaspoon ground pepper
10　mushrooms, sliced
4　green onions, sliced
3　large tomatoes, peeled and cut in wedges
1　green pepper, sliced
½　pound shredded Swiss cheese
4　hard-boiled eggs, peeled and sliced

Sprinkle cucumbers with salt and let stand 30 minutes. Combine oil, vinegar, garlic, basil, tarragon, salt, and pepper in a bowl. Add mushrooms and green onions. Drain cucumbers and pat dry, then combine with the tomatoes and green pepper, mixing gently. In a large bowl, put a layer of the mixed vegetables, then the dressing with the mushrooms and onions, and keep alternating. Cover bowl and refrigerate for 4 hours. Just before serving, add cheese and eggs. Toss.

GREEN CHILI SALAD

8 servings

4　tomatoes, cut in wedges
1　4-ounce can whole green chilies, drained and sliced
¼　pound fresh mushrooms, sliced
16　pitted black olives
2　tablespoons scallions, minced
1　lemon, thinly sliced
¼　cup oil
2　tablespoons olive oil
3　tablespoons wine vinegar
¼　teaspoon salt
¼　teaspoon pepper
¼　teaspoon oregano
¼　teaspoon cumin

Toss together tomatoes, chilies, mushrooms, olives, onion and lemon. Mix remaining ingredients and pour over vegetables; refrigerate for three hours. Remove lemon before serving. Serve on beds of lettuce.

GREEK RADISH SALAD

10 servings

⅓ cup olive oil
¼ cup fresh lemon juice
1 tablespoon prepared mustard
1 teaspoon sugar
½ teaspoon cracked pepper
3 6-ounce packages radishes
½ pound feta cheese, crumbled
1 6-ounce can pitted ripe olives, drained
¼ cup minced fresh parsley

In medium bowl with wire whisk, mix well olive oil, lemon juice, mustard, sugar and pepper. Add radishes, cut into bite sized pieces, cheese, olives and parsley. With rubber spatula, toss gently to mix well. Cover and refrigerate at least 45 minutes to blend flavors.

GUAYMAS SALAD

8 servings

3 ripe avocados
2 tablespoons fresh lime juice
3 seedless oranges
1 jicama
1 small head lettuce
Pitted ripe olives

AVOCADO DRESSING:

1 ripe avocado, pitted, peeled, cut into cubes
⅓ cup orange juice
¼ cup fresh lime juice
1 tablespoon honey
½ teaspoon salt
Dash cayenne pepper

Cut avocados in half; peel and remove pits. Cut into thin slices and immediately dip all sides in lime juice to prevent discoloring. With sharp knife, cut peel off oranges, cutting deep enough to remove all white membrane. Cut into thin slices. Peel jicama; shred, using the large holes of shredder or shredding blade of food processor. Line serving platter with lettuce leaves. Arrange avocado and orange slices overlapping slightly around the shredded jicama. Garnish with olives. Serve with avocado dressing. To make dressing; put all dressing ingredients in blender or food processor. Blend until smooth.

Excellent with Mexican food!

LETTUCE WITH WALNUT DRESSING

6-8 servings

6 slices bacon
¾ cup chopped walnuts
1 tablespoon flour
1 cup sour cream
2 tablespoons lemon juice
2 teaspoons sugar
1 teaspoon salt
1 head lettuce

Cook bacon until crisp; drain well on paper towel. Add walnuts to bacon pan, cook 2 minutes. Transfer to paper towel; drain well. Add flour to pan and cook, stirring, until smooth. Stir in sour cream, lemon juice, sugar, salt and heat. Break lettuce into bite-size pieces and place in salad bowl. Pour hot dressing over lettuce and top with crumbled bacon and walnuts. Serve immediately.

HOT GERMAN POTATO SALAD
12 servings

4½	pounds peeled and boiled potatoes
9	slices bacon, diced
1½	cup chopped onion
¾	cup chopped celery
3	tablespoons flour
4	teaspoons salt
1½	cups water
1	cup cider vinegar
1	cup sugar
⅓	cup snipped parsley
1½	cup sliced radishes

Boil potatoes. Fry bacon until crisp in large skillet. Remove and drain on paper towel. Cook onion and celery in bacon fat until tender. Stir in flour and salt. Cook over low heat, stirring constantly until bubbly. Remove from heat, stir in water, vinegar, and sugar. Heat to boiling, stirring constantly. Boil and stir 1 minute. Stir in parsley and bacon. Cut potatoes into thin slices. Toss potatoes with bacon mixture in 3½ quart casserole. Cover and bake in 350° oven for 30 minutes. Stir in radishes.

ITALIAN PEPPER SALAD
10 servings

¼	cup salad oil
1	large clove garlic, mashed
8	medium green peppers, cut into ½ inch strips
3	medium onions, each cut into 8 wedges
2	tablespoons cider vinegar
2	teaspoons salt
1½	teaspoons oregano leaves
¼	teaspoon pepper
3	medium tomatoes, each cut into 8 wedges

In a 5-quart Dutch oven over medium high heat, cook garlic in salad oil until browned. Add peppers and remaining ingredients except tomatoes; cook until vegetables are tender-crisp, about 15 minutes, stirring often. Remove from heat and stir in tomatoes. Cover and refrigerate until chilled, about 2 hours.

This is a nice change-of-pace salad for Italian menus or makes an excellent accompaniment to grilled meats or other barbecue fare.

MUSHROOM-PROVOLONE SALAD
4-6 servings

2	cups fresh mushrooms, sliced
1½	cups celery, sliced
1½	cups provolone cheese, diced
⅔	cup Italian dressing
	Salt to taste
	Pepper to taste

Combine all ingredients and chill thoroughly.

SPINACH SALAD

1½   pound spinach, washed and chilled
½   cup tarragon vinegar
1   cup olive oil
¼   teaspoon celery seed
1   teaspoon dry mustard
½   teaspoon Worcestershire sauce
1   clove of garlic, crushed
  Dash of salt
  Dash of MSG
10   strips of bacon, fried crisp and crushed
3   tablespoons hot bacon grease
¼   teaspoon garlic salt
3   hard-boiled eggs, grated

Tear spinach into bite-size pieces. Mix vinegar, oil, celery seed, mustard, Worcestershire sauce, garlic, salt and MSG. Pour the dressing over the spinach. Add bacon, bacon grease and garlic salt. Toss. Top with hard-boiled eggs.

SALADS

THE BEAN THING

10-12 servings

1   16-ounce can kidney beans, drained and rinsed
1   16-ounce can pinto beans, drained and rinsed
1   16-ounce can yellow niblet corn, drained
1   16-ounce can chick peas, drained and rinsed
1   small green pepper, chopped
½   cup chopped celery
½   cup chopped scallions
¾   cup olive oil
3   tablespoons vinegar
1   clove crushed garlic
½   teaspoon salt
  Dash pepper
2   tablespoons chianti or other red wine

In a large bowl combine beans, corn and chick peas with chopped scallions, green pepper and celery. Mix remaining ingredients well. Pour over bean mixture and toss well to coat. Cover and refrigerate for several hours or overnight.

Good with most New Mexican dishes.

POTATO SALAD WITH WALNUTS   8 servings

3   pounds potatoes
    Salt to taste
1   tablespoon Dijon
    mustard
1   teaspoon finely
    minced garlic
⅓   cup dry white wine
¼   cup red wine vinegar
¼   teaspoon freshly
    ground pepper
½   cup peanut, vegetable
    or corn oil
½   cup finely chopped
    parsley
2   cups broken walnuts,
    toasted

Put unpeeled potatoes in a kettle and add cold water to cover. Add salt to taste. Bring to a boil and let simmer about 20 minutes or longer until potatoes are tender. Drain. When the potatoes are cool enough to handle, peel them. Cut them into small cubes. Set aside. Put the mustard, garlic, wine, vinegar and pepper in a mixing bowl. Stir with a wire whisk while gradually adding the oil. Add the potatoes, parsley and toasted walnuts. Toss to blend. Serve at room temperature.

SOUTHWESTERN POTATO SALAD   6-8 servings

4   medium potatoes
⅓   cup salad oil
¼   cup vinegar
1   tablespoon sugar
1½ teaspoons chili powder
1   teaspoon seasoned
    salt
    Dash bottled hot pep-
    per sauce
1   small onion, thinly
    sliced
1   8-ounce can whole
    kernel corn, drained
½   cup shredded carrot
½   cup chopped green
    pepper
½   cup sliced pitted ripe
    olives

Cook potatoes in boiling salted water until tender; drain, pare and cube. Combine oil, vinegar, sugar, chili powder, seasoned salt and hot pepper sauce. Add to warm potatoes; toss gently to coat. Cover and chill 1 hour. Fold in remaining ingredients. Garnish with additional halved ripe olives, if desired. Serve well chilled.

A new twist to an old favorite!

ORANGE-ALMOND SALAD

6-8 servings

¼ cup salad oil
2 tablespoons sugar
2 tablespoons malt vinegar
¼ teaspoon salt
⅛ teaspoon almond extract
6 cups torn mixed greens
3 medium oranges, peeled, sliced crosswise and halved
1 cup thinly sliced celery
3 tablespoons sliced green onion
⅓ cup toasted slivered almonds

In a screw-top jar combine oil, sugar, vinegar, salt and almond extract. Cover and shake well to dissolve sugar and salt. Chill. In a large salad bowl, combine greens, oranges, celery and onion. Sprinkle with almonds. Pour dressing over and toss gently to coat. Serve at once.

RAITA

4 servings

1 small cucumber, peeled, seeded and shredded
1 carrot, shredded
1 green onion, finely chopped
1 small green chili, finely chopped (optional)
1 small tomato, finely chopped (optional)
1 cup plain yogurt
½ teaspoon salt

Combine all the ingredients and chill.

A salad that cools the palate.

ASPIC OLÉ

9 servings

2 3-ounce packages lemon-flavored gelatin
1½ cups hot water
¾ cup chopped celery
½ cup chopped bell pepper
1 7-ounce can green chili salsa
1 8-ounce can tomato sauce
½ cup chopped onion

Dissolve gelatin in hot water. Stir in remaining ingredients. Pour into 8″ square pan. When chilled and set cut in squares and serve on a bed of chopped lettuce and, if desired, top with a dollup of salad dressing or sour cream.

135

TOMATO AND CREAM CHEESE ASPIC   6-8 servings

1   tablespoon unflavored
     gelatin
¼   cup cold water
3   3-ounce packages
     cream cheese
1   10½-ounce can con-
     densed tomato soup
1   cup mayonnaise
½   cup green pepper,
     chopped
½   cup celery, chopped

Dissolve gelatin in water. Melt cheese in soup. Add mayonnaise, dissolved gelatin, green pepper and celery. Pour into a mold and chill until firm.

AVOCADO SALAD RING   6-8 servings

1   envelope unflavored
     gelatin
¼   cup ice cold water
1   cup boiling water
1   tablespoon lemon
     juice
1   teaspoon sugar
1   cup mashed avocados
1   tablespoon lemon
     juice
½   cup sour cream
½   cup mayonnaise
     Salt
     Pepper
     Cayenne

Soak gelatin in ice water. Dissolve this in the hot water. Add lemon juice and sugar; chill until slightly thickened. Rub the mashed avocado through a sieve and add to lemon mixture. Add sour cream and mayonnaise and season according to taste. Pour into oiled ring mold. Chill 2-3 hours. Unmold on lettuce and fill center with chopped tomatoes and onions.

FROZEN FRUIT CUPS   40 fruit cups

6   ripe bananas, mashed
1   20-ounce can crushed
     pineapple, drained
2   17-ounce cans
     apricots, drained and
     cut up
2   tablespoons lemon
     juice
1   cup sugar
1   12-ounce can frozen
     orange juice
1   12-ounce juice can of
     water
40   fluted paper cupcake
     cups

Combine all of the ingredients, using a blender, if desired, for a smoother texture. Freeze in cupcake papers in muffin tins. Can remove from muffin tins and store in plastic bags in freezer. They will keep well for weeks.

Great for breakfast or brunch and as a snack for kids.

BEAUTIFUL CRANBERRY MOLD

8-10 servings

1 8¼-ounce can crushed pineapple
1 3-ounce package raspberry-flavored gelatin
1 16-ounce can whole cranberry sauce
1 teaspoon orange peel, grated
1 11-ounce can mandarin orange segments, drained
1 cup whipping cream

Drain pineapple, reserving syrup. Add enough water to syrup to make 1 cup. Heat to boiling. Dissolve gelatin in hot liquid. Stir cranberry sauce and orange peel into gelatin. Chill until partially set. Fold in oranges and pineapple. Whip cream and fold into fruit. Pour into a six-cup mold and chill until set.

This is light and beautiful and perfect for a special dinner, particularly during the holidays. This recipe can be doubled and prepared in a 12-cup tube pan.

BLUEBERRY HILL MOLD

6-8 servings

1 3-ounce package lemon-flavored gelatin
1 cup pineapple juice heated or rather hot
1 15-ounce can blueberries, liquid drained and reserved to measure 1 cup
2½ medium bananas, mashed
½ pint whipping cream, whipped

Dissolve gelatin in hot pineapple juice. Stir in juice from can of blueberries, add blueberries and mashed bananas. Fold in whipped cream. Pour into a decorative 6 cup mold. Best made day before serving.

Beautiful and tasty!

ORANGE-APRICOT SALAD MOLD

6-8 servings

1 3-ounce package orange-flavored gelatin
1½ cups boiling water
½ tablespoon unflavored gelatin
2 tablespoons cold water
1 6-ounce can frozen orange juice, concentrate, thawed
2 4½-ounce jars strained apricots
2 11-ounce cans mandarin oranges, drained
3 tablespoons sugar

Dissolve the orange-flavored gelatin in the boiling water. Dissolve the unflavored gelatin in cold water and add to the orange-flavored gelatin. Add orange juice, strained apricots, mandarin oranges and sugar. Pour into a mold and chill until firm.

APPLESAUCE SALAD

6 servings

2 cups applesauce
2 3-ounce packages
   cherry-flavored gelatin
½ cup orange juice
2 cups lemon-lime car-
   bonated beverage

Heat applesauce and gelatin until gelatin is dissolved. Add orange juice and carbonated beverage and pour into a 5-cup mold. Chill until set.

CURRIED RICE ARTICHOKE SALAD

6-8 servings

1 6-ounce package
   chicken flavored rice
   mix
4 green onions, sliced
   fine
½ green pepper, chop-
   ped
12 pimiento-stuffed
   olives, sliced
2 6-ounce jars marinated
   artichoke hearts
¾ teaspoon curry powder
½ cup mayonnaise

Cook rice according to package directions but omit butter; cool. Place rice mix in large bowl and add onions, peppers, and olives. Drain artichoke marinade into the mayonnaise and add curry; mix well. Cut artichokes in small pieces and add to rice. Add mayonnaise and curry mixture and toss well. Chill overnight or several hours before serving.

POLYNESIAN RICE SALAD

6 servings

½ cup salad oil
¼ cup cider vinegar
2 tablespoons soy sauce
½ teaspoon salt
1 ✦ cup thinly sliced
   celery
¼ cup thinly sliced green
   onion tops
3 cups cooked long-
   grain rice, cooled to
   room temperature
1 8½-ounce can water
   chestnuts, drained and
   sliced
1 cup sliced fresh
   mushrooms
1 11-ounce can man-
   darin oranges, drained
   Lettuce (optional)

Combine salad oil, vinegar, soy sauce, salt, celery, and onion; stir in rice and toss well. Fold in water chestnuts, mushrooms and oranges just until blended. Chill thoroughly and serve in a lettuce-lined bowl.

Great with grilled meats or chicken.

TABOOLEH WHEAT SALAD

6 servings

1 cup finely cracked wheat
  Warm water
1 small bunch green onions
2 bunches of parsley
½ cup fresh mint leaves
4 large tomatoes
  Juice of 4 lemons or 8 tablespoons lemon juice
¼ cup olive oil
¼ cup salad oil
¼ teaspoon salt
⅛ teaspoon pepper

Soak wheat in water for one hour. Squeeze dry by pressing between palms. Chop onion, parsley, mint and tomatoes very fine. Add wheat, lemon juice, oils, salt and pepper to vegetable mixture. Mix well. Serve in lettuce lined bowl or on grape leaves or cabbage leaves.

SPAGHETTI SALAD

24 servings

2 pounds spaghetti
2 tablespoons olive oil
3 pounds mozzarella cheese, shredded
12 tomatoes, chopped
6 bunches watercress, finely chopped
5 garlic cloves, finely minced
2½ pounds fresh pea pods
3 10-ounce packages frozen green peas, thawed
  Salt and freshly ground pepper
  Freshly grated Parmesan cheese

Cook spaghetti in large pot of boiling water with olive oil until al dente. Drain well. Return to pot, add mozzarella and toss until cheese melts (cheese will be very gummy and seemingly inseparable but will break up as other ingredients are added). Cook over low heat 15 minutes. Remove from heat, add remaining ingredients except Parmesan and toss gently but thoroughly (using hands if necessary). Serve at room temperature lavishly sprinkled with Parmesan cheese. Pass a bowl of Parmesan separately, if desired.

Let your food processor make easy work of this delicious and unusual salad.

CHICKEN SALAD DIVINE

4 servings

2   tablespoons butter
1   tablespoon oil
2   whole chicken breasts, halved, skinned and boned
1   teaspoon fresh lemon juice
     Salt
     Pepper
6   tablespoons oil
3   tablespoons vinegar
½   teaspoon dry mustard
2   stalks celery, julienned
1   cup Cheddar cheese, shredded
½   cup sliced almonds toasted in butter
1   head leaf lettuce

Melt 2 tablespoons butter with 1 tablespoon oil in medium skillet over low heat. Add chicken, turning to coat all sides. Sprinkle with lemon juice, salt and pepper. Cover with circle of waxed paper and lid and poach until chicken feels just firm to the touch (about 10-12 minutes). Remove from heat and let cool, covered in pan. Combine oil, vinegar, mustard, salt and pepper in bowl and whisk well to make dressing. Shred chicken coarsely with fingers and return to skillet with some of the poaching liquid. Add half of dressing and toss gently. Toss remaining ingredients with remaining dressing. Add chicken with its liquid and toss again. Serve at room temperature.

CHINESE CHICKEN AND LETTUCE SALAD

4 servings

3   cups water
2   tablespoons lemon juice
1   tablespoon salt
2   medium chicken breasts, skinned, boned and split (1 pound boneless)
2   tablespoons sesame oil
2   tablespoons soy sauce
2   teaspoons lemon juice
1   large bunch watercress or 1 head leafy green lettuce
1   sweet red pepper, cored, seeded and finely slivered

In a medium saucepan place water, 2 tablespoons lemon juice and salt and bring to boil. Add chicken breasts; cover and simmer over moderate heat for 15 minutes. Remove pan from heat; cool chicken slightly and then chill in broth several hours or overnight. Just before serving, slice chicken in 3″ x ¼″ strips and place in a bowl. Put the oil, soy sauce and 2 teaspoons lemon juice in a screw-top jar; cover and shake well. Add half of the dressing to the chicken and toss well. Place watercress and pepper strips on a medium-sized platter; add remaining dressing and toss well. Pile chicken strips in center of watercress. Toss again just before serving.

An excellent salad to serve for lunch with crusty bread, butter and hot or iced tea.

PEANUT-CHICKEN SALAD

6 servings

½ cup plain yogurt
⅓ cup peanut butter
½ cup milk
3 tablespoons white wine vinegar
1 tablespoon salad oil
1 tablespoon sugar
½ teaspoon soy sauce
¼ teaspoon garlic powder
Dash cayenne
6 cups torn greens
2 cups diced cooked chicken
1 tart apple, cored and diced
1 cup shredded red cabbage
¼ cup raisins
1 tablespoon thinly sliced green onion
½ cup roasted and salted peanuts

In a small mixing bowl stir together yogurt, peanut butter, milk, vinegar, oil, sugar, soy sauce, garlic powder, and cayenne. In large salad bowl arrange lettuce, chicken, apple, cabbage, raisins, onion, and peanuts. Add dressing and toss.

TURKEY SALAD INDIENNE

6-8 servings

4 cups diced cooked turkey
1 8-ounce can water chestnuts, drained and sliced
1½ cups seedless grapes
1 cup diagonally sliced celery
1 5-ounce can toasted slivered almonds
1½ cups mayonnaise
1-2 teaspoons curry powder
2 teaspoons soy sauce
1 20-ounce can sliced pineapple, drained (reserve 2 tablespoons)
Lettuce

Combine turkey, water chestnuts, grapes, celery, and almonds. Blend mayonnaise with curry powder, soy sauce, and 2 tablespoons reserved pineapple juice. Combine with turkey mixture; chill. Serve on pineapple slices and lettuce.

CRAB AND WILD RICE SALAD

1   **6-ounce package long grain and wild rice**
1   **6½-ounce can crabmeat, drained and flaked**
2   **tablespoons lemon juice**
2   **tablespoons chopped green pepper**
2   **tablespoons chopped pimiento**
2   **tablespoons chopped parsley**
½   **cup mayonnaise**
2   **tablespoons bottled Russian dressing**
2   **medium avocados, sliced**

Cook rice according to package directions; cool. Mix crabmeat with lemon juice. Add green pepper, pimiento and parsley. Blend together mayonnaise and Russian dressing. Pour over crab mixture and mix well. Chill. Serve on avocado slices.

SHRIMP SALAD

3   **cups cooked rice**
1   **green bell pepper, chopped**
2   **cups raw cauliflower, chopped**
16   **stuffed green olives, sliced**
8   **green onions, chopped with tops**
2   **4½-ounce cans small shrimp, drained and rinsed**

DRESSING:

1½   **cups mayonnaise**
2   **medium-size lemons, juiced**

Combine rice, bell pepper, cauliflower, green olives, green onions and shrimp. Mix salt, mayonnaise and the juice of the 2 lemons thoroughly. Pour dressing over salad mixture and toss.

SICILIAN SALAD

4-6 servings

1   **10 ounce package
frozen green beans**
1   **10 ounce package
frozen wax beans**
1   **7-ounce can tuna fish,
oil packed**
1   **red onion**
1   **2-ounce jar sliced
pimientos**
2   **tablespoons olive oil**
½   **cup pine nuts
Herb Vinaigrette (See
Index)
Salt and pepper
Parsley**

Cook green beans and wax beans until barely tender. Drain beans, rinse with cold water and drain again. Place in a salad bowl. Drain tuna and break it up; add to the beans. Thinly slice the onion and add to the bowl. Drain pimientos and place in bowl. In a small skillet, heat the oil and saute' the pine nuts until golden brown. Drain the nuts and add them to the salad bowl. Add the Vinaigrette to taste and toss carefully. Season with salt and pepper and garnish with the parsley.

DIJON SALAD

4-6 servings

1   **pound lean pork, cooked and sliced thinly**
2   **tablespoons olive oil**
¼   **cup wine vinegar**
2   **green onions, minced**
2-3   **large potatoes, cooked
and diced**
¼   **cup wine vinegar**
4   **tablespoons olive oil**
¼   **cup red onion,
chopped**
1   **teaspoon Dijon style
mustard
Salt
Freshly ground pepper**
1   **head Romaine lettuce**
2   **roasted green or red
peppers, julienne**
2   **green onions, thinly
sliced**
2   **tablespoons capers**

Combine pork, oil, vinegar and green onions; cover and refrigerate 1-2 days. Combine potatoes, vinegar, oil, red onion, mustard, salt, pepper and toss. Cover and refrigerate overnight. Arrange lettuce leaves on large platter. Add peppers to pork mixture and toss. Taste and season with salt and pepper. Arrange potato salad over lettuce in a ring and sprinkle with onions. Mound pork in center and top with capers.

This is especially good with beer or dry white wine and dark bread.

LENTIL AND SAUSAGE SALAD

4-6 servings

1   pound kielbasa or knockwurst
2-3   cups cooked lentils
1   large green pepper, seeded and diced
1   sweet red onion, peeled and sliced thin
2   large tomatoes, cut into eighths
½   cup Garlic and Mustard Vinaigrette (recipe below)
    Crisp romaine or spinach leaves
2-4   hard-cooked eggs, peeled and quartered

On the rack of a broiler pan broil the kielbasa or knockwurst 3-5 inches from heat source for 3 to 5 minutes, turning several times. Meanwhile, put lentils, pepper, onion and tomatoes into a medium-sized bowl. Add ¼ cup vinaigrette dressing and toss to coat. Cut sausage into thin slices and add to salad. Add remaining ¼ cup dressing and toss again. Mound salad on a bed of romaine and garnish with eggs. Serve at room temperature.

Garlic and mustard vinaigrette:

5   tablespoons olive oil
3   tablespoons red wine vinegar
½   teaspoon minced, peeled garlic
1   teaspoon Dijon-style mustard
½   teaspoon salt
¼   teaspoon ground pepper

Put all ingredients into a screw-top jar; cover and shake well. Makes ½ cup dressing.

A hearty salad great for picnics or other summer pleasures.

BEEF CAESAR SALAD

4 servings

¼   teaspoon salt
1   garlic clove, crushed
1   teaspoon dry mustard
1   tablespoon lemon juice
3   tablespoons olive oil
2   bunches Romaine, washed, drained and chilled
2   tablespoons Parmesan cheese
1   2-ounce can anchovy fillets, washed and drained
1   egg, coddled
1½   cups julienne strips of rare roast beef
1   cup toasted croutons

Mix salt, garlic, mustard, lemon juice and olive oil in large wooden bowl. Add Romaine, cheese and anchovies. Break egg over salad. Distribute beef and croutons over salad. Mix gently but well.

🦃 MEXICAN CHEF SALAD

1   6-ounce can pitted ripe olives, sliced
1   head shredded iceberg lettuce
1   16-ounce can kidney beans, drained and rinsed
2   tomatoes, chopped and drained
1   tablespoon chopped green chile
½   pound ground beef, cooked and seasoned (optional)
1   large avocado, diced
½   cup sour cream
2   tablespoons bottled Italian salad dressing
1   teaspoon instant minced onion
¾   teaspoon chili powder
½   teaspoon salt
⅛   teaspoon pepper
½   cup grated Cheddar cheese
½   cup coarsely crushed corn chips

Combine olives, lettuce, beans, tomatoes, and chili and beef; chill thoroughly. Blend avocado, sour cream, dressing and seasonings; chill. Toss lettuce mixture with dressing; top with cheese and chips.

SZECHWAN BROCCOLI AND BEEF SALAD 12 servings

2   bunches (2 pounds each) broccoli
¾   cup vegetable oil
2   sweet red peppers, cut in strips
4   cups sliced fresh mushrooms
½   cup white vinegar
¼   cup naturally brewed soy sauce
2½   teaspoons salt
5   dried, hot red peppers, crushed
2   pounds rare roast beef, julienned
1   8-ounce can water chestnuts, drained and sliced
1   4-ounce can bamboo shoots

Wash broccoli; cut into large flowerets; place in bowl. Cut stalks into 3/8″ slices and put in separate bowl. Stir-fry stalk 1 minute in hot oil; add flowers, stir-fry 1 minute more. Cover pan and cook over moderate heat 2-3 minutes. Transfer broccoli to a large bowl. Stir-fry red pepper strips in same pan 1-2 minutes (add more oil if necessary). Add to broccoli. Stir-fry mushroom slices in same pan 3-4 minutes; add to broccoli. Combine vinegar, soy sauce and crushed red peppers. Pour over broccoli and toss. Add beef, water chestnuts and bamboo shoots. Toss; cover and chill 2-3 hours.

HERB VINAIGRETTE

1¼ cups

4 tablespoons tarragon
vinegar
2 teaspoons Dijon
mustard
2 teaspoons salt
2 cloves garlic, minced
2 tablespoons fresh
parsley, minced
2 teaspoons dried
chervil
¾ cup olive oil

In a covered jar combine the vinegar, mustard, salt, garlic and herbs; blend well. Let mixture stand for 30 minutes to develop the full flavor of the herbs. Blend in the olive oil a little at a time. Shake dressing vigorously before using.

MINI SKINNY MAYONNAISE

1 cup

4 ounces Neufchatel
cheese
1 hard-cooked egg yolk
1 raw egg yolk
½ cup plain low-fat
yogurt
1 teaspoon lemon juice
½ teaspoon Dijon-style
mustard
Salt and pepper

Combine cheese, hard-cooked and raw egg yolks in blender and mix until smooth. Transfer to bowl and stir in yogurt, lemon juice, mustard and seasonings. Refrigerate.

Wonderful on fish, especially salmon.

ORANGE YOGURT SALAD DRESSING

1⅓ cups

1 medium banana,
mashed
1 tablespoon orange
juice concentrate
2 teaspoons honey
⅛ teaspoon ground
ginger
⅛ teaspoon cinnamon
1 cup orange yogurt

Combine all ingredients and mix well. Chill and serve with fresh fruit.

A subtle touch of the tropics.

POPPY SEED DRESSING

3½ cups

1½ cups sugar
2 teaspoons dry mustard
2 teaspoons salt
⅔ cup vinegar
3 tablespoons onion
juice
2 cups salad oil (not
olive oil)
3 tablespoons poppy
seeds

Mix sugar, mustard, salt and vinegar. Add onion juice and stir it in thoroughly. Add oil slowly while beating and continue to beat until thick. Add poppy seeds and beat a few seconds longer.

SLENDERIZED ROQUEFORT DRESSING 1½ cups

1 cup low-fat cottage
   cheese
½ cup buttermilk
2 tablespoons wine
   vinegar
2 ounces Roquefort or
   blue cheese
   Salt and freshly
   ground pepper

Mix cottage cheese, buttermilk and vinegar in blender. Add half blue cheese and mix until smooth. Crumble remaining cheese and stir into dressing with salt and pepper to taste.

A dieter's delight.

SWISS SALAD SAUCE 1 cup

⅛ cup oil
2 tablespoons vinegar
1 clove garlic, crushed
2 tablespoons Maggi
   Liquid Wurze or soy
   sauce
3 tablespoons milk or
   cream
4 tablespoons mayon-
   naise
1 teaspoon prepared
   mustard

Combine all ingredients in a shaker bottle; chill. Shake thoroughly before serving.

Delicious on green salads, this "sauce" is popular in family owned restaurants and guest houses throughout Switzerland and Austria.

TANGY SALAD DRESSING 2 cups

1 cup salad oil
⅔ cup sugar
⅓ cup ketchup
¼ cup cider vinegar
3 tablespoons grated
   onion
1 teaspoon celery seed
1 teaspoon dry mustard
1 teaspoon salt
½ teaspoon sweet
   paprika

In a blender or food processor blend all ingredients well. Transfer dressing to a bowl and chill covered at least 24 hours.

YOGURT SALAD DRESSING 1⅓ cups

3 tablespoons orange
   juice
2 tablespoons honey
1 tablespoon lemon
   juice
1 tablespoon fresh mint,
   minced
1 cup plain yogurt

In a bowl combine first four ingredients and mix well. Whisk in the yogurt; chill.

This refreshing dressing is especially tasty tossed with orange sections and seedless grapes. It makes any fresh fruit combination shine.

Let the Sunshine In.....

The word on solar energy -- though they may not have called it that -- was out among New Mexico's early inhabitants, the cliff dwellers and pueblo-builders. Later settlers, however, must have had other things on their minds and somehow lost sight of those ancient ways of harnessing the sun for human needs. In recent years worldwide energy shortages have accentuated the need for man to live more symbiotically with his environment. And in New Mexico there is a rush to find the most effective and efficient ways of utilizing solar energy. Millions of dollars each year are going into solar energy research in this state and because the sun shines here almost every day of the year, more and more individuals are adapting solar energy concepts to home heating and cooling needs. True solar homes -- those designed to collect solar heat, store solar heat and minimize heat gain in summer -- are common sights in all parts of New Mexico.

Accompaniments

COCHITI JUG

APPLE MINT SAUCE FOR LAMB

about 1½ cups

1 cup apple juice or cider
1 tablespoon cornstarch
⅛ teaspoon salt
1 teaspoon grated lemon rind
1½ teaspoons butter
½ teaspoon peppermint extract
3 tablespoons apple jelly
⅛ teaspoon garlic salt
1 teaspoon liquid gravy base

Combine apple juice and cornstarch in small saucepan and bring to a boil, stirring constantly. Add remaining ingredients, and mix well. Serve with lamb chops or leg of lamb.

BUTTERY BARBEQUE SAUCE

1½ cups

½ cup butter
¾ cup catsup
½ cup brown sugar
3 tablespoons lemon juice
1 tablespoon Dijon-style mustard
2 teaspoons hot pepper sauce
2 teaspoons Worcester-shire sauce
2 teaspoons bottled steak sauce

Melt butter and stir in remaining ingredients. Cook 5 minutes uncovered over low heat.

🐦 CHILI CARIBE SAUCE

1 quart

34 medium sized whole dried red chili pods, seeded and stemmed
1 quart water
½ teaspoon onion, minced
½ teaspoon oregano
½ teaspoon salt
½ teaspoon garlic salt
¼ teaspoon white pepper
¼ teaspoon monosodium glutamate
¼ teaspoon Worcester-shire sauce

Roast chili pods in a 350° oven for about 4 minutes. Wash, then break up pods into a container; add water. Place pods and water to cover in blender, a little at a time. Mix the quart of blended chilies with all other ingredients and simmer in a saucepan for at least 20 minutes to blend flavors.

This fiery sauce has a multitude of uses: over enchiladas, beans, eggs or posole. It will keep well for two weeks in the refrigerator and freezes beautifully.

CAPER SAUCE

1½ cups

1   cup mayonnaise
¼   cup lemon juice
¼   cup capers
1   hard-boiled egg, finely chopped
    Dash onion salt
    Dash liquid hot pepper sauce.

Combine all ingredients well and chill at least 1 hour before serving. Serve with cooked vegetables.

CONTINENTAL MUSTARD SAUCE

3½ cups

2   cups light cream
¼   cup dry mustard
½   cup sugar
½   cup tarragon vinegar
2   egg yolks, well beaten
2   tablespoons flour
    Salt to taste

Pour cream in top of double boiler and heat. Stir remaining ingredients into cream and cook slowly in double boiler until thick, 1 hour or more. Do not let boil. Stir occasionally. Serve hot or cold. If serving cold, drained horseradish or whipped cream may be added. Serve with ham, corned beef or roast beef.

DILL SAUCE

1¼ cups

1   cup sour cream
¼   cup mayonnaise
1   tablespoon chopped chives
1   teaspoon vinegar
¼   teaspoon salt
½   teaspoon dill weed
½   teaspoon grated onion, optional

Combine all ingredients and mix well. Chill and let stand at least an hour before serving. Serve with beef fondue or salmon.

HORSERADISH-SOUR CREAM DRESSING

1½ cups

1   cup sour cream
½   cup mayonnaise
1   teaspoon lemon juice
¼   teaspoon dry mustard
1   tablespoon prepared horseradish
¼   teaspoon onion juice
2   teaspoons chopped chives

Thoroughly combine all ingredients and chill. Store refrigerated in a covered container. Serve with prime rib or beef brisket.

ACCOMPANIMENTS

MANDARIN ORANGE-GRAPE SAUCE FOR FOWL

about 1 cup

½ stick butter
1 tablespoon Worcester-
 shire sauce
1 teaspoon fines herbes
 seasoning
1 10-ounce jar sweet
 orange marmalade
½ pound seedless
 grapes
1 small can Mandarin
 oranges, drained

Melt butter in saucepan over low heat. Add Worcestershire sauce and fines herbes. Stir. Add marmalade and grapes. Allow jelly to melt and simmer. Add oranges and simmer 20 minutes, stirring frequently. Let sit 5 minutes before serving.

ORANGE BASTING SAUCE

⅔ cup

1 teaspoon orange peel,
 grated
⅓ cup orange juice
⅓ cup salad oil
¼ teaspoon seasoned
 salt
1 teaspoon soy sauce
½ teaspoon sugar

Combine ingredients and blend thoroughly. Use to baste chicken, fish or pork in 325° oven.

REMOULADE SAUCE

1 cup

3 tablespoons wine
 vinegar
2 tablespoons Dijon-style
 mustard
2 tablespoons minced
 green onions
1 teaspoon horseradish
1 tablespoon minced
 parsley
½ cup plus 1 tablespoon
 olive oil
 Dash hot pepper sauce
 Salt to taste
 Pepper to taste,
 freshly ground
2 tablespoons drained
 capers

Combine vinegar, mustard, onions, horseradish and parsley. Beat in olive oil a little at a time. Season to taste with pepper sauce, salt and pepper. Add capers. Chill. Serve with cold boiled shrimp or lobster.

Easy and very good.

🐦 MILD HOMEMADE TACO SAUCE

2 cups

1   **16-ounce can plum tomatoes, undrained**
1   **large onion, minced**
2   **large garlic cloves, crushed**
1½   **tablespoons cooking oil**
1   **teaspoon oregano**
¾   **teaspoon ground cumin**
¾   **teaspoon ground coriander**
2   **tablespoons (or more to taste) chopped green chili**
1   **tablespoon tomato paste**
1½   **teaspoons sugar**
1   **teaspoon chopped fresh coriander**
1   **teaspoon white vinegar**
   Salt and pepper to taste

In a food processor fitted with the steel blade or in a blender coarsely puree the tomatoes with juice. In a large skillet cook onion and garlic in oil over moderate heat, stirring, until onion is softened. Add oregano, cumin and ground coriander and cook the mixture, stirring, for 2 minutes. Add the tomato puree, chopped green chili, tomato paste, sugar, chopped coriander, vinegar, salt and pepper. Simmer the mixture, stirring often, for 15 minutes or until sauce is thickened.

Serve this mild but zesty sauce with any favorite Mexican entree. It also goes well with grilled steaks or hamburgers.

SPICY SPAGHETTI SAUCE

3 quarts

1   **pound hot bulk sausage**
1   **pound ground beef**
1½   **cups chopped onions**
½   **pound fresh mushrooms, sliced**
2   **teaspoons salt**
½   **teaspoon marjoram**
½   **teaspoon garlic powder**
1   **cup chopped parsley**
2   **6-ounce cans tomato paste**
3   **8-ounce cans tomato sauce**
1   **teaspoon rosemary**
1   **teaspoon oregano**
½   **teaspoon freshly ground pepper**
1   **cup dry red wine**
1   **cup water**

Brown sausage and beef in skillet. Drain off excess fat and put in a large crockery slow cooker or large pot. Add remaining ingredients and mix well. For slow cooker cook on high heat for 2 hours and then low heat for 4 hours. On stove top simmer slowly, covered, for 4 hours.

Now, that's Italian!

INDONESIAN PEANUT SAUCE 1½ cups

6   tablespoons peanut butter
1   teaspoon Sambal Ulek (or 2 drops hot pepper sauce)
1   teaspoon lemon rind, grated
1   teaspoon brown sugar
½   cup hot water
½   cup soy sauce
1   clove garlic, minced

Combine ingredients in a saucepan over low heat. Serve hot with beef fondue or pork sate.

SOUR CREAM AND ONION SAUCE 1 cup

1   tablespoon butter
½   onion, chopped
1   teaspoon grated Parmesan cheese
½   cup sour cream
    Salt and pepper to taste

Melt butter in frying pan. Cook onion until tender; stir in cheese and sour cream. Season to taste. Serve with sliced cooked zucchini.

SPICED CHERRY SAUCE 2 cups

1   16-ounce can dark sweet cherries
5   teaspoons cornstarch
½   cup sugar
2   tablespoons white vinegar
2   tablespoons water
⅛   teaspoon cinnamon
⅛   teaspoon allspice
⅛   teaspoon nutmeg
½   cup rose' wine

Drain cherries and reserve syrup. Combine cherry syrup in saucepan with cornstarch, sugar, vinegar, water, and spices. Cook, stirring constantly, until thick and clear. Add wine and cherries. Can use as a dessert topping or as a glaze for ham, pork, or poultry.

SWEET AND SOUR SAUCE 2 cups

¾   cup sugar
¼   cup soy sauce
¼   cup vinegar
⅔   cup water
3   tablespoons cornstarch
    Pineapple chunks (optional)
    Chopped green pepper (optional)

Combine sugar, soy sauce, vinegar, water and cornstarch in a saucepan. Cook over low heat until thickened, stirring constantly. May add a few pineapple chunks and chopped green pepper, if desired. Use with meat, chicken or fish.

SUPER SEASONING SALT

1¼ cups

1 cup salt
2 tablespoons paprika
1 teaspoon dried marjoram
¼ teaspoon garlic powder
1 teaspoon black pepper
½ teaspoon celery seed
½ teaspoon curry powder
⅛ teaspoon cayenne pepper

Measure all ingredients into electric blender container. Cover and blend until mixture is smooth. Store in tightly covered jar.

Package in small shaker-top jars for a gift.

NEW MEXICAN SEASONING MIX

¾ cup

⅓ cup minced dried onion
¼ cup dried parsley flakes
1 tablespoon instant chicken bouillon granules
1 tablespoon chili powder
2 teaspoons crushed red pepper
1 teaspoon dried oregano
¼ teaspoon garlic powder
½ teaspoon salt

In a small bowl combine all ingredients. Transfer to a tightly covered container. Use mix to season burgers, chili, tacos, tostadas and other New Mexican foods. Mix ingredients well before measuring the seasoning.

HONEY BUTTER

¾ cup

½ cup butter, softened
¼ cup honey
½ teaspoon finely shredded lemon peel (optional)

Place all ingredients in a medium mixing bowl and beat at high speed until mixture is light and fluffy. Variation: substitute maple syrup for the honey and omit lemon peel. Variation: omit honey and lemon peel and substitute 1 tablespoon powdered sugar and ½ teaspoon finely shredded orange peel.

Delicious with hot biscuits, home-baked bread, sopaipillas or flour tortillas. Be sure to serve in small bowls or crocks.

ACCOMPANIMENTS

155

ANCHOVY BUTTER

½ cup

½ cup butter, softened
1 teaspoon anchovy paste
1 teaspoon chopped parsley

Cream butter, anchovy paste and parsley together. Serve with steaks, chops or fish.

ONION BUTTER

½ cup

4 tablespoons red onion, grated very fine
4 tablespoons fresh or dried parsley, minced
4 tablespoons butter, softened
2 teaspoons Worcestershire sauce
½ teaspoon salt
¼ teaspoon dry mustard
¼ teaspoon coarsely ground pepper

Mix all ingredients together in small bowl. Place a heaping tablespoon of the mixture atop a steak or chop as soon as it is removed from the broiler. Or, the mixture can be heated just until the butter melts and served as a sauce. Serve on salmon steaks as well as any type of beef.

APPLE BUTTER

2 quarts

4 pounds Jonathan or Winesap apples
2 cups cider
½ cup sugar
1½ teaspoons cinnamon
1 teaspoon whole cloves
½ teaspoon whole allspice
½ teaspoon nutmeg
Juice and grated rind of 1 lemon

Remove stems from apples; quarter and cook in cider until soft. Put through strainer and add other ingredients. Cook the apple butter very slowly, stirring often, until butter falls in sheets from a spoon. This does not have to be sealed and will keep in the refrigerator.

SANGRÍA JELLY

4 cups

1½ cups burgundy
¼ cup orange juice
2 tablespoons lemon juice
2 tablespoons orange-flavored liqueur
3 cups sugar
½ of 6-ounce bottle liquid pectin

Combine wine, juices and liqueur in top of double boiler. Stir in sugar. Place over, but not touching, boiling water and stir till sugar is dissolved, about 3-4 minutes. Remove from heat. At once add pectin and mix well. Skim off foam. Pour into clean, hot wine glasses, using metal spoon to prevent breaking. Seal with paraffin.

Spread the holiday spirit with a gift from your kitchen.

🦃 JALAPEÑO JELLY

6 cups

1½ cups finely chopped, seeded green pepper
1 cup finely chopped, seeded jalapeno peppers
6½ cups granulated sugar
1½ cups cider vinegar
¼ teaspoon green food coloring
1 6-ounce bottle liquid fruit pectin

Remove seeds from bell peppers and grind, saving the pulp and juice. This may be done in a blender, but be careful not to grind the peppers too finely. Mix the peppers, hot peppers, cider vinegar and sugar in a 4-6 quart saucepan and bring to a rolling boil. Add liquid fruit pectin and bring to a full, rolling boil again, stirring constantly for 1 minute. Remove from burner and let stand for a minute or two and then skim off foam. Add food coloring to achieve desired coloring. Pour through a strainer into hot sterilized jelly jars and seal. Serve with game or over cream cheese with crackers.

Delightful to look at, this unusual jelly makes a special gift from your kitchen.

SPICY PEACH PRESERVES

6½ pints

5 cups sugar
½ cup cider vinegar
1 teaspoon cinnamon
1 teaspoon ground cloves
6 pounds firm-ripe peaches, peeled, pitted and thinly sliced

Mix together and let stand 1 hour to draw some juices from the peaches. Bring peach-sugar mixture to boil over high heat and stir just until sugar dissolves. Pour through a colander; reserving peaches, then measure syrup; you should have about 6 cups. Return syrup to medium high heat and cook until reduced by half, to about 3 cups; add peach slices. Cook over medium heat, stirring often to prevent sticking, until preserves are golden brown and thick, about 25 minutes. Skim off foam. Ladle hot preserves into 6 sterilized ½-pint jars. Leave 1/8″ head space. Wipe jar rims with a clean, damp cloth; put on hot, scalded lids and screw on ring bands. Invert jars for 15 seconds, then set upright on a rack or several layers of towels until completely cooled.

BARON OF BEEF CHUTNEY

2-3 cups

3   green apples, peeled, cored, cut into ¾" cubes
2   green tomatoes, cut into ¾" cubes
1"   square fresh ginger, thinly sliced
2   medium onions, cut into ¾" cubes
4-6 garlic cloves, chopped
     Handful of raisins
¼   cup mustard seed
1   teaspoon curry powder
½-¾ cup wine vinegar
1   tablespoon brown sugar
3-12 small hot red chilies
     Dash of tumeric
     Dash of salt
     Sprinkle of cinnamon
     Sprinkle of black pepper

Mix all ingredients and simmer slowly until tender about 20 minutes. Stir gently to avoid scorching but try not to break up the pieces too much. This chutney will keep in the refrigerator for several weeks. Its flavor is enhanced if made a few days ahead.

GINGER PEACH CHUTNEY

about 4 pints

1½ cups raisins
½   pound pitted dates, chopped
3   tablespoons lemon juice
3   tablespoons lime juice
½   teaspoon lemon peel
½   teaspoon lime peel
2   cups cider vinegar
3   cups sugar
½   cup chopped candied ginger
10   cups peeled, pitted and thinly sliced peaches (about 5 pounds)

In a heavy 4 to 5 quart saucepan combine raisins, dates, lemon juice, lime juice, lemon and lime peels, vinegar, sugar and ginger. Bring mixture to a boil over high heat; reduce heat to low and simmer, stirring frequently, for 20 minutes. Add peaches to the hot syrup and bring mixture to a boil over high heat. Reduce heat to medium and cook, stirring frequently to prevent sticking, until chutney is thick, about 40 minutes. Ladle hot chutney into 8 clean, hot half-pint canning jars, leaving 1/8" head space. Wipe jar rims with a clean, damp cloth; then put on hot, scalded lids and screw on ring bands. Process jars in a water bath 5 minutes.

DIETERS' BREAD-AND-BUTTER PICKLES 3 18-ounce jars

4	medium cucumbers, sliced thin
2	tablespoons onion flakes
½	teaspoon dehydrated garlic chips
2	tablespoons salt
¼	cup cracked ice
	Artificial sweetener to equal 2 tablespoons sugar
½	cup cider vinegar
¼	teaspoon turmeric
½	teaspoon mustard seed
½	teaspoon celery seed

Combine cucumbers, onion flakes, garlic chips, salt, ice and sweetener. Mix well and let stand at room temperature for 3 hours. Drain well. Pour remaining ingredients over cucumbers in saucepan. Bring to a boil and simmer 3 minutes. Cool and refrigerate in a jar.

CRANBERRY PINEAPPLE SORBET 10 servings

1	pound cranberries
2	cups coarsely chopped fresh pineapple
1	cup superfine sugar
½	cup seeded chopped orange pulp
1	tablespoon orange peel, finely slivered
1	tablespoon Grand Marnier
	Curls of orange peel

Stir together cranberries, pineapple, sugar, orange pulp and orange peel. Process mixture in a food processor with rapid on/off turns until coarsely chopped. Transfer to a large metal bowl and stir in Grand Marnier. Cover and freeze until mixture is frozen 2″ in from the sides, about 2 hours. Scrape down frozen part, beat with electric mixer and return to the freezer. Repeat this procedure twice, freezing completely after final beating. Spoon into serving dishes and garnish with orange peel.

A delightful palate-refresher to serve with a turkey dinner.

CRANBERRY RELISH about 4 cups

1	pound (4 cups) fresh cranberries
1	whole orange
1	apple, cored and finely chopped
½	cup dates, chopped fine
1½	cups sugar

Wash all the fruit. Cut orange into quarters; leave peel on; remove seeds. Put cranberries and orange through meat grinder or blender. Add chopped apple and dates. Stir in sugar and refrigerate for at least three days before using. Serve with turkey or any meat dish.

APPLE-ONION CASSEROLE

2   tablespoons sugar
2   tablespoons cinnamon
1   stick butter
1   large onion, thinly sliced
6   large tart apples, pared and sliced ¼″ thick
30   rich buttery crackers, crushed
1   cup apple juice or cider

Combine sugar and cinnamon in a small bowl. Melt 2 tablespoons butter in a large skillet over medium-high heat. Add onion and saute' until golden, about 10 minutes. Remove onion and set aside. Melt 3 tablespoons butter in same skillet over medium-high heat. Add apples and cook about 12 minutes. Spread half of apples in a buttered 1-quart baking dish. Top with half of onion. Sprinkle with half of sugar-cinnamon mixture and half of cracker crumbs. Repeat layering. Pour apple juice or cider over top. Dot with remaining 3 tablespoons butter. Cover and bake in a 350° oven until bubbly, about 1 hour.

Wonderful with pork roast or other grilled meats!

BANANA CASSEROLE

3   bananas
1   cup brown sugar
¼   pound butter
½   cup raisins
½   cup pecan halves
    Brandy

Preheat oven to 325°. Butter a 9″ square casserole. Cut bananas in half lengthwise then crosswise in 3″ sections. Cover the bottom with a single layer of bananas, sprinkle with brown sugar and dot with butter. Add a layer of raisins and pecans. Repeat layers. Bake in 325° oven for 30 minutes. Before serving, pour a little brandy on top. Good with pork, chicken and turkey dishes.

Sweet enough to spoon over vanilla ice cream for dessert.

BANANAS A L'ORANGE

6   firm bananas
½   cup orange-flavored liqueur
2   eggs, beaten
¾   cup bread crumbs
½   teaspoon cinnamon
¼   teaspoon ginger
⅛   teaspoon salt
½   cup butter

Peel bananas, cut in half lengthwise then in half crosswise. Place bananas in single layer in a shallow dish, cover with liqueur and marinate at least 1 hour. Beat eggs and add 2 teaspoons liqueur in which bananas have been marinating. Mix breadcrumbs, spices and salt. Dip bananas in eggs and then in bread crumbs. Saute' in butter until slightly brown. Serve with pork roast, ham, turkey or hot curry dishes.

CHEESE-STUFFED PEACHES

16 halves

2   **3-ounce packages cream cheese, softened**
4   **teaspoons orange peel, grated**
¼   **cup orange juice**
¼   **cup candied ginger, slivered**
16   **peach halves**
     Paprika

Cream the cheese. Blend in grated orange peel and orange juice. Add ginger. Fill peach halves and chill. If desired, fit halves together and secure with toothpicks. Sprinkle paprika on cheese mixture peeking from between halves.

Pretty and delicious with meat and poultry dishes and luncheon salads.

CURRIED FRUIT

8-10 servings

1   **16-ounce can pineapple chunks**
1   **16-ounce can apricot halves**
1   **16-ounce can pear halves or slices**
1   **16-ounce can peach halves or slices**
⅓   **cup butter**
½   **cup brown sugar**
2   **teaspoons curry powder**

Preheat oven to 325°. Drain fruits and place in a 3-quart baking dish. Melt butter and stir in brown sugar and curry powder. Pour over fruit, and let stand one hour. Bake 20 minutes at 325°. Serve hot.

Great for brunches. Good accompaniment for roast meat, poultry, ham or egg dishes.

HOT FRUIT COMPOTE

10-12 servings

12   **macaroons, crumbled**
4   **cups canned fruit, drained (peaches, pears, pineapple, apricots, cherries)**
¼   **cup brown sugar**
½   **cup slivered almonds**
½   **cup sherry**
¼   **cup melted butter**

Butter 2½ quart casserole; cover bottom with macaroon crumbs. Alternate fruit and crumbs, finishing with crumbs. Sprinkle brown sugar, almonds and sherry over top. Bake in 350° oven, covered for 30 minutes, uncovered for 15 minutes. Add melted butter and serve hot.

ACCOMPANIMENTS

161

Chuckwagon Gourmets.....

Cattle ranching became an important eco//
nomic activity in New Mexico in the late 1800s.
For cattlemen, the principal work force was made
up of vaqueros -- or cowboys -- who performed
the hard labor. They conducted the spring round//
up of horses, the long summer roundup of
cattle and the winter roundup from water hole
to water hole to find calves overlooked in the
summer. Cowboys were a wild, simple group
with a lore of their own, a swatch of songs
and tales and personal recollections of bears,
wolves, lions and storm calamities. A few,
like William Bonney -- Billy the Kid -- achieved
notoriety when they got involved in rustling
or in range wars. On cattle drives the cowboys
were awakened at four in the morning by the
chuckwagon boss yelling, "Roll out and roll up!
Chuck!" Coffee was over the fire, beans were
boiling and, buried in the coals of the camp//
fire, were bread and biscuits ∻

Eggs and Cheese

SANTO DOMINGO
WICKER BASKET

CURRIED EGGS

½   cup minced onion
3   tablespoons butter
2   tablespoons curry
    powder
1   tablespoon flour
2   cups rich chicken
    broth
1   cup heavy cream
1   tablespoon lemon
    juice
    Salt and white pepper
    to taste
2   teaspoons cumin seed
12 hot, hard-boiled eggs,
    quartered lengthwise

In a saucepan cook onion in butter over moderate heat for about 3 minutes. Add curry powder, and flour and cook the roux, stirring, for 2 minutes. Add chicken broth and bring to a boil; simmer for 20 minutes. Add cream; bring liquid to a boil and cook the sauce over moderate heat, stirring constantly, for 15 minutes. Add lemon juice, salt and pepper. In a dry small skillet toast cumin seed over moderate heat until it crackles and turns several shades darker. Arrange the egg quarters in a chafing dish, pour the sauce over them and garnish with cumin seed. Serve with slices of toasted raisin bread.

Perfect for brunch!

EGGS RACHEL

6 servings

1   10-ounce package
    frozen pastry shells
1   cup sliced mushrooms
2   tablespoons butter
1   tablespoon flour
1   cup milk
2   tablespoons sherry
½   teaspoon salt
¼   cup butter
8   eggs, well-beaten
½   cup sour cream
¼   cup frozen chives
½   teaspoon salt
¼   teaspoon pepper

Prepare pastry shells according to package directions. Saute' mushrooms in butter. Add flour and stir. Add milk, sherry, and salt and cook stirring constantly until thick. In another pan, melt butter. Add the eggs, sour cream, chives, salt, and pepper and scramble. Place cooked eggs in baked pastry shells and top with sauce.

EGGS SUPREME

4 servings

4   slices bread, crusts
    trimmed
    Butter
2   strips bacon, cooked
⅓   cup milk
4   eggs
½   cup grated Swiss
    cheese

Butter bread and press slices into 4 buttered custard cups. Place ½ strip bacon in each cup. Combine the milk, eggs and cheese, beating well. Spoon egg mixture over bacon. Place cups in shallow pan of water and bake at 375° until set, about 20-25 minutes.

🦃 EGGS RIO GRANDE

⅓ cup tomato, chopped
2 tablespoons celery, chopped
1 tablespoon onion, chopped
1 4-ounce can green chilies, chopped
½ teaspoon sugar
1 teaspoon vinegar
¼ teaspoon rosemary
6 eggs
½ teaspoon salt
⅛ teaspoon pepper
1 tablespoon butter
4 flour tortillas

Mix tomato, celery, onion, green chilies, sugar, vinegar and rosemary and let blend while preparing the eggs. In a skillet over medium heat mix the eggs with salt and pepper and cook with the butter, stirring occasionally. Add the tomato mixture just before the eggs set. Meanwhile, in 300° oven, heat the tortillas slightly; pile the hot egg mixture on the warmed tortillas. Serve with a chili salsa to pour over, if desired.

🦃 SPANISH OMELET

4 servings

1 tablespoon butter
1 tablespoon flour
½ cup milk
½ teaspoon salt
⅛ teaspoon pepper
4 eggs, well-beaten
½ cup grated Cheddar cheese
¼ cup green pepper, chopped
1 small tomato, peeled, seeded and chopped
¼ cup minced onion
1 4-ounce can green chilies
1 2-ounce jar pimientos, chopped
1 8-ounce package breakfast sausage, cooked as label directs

Melt butter in a 9" square glass baking dish. Mix in flour, stirring until smooth and slowly stir in milk and seasonings. Fold in eggs and remaining ingredients except for the sausage. Bake in a preheated 425° oven 10 minutes; reduce heat to 350° and continue baking 35-45 minutes. When done, top with cooked sausage and serve at once.

This versatile dish pleases diners at breakfast, lunch or dinner. Or use it as the main attraction for an unforgettable New Mexican-style brunch.

EGGS & CHEESE

🐦 TIERED OMELET RANCHEROS 4 servings

8	eggs
2	tablespoons milk
¾	teaspoon salt
⅛	teaspoon pepper
	Butter or margarine
1	16-ounce can stewed tomatoes, cut up
1	4-ounce can green chilies, chopped
⅛	teaspoon salt
	Bottled hot pepper sauce to taste
1	tablespoon cold water
1	tablespoon cornstarch
½	cup sour cream
1	large avocado, peeled, seeded and sliced
	Lemon juice
1¼	cups shredded Monterey Jack cheese

Combine eggs, milk, salt and pepper with a rotary beater until well-combined. Heat 1 tablespoon butter or margarine in a 6″ skillet or omelet pan. Pour a scant ½ cup egg mixture into pan. Tilt skillet to spread mixture over the bottom of the pan. As mixture begins to set, use a metal spatula to lift omelet at edges so uncooked egg flows underneath. Cook until eggs are set. Invert omelet onto waxed paper. Repeat with remaining egg mixture and butter or margarine to make four omelets. In saucepan combine tomatoes, chilies, 1/8 teaspoon salt and a few drops hot pepper sauce. Stir together cold water and cornstarch; add to tomato mixture. Cook and stir until thickened and bubbly. To assemble place 1 omelet in 8″ round baking dish or pie plate. Spread on half the tomato mixture. Set aside 1 tablespoon sour cream; spread remaining sour cream atop a second omelet; place omelet, sour cream side up, over tomato-topped omelet. Dip avocado slices in lemon juice to prevent browning. Set aside 2 slices. Arrange remaining avocado slices atop sour cream. Top with another omelet. Sprinkle with 1 cup cheese. Top with remaining omelet. Bake, covered, in a 350° oven for 35 minutes. Uncover and sprinkle with remaining cheese, bake 5 minutes more. Add 2 tablespoons water to remaining tomato sauce; heat through. Top omelet stack with some of the sauce, the reserved sour cream and avocado slices. Cut omelet in wedges to serve. Pass remaining sauce.

A delicious and eye-catching brunch or luncheon entree.

🐦 HUEVOS RANCHEROS   6 servings

1   tablespoon butter
1   tablespoon flour
1   medium onion,
     chopped
1   4-ounce can chopped
     green chilies
2   medium tomatoes,
     chopped
1   clove garlic, crushed
½   teaspoon salt
1½   cups water
1   chicken bouillon cube
6   warmed tortillas
1½   cups grated Monterey
     Jack cheese
6   poached or fried eggs
     Shredded lettuce
     Tomato wedges

To prepare sauce, melt butter in a medium saucepan; add flour and stir. Add the onion, chilies, tomatoes and garlic and cook until onion is transparent. Add the salt, water and bouillon cube and cook until cube is dissolved and sauce becomes smooth. Simmer, covered, about 10 minutes to blend flavors. Preheat oven to 350°. To assemble huevos rancheros, place 1 or 2 warmed corn tortillas on a warmed serving plate. Top with a generous amount of the sauce and cheese and place in oven just until cheese is melted. Top with 1 or 2 fried or poached eggs. Garnish with lettuce and tomato wedges and pass additional sauce.

SCRAMBLED EGGS DELUXE EN CROUTE   10 servings

18   eggs
¾   cup milk
1¼   teaspoons salt
     Dash pepper
2   tablespoons butter or
     margarine
3   3-ounce packages
     chive cream cheese,
     cut into ½" cubes
2   tablespoons chopped
     fresh chives
1   freshly baked Italian
     bread loaf
¼   cup melted butter

Split Italian bread loaf in half lengthwise. With a fork scoop some of soft insides from center. Brush inside of loaf with melted butter. To make scrambled eggs, combine eggs, milk and salt and pepper in a medium bowl and beat with a rotary beater until just combined. Heat 2 tablespoons butter in a large skillet. Pour in egg mixture; cook over low heat. As eggs start to set on bottom, gently lift cooked portion with spatula to form flakes, letting uncooked portion flow to bottom of pan. Add cheese and chives; cook until eggs are moist and shiny but no longer runny. Allow cheese to remain partially unmelted. Spoon eggs into hot bread and serve.

🦃 GOLD RUSH BRUNCH

8-12 servings

1   2-pound package
    frozen hash browns
½   cup chopped onions
2   tablespoons chopped
    parsley
1   4-ounce can chopped
    green chilies
¼   cup melted butter
½   cup flour
1   teaspoon salt
¼   teaspoon pepper
1½ cups milk
½   cup sour cream
12 slices Canadian bacon
12 eggs

Cook potatoes as directed on package. Add onion, parsley and green chilies. Mix and heat butter, flour, salt, pepper and milk. Cook until thick. Remove from heat and add sour cream. Place potatoes in 9" x 13" greased pan. Top with sauce and mix lightly. Place bacon rounds on top and press down to form cups. Mixture may be frozen at this stage. Bake at 350° 45 minutes. Remove from oven and break 1 egg into each cup; season with salt and pepper; bake at 350° 15-20 minutes.

GOURMET BREAKFAST

6 servings

¼   cup butter
8   hard-boiled eggs,
    sliced
½   pound cooked shrimp
3   ounces salami, sliced
    thin
3   pimientos, diced
¾   cup heavy cream
2   teaspoons sharp
    mustard
    Salt and pepper to
    taste
½   cup grated Swiss
    cheese
3   tablespoons parsley,
    chopped

Preheat oven to 400°. Melt half the butter in a shallow 9" x 13" dish. Arrange egg slices, shrimp, salami and pimiento in it. Beat cream with mustard and seasonings and pour over the top. Sprinkle with mixture of cheese and parsley and dot with remaining butter. Bake 15 minutes or until golden.

🐏 GREEN CHILI TREAT

Pastry for 2-crust 9" pie
2 4-ounce cans chopped green chilies
¼ cup flour
½ teaspoon salt
¼ teaspoon pepper
2 tablespoons minced dried onion
4 cups (1 pound) grated Swiss cheese
6 large eggs
2 cups hot milk

Press pastry on bottom and sides of a 12" x 15" pan. Spread chilies over pastry. Mix flour, salt, pepper, onion and cheese. Beat eggs and milk. Pour over chilies and bake at 325° 30-40 minutes or until top is lightly browned and a knife comes out clean. Remove from oven and cut into rectangles. Serve warm or cold.

🐏 JACK JUBILEE

8 servings

1 onion, chopped
2 tablespoons butter
1 8-ounce can tomato sauce
1 4-ounce can chopped green chilies
1 teaspoon oregano
1 cup milk
2 eggs, beaten
6 ounces corn chips
½ pound cubed Monterey Jack cheese
½ pound Cheddar cheese, grated
½ pint sour cream

Saute' onions in butter; add tomato sauce and chilies and simmer 5 minutes. Add oregano, milk and eggs. In buttered 9" x 13" casserole layer the corn chips and Monterey Jack cheese and some of the grated Cheddar cheese. Pour sauce over top. Top with sour cream and remaining Cheddar cheese. Bake 30 minutes at 350°.

CHILI CHEESE CASSEROLE

8 servings

2	7½-ounce cans whole green chilies
1½	pounds Monterey Jack cheese, sliced
	Salt and pepper
2	green onions, minced
1	2¼-ounce can sliced black olives
1	7-ounce can pimientos
6	eggs, well beaten
1	13-ounce can evaporated milk
1	pound Cheddar cheese, shredded
2	8-ounce cans tomato sauce

Butter sides and bottom of 13" x 9" baking dish. Preheat oven to 350°. Slit and remove seeds from chilies; pat dry with paper towel. Spread chilies on bottom of baking dish. Cover with a layer of half the Monterey Jack cheese. Sprinkle with salt and pepper to taste. Spread onions, olives and pimientos over cheese; top with remaining Monterey Jack cheese. Beat eggs and milk together and pour over cheese. Sprinkle shredded Cheddar on top. Bake for 45 minutes. Remove from oven, cover with tomato sauce and bake an additional 15 minutes.

CHAMA CHILI SOUFFLÉ

4 servings

3	tablespoons butter
3	tablespoons flour
1	cup milk
3	egg yolks
½	cup cottage cheese
½	cup chopped drained tomato pulp
2	tablespoons chopped green onions
1	4-ounce can chopped green chilies
	Salt and pepper
4	egg whites

Preheat oven to 350°. Melt butter in saucepan and stir in flour. Using a whisk, blend in milk. Cook over medium heat until thick. Remove from heat and whisk in egg yolks, one at a time. Fold in cottage cheese, tomatoes, onions, chilies and salt and pepper to taste. Beat egg whites until stiff peaks form. Thoroughly fold about ⅓ of egg whites into yolk mixture. Add remaining whites and fold in quickly, leaving some streaks of the whites showing. Pour mixture into one-quart souffle dish. To make the center rise higher than the edges, run a finger around inner rim of the dish to make a trough in the egg mixture. Bake 30-35 minutes, until deep golden brown.

🦃 MEXICAN GREEN CHILI STRATA

8 servings

6	slices firm bread
	Butter
2	cups shredded sharp Cheddar cheese
2	cups shredded Monterey Jack cheese
8	ounces chopped green chili
6	eggs
2	cups milk
2	teaspoons salt
2	teaspoons paprika
1	teaspoon crumbled oregano
¼	teaspoon pepper
½	teaspoon garlic powder
¼	teaspoon dry mustard

Trim crusts from bread and spread one side of each with butter. Arrange bread, butter side down in a 9" x 12" baking pan. Sprinkle cheeses evenly over bread. Distribute the chilies evenly over the cheese layer. In a bowl beat eggs with milk and all seasonings until well blended. Pour egg mixture over cheese. Cover and chill overnight or at least 4 hours. Bake, uncovered, at 325° for about 50 minutes, or until top is lightly browned. Let stand 10 minutes before serving.

🦃 MEXICAN-STYLE QUICHE

4 servings

4	6" flour tortillas
4	ounces Monterey Jack cheese with peppers, sliced
1	3-ounce can French fried onions
2	cups milk
4	beaten eggs
½	teaspoon salt
½	teaspoon chili powder
¼	teaspoon dry mustard

Gently press one flour tortilla in each of 4 individual greased casseroles. Top with cheese slices and about three-fourths of onion (reserving remaining for garnish). In saucepan, heat milk almost to boiling. Gradually add milk to beaten eggs, blending well. Stir in salt, chili powder and mustard. Place casseroles in shallow baking pan on oven rack. Divide egg mixture evenly between casseroles. Bake at 350° for 23 minutes. Sprinkle reserved onion atop. Bake 5 minutes more or until knife inserted just off center comes out clean. Let stand at room temperature 5 minutes before serving.

❧ ELEGANT FLAUTA TART

6-8 servings

1 unbaked 9″ pastry shell
1 egg white, lightly beaten
1 tablespoon oil
1 pound boneless lean chuck roast
1½ teaspoons paprika
¼ teaspoon chili powder
1 large onion, chopped
1 large garlic clove, crushed
1½ cups grated Monterey Jack cheese
1 cup sour cream
¾ cup chopped green onion
1 4-ounce can chopped green chilies
3 eggs, beaten
1 teaspoon salt
¼ teaspoon pepper
   Sour cream and sliced avocado (garnish)
   Salsa (optional)

Preheat oven to 400°. Brush pastry shell with egg white and bake 5 minutes. Cool. Heat oil in large skillet over medium-high heat. Pat meat with mixture of paprika and chili powder. Add meat, onion and garlic to skillet and brown well. Reduce heat and braise, tightly covered, for 1½ hours or until meat shreds easily. Let meat cool; shred coarsely. Preheat oven to 325°. Combine meat, cooked onion and garlic, cheese, sour cream, green onion, chilies, eggs, salt and pepper and mix well. Turn into pastry and spread evenly. Bake 60 minutes or until filling is set and crust is nicely browned. Cool slightly, then spread top with sour cream and decorate with avocado slices. Serve with salsa if desired.

Appropriate for lunch and dinner and may double as an appetizer if sliced into miniature wedges. This flauta also makes delightful picnic fair.

❧ MICROWAVE NEW MEXICO QUICHE

6 servings

9 strips bacon, crisply cooked and crumbled
2 cups grated Monterey Jack cheese
1 4-ounce can diced green chilies
3 green onions, thinly sliced
1 baked 9″ deep-dish pie shell
1 13-ounce can evaporated milk
4 eggs

Combine first 4 ingredients and toss lightly. Sprinkle about ¾ of mixture over pie shell. Heat milk in measuring cup on high 2½ minutes. Beat eggs in separate bowl. Add hot milk and beat again. Pour evenly into pie shell. Sprinkle with remaining bacon mixture. Cook on bake setting (60% power) until center is barely set, about 12-15 minutes. Let stand 5 minutes before cutting into wedges and serving.

FRITTATA SAN REMO

1 cup thinly-sliced white onion
¼ cup olive oil
2 tablespoons butter or margarine
8 eggs
¼ cup grated Parmesan cheese
1 teaspoon salt
¼ teaspoon black pepper
2 cups thinly sliced zucchini

Saute' onion in 2 tablespoons of the oil and 1 tablespoon of the butter in a large skillet until soft, about 5 minutes. Remove and place in a sieve to drain. Beat eggs, cheese, salt and pepper in a large bowl until well-blended. Add the drained onions and the zucchini and mix thoroughly. Heat remaining butter and oil in 9" skillet. When very hot, pour in the egg mixture; cook 5 minutes or until the bottom and side are set. Loosen edge with a spatula. Flip the frittata and cook 4 minutes longer or until the bottom is set.

ITALIAN SAUSAGE FRITTATA

4 servings

3 hot Italian sausage links
½ cup butter or margarine
¼ cup olive oil
3 medium-size potatoes, pared and cut into thick slices (2 cups)
1½ teaspoons salt
½ cup chopped white onions
5 eggs

Prick sausages with a fork; plunge into boiling water and parboil 5 minutes. Place sausages on rack under broiler for 10 minutes, turning once. Cut into ¼" thick rounds. Melt ¼ cup of the butter with 2 tablespoons of the olive oil in a large skillet. Add potatoes; sprinkle with 1 teaspoon salt and turn them several times until they are well-coated with the butter-oil mixture. Cook over medium heat 10 minutes until potatoes are lightly browned. Push potatoes to one side of the pan; add onions and cook 5 minutes. Add sausages. Mix potatoes, onions and sausage together and cook 5 minutes longer. Remove to a sieve to drain off fat. Beat eggs with remaining ½ teaspoon salt in a large bowl; add vegetable and sausage mixture. Heat remaining butter and oil in a 9" skillet over medium heat. When very hot, pour in egg mixture, spreading it so it will cook evenly. From time to time remove the skillet from the heat and give it a vigorous shake to prevent the eggs from sticking. When eggs become firm in about 4 minutes, remove skillet from heat. Place a plate over the skillet; flip the egg cake onto the plate and slide back into the skillet, uncooked side down. Cook 3 minutes longer. Cut into wedges to serve.

Spicy Italian sausages provide the seasoning in this unusual main dish.

EGGS & CHEESE

173

ZUCCHINI-SPINACH FRITTATA   8 servings

8   zucchini, thinly sliced
4   tablespoons butter
1   onion, thinly sliced
¾   pound fresh mush-
        rooms, sliced
3   cups finely chopped
        fresh spinach
4   eggs
1½   cups light cream
¼   teaspoon salt
¼   teaspoon pepper
½   teaspoon thyme
½   teaspoon basil
        Grated cheese, Ched-
        dar or mozzarella

In 12" skillet, saute' zucchini in 2 table-spoons butter over high heat for 15 minutes. Remove with slotted spoon and put in bottom of shallow 2 quart casserole. Add 1 more tablespoon butter to same skillet and saute' onion over high heat for 5 minutes. Layer over zucchini. Add rest of butter and saute' mushrooms over moderate heat for 3 minutes. Add spinach and saute' 3 minutes, stirring constantly. Place mixture on top of zucchini. In medium mixing bowl, beat eggs with whisk, adding cream gradually. Quickly mix in salt, pepper and herbs and pour this over vegetables. Sprinkle generously with cheese and bake in 375° oven for 25-30 minutes. Serve very hot, cut in wedges. The vegetables can be done and layered several hours ahead. Eggs, cream and seasonings can be prepared 30 minutes ahead.

QUICHE SICILIANO   6 servings

1   pound sweet Italian
        sausage links,
        chopped
6   eggs
2   10-ounce packages
        frozen chopped
        spinach, thawed and
        drained
1   pound mozzarella
        cheese, shredded
⅔   cup ricotta cheese
¾   teaspoon salt
⅛   teaspoon pepper
⅛   teaspoon garlic
        powder
        Pastry for a 9" double
        crust pie
1   tablespoon water

Cook sausage over medium heat until brown, about 10 minutes. Drain. Reserve 1 egg yolk. In a large bowl combine remaining eggs with sausage, spinach, mozzarella, ricotta, salt, pepper and garlic powder. Prepare pie crust. Line a 9" pie plate with one crust. Spoon sausage mixture onto crust. Place second crust over filling. Trim edges and cut slits in pastry top. Combine reserved egg yolk and water. Brush over pastry. Bake at 375° for 1 hour and 15 minutes or until pie is golden. Let pie stand for 10 minutes before cutting.

PROSCUITTO AND SAUSAGE PIE

6-8 servings

Pastry for a 2-crust
10" pie
¼ pound proscuitto (or
regular ham), cubed
½ pound Italian sausage,
cubed
3 eggs, well-beaten
1 pound ricotta cheese
¼ cup Parmesan cheese
¼ teaspoon cinnamon
5-6 sprigs parsley,
chopped
Salt and pepper

Line a 9" or 10" deep-dish pie pan with pastry. Refrigerate while making filling. Combine eggs, ricotta, Parmesan, cinnamon, parsley, salt and pepper. Mix with the meats and pile in pie pan, mounding it in the center. Cover with a top crust, seal and flute. Bake in preheated 450° oven for 10 minutes; reduce heat to 325° and bake an additional 45-60 minutes, or until browned. Serve hot or cold.

SPINACH AND ARTICHOKE PIE

6-8 servings

CRUST:

2 cups mild Cheddar
cheese, grated
¾ cup flour
½ teaspoon salt
¼ teaspoon dry mustard
½ cup melted butter

FILLING:

2 10-ounce packages
frozen chopped
spinach
¼ cup lemon juice
1 cup half-and-half
1 medium onion, finely
chopped
1 cup fresh mushrooms
sauteed in 3 table-
spoons butter 5
minutes
1 teaspoon salt
¼ teaspoon pepper
¼ teaspoon nutmeg
2 eggs, well beaten
1 14½-ounce can arti-
choke hearts, drained
and sliced in half

For crust mix all ingredients together with fork and press firmly into a 10" pie plate. Set aside while preparing filling. For filling cook spinach according to package directions. Drain well and add lemon juice. In saucepan combine all other ingredients except spinach and artichoke hearts. Simmer together 1 minute, stirring constantly. Stir in spinach and artichoke hearts. Pour into cheese crust. Bake at 400° 15 minutes, then at 325° 20 minutes or until knife inserted comes out clean.

This also is a delicious appetizer.

EGGS & CHEESE

ROQUEFORT-MUSHROOM QUICHE

8 servings

4 tablespoons butter
¾ pounds mushrooms
⅓ cup finely chopped onions
3 eggs lightly beaten
2 cups heavy cream
¼ teaspoon dry mustard
2 tablespoons flour
4 ounces Roquefort cheese
Salt and freshly ground pepper to taste
1 9″ pie crust, unbaked

Slice mushrooms, chop onions in food processor. Melt 2 tablespoons butter. Add onions and mushrooms and stir until mushrooms wilt. Cover and simmer slowly 30 minutes. Let cool. Preheat oven to 450°. Bake pie crust 5 minutes. Combine eggs, cream, mustard, salt and pepper. Melt remaining butter and add slowly while beating. Line pie shell with mushrooms, onions, and Roquefort cheese. Pour egg mixture through strainer into partly baked shell. Bake 15 minutes, reduce oven to 350° bake about 20 minutes longer until knife inserted comes out clean.

Good food processor recipe! The Roquefort cheese makes the difference.

ITALIAN ZUCCHINI PIE

6-8 servings

4 cups thinly sliced, unpeeled zucchini
1 cup onion, chopped
½ cup butter
½ cup chopped parsley or 2 tablespoons parsley flakes
½ teaspoon salt
½ teaspoon pepper
¼ teaspoon garlic salt
¼ teaspoon sweet basil
¼ teaspoon oregano
2 eggs, well beaten
8 ounces mozzarella cheese, shredded
1 8 ounce can refrigerated crescent dinner rolls
2 teaspoons Dijon or prepared mustard

In a 10-inch skillet, cook zucchini and onion in butter until tender. Drain excess liquid. Stir in parsley and seasonings. In a large bowl blend eggs and cheese; then stir in vegetable mixture. Separate dough into 8 triangles and place in ungreased 10″ pie pan or 12″ x 8″ baking dish. Press over bottom and up sides to form crust. Spread crust with mustard. Spoon vegetable mixture evenly over crust. Bake at 375° for 20 minutes or until knife inserted in center comes out clean. Let stand 10 minutes before serving.

TOMATO CHEESE TART

6-8 servings

½   11-ounce package pie crust mix
½   cup Cheddar cheese, grated
2   medium sized ripe tomatoes, peeled and sliced
6   green onions, chopped
2   tablespoons melted butter
½   cup grated Cheddar cheese
2   ounces grated Gruyere cheese
1   teaspoon salt
⅛   teaspoon pepper
1   teaspoon oregano
2   tablespoons soft bread crumbs

Combine pie crust mix with Cheddar cheese and mix according to package directions, using only half the amount of water called for in directions because you are using only half the mix. Blend well. Press into 8″ or 9″ pie pan and prick well around sides and on bottom of crust. Bake at 425° for 10 minutes. Cool. Peel tomatoes and slice in thin slices. Saute' green onions in butter until bright green. Do not drain. Sprinkle both cheeses into bottom of cooled crust. Arrange sliced tomatoes around edge of pie crust and sprinkle with seasonings. Spoon onions into center of tomato ring and top entire pie with bread crumbs. Bake uncovered at 325° for 20 minutes.

CELEBRATION CREPES

4-6 servings

2   tablespoon butter
½   pound minced mushrooms
2   tablespoons minced green onions
8   ounces cream cheese, room temperature
2   cups sour cream
3   tablespoons minced fresh dill
12 crepes
6   tablespoons butter, melted

Preheat oven to 325°. Butter a large shallow baking dish. Melt 2 tablespoons butter; add mushrooms and green onions and cook until liquid has evaporated. Season with salt and pepper; set aside. Combine cream cheese and sour cream and mash with fork. Add mushrooms mixture, Parmesan cheese and dill. Mix well. Divide mixture evenly among crepes. Place seamside down in baking dish. Pour butter over top. Bake 20 minutes.

Historic Kitchens.....

A segment of American history -- that cre-
ated by early Southwestern cooks preparing their
regional specialties over hot fire pits and, later,
slightly elevated corner cooking hearths -- is
recreated at El Rancho de las Golondrinas (The
Ranch of the Swallows), also known as the
Old Cienega Village Museum. This complex
lies about 15 miles south of Santa Fé, and
includes a sequence of three beautiful adobe
kitchens, spaced about 100 years apart in time
and stemming from the late 17th, 18th and 19th
centuries. Earliest of the three, the "cocina
con fogón de pastor," is the only one of its kind
still in existence. The ranch, a living museum,
presents history in a very animated way. Wheat
is threshed under the hooves of a herd of goats.
Women weave, water mills grind, craftsmen and
artisans follow their ancient skills and everyone
is so busy that the ranch is open to the public
only on certain days, for two annual fiestas
and by appointment ❖

Rice, Pasta and Grains

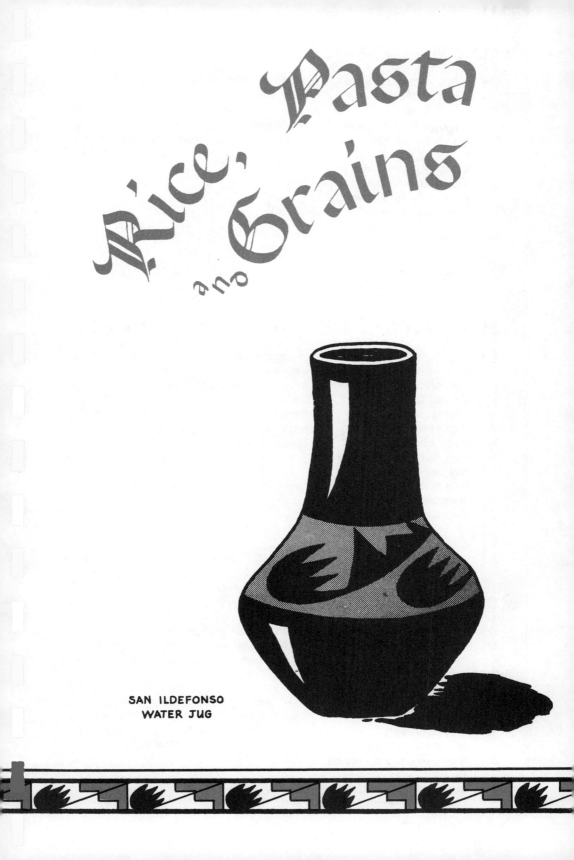

SAN ILDEFONSO
WATER JUG

ALMOND RUMBA RICE

6-8 servings

1½ cups uncooked long grain converted rice
¼ cup butter
1 onion, finely chopped
⅛ teaspoon pepper, scant
3 cups chicken broth
3 3-ounce cans button mushrooms, drained
½ cups almonds, chopped or sliced
1½ tablespoons poppy seeds
Salt to taste

In heavy skillet brown rice in butter. Add onion and pepper, cooking until onion is tender. Spoon into a buttered 2-quart casserole. Add broth, mushrooms, almonds, poppy seeds and salt, if necessary. Mix well. Bake uncovered for one hour at 375°.

BURGUNDY RICE AND MUSHROOMS

6-8 servings

½ cup butter
1 cup rice
1 cup chopped tomatoes
1 pound fresh mushrooms, sliced
½ cup chopped onions
3 cups chicken broth
½ cup Burgundy (or other dry red wine)
1-2 teaspoons salt
⅛ teaspoon pepper
1 cup cooked peas (optional)
¼ cup Parmesan cheese

In large skillet, melt butter and cook rice, tomatoes, mushrooms and onions for 10 minutes. Add broth, wine and seasonings and mix well. Cover and simmer for 45 minutes or until rice is tender and the liquid is absorbed. Stir in peas, if desired. Sprinkle with cheese.

CORONADO RICE CASSEROLE

10 servings

¼ cup margarine
1 cup chopped onion
4 cups cooked rice
2 cups sour cream
1 cup cream-style cottage cheese
1 large bay leaf
½ teaspoon salt
⅛ teaspoon pepper
2 4-ounce cans chopped green chilies, drained
2 cups grated sharp Cheddar cheese

Saute' onion in margarine until golden. Remove from heat and stir in cooked rice, sour cream, cottage cheese, bay leaf, salt and pepper. Layer half the rice mixture in a lightly buttered 3-quart baking dish. Add half the chopped chilies and sprinkle with half the cheese. Repeat layers, ending with cheese. Bake uncovered at 375° for 30 minutes.

GREEN RICE CASSEROLE

6-8 servings

1½   cups long grain rice
3   cups water
1   teaspoon salt
1   10-ounce package frozen chopped spianch, cooked and squeezed dry
⅛   cup parsley, chopped
½   cup Parmesan cheese
   Salt and pepper to taste
1   teaspoon oregano
1   teaspoon thyme
⅓   cup butter, melted
2   eggs, beaten
1   cup milk
2   tablespoons butter

Cook rice in 3 cups water and salt for 20 minutes. Add spinach, parsley, ⅓ cup cheese, salt and pepper. Stir in herbs and melted butter. Put mixture in casserole and add eggs beaten with milk. Sprinkle with remaining cheese, dot with butter and bake 1¼ hours.

SAUSAGE RICE

16-18 servings

3   pounds bulk sausage
1   chopped onion
1   small chopped green pepper
2   cups uncooked celery
2   cups dehydrated chicken noodle soup mix
9   cups boiling water
⅓   cup toasted slivered almonds

Brown sausage and drain. Add onion, pepper and celery and saute' until onion is limp. Add raw rice, soup mix, and boiling water. Mix well and add almonds. Bake at 350° for approximately 1 hour.

SPICED RICE WITH PEAS AND CASHEWS

6 servings

1   cup cashews
3   tablespoons peanut oil
¼   cup raisins
1½   cups long grain rice
2   teaspoons curry powder
3   cups boiling water
1   teaspoon salt
1   10-ounce package frozen peas
2   tablespoons lime juice

Saute' cashews in oil over medium low heat until golden, about 4 minutes. Remove to paper towel to drain. Saute' raisins about 30 seconds; remove. Heat oven to 350°. Saute' rice and curry powder about 4 minutes. Bake on center oven rack 45-50 minutes. Remove from oven. Stir in peas; let stand covered 6 minutes. Chop cashews. Stir lime juice into rice; sprinkle with cashews and raisins.

A wonderful buffet dish.

ARMENIAN FESTIVE RICE
6-8 servings

1   tablespoon oil
½   cup crushed vermicelli
¼   cup butter
1   cup rice
2   cups chicken broth
      Salt to taste

Heat oil. Add vermicelli and saute' until golden. Add butter and rice; saute' 5 minutes. Bring broth to a boil; pour over rice. Reduce heat, cover and simmer 15-20 minutes. Add salt. Cover with almond-fruit topping.

TOPPING:

¼   cup butter
½   cup slivered almonds
½   cup coarsely chopped
      dried apricots
½   cup raisins
½   cup chopped dates
½   cup brown sugar

Melt butter. Add almonds and saute' until golden brown. Add fruit and brown sugar; cook 2-3 minutes. Pour over rice. Additional apricot may be added for garnish.

Wonderful with lamb or pork dishes.

RICE CHILI VERDE
6-8 servings

1   pint sour cream
1   cup chopped green
      chili
      Pinch of salt
3   cups cooked rice
½   pound grated Monterey Jack cheese
      Parmesan cheese

Combine sour cream, chili and salt. In 9x13 casserole layer rice, sour cream mixutre, and Jack cheese. Add another layer, ending with rice. Bake at 350° for 25 minutes. Sprinkle with Parmesan cheese.

BROCCOLI AND RICE PICANTE
8-10 servings

2   cups uncooked rice
1   10-ounce package frozen chopped broccoli
1   medium onion, chopped
2   tablespoons butter
1   10½-ounce can condensed cream of celery soup
1   16-ounce jar pasteurized processed cheese spread with jalapenos

Prepare rice and broccoli according to package directions. Drain broccoli well. Saute' chopped onion in butter until soft. Combine rice, broccoli, soup and cheese spread with onions. Place in buttered 2 quart casserole and bake at 350° for 30 minutes.

NOODLES WITH CHINESE MEAT SAUCE   4-6 servings

½   pound (4 cups) very fine egg noodles (about 4 cups cooked)
2   teaspoons peanut oil
1   clove garlic, minced
1   pound lean ground pork
3   tablespoons chopped green onions or scallions
2   tablespoons mirin (sweet rice wine) or sweet sherry wine
1   tablespoon hot sesame chili oil
3   tablespoons soy sauce
¼   cup chicken broth
1   tablespoon wine vinegar
1   cucumber, peeled and diced
1   tablespoon finely chopped, peeled garlic (optional)
4   tablespoons chopped green onions or scallions

The sauce can wait for the noodles, but the noodles shouldn't wait for the sauce. Boil the water while you make the sauce, add noodles while the sauce is simmering and cook 5 to 6 minutes. In a medium-sized skillet heat oil over moderately high heat; add the minced garlic, and when it begins to brown, add the pork. Stir-fry the pork, breaking it up with a spoon as it cooks. When meat loses its pink color, add the 3 tablespoons green onions, the wine, hot oil, soy sauce, chicken broth and vinegar. Bring mixture to a boil and cook until most of the liquid has evaporated, about 8 minutes. Remove skillet from heat and cover to keep hot until ready to serve. Place drained, cooked noodles on a platter and pour sauce over it; top with cucumbers, the 1 tablespoon chopped garlic and the 4 tablespoons green onions.

WINE NOODLES   4-6 servings

8   ounces uncooked thin noodles
    Salt water
1   cup white wine
6   tablespoons sugar
4   tablespoons butter
3   eggs, separated
1   tablespoon grated lemon rind
    Juice of half a lemon

Drop noodles in boiling salted water and cook about 5 minutes until almost tender. Drain. Combine wine and 3 tablespoons sugar in saucepan. Bring to a boil stirring until sugar dissolves. Pour mixture into mixing bowl. Add noodles and stir. Set aside. Cream butter and remaining 3 tablespoons sugar, egg yolks, lemon rind and lemon juice. Add lemon mixture to noodles. Beat egg whites until stiff and fold into noodle mixture. Pour into a greased casserole and bake 15 minutes at 350°.

A tangy side dish with pork or turkey.

NOODLE KUGEL

¾   cup butter, melted
¾   cup sugar
1   cup sour cream
½   cup milk
1   12-ounce carton cot-
    tage cheese
½   teaspoon salt
1   teaspoon vanilla
½   pound cream cheese,
    softened
6   eggs, beaten
1½ teaspoons cinnamon
½   cup raisins (or more to
    taste)
1   12-ounce and 1
    8-ounce package extra
    wide noodles, cooked
    according to package
    directions.

Mix all ingredients, except noodles, together. Stir by hand until well blended. Stir in noodles and pour into a 9" x 13" buttered casserole. Combine topping and spread over noodles. Bake at 350° for 1 hour.

TOPPING:

½   cup brown sugar
½   cup silvered almonds
2   tablespoons melted
    butter

PASTA LA SCALA

6-8 servings

6   tablespoons unsalted
    butter
3   cloves garlic, crushed
1   pound mushrooms,
    sliced
2   tablespoons fresh
    lemon juice
4   small unpeeled zuc-
    chini (1 pound total)
    cut into ¼" julienne
4   tablespoons minced
    parsley
1½ teaspoons dried basil
1   teaspoon salt
    Freshly ground black
    pepper
1   pound freshly cooked
    spaghetti

Melt 2 tablespoons butter in large skillet over medium heat. Add 1 garlic clove and cook 3 minutes. Add mushrooms and lemon juice and toss until well combined. Add zucchini, 2 tablespoons parsley and seasonings and blend well. Cover, increase heat to medium-high and cook until vegetables are steamed through, 3 to 5 minutes, shaking pan frequently. Place remaining butter and garlic in large serving bowl. Add hot pasta and remaining parsley and toss well. Top with vegetables and toss again.

INDONESIAN NOODLES

6 servings

1	pound pork, cut into thin strips
½	cup water
4	cloves garlic, minced
1	slice fresh ginger, minced
1	teaspoon salt
¼	teaspoon pepper
1	tablespoon lemon juice
2	tablespoons peanut oil
2½	cups Chinese cabbage, shredded
1	cup bean sprouts
1	cup bamboo shoots, cut into thin strips
5	green onions, chopped
½	cup Chinese snow peas
3	tablespoons soy sauce
2	teaspoons molasses
1	teaspoon hot sauce or oil
1	pound Indonesian noodles or egg noodles, cooked and drained
1	cup celery, chopped

Cook pork in water for 10 minutes; drain. In a wok combine garlic, ginger, salt, pepper, lemon juice and oil. Stir fry for 1 minute. Add pork and vegetables. Stir fry for 3 minutes. Add soy sauce, molasses, hot oil and stir thoroughly. Combine cooked noodles with vegetables. Adjust seasonings if desired. Place on platter and sprinkle with celery.

EASY SPINACH-STUFFED SHELLS

8 servings

2	tablespoons salad oil
1	small onion, diced
1	28-ounce can tomatoes
1	6-ounce can tomato paste
2	teaspoons brown sugar
1½	teaspoons oregano leaves
	Salt and pepper
1	12-ounce package jumbo macaroni shells
2	10-ounce packages frozen creamed spinach in boilable bag
1	15-ounce container ricotta cheese
8	ounces mozzarella cheese, shredded

In a large saucepan over medium heat, in hot oil, cook onion until tender, stirring often. Add tomatoes with their liquid, tomato paste, brown sugar, oregano, 1½ teaspoons salt and ¼ teaspoon pepper. Heat to boiling; reduce heat to low; cover and simmer 20 minutes. Meanwhile, prepare macaroni shells as label directs. Prepare creamed spinach as labels direct; pour into large bowl and cool slightly. Stir in ricotta and mozzarella cheese, 1 teaspoon salt and ¼ teaspoon pepper. Fill each cooked shell with about 1 tablespoon cheese mixture. Preheat oven to 350°. Spoon sauce evenly into 14"x10" roasting pan; arrange filled shells in sauce. Cover roasting pan with foil; bake 30 minutes or until hot and bubbly.

PASTA VERONESE

½ pound medium egg noodles
2 tablespoons olive oil
2 tablespoons butter
½ cup onion, finely chopped
½ teaspoon garlic, minced
2 chicken breasts (about 1 pound), boned, skinned and cut into ½" cubes
¾ pounds zucchini, sliced ¼" thick
2 cups halved cherry tomatoes
1½ teaspoons salt
¼ teaspoon pepper
¼ teaspoon basil leaves
2 tablespoons butter, softened
1 cup coarsely shredded Swiss cheese

Cook noodles in 4 quarts boiling salt water for 8 minutes; drain. Meanwhile, heat the olive oil and 2 tablespoons butter in skillet over moderately high heat. Add onion and garlic and cook until onion is translucent. Increase heat slightly, add chicken and cook, stirring briskly, until chicken turns white. Add zucchini, tomatoes, salt, pepper and basil to the skillet; reduce heat to moderate, cover skillet and cook 10 minutes. Mix hot, drained noodles with the remaining butter; add chicken mixture and toss gently to mix. Serve with shredded cheese.

A quick and colorful main dish that is excellent served to family or last-minute guests.

PASTA WITH SPINACH PESTO

3 cups fresh spinach leaves, stems discarded
2 cups fresh parsley (preferably Italian flat-leaf type)
½ cup grated Parmesan cheese
½ cup grated Romano cheese
½ cup oil
¼ cup blanched almonds
¼ cup butter, melted
2 tablespoons pine nuts
4 large cloves garlic, crushed
1 teaspoon salt
1 teaspoon oil
Salt
1 pound spaghetti or linguini
Grated Parmesan cheese

Combine first 10 ingredients in food processor or blender and puree until smooth; set aside. Bring water to boil in large pan. Add oil and salt. Add pasta and cook until al dente. Strain in colander, reserving ⅓ cup liquid. Blend hot liquid into puree and toss with pasta. Serve with additional grated Parmesan cheese.

CHICKEN, SAUSAGE AND BEEF LASAGNE

10-12 servings

2	cups chopped tomatoes
5	tablespoons butter
4	tablespoons flour
2	cups rich chicken broth
1	cup heavy cream
	Salt and freshly ground pepper to taste
⅛	teaspoon nutmeg
½	pound hot or sweet Italian sausages
1	cup finely chopped green pepper
1	cup finely chopped celery
1	cup finely chopped onion
1-2	tablespoons finely chopped garlic
½	pound ground sirloin
2	cups thinly sliced mushrooms
	Hot pepper sauce to taste
1	teaspoon Worcestershire sauce
1	cup frozen or freshly shelled green peas
9	lasagne noodles
2	cups shredded, skinless, cooked chicken
2	cups grated Cheddar cheese
¾	cup freshly grated Parmesan cheese

Put the tomatoes in a saucepan and cook down about 30 minutes, or about 1½ cups. Heat 3 tablespoons of the butter in a saucepan and add the flour, stirring with a wire whisk. When blended add the broth, stirring rapidly with the whisk. Cook about 10 minutes, stirring occasionally. Add the cream, salt, pepper and nutmeg. Remove and discard the skin of the sausage. Add the meat to a skillet and cook, stirring with the side of a heavy, metal kitchen spoon to break up any lumps. Cook until meat loses its raw color. Drain off the fat. Set the meat aside. Heat remaining 2 tablespoons of butter in a skillet and add the green peppers, celery, onion and garlic. Cook, stirring briefly, until tender, but crisp. Add the beef and cook, cutting down with the side of a heavy metal kitchen spoon to break up any lumps. Add the sausage and mushrooms and cook briefly. Add salt and pepper to taste. Add the tomatoes to the cream sauce. Pour this combined sauce over the meat mixture and stir to blend. Add the hot pepper sauce and Worcestershire sauce and salt and pepper to taste. Add the peas and bring to a boil. Preheat oven to 375°. Cook the lasagne according to package directions. Drain. Butter a 9" x 13" baking dish. Arrange 3 lasagne strips over the dish. Add a layer of chicken and spoon some of the meat sauce over. Add about ⅓ of the grated Cheddar cheese. Cover with 3 lasagne strips. Add a layer of chicken and another layer of meat sauce and grated cheese. Add a third layer of lasagne. Add the remaining chicken and spoon the remaining meat sauce over all. Sprinkle with remaining grated Cheddar cheese. Bake 30 minutes. Serve with grated Parmesan cheese on the side.

ITALIAN FLAG CASSEROLE

6-8 servings

2½   cups green egg
       noodles
       Boiling salted water
1   tablespoon cooking oil
1   pint small curd cottage
       cheese
1   pint dairy sour cream
1½   teaspoons oregano,
       crumbled
½   teaspoon thyme
¾   teaspoon salt
⅓   cup minced parsley
1   pound lean ground
       beef
1   cup chopped onion
2   cloves garlic, minced
1   6-ounce can tomato
       paste
½   cup Monterey Jack
       cheese, shredded

Cook noodles in boiling salted water 10 minutes. Drain in colander and rinse with cold water. Mix with oil and turn into 3-quart baking dish. Mix cottage cheese, sour cream, oregano, thyme and ½ teaspoon salt. Spoon in layer over noodles. Sprinkle with parsley. Saute' beef with onion and garlic until browned. Mix in ¼ teaspoon salt and tomato paste. Spoon over cottage cheese and sour cream layer. Sprinkle with cheese. Cover. Bake in 400° oven for 30 minutes or until hot in center. Can be made ahead and refrigerated. If refrigerated, allow an additional 20 minutes baking time.

PASTA PROVENCALE WITH SCALLOPS

4 servings

3   tablespoons light olive
       oil
3   tablespoons unsalted
       butter
1   pound sea scallops,
       quartered
8   shallots, minced
8   green onions, minced
3   large garlic cloves,
       crushed
2   teaspoons dried basil
1   teaspoon dried tar-
       ragon
¼   teaspoon dried thyme
½   cup dry white wine
4   cups well-drained,
       crushed canned
       tomatoes
½   cup whipping cream
2   teaspoons sugar
       Salt and freshly
       ground black pepper
1   pound freshly cooked
       linguine
1   large ripe avocado,
       peeled, seeded and
       chopped

Heat oil and butter in large skillet over medium heat. Add scallops and saute' until barely firm, about 3 minutes. Using slotted spoon, transfer to mixing bowl. Increase heat to medium-high. Add shallots and onions and saute' until soft. Stir in garlic and herbs; cook 2 minutes. Add wine and cook 2 minutes more. Stir in tomatoes. Increase heat to high and boil briefly until sauce is thick. Stir in cream and sugar and cook another 30 seconds. Season with salt and pepper. Add to scallops, mixing gently. Toss with hot pasta and divide evenly among serving plates. Top with chopped avocado.

A memorable combination of flavors and textures.

FELLINI'S LINGUINI

¼ cup olive oil
¼ cup unsalted butter
1 tablespoon flour
1 cup chicken broth
1 garlic clove, minced
2 teaspoons parsley, dried
2 teaspoons lemon juice
Salt
Freshly ground pepper
1 14-ounce can artichoke hearts, drained and quartered
3 tablespoons Parmesan cheese
2 teaspoons capers
1 tablespoon unsalted butter
1 tablespoon olive oil
1 tablespoon Parmesan cheese
1 pound linguini, cooked and drained
Proscuitto or ham for garnish

Melt oil and butter. Add flour and stir until smooth, about 2-3 minutes. Add broth stirring until thickened, about 1 minute. Add garlic, parsley, lemon juice, salt and pepper; cook 5 minutes, stirring constantly. Add artichokes, cheese and capers. Cover and simmer about 10 minutes. Melt remaining butter and oil in pan. Add 1 tablespoon cheese and linguini. Toss lightly. Arrange pasta on platter and pour sauce over. Garnish with proscuitto or ham.

Wonderful with a tossed green salad, crusty bread and Zuppa Inglese as dessert.

LINGUINI WITH WHITE CLAM SAUCE

3 6-ounce cans minced clams
Bottled clam juice or canned chicken broth
¼ cup butter or margarine
2 cloves garlic, crushed
2 tablespoons flour
½ cup dry white wine
⅛ teaspoon dried thyme leaves
Pinch dried red pepper flakes (optional)
¼ cup chopped fresh parsley
1 tablespoon lemon juice
Salt and pepper
1 pound linguini or spaghetti, cooked according to label

Drain clams into a 2-cup measure; add enough bottled clam juice or chicken broth to make 2 cups liquid. In a medium skillet melt butter over moderately high heat. Stir in garlic and cook just until it begins to brown. Remove pan from heat and stir in flour. Cook over low heat about 1 minute stirring constantly. Gradually stir in clam liquid, wine, thyme and red pepper flakes; bring to a boil and then simmer 1 to 2 minutes. Stir in clams, parsley and lemon juice and heat through. Taste sauce; add salt and pepper if needed. Serve over hot linguini.

A slightly extravagant pasta treat!

VERMICELLI WITH SHRIMP SAUCE

2 servings

3½ tablespoons lightly salted butter
1 teaspoon minced garlic
6 ounced peeled and de-veined shrimp (about 1 cup)
2 tablespoons chopped fresh parsley
2 tablespoons dry ver-mouth or white wine
¼ cup Parmesan cheese, preferably fresh-grated
½ cup heavy cream
Pinch crushed red pepper flakes
4 ounces vermicelli, cooked according to label
½ ripe avocado, peeled, pitted and diced (about 1 cup)

In a large skillet heat 1 tablespoon of the butter over moderately high heat. When melted, add garlic and cook 1 minute. Add shrimp, parsley and vermouth and cook about 2 minutes longer, stirring con-stantly, until shrimp turn pink and are just tender. Transfer shrimp mixture to a small bowl. Add remaining butter to pan and heat until melted. Reduce heat to low; add cheese, cream and pepper and cook 3 minutes longer, stirring constantly, until cheese melts and sauce is smooth, remove from heat; add hot spaghetti, the avocado and the shrimp mixture; toss gently to coat. Serve immediately on heated plates.

SPAGHETTI ALLA EMILIO

6 servings

1 cup whipping cream
3 ounces Gorgonzola cheese (or blue cheese)
3 tablespoons butter
1 ounce vodka
Salt and freshly ground pepper
10 ounces frozen spinach, cooked, drained and chopped
3 ounces ricotta cheese
1 pound spaghetti
3 ounces freshly grated Parmesan cheese

Bring cream to simmer but not boil over low heat. Add Gorgonzola, butter and vodka. Season with salt and pepper. Add spinach and ricotta. Stir until smooth. Remove from heat and keep warm. Cook spaghetti al dente about 8-10 minutes. Drain well. Return pasta to pot. Add sauce and toss. Transfer to a large bowl and sprinkle with Parmesan cheese.

SPAGHETTI PIE

6-8 servings

6 ounces spaghetti
3 tablespoons butter
2 eggs, beaten
⅓ cup grated Parmesan cheese
1½ pound ground beef
½ cup chopped onion
½ cup chopped green pepper
1 4-ounce can chopped mushrooms, drained
1 8-ounce can tomatoes, chopped
1 6-ounce can tomato paste
1½ teaspoons oregano
¾ teaspoon basil
¼ teaspoon salt
2 cloves fresh garlic, minced
1 cup cottage cheese, well drained
1 cup shredded mozzarella cheese

Cook spaghetti until just tender — do not overcook. Drain. Stir butter, eggs, and Parmesan cheese into spaghetti. Make spaghetti mixture into a "crust" and press into a buttered 10" pie plate. In a skillet, cook ground beef, onion, and green pepper until meat is done. Drain off excess fat. Stir in mushrooms, tomatoes, tomato paste, oregano, basil, salt, and garlic. Simmer for 30 minutes. Spread cottage cheese over bottom of spaghetti "crust." Fill pie with meat-tomato mixture. Cover with foil and bake at 350° for 45 minutes. Uncover. Top with shredded mozzarella cheese. Bake an additional 7-8 minutes, or until cheese has melted.

Freezes well.

GRITS GRUYERE

8-12 servings

1 quart milk
½ cup butter
1 cup hominy grits (not the quick-cooking kind)
1 teaspoon salt
¼ teaspoon pepper
⅓ cup butter, melted
1 cup grated Gruyere cheese
⅓ cup grated Parmesan cheese

Bring milk to boil with ½ cup butter. Stir in grits. Bring to boil and cook, stirring constantly over medium heat for 15 minutes. Remove from heat and add salt and pepper. Beat with electric mixer at high speed 5 minutes. Pour into a 2-quart mold and chill. Unmold and slice ¼" thick. Place slices one over another like fallen dominoes in a buttered shallow 9" x 5" loaf pan. Pour ⅓ cup melted butter over and sprinkle with grated cheeses. Bake in 400° oven 30-35 minutes. Place under heated broiler unit and broil 1 minute.

The cheeses give grits a touch of class.

Centerpieces of Enchantment......

New Mexico's distinctive state flag features a dark red sun symbol from ancient Zia Pueblo centered on a field of yellow -- the color combination influenced by the banners carried by the Spanish conquistadores as they explored the New World for Spain's King Ferdinand and Queen Isabella in the 16th century. The yucca plant or "God's candle" was chosen as the state flower because of its widespread growth, resistance to drought and its regal beauty. The state bird is the roadrunner, a quick and elusive member of the cuckoo family. Like all cuckoos, the roadrunner has two toes forward and two toes back, prompting Indians to adapt their tracks as symbols capable of warding off evil spirits. The roadrunner's erect tail and tall crest feathers present a striking picture and New Mexicans never fail to take delight in spotting one of these birds running along the roadside·

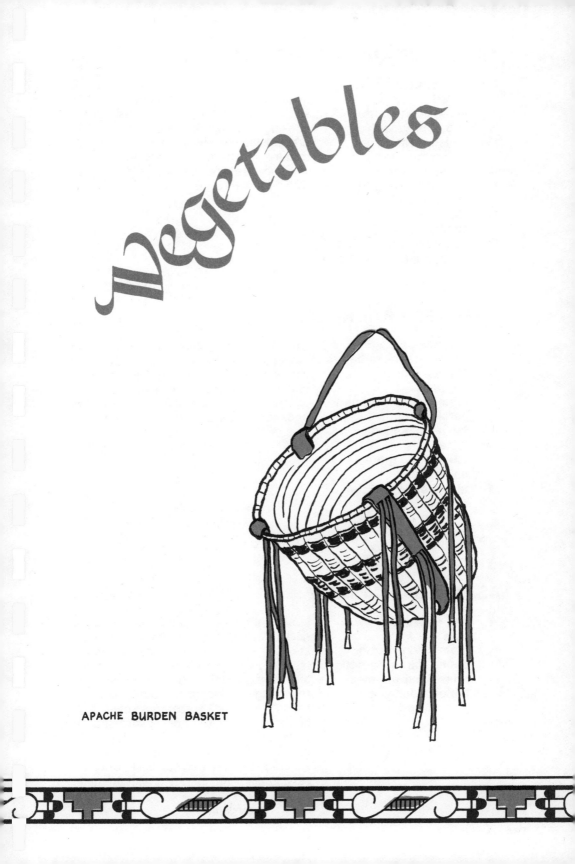

Vegetables

APACHE BURDEN BASKET

ARTICHOKE AND MUSHROOMS

4-6 servings

1 pound mushrooms, sliced
2 tablespoons butter
½ cup sour cream
1½ tablespoons flour
¾ teaspoon salt
¼ teaspoon pepper
1 14-ounce can artichoke hearts
¾ cup shredded Swiss cheese
¼ cup fresh parsley, finely chopped

Saute' mushrooms in butter for 2 minutes. Blend sour cream with flour. Add salt and pepper and stir into mushrooms, cooking until mixture comes to a boil. Add drained artichoke hearts and mix well. Put mixture in a 1 quart casserole, sprinkle with cheese and parsley and bake at 425° for 10-15 minutes.

CREAMED ARTICHOKES

6 servings

2 9-ounce packages frozen artichoke hearts
¾ cup mayonnaise
¼ cup milk
2 tablespoons chopped parsley
2 tablespoons lemon juice
1 tablespoon grated onion
¼ teaspoon Worcestershire sauce
2 hard-cooked eggs, chopped

Cook artichoke hearts according to package directions; drain. Combine mayonnaise, milk, parsley, lemon juice, onion and Worcestershire sauce and heat just until hot. Add eggs; pour over hot cooked artichoke hearts.

ASPARAGUS CASHEW

4-6 servings

¼ cup salted cashew nuts
4 tablespoons butter
1 pound thin asparagus, rinsed and trimmed
2 tablespoons water

In a large heavy saucepan cook cashew nuts in 2 tablespoons butter over moderate heat, stirring, for 2 minutes and transfer them with a slotted spoon to paper towels to drain. Add to the pan the remaining 2 tablespoons butter and the asparagus. Cook asparagus over high heat for 1 minute. Add 2 tablespoons water and cook covered for 3-4 minutes or until asparagus is tender. Transfer the asparagus with slotted spatula to a heated serving dish and sprinkle it with the nuts.

Easy and elegant.

CURRIED ASPARAGUS BUNDLES

4 servings

1 pound fresh asparagus
1 egg
2 tablespoons water
¾ teaspoon curry powder
Dash of salt and pepper
¾ cup dry bread crumbs
3 tablespoons butter
4 green pepper rings

Lay asparagus flat in large skillet. Cook covered in a small amount of salted boiling water, just until tender, about 10 minutes; drain. Beat together egg and 2 tablespoons water, curry, salt and pepper. Roll asparagus spears in crumbs, dip in egg mixture and roll again in crumbs. Brown slowly in skillet in butter for 5-10 minutes, turning occasionally. To serve, make 4 "bundles" by inserting spears through green pepper rings.

BRAISED GREEN BEANS

4 servings

1 pound green beans
Salted water
¼ cup olive oil
1 dried hot chili pepper
6 tomatoes, peeled, seeded and chopped
¼ cup fresh parsley, finely chopped
3 basil leaves, finely chopped
4 garlic cloves, finely chopped
1 teaspoon dried thyme
1 teaspoon dried oregano leaves
½ teaspoon salt
Pepper to taste
¼ cup Parmesan cheese, freshly grated

Snap off ends of beans, leaving them whole. Rinse under cold water and drain well. Bring salted water to boil, add beans, cover and cook 10-15 minutes, or until crisp tender. Drain well and immediately plunge beans in cold water to stop cooking process. Set aside. Heat olive oil in large fry pan over high heat. Add chili pepper and cook until darkened. Discard pepper. Add tomatoes, parsley, basil, garlic, thyme, oregano, salt and pepper. Reduce heat and simmer 20-30 minutes, or until liquid from tomatoes has evaporated and the sauce is thick. Add green beans, mix well and cook an additional 5 minutes. Place in serving dish and sprinkle with Parmesan cheese.

HERBED GREEN BEANS

4 servings

1   **pound fresh green beans**
      Boiling salted water
⅓   **cup pine nuts**
¼   **cup olive oil**
¼   **cup vinegar**
1   **teaspoon oregano leaves**
½   **teaspoon basil leaves**
½   **teaspoon garlic salt**
      Salt and pepper to taste
¼   **cup grated Parmesan cheese**

Snip ends from beans; cut in half. Rinse well. Cook beans uncovered in a large amount of boiling water until barely tender when pierced with a fork, 5-8 minutes. Drain, plunge in cold water, and drain again. Cover and chill. Spread pine nuts in shallow baking pan and place in 350° oven until light brown, approximately 15 minutes. In large pan combine oil, vinegar, oregano, basil, garlic salt and toasted pine nuts. Add beans and place over medium low heat until heated thoroughly, turning several times so beans are well-coated. Season to taste with salt and pepper. Transfer to serving dish and sprinkle with Parmesan cheese.

Also delicious as a chilled vegetable accompaniment. After refrigerating, let stand at room temperature 30 minutes before serving.

BEETS AND ORANGES

5 servings

2   **tablespoons flour**
2   **tablespoons butter**
¾   **cup orange juice**
½   **teaspoon salt**
3   **cups sliced cooked beets**
¼   **cup sugar**
1   **11-ounce can mandarin oranges, well drained**

Make a roux of flour and butter. Slowly add orange juice, stirring constantly. Add salt and sugar and continue stirring until well-blended and slightly thick. Add beets. Bake covered in 1 quart casserole for 15 minutes at 350°. Five minutes before serving, add mandarin oranges.

BROCCOLI LOAF

3   tablespoons butter
1   cup chopped onion
4   eggs, slightly beaten
1   cup milk
2   teaspoons dry mustard
1   teaspoon salt
¼   teaspoon garlic powder
¼   teaspoon pepper
2   10-ounce packages frozen broccoli, thawed and well-drained
½   cup dry bread crumbs
1¼   cups shredded Cheddar cheese
1   hard-cooked egg, sliced, for garnish

SAUCE:

2   tablespoons butter
2   tablespoons flour
¼   teaspoon salt
1   cup milk
½   teaspoon Worcestershire sauce
1   cup shredded Cheddar cheese

Preheat oven to 350°. Saute' onion in butter until tender; set aside. Combine eggs, milk, mustard, salt, garlic powder and pepper in large bowl. Stir in broccoli, bread crumbs, cheese and onion. Spoon mixture into well-buttered 9" x 5" loaf pan. Place loaf pan in shallow baking pan on oven rack; pour 2" hot water into the larger pan. Bake 1 hour or until knife inserted near center comes out clean. In the meantime for sauce: melt butter in saucepan. Stir in flour and salt until smooth. Remove from heat. Gradually stir in milk and Worcestershire sauce. Bring to boil, stirring constantly. Lower heat and add cheese; stir until melted. When Broccoli Loaf is done, remove loaf pan from hot water and let stand 10 minutes. Unmold on serving platter, garnish with egg and serve with sauce.

BROCCOLI-ONIONS SUPREME

2   10-ounce packages frozen cut broccoli
2   cups frozen whole small onions
2   tablespoons butter
2   tablespoons flour
¼   teaspoon salt
   Dash pepper
¾   cup milk
1   3-ounce package cream cheese, cut up
⅓   cup dry white wine
   Toasted sliced almonds

Cook broccoli and onions in boiling salted water until tender, about 10 minutes; drain. In saucepan melt butter, blend in flour, salt and a dash of pepper. Add milk and stir until bubbly. Blend in cream cheese until smooth. Remove from heat, stir in wine and then fold in vegetables. Turn into a 1½-quart casserole. Bake uncovered in 350° oven for 30-35 minutes. Sprinkle almonds on top.

BROCCOLI SUPREME

6-8 servings

2   10-ounce packages
    frozen chopped broc-
    coli, cooked according
    to package directions
    and drained
1   4-ounce jar pimientos,
    chopped
1   cup celery, chopped
½   cup onion, chopped
1   10½-ounce can con-
    densed cream of
    mushroom soup
1   cup sour cream
1   cup Cheddar cheese,
    shredded
½   cup slivered almonds

Combine all ingredients except cheese and almonds. Put in 1½-quart casserole, top with cheese. Bake at 350° for 30-40 minutes. During the last 5 minutes, sprinkle with almonds and continue to bake.

CONFETTI CUSTARD

6 servings

½   cup butter
2   cups fresh broccoli,
    sliced diagonally
2   cups sliced yellow
    squash
¾   cup Swiss cheese,
    shredded
1   egg
¼   cup milk
¼   teaspoon dry mustard
1   teaspoon salt
    Dash cayenne
½   cup grated Parmesan
    cheese

In a large skillet, melt butter and saute' vegetables until soft. Beat egg. Stir in milk, mustard, salt, cayenne and Swiss cheese. Place vegetables in 1-quart casserole. Pour egg mixture over vegetables and sprinkle Parmesan cheese on top. Bake at 375° for 15 to 20 minutes or until cheese is slightly browned and custard is set.

BRUSSELS SPROUTS WITH CARAWAY   8 servings

1½   pounds Brussels
      sprouts, rinsed in cold
      water
2½   cups chicken broth
¼   cup melted butter
2   tablespoons lemon
      juice
1½   tablespoons caraway
      seeds
½   teaspoon salt
      Fresh pepper
4   tablespoons seasoned
      breadcrumbs
2   tablespoons butter

Combine Brussels sprouts and chicken broth in medium saucepan and cook over medium heat for 5 or 6 minutes, or until just tender. Drain well. Preheat broiler. Toss sprouts with melted butter, lemon juice, caraway seeds, salt and pepper. Place in 1-quart baking dish, sprinkle with breadcrumbs, and dot with remaining 2 tablespoons butter. Place under broiler for 1 minute or until crumbs are crisp and golden brown.

BRUSSELS SPROUTS IN SOUR CREAM   6 servings

2   10-ounce packages
      frozen Brussels
      sprouts
¾   cup sour cream
½   cup toasted slivered
      almonds
¼   cup chopped pimiento
1   teaspoon sugar
½   teaspoon fresh ground
      pepper
1   teaspoon salt

Cook Brussels sprouts according to directions for 7-8 minutes or until crisp tender; drain. Combine Brussels sprouts, sour cream, almonds, pimiento, sugar, pepper and salt in the top of a double boiler and mix ingredients together lightly. Place over hot water until heated through. Transfer to a warm serving dish and serve hot.

MARINATED BRUSSELS SPROUTS   4-6 servings

½   cup tarragon vinegar
½   cup cooking oil
1   clove garlic, crushed
1   tablespoon sugar
1   teaspoon salt
2   small onions, cut in
      rings
2   10-ounce packages
      frozen Brussels
      sprouts, cooked
      according to package
      directions

Combine first 5 ingredients and pour over onion rings and cooked Brussels sprouts. Cover and refrigerate at least 24 hours. If desired, cooked asparagus, artichoke hearts or fresh mushrooms may be combined with the Brussels sprouts.

PICKLED BRUSSELS SPROUTS

6-8 servings

Boiling water
1 10-ounce package frozen Brussels sprouts
1 8-ounce jar pearl onions, drained
2 6-ounce cans mushroom caps, drained
1½ cups white vinegar
Salt
1 cup sugar
1 teaspoon celery seeds
1 teaspoon turmeric
½ teaspoon dry mustard
1 teaspoon mustard seeds

Pour boiling water over Brussels sprouts; cover and set aside for 10 minutes. Drain, add onions and mushroom caps, mix gently. Combine remaining ingredients in a saucepan and bring to a boil; cook 3 minutes. Pour hot vinegar mixture over vegetables; toss gently. Cover and store in refrigerator at least a week before serving. Liquid may be saved and used again.

HOT CURRIED CABBAGE

12-15 servings

1 10¾-ounce can beef consomme
1 cup water
1 bay leaf
3 whole cloves
½ teaspoon salt
3 pounds cabbage, shredded
4 tablespoons butter
1 onion, chopped
1 clove garlic, crushed
2 tablespoons flour
1 tablespoon curry powder
1 teaspoon salt
¼ teaspoon nutmeg
½ cup stock (made by boiling first 6 ingredients)
1½ cups sour cream
¼ cup bread crumbs
2 tablespoons Parmesan cheese

Boil first 5 ingredients together 5 minutes; add shredded cabbage and cook covered for 10 minutes. Remove bay leaf and cloves and drain saving ½ cup stock. In saucepan melt butter and saute' onion and garlic 3 minutes. Add flour, curry powder, salt, nutmeg, ½ cup reserved stock and sour cream. Blend until smooth and thickened, then add to cabbage. Place in buttered 2-quart casserole and top with bread crumbs and Parmesan cheese. Bake at 425° 15 minutes or until brown on top.

DANISH RED CABBAGE

1 medium head red cab-
bage, shredded
¼ pound butter
1 10-ounce jar red cur-
rant jelly
Salt to taste
¼ cup red wine vinegar

Mix first 3 ingredients in saucepan. Cook over very low heat about 40 minutes. Add salt and red wine vinegar just before serving.

CARROTS VERONIQUE

6-8 servings

2 pounds carrots, cut in-
to thick diagonal slices
¼ cup butter
⅛ teaspoon sugar
1 tablespoon vodka
1 cup seedless green
grapes
¼ cup water
Salt and pepper to
taste

Saute' carrots in butter for 5 minutes. Sprinkle carrots with sugar and cook them an additional 2 minutes, stirring constantly. Add vodka and ½ cup water and cook carrots until almost tender. Add grapes, season to taste with salt and pepper and serve.

MARINATED CARROTS

8-10 servings

3 1-pound cans sliced
carrots, drained
2 medium sized onions,
sliced in thin rings
1 bell pepper, cut in
strips

Combine carrots, onions and bell pepper in a large bowl. Combine remaining ingredients and pour over vegetables. Refrigerate at least 24 hours before serving.

MARINADE:

1 cup sugar
¾ cup vinegar
½ cup oil
1 10¾-ounce can con-
densed tomato soup
1 teaspoon salt
1 teaspoon pepper
1 teaspoon prepared
mustard
1 teaspoon Worcester-
shire sauce

VEGETABLES

🦃 CHIMAYO CORN PUDDING

1½   cups creamed corn
1   cup yellow cornmeal
1   cup (2 sticks) butter, melted
¾   cup buttermilk
2   medium onions, chopped
2   eggs, beaten
½   teaspoon baking soda
2   cups grated sharp Cheddar cheese
1   4-ounce can green chilies, drained

Preheat oven to 350°. Grease a 9" square baking pan. Combine first 7 ingredients and mix well. Turn half the batter into prepared pan; cover evenly with half the cheese, all of the chilies, then remaining cheese. Top with remaining batter. Bake 1 hour. Let cool 15 minutes before serving.

Here's a spicy side dish that's sure to become a family favorite.

CONFETTI CORN

2   10-ounce packages frozen corn
6   tablespoons butter
1   green pepper, chopped
1   red sweet pepper, chopped
1½   tablespoons fresh parsley
1½   teaspoons tarragon
2   teaspoons chives
¼   cup white wine
     Salt and pepper to taste
2   tablespoons brandy
2   tablespoons creamy peanut butter

Saute' frozen corn in 3 tablespoons butter until kernels are separated. Add peppers, parsley, tarragon, chives, wine and remaining 3 tablespoons of butter and simmer for about 20-25 minutes, covered. Uncover pan. Add brandy and peanut butter; mix well and serve.

CELERY WITH WATER CHESTNUTS

6-8 servings

1 bunch celery, cut into 1" pieces
1¾ cups chicken broth
½ teaspoon sweet basil
½ teaspoon salt
¼ teaspoon pepper
2 tablespoons corn-starch
2 tablespoons cold water
1 6½-ounce can water chestnuts, drained and sliced
½ cup bell pepper, chopped
1 cup mushrooms, sliced
½ cup sliced almonds

Put celery, broth, basil, salt and pepper into a large saucepan and cook, covered, until celery is almost tender but slightly crisp, about 10 minutes. Blend cornstarch and water; gradually add to hot stock, stirring just until thickened. Add water chestnuts, bell pepper and mushrooms to sauce. Pour into a 2-quart casserole and bake uncovered in a 350° oven for 30 minutes.

🐦BAKED CHILIES RELLENOS

4 servings

10 whole green chilies, peeled
½ pound Monterey Jack cheese, cut in 10 strips
1 cup grated Cheddar cheese
3 eggs
¼ cup flour
¾ cup milk
¼ teaspoon salt
¼ teaspoon black pepper
Dash of liquid hot pepper sauce

Preheat oven to 350°. Cut green chilies in half, seed, leaving a few seeds for extra flavor. Spread chilies on paper towel and pat dry. Slip a strip of Monterey Jack cheese in each chili and lay them side-by-side in a greased 9" x 13" baking dish. Sprinkle with Cheddar cheese. Beat eggs with flour until smooth. Add milk, seasonings and pepper sauce. Carefully pour egg mixture over chilies. Bake uncovered for 45 minutes or until knife inserted in custard comes out clean.

A fine accompaniment to steaks, hamburgers or meat loaf or can stand alone as a meatless main dish.

🐦SUSAN'S HOMINY CASSEROLE

6-8 servings

2 16-ounce cans yellow hominy, drained
1 4-ounce can chopped green chilies
1 2-ounce jar diced pimientos
¼ cup butter, melted
1 cup sour cream
½ pound Cheddar cheese, grated

Combine first 5 ingredients and mix thoroughly. Sprinkle cheese over top. Bake 1 hour at 350°.

⚜ EGGPLANT MEXICANA 6-8 servings

2	medium eggplants
½	cup or more salad oil (enough to brush on eggplant)
1	15-ounce can tomato sauce
1	4-ounce can chopped green chilies
½	cup thinly sliced green onions
½	teaspoon ground cumin
½	teaspoon garlic salt
1	2¼-ounce can sliced black olives, well-drained
2½	cups shredded Cheddar cheese
½	cup (or more) sour cream, for topping

Cut unpeeled eggplant into ½" slices. Brush slices with oil on both sides and arrange in a single layer on rimmed baking sheet. Bake uncovered, at 350° for 15-20 minutes, or until soft. Watch eggplant carefully to prevent it from burning. Meanwhile, in saucepan combine remaining ingredients, except cheese and sour cream, and simmer, uncovered, 10 minutes. Layer in a 9" x 13" casserole: a single layer of eggplant, half of the tomato sauce mixture and half of the shredded cheese. Repeat layers, topping with cheese. Bake at 350° for 25 minutes or until bubbly. Pass sour cream to spoon over individual servings.

EGGPLANT TORTA 8 servings

1	large eggplant
	Flour, seasoned with salt and pepper
	Oil
	Salt, pepper and thyme to taste
¾	cup chopped parsley
6	large tomatoes, skinned and sliced
1	onion, finely chopped
2	green peppers, finely chopped
2	8-ounce packages sliced mozzarella cheese
1	cup whipping cream
½	cup half-and-half
3	eggs
2	egg yolks

Peel and slice eggplant. Dredge in seasoned flour. Fry in hot oil until browned. Place half the eggplant slices in a 9" x 13" baking dish. Sprinkle with salt, pepper and thyme and 3 tablespoons chopped parsley. Cover eggplant slices with half the tomatoes. Sprinkle tomatoes with salt, pepper, thyme, more parsley, half the onion and half the peppers. Cover with half the cheese slices. Repeat layers ending with cheese. Beat remaining ingredients together. Pour over layered ingredients. Bake in 425° oven 30-40 minutes or until the custard is set and the cheese is nicely browned. Remove from oven and let rest 5 minutes before serving.

MUSHROOM FRITTERS WITH HOT HERB CREAM

4 servings

½   pound small fresh
    mushrooms
1   recipe Basic Fritter
    Batter
1   recipe Hot Herb Cream

**BASIC FRITTER
BATTER:**

1½ cups sifted all-purpose
    flour
1   teaspoon salt
2   tablespoons oil
1   egg, well beaten
    Cold water

**HOT HERB
CREAM:**

¾   cup half-and-half
1   teaspoon basil leaves
1   teaspoon chopped
    parsley
¼   teaspoon thyme leaves
    Salt and fresh ground
    pepper to taste

Remove stems from mushrooms. Dip mushrooms in batter and coat entire surface. Drop in hot oil at 370° in a deep fat fryer. Fry until lightly browned. Remove from oil and drain well. Serve with Hot Herb Cream. To make Basic Fritter Batter; sift flour and salt together in a medium bowl. Add the oil, egg, and about 1 cup of cold water or enough to make a thick batter. If the batter does not adhere to the vegetables, add 1 or 2 tablespoons of water to the batter. To make Hot Herb Cream; combine all ingredients in a small saucepan and bring just to a boil. Serve hot with vegetable fritters.

STUFFED MUSHROOMS IMPERIAL

4 servings

½   stick butter (¼ cup)
4   tablespoons minced
    shallots
½   cup chopped walnuts
    or pecans
8   giant mushroom caps,
    stems reserved and
    chopped
½   cup breadcrumbs
¼   teaspoon thyme
    Salt and pepper to
    taste

Preheat oven to 350°. Butter a 8" square baking dish. Melt butter in skillet over medium heat. Add shallots and saute until limp. Add nuts and chopped mushroom stems and saute an additional 3 minutes. Mix in breadcrumbs, thyme, salt and pepper to taste. Fill mushroom caps with mixture. Place in baking dish and bake 15 minutes.

MUSHROOM CASSEROLE

6-10 servings

1   **pound fresh mushrooms**
2   **tablespoons butter**
9   **slices of buttered toasted white bread**
½   **cup chopped onions**
½   **cup bell pepper**
½   **cup celery**
¾   **teaspoon salt**
¼   **teaspoon pepper**
½   **cup mayonnaise**
2   **large eggs**
½   **cup milk**
10½ **-ounce can condensed cream of mushroom soup**
1½   **cup grated mild Cheddar cheese**

Wash mushrooms and slice. Saute mushrooms in butter 3 minutes; set aside. Butter the white bread and cut each into 9 squares. Place 3 slices (27 pieces) of bread on the bottom of an ungreased 3 quart casserole. Set the rest aside for layering. Mix chopped onions, bell pepper, celery, salt, pepper, mayonnaise, and cooked mushrooms; pour over bread in pan. Put 3 more slices (27 pieces) of bread on top. Beat eggs with milk, and pour over the top. Place last 3 slices of bread on top and spread undiluted can of soup over all. Bake uncovered, in 325° oven for 50-60 minutes. During the last 10 minutes, top with grated cheese. Can be made 24 hours ahead but do not add soup or cheese until cooking time.

HERBED ONION SLICES

6 servings

3   **tablespoons butter**
1   **tablespoon brown sugar**
½   **teaspoon salt**
     Dash pepper
2   **large mild onions, cut in ½" slices**
¼   **cup finely chopped celery**
2   **tablespoons minced parsley**
¼   **teaspoon dried oregano**

In large skillet melt butter; add brown sugar, salt and pepper. Place onion slices in a single layer in butter mixture. Cover and cook slowly for 10 minutes without turning. Turn slices, sprinkle with celery, parsley and oregano. Cook uncovered 10 minutes more.

Delicious with steak or roast beef.

SOUTHERN FRIED OKRA

6 servings

1   **cup yellow cornmeal**
½   **cup flour**
1½   **teaspoons salt**
⅛   **teaspoon pepper**
¾   **pound (about 3 cups) fresh okra, cut in ½" slices**
⅓   **cup bacon drippings**

In medium bowl combine cornmeal, flour, salt and pepper. Add okra and toss until well coated. In a 10" skillet heat enough bacon drippings (about 3 tablespoons) to cover bottom of pan. Add some okra and cook, turning frequently, until crispy and brown. Drain on paper towels. Keep warm. Repeat, adding more bacon drippings as needed.

Some Southerners say if you haven't eaten fried okra you haven't lived!

SHERRIED ONION CASSEROLE

4-6 servings

4   **medium onions, sliced**
4   **tablespoons butter**
2   **tablespoons flour**
¾   **cup beef bouillon**
⅛   **teaspoon pepper**
¼   **cup dry sherry**
1½ **cups cheese and onion croutons**
3   **tablespoons butter, melted**
1   **cup Swiss cheese, grated**
3-4 **tablespoons grated Parmesan cheese**

Cook onions in 4 tablespoons butter until barely tender. Mix flour and bouillon together, then add to onion mixture. Stir in pepper, then add sherry; cook and stir until thickened and bubbly. Turn into a 1-quart casserole. Toss croutons with the 3 tablespoons melted butter and spoon over onion mixture. Sprinkle with Swiss and Parmesan cheese. Place under broiler just until cheese melts, about 1 minute.

FRENCH SPRING PEAS

6 servings

2   **pounds fresh or 1 pound frozen peas**
3-6 **moist lettuce leaves**
⅓   **cup sliced green onions**
½   **teaspoon sugar**
½   **teaspoon salt**
     Dash of pepper
¼   **teaspoon chervil**
¼   **teaspoon thyme**
1   **teaspoon chopped parsley**
1   **tablespoon butter**

Shell peas if fresh. Cover bottom of a 10" skillet with lettuce leaves; top with peas and onion. Sprinkle with sugar, salt, pepper, chervil, thyme and parsley. Cover tightly and cook over low heat for 10-15 minutes or until peas are tender; remove lettuce leaves. Drain peas; season with additional salt to taste; dot with butter.

TANGY NEW POTATOES

4 servings

1½ **pounds new potatoes**
⅓   **cup butter**
4   **teaspoons fresh parsley, chopped**
4   **teaspoons minced chives**
1   **tablespoon lemon juice**
1   **teaspoon grated lemon peel**
½   **teaspoon salt**
⅛   **teaspoon white pepper**

Boil potatoes until done in salted water. Drain well and peel. Melt the butter in small saucepan. Stir in minced chives, parsley, lemon juice, lemon peel, salt and pepper. Pour mixture over hot potatoes coating thoroughly.

HASH BROWN CASSEROLE

8-12 servings

1   2-pound package frozen hash brown potatoes
1   cup half-and-half
1   cup sour cream
1   can condensed cream of chicken soup
½   cup chopped onions
2   cups grated Cheddar cheese
     Salt and pepper

Combine all ingredients and mix well. Place in a greased 9" x 15" pan. Bake at 350° for 1-1½ hours.

POTATOES IN BROWN SAUCE

6-8 servings

2   pounds potatoes
3   tablespoons butter
1   tablespoon chopped onion
½   teaspoon chopped parsley
2   tablespoons flour
1   cup beef stock
1   tablespoon vinegar
½   bay leaf, crushed
     Dash of ground thyme
     Salt to taste
¼   cup sour cream
2   tablespoons chopped pickle

Boil potatoes in their jackets. Peel and slice. Melt butter and fry onion and parsley in it. Add flour and brown lightly. Add stock, vinegar, bay leaf, thyme, salt and sour cream and blend well. Bring almost to a boil. Add potatoes and pickles and allow to heat through.

SHRIMP-STUFFED BAKED POTATOES

4 servings

4   large baking potatoes
2   egg yolks
     Half-and-half
5   tablespoons chopped parsley
2   tablespoons chopped chives
1   cup cooked shrimp, chopped
½   cup grated Cheddar cheese

Bake potatoes in a 375° oven for 1 hour or until the potatoes are tender. Remove potatoes from oven; split potatoes open and scoop out the pulp, leaving a firm shell. Place shells aside. Place pulp in a medium-sized bowl; add egg yolks and beat until smooth. Add enough half-and-half to make the mixture light and fluffy. Fold in 3 tablespoons of the fresh parsley, the chives and shrimp and place mixture back in the potato skins. Sprinkle tops with Cheddar cheese. Place in baking pan and bake 15 minutes longer or until the cheese is melted and golden brown. Sprinkle each potato with remaining parsley.

VIENNESE POTATO CROQUETTES

6-8 servings

1   pound potatoes, peeled and quartered
2   eggs
½   cup flour
½   cup cornmeal
3   tablespoons butter
2   teaspoons salt
¼   teaspoon pepper
    Vegetable oil

Cook potatoes in boiling salted water to cover until tender, about 25-30 minutes. Mash. Stir in remaining ingredients except oil. Cool. Pour 5″ oil into large pan. Heat to 375°. Drop heaping tablespoons of dough into oil; fry until brown, about 4 minutes. Remove with slotted spoon; drain on paper towels. Repeat until all dough is used.

REFRIED BEANS

6-8 servings

1   1-pound package of pinto beans
6   slices bacon
¼   cup chopped onion
¼   cup chopped green pepper
1   clove garlic, crushed
2   teaspoons salt
1   teaspoon chili powder
    Chopped green pepper or shredded Cheddar cheese

Wash beans. Turn into a large saucepan or Dutch oven; cover with 8 cups cold water. Cover pan and let beans soak overnight. Next day, bring beans and liquid to boiling; reduce heat and simmer, covered, about 2 hours or until tender. Drain beans, reserving liquid. In a large skillet, saute' bacon until crisp. Drain on paper towels and crumble. In bacon drippings in skillet, saute' onion, green pepper and garlic until tender, about 5 minutes. With wooden spoon, stir in beans, bacon, salt and chili powder. Cook over medium heat, stirring in reserved bean liquid a little at a time and mashing beans until all are mashed and mixture is creamy. Turn beans into serving dish. If desired, sprinkle with chopped green pepper, crisp bacon bits or grated cheese.

MAMACITA'S PINTO BEANS

6 servings

3   cups dried pinto beans
½   cup oil
4   cloves garlic
½   teaspoon pepper
2   tablespoons powdered red chili
½   pound salt pork
1   medium onion, quartered
1   tablespoon sugar

Soak clean beans in water to cover in refrigerator overnight. Drain. Put beans in pressure cooker. Add water to within 2 inches of top. Add all other ingredients. Boil 30 minutes, skimming top, if necessary. Add water, leaving two inches top space. Pressure-cook at 10 pounds 30 minutes longer. Let cool until pressure is down. Uncover and mash beans slightly. Cook for another 30 minutes, adding water as it boils off. May be served at this point, or simmered all day for fullest flavor, adding water when necessary. Add salt just before serving.

Freezes well.

POTATO RING WITH GLAZED CARROTS   8 servings

POTATO RING:

1   cup coarsely grated
    sharp Cheddar cheese
6   cups mashed potatoes,
    seasoned with salt and
    pepper (do not add
    milk or butter)
3   tablespoons melted
    butter

GLAZED CARROTS:

6   cups carrots, sliced on
    diagonal
2   tablespoons butter
¼   cup chicken stock
¼   teaspoon salt
¼   teaspoon pepper
1   cup orange marmalade
    Dash of orange-
    flavored liqueur

Preheat oven to 400°. Heavily butter a smooth 2-quart ring mold. Stir cheese into mashed potatoes to give a marbled effect. Pour into mold and brush with 1½ tablespoons melted butter. Bake 20-25 minutes or until top is golden brown. Unmold on heated serving platter. Preheat broiler. Brush top of mold with remaining butter and run under broiler 4-5 minutes or until evenly browned. Remove from oven and fill center of mold with glazed carrots. To glaze carrots, put carrots, butter and stock in saucepan. Cook covered over high heat for 3 minutes. Add remaining ingredients and cook uncovered over low heat until carrots are tender. Stir often as the sauce thickens.

SPINACH ALBUQUERQUE   4-6 servings

1   pound fresh spinach
    or 1 10-ounce package
    frozen spinach
½   cup lightly salted
    water
2   teaspoons bacon drip-
    pings (optional)
¼   teaspoon grated
    orange peel
¼   teaspoon crushed
    basil
4   ounces chopped green
    chilies (canned or
    fresh)
1   10½-ounce can con-
    densed cream of
    celery soup
½   cup grated sharp
    Cheddar cheese
1   egg, well beaten
¼-½ teaspoon salt
⅛   teaspoon black pepper

If using fresh spinach, cut coarsely, then simmer covered in salted water until tender. If using frozen spinach, cook according to package directions. Drain well. Add all other ingredients, reserving half the cheese. Stir gently with a fork over low heat until blended well. Pour into 1½-2 quart casserole dish and cover with remaining cheese. Bake uncovered at 350° for 15 to 20 minutes until mixture bubbles gently and cheese is melted.

CREAMED SPINACH

4 servings

1   10-ounce package
    frozen chopped
    spinach
1   3-ounce package
    cream cheese
¼   teaspoon onion salt
    Pepper to taste
    Dash of nutmeg

Prepare spinach according to package directions. Drain well and add cream cheese, onion salt, pepper and nutmeg. Heat slowly, stirring until well-blended. (For variation, spoon spinach mixture into tomato shells, artichoke bottoms, or fresh mushrooms, sprinkle with Parmesan cheese and butter and broil until hot and bubbly.)

SPINACH WITH PINE NUTS

6-8 servings

2   10-ounce packages
    frozen leaf spinach (or
    2 bunches fresh
    spinach)
4   ounces butter
3   medium cloves garlic
6   green onions
½   teaspoon salt
1   4-ounce package pine
    nuts

Cook spinach according to package directions. If fresh spinach is used, cook in lightly salted water until tender. Drain and squeeze dry throughly. Melt butter in saucepan. Add minced garlic and chopped green onion. Add salt and mix well. Pour butter mixture over spinach and toss lightly to coat. Place in 1 quart casserole dish and sprinkle pine nuts over top. Place under broiler to brown the nuts. Can be made ahead and broiled at the last minute,

DIXIE YAM CASSEROLE

6-8 servings

2   30-ounce cans yams,
    drained and mashed
2   tablespoons butter,
    melted
½   teaspoon cinnamon
½   teaspoon nutmeg
1   cup miniature marsh-
    mallows, plus extra for
    topping
½   cup orange marmalade
¼   cup slivered almonds
    or chopped pecans

Preheat oven to 350°. Grease a 2½-to 3-quart casserole. Combine yams, butter, cinnamon and nutmeg in large bowl and mix well. Fold in marshmallows, marmalade and nuts. Pour into casserole, top with extra marshmallows and bake about 20-25 minutes or until top is nicely browned.

COMPANY SWEET POTATOES

6 servings

6   yams
½   cup brown sugar
⅓   cup chopped pecans
1   cup orange juice
1   tablespoon grated
     orange rind
⅓   cup sherry
2   tablespoons butter

Cook yams in salted, boiling water until tender. Peel and cut in half lengthwise. Place in large casserole and sprinkle with sugar and pecans. Pour mixture of orange juice, rind, and sherry on top and dot with butter. Cover and bake at 350° for 45 minutes or until all juice has cooked into potatoes.

ORANGE SWEET POTATOES FLAMBÉ

10 servings

5   sweet potatoes
6   tablespoons butter
4   tablespoons honey
2   small oranges
     Dash of salt
2   tablespoons poppy
     seed
1   tablespoon sugar
4   tablespoons rum,
     heated

Peel and cook fresh sweet potatoes until barely tender. Slice in half and place in one layer in baking dish. Blend over low heat the butter, honey, the peel and juice of two oranges and salt. Pour over sweet potatoes. Top with mixture of poppy seeds and sugar. Bake at 450° for 30-35 minutes or until potatoes are glazed. Before serving, heat the rum, set it aflame, and pour over the potatoes. Baste and serve immediately.

🦆GUACAMOLE STUFFED TOMATOES

6 servings

6   medium tomatoes
     Salt
½   cup finely chopped
     onion
1   clove garlic, minced
2   canned green chilies,
     finely chopped
2   teaspoons lemon juice
2   very ripe avocados
3   slices bacon, crisp-
     cooked and crumbled
     Crisp lettuce

Cut ½ inch thick slice from stem end of each tomato. Scoop out centers and chop finely. Lightly sprinkle the insides of tomato cups with salt; turn upside down on paper towels to drain. Refrigerate. Stir chopped onion, garlic, chili, lemon juice and 1½ teaspoon salt into chopped tomato. Refrigerate, covered. Just before serving, peel and pit avocados; mash. Stir in chopped tomato mixture. Spoon guacamole into tomato cups; top with crumbled bacon. Arrange on lettuce leaves on serving platter. Pass any remaining guacamole. If desired, surround each tomato with crisp corn chips.

CELEBRITY TOMATOES

8 servings

1	teaspoon garlic salt
2	tablespoons basil
2	tablespoons parsley, minced
6	tablespoons Parmesan cheese
¼	cup chopped walnuts
¼-½	cup olive oil
4	tomatoes cut in half crosswise and allowed to drain

Combine first 6 ingredients and spread over tomato halves in a shallow baking dish. Bake at 350° for 10 minutes. Serve hot.

STUFFED TOMATOES ITALIAN

4 servings

4	large, ripe tomatoes
½	cup olive oil
1	teaspoon salt
¼	teaspoon freshly ground pepper
1	cup water
¼	cup raw long-grain rice or Italian arborio rice
1	small clove garlic
2	tablespoons chopped flat-leaved parsley
10	large fresh basil leaves or 1½ teaspoons dried basil
¼	teaspoon oregano
2	medium potatoes

Preheat oven to 375°. Cut the tops off the tomatoes about one-quarter of the way down. Reserve the tops, scoop out the insides and mash them through a sieve, saving the resulting juice. Sprinkle the inside of the tomatoes with a little of the olive oil, ¾ teaspoon salt and pepper. Bring water to a boil in a medium saucepan. Add the rice and remaining ¼ teaspoon salt. Cook 8 minutes. Drain well and place in a bowl. Mince the garlic, parsley, basil and oregano together and add to the rice along with 3 tablespoons of the olive oil and ¼ cup of the reserved tomato juice. Fill the tomatoes loosely with the rice and cover each with its own top. Peel the potatoes. Cut 4 ½" slices from one and cut the rest in bite-size chunks. Put the slices evenly spaced in the bottom of an oiled baking dish. Place the stuffed tomatoes on the rounds and fill the spaces around the tomatoes with the remaining chunks of potatoes. Dribble remaining oil over the vegetables and bake 30 to 45 minutes or until the potatoes are done and the rice is tender. Serve cold as an antipasto, or hot as a side dish.

BAKED STUFFED TOMATOES

6 servings

6 tomatoes
½ cup cooked bacon, chopped
¼ cup celery, chopped
1 small onion, minced
1 cup bread crumbs
½ teaspoon salt
2 tablespoons butter
½ cup Cheddar or Monterey Jack cheese, grated

Preheat oven to 350°. Cut off top of tomatoes and scoop out the centers. Mix pulp and next six ingredients and ¼ cup cheese. Fill tomatoes and sprinkle remaining cheese on top. Bake in greased muffin cups or baking dish in 350° oven for 30 minutes.

Good with seafood or pasta dinners.

SQUASH DELIGHT

6 servings

1 pound yellow squash
¼ pound butter, melted
¾ cup chopped bell pepper
¾ cup chopped onion
¾ cup grated Cheddar cheese
¾ cup sliced water chestnuts
½ cup mayonnaise
1 teaspoon sugar
1 beaten egg
   Cayenne pepper to taste
¼ cup cracker crumbs

Slice squash. Boil in salted water until barely tender. Drain well. Add remaining ingredients. Mix well and place in 1 quart buttered casserole and cover with the crumbs. Bake at 350° for 30-40 minutes.

ZUCCHINI ST. MORITZ

4 servings

1 12" long zucchini, about 3" in diameter
1 cup finely chopped onions
2 cups chopped mushrooms
4 tablespoons olive oil
2½ cups grated Swiss cheese
1 cup cooked brown rice
1 cup finely chopped walnuts
3 large eggs, well-beaten
¾ teaspoon curry powder
   Salt and pepper to taste

Parboil zucchini in water to cover until tender but not mushy, approximately 7-8 minutes. Drain, halve lengthwise and let cool. Scoop out inside, leaving about ¼" shell. Retain 1 cup of pulp. Preheat oven to 325°. Saute' onions and mushrooms in oil about 5 minutes. Drain off excess liquid and transfer to bowl. Blend in zucchini pulp, 1 cup of the cheese, the rice, nuts and eggs. Add curry, and salt and pepper to taste. Heap in squash shell and sprinkle with remaining cheese. Place in baking dish with a little water and cover with foil. Bake 20-30 minutes or until stuffing is set and cheese is melted.

SAUSAGE ZUCCHINI BOATS

4 servings

4	medium unpeeled zucchini
¼	pound bulk pork sausage
¼	cup chopped onion
½	cup fine cracker crumbs
1	slightly beaten egg
½	cup grated Monterey Jack cheese
¼	teaspoon thyme
½	teaspoon garlic salt
¼	teaspoon pepper to taste
¼	cup additional grated cheese

Cook zucchini in boiling water to cover for 10 minutes. Drain and cut in half lengthwise. Scoop out pulp, leaving ¼" shell. Chop pulp. Crumble sausage into heated skillet; add onion and cook well. Drain off grease. Add pulp, crumbs, egg, ½ cup cheese, thyme, garlic salt and pepper. Fill shells; place in shallow, greased, close-fitting pan. Sprinkle top with cheese. Bake for 25 minutes at 350°.

VEGETABLE BURRITOS FOR A CROWD

24 servings

¼	cup oil
2	garlic cloves, crushed
2	medium onions, chopped
5	6-ounce cans water chestnuts, drained, sliced and cut julienne
6	large zucchini, grated
1½	pounds mushrooms, sliced
1	teaspoon celery salt
4	large tomatoes, seeded and chopped
	Salt and freshly ground black pepper to taste
24	large flour tortillas
4	cups shredded Cheddar cheese
2	large avocados, peeled, seeded and chopped
2	cups sour cream
1	tablespoon fresh lemon juice
24	avocado slices for garnish

Heat oil in large skillet. Add garlic and onion and saute' until golden. Add water chestnuts and stir-fry until warmed. Add zucchini and heat through. Add mushrooms and saute' briefly. Sprinkle with celery salt. Add tomatoes and stir to heat through. Remove from heat. (Do not overcook; vegetables should remain firm.) Add salt and pepper. Preheat oven to 350°. Cook tortillas one at a time in ungreased skillet over medium-high heat; turning frequently until softened. Remove tortillas from heat. Place 2 heaping tablespoons cheese and 2 tablespoons vegetable mixture down center. Roll up and transfer to baking dish. Repeat with remaining tortillas. Bake until heated through, about 10-15 minutes. While burritos are baking, make avocado sauce by combining chopped avocados, sour cream and lemon juice and beating until smooth. Spoon some of sauce down the center of burritos as they come from the oven and lay an avocado slice across the top of each burrito. Serve immediately with remaining avocado sauce.

So delicious and unusual your guests will adore you.

Mountain Magic.....

The rugged mountains of New Mexico -- forming the southernmost peaks of the Rocky Mountain chain -- command the landscape with a haunting beauty. The mountains are home to a large variety of game and fish. Elk can be found in the northern mountains along with bighorn sheep, antelope, deer, mountain lions and other big game animals. The cool mountain streams are a wonderful habitat for several varieties of trout and some Kokanee salmon. From Thanksgiving to Easter, skiers from all over the United States flock to a half-dozen ski resorts and snow bowls located throughout the New Mexico mountains. Some of the largest and most famous are located conveniently close to Albuquerque, Taos and Santa Fé and offer skiing that many experts rate "better than Switzerland." Sandia Peak Ski Area is just 30 minutes by car from Albuquerque. Or anxious skiers may take the aerial tram that, in 20 minutes, ascends spectacularly from the mountain base to the ski area at the crest ❖

Fish, Shellfish and Game

ZUNI OWLS

BAKED SUMMERTIME FISH

4 servings

Olive oil
2 pounds fresh fish, dressed (trout is good)
Juice of one lemon
2 tablespoons parsley, chopped
1 onion, thinly sliced
2 garlic cloves, crushed
1 bunch fresh spinach, finely chopped
3 tomatoes, coarsely chopped
Salt and pepper to taste

Preheat oven to 450°. Oil a large baking pan, place whole fish or fillets in pan skin-side down. Drizzle a little olive oil over fish and sprinkle with juice of one lemon. Cover with remaining ingredients. Bake for 3-5 minutes or until slightly browned. Lower heat to 350° and bake 10-30 minutes longer depending on size of fish pieces (whole fish takes longer than pieces).

BROILED LEMON FISH

4 servings

Butter
2 pounds sole, cod or flounder fillets
1 cup mayonnaise
¾ cup chopped, un-peeled cucumber
1 teaspoon dried dillweed
3 green onions, sliced
5 dashes hot pepper sauce
½ teaspoon salt
Lemon slices or green onion for garnish

Butter a large oven-to-table platter; arrange fish on platter in single layer. Combine remaining ingredients except lemon slices and onion in bowl and spread evenly over fish. Broil 3-5 inches from heat for 5-7 minutes or until top is brown and bubbly and fish is opaque. Garnish with lemon slices and sliced green onions.

LOW-CAL GOURMET FISH

6 servings

2 pounds fillets of sole, cod or flounder
2 tablespoons prepared horseradish, drained
2 tablespoons Dijon-style mustard
2 tablespoons lemon juice
4 tablespoons grated Parmesan cheese
⅓ cup plain yogurt
2 tablespoons unsalted butter or margarine, melted

Arrange fish in a single layer in a foil-lined broiler pan. Preheat broiler. Combine horseradish, mustard, lemon juice, 3 tablespoons Parmesan cheese and yogurt in a small bowl. Add butter; stir until smooth. Spread mixture over fish fillets in a thin even layer. Top with 1 tablespoon Parmesan cheese. Broil about 5-6 minutes until fish is just cooked through and sauce is bubbly and slightly glazed.

Elegant enough for company but great for the waistline.

PORTUGUESE FISH STEW

6-8 servings

3	tablespoons oil
4	onions, thinly sliced
3	garlic cloves, minced
¼	cup sherry (dry)
3	tomatoes, cubed
3	medium potatoes, peeled and cubed
4	whole cloves
2	bay leaves
1	tablespoon parsley
½	teaspoon tarragon
½	teaspoon marjoram
¼	teaspoon pepper
7-8	cups water
1	pound halibut, haddock or cod fillets
1	pound boned trout fillets
	Salt
¼	cup butter
1	garlic clove, minced
12-16	slices French or Italian bread
8	tablespoons Parmesan cheese
1	tablespoon parsley

Heat oil and add onion and garlic; cook about 15 minutes. Add next 10 ingredients. Cover and simmer 50-60 minutes. Uncover and simmer until liquid is reduced, at least two hours. Break fish into chunks; add to liquid and simmer 5 minutes. Season with salt. Melt butter in skillet, add garlic and saute until soft. Add bread slices and brown on both sides. Remove. Ladle stew into soup bowls and top with 2 slices bread and 1 tablespoon cheese and some parsley.

SWEET AND SOUR FISH

3-4 servings

1½	pounds fish fillets (flounder or cod)
3	tablespoons water
3	tablespoons cornstarch
3	tablespoons flour
	Peanut oil
5	tablespoons sugar
3	tablespoons white vinegar
2	tablespoons soy sauce
1	tablespoon dry vermouth or sake
1	tablespoon catsup

Coat fish with a batter made of the water, cornstarch and flour. Fry in hot peanut oil until crisp and golden brown, about 15 minutes. Remove to platter and keep warm. Combine sugar, vinegar, soy sauce, vermouth or sake, and catsup and heat until thickened, about 10-15 minutes. Pour over fish.

FESTIVE FISH

2   pounds fish fillets
½   cup bottled Italian
     salad dressing
1½   cups cheese crackers,
     crushed
2   tablespoons butter,
     melted
     Paprika

Preheat oven to 500°. Dip fillets in dressing and coat with cracker crumbs. Place on a well-greased cookie sheet; drizzle with butter and sprinkle with paprika. Bake at 500° 10-12 minutes.

FLOUNDER KIEV

½   cup butter, softened
1   tablespoon lemon
     juice
2   tablespoons parsley,
     minced
1   clove garlic, minced
1   teaspoon Worcester-
     shire sauce
¼   teaspoon hot pepper
     sauce
2   pounds flounder fillets
1   egg, beaten
1   tablespoon water
¼   cup flour
1½   cups bread or cracker
     crumbs
     Safflower oil

Mix together butter, lemon juice, parsley, garlic and 2 sauces and chill well. When hardened cut into 12 pieces. Cut flounder into 12 2" x 5" strips. Place a section of the hard butter in the middle of each fish strip and roll fish around butter. Secure with a toothpick. Beat egg with water. Roll fillet in flour, then in egg mixture and finally in bread crumbs. Chill. Fry in hot oil 5 minutes or until fish flakes easily. Drain on paper towels and serve hot. Can be made early and chilled until just before frying.

FLOUNDER SUPREME

1   4-ounce can mush-
     rooms, sliced
6   flounder fillets
     Seasoned salt
6   slices Swiss cheese,
     folded in half
1   tomato, cut in 6 slices
2   onions, sliced
2   tablespoons butter,
     melted
1½   tablespoons flour
1½   teaspoons seasoned
     salt
1   cup half-and-half
½   cup dry sherry
     Hot cooked rice

Preheat oven to 400°. Drain mushrooms, reserving liquid. Add enough water to make ½ cup; set aside. Sprinkle fillets on all sides with seasoned salt. Place a cheese slice and a tomato slice on each fillet. Starting at wide end, roll up each fillet. Place seam side down in greased 13" x 9" x 2" dish. Set aside. Saute' onions and mushrooms in butter until golden. Stir in flour, seasoned salt, half-and-half, mushroom liquid and sherry. Bring to a boil and pour over fish. Bake at 400° 20 minutes or until fish flakes easily. Serve with cooked rice.

GRILLED OR BROILED SALMON

6-8 servings

8   **fresh salmon steaks or one very large boned fillet**
⅔   **cup salad oil**
⅔   **cup soy sauce**
⅔   **cup bourbon**
1   **stick butter, melted**
     Juice of one lemon
1   **lemon, sliced**

Rinse fish and dry with paper towel. Mix oil, soy sauce, bourbon and pour into shallow pan. Place fish in mixture, refrigerate 2 hours, turning once. Remove fish from marinade and grill or broil 5-10 minutes. Fish should just barely flake and be lightly pink. Do not overcook. Remove to platter and top with some of the melted butter and lemon juice. Garnish with lemon slices. Pass additional butter.

SIMPLE SALMON PIES

4-6 servings

3   **slices bread**
1   **16-ounce can salmon, flaked and drained, liquid reserved**
1   **egg**
1   **medium onion, cut into eighths**
2   **tablespoons flour**
2   **tablespoons lemon juice**
¼   **teaspoon salt**
     Dash pepper
2   **sprigs parsley**
1   **teaspoon Worcestershire sauce**

Crumb bread in blender. Place salmon in large bowl. In blender or food processor place reserved salmon liquid, egg, onion, flour, lemon juice, salt, pepper, parsley and Worcestershire sauce. Cover and process until onion and parsley are grated fine. Pour over salmon, stir in bread crumbs and mix well. Form salmon mixture into 12 patties. Melt butter and saute' patties on a moderately hot (325°) griddle until well browned. Serve with cocktail sauce or catsup.

Also good served on toasted English muffin halves topped with Hollandaise sauce.

SMOKED SALMON TART

6-8 servings

1   **unbaked 9″ pastry shell**
1   **egg white, lightly beaten**
½   **pound smoked salmon, chopped**
1   **cup grated Swiss cheese**
4   **eggs**
1¼   **cups heavy cream**
1   **tablespoon dill**
½   **teaspoon salt**
¼   **teaspoon pepper**
     Red caviar for garnish, optional

Preheat oven to 450°. Brush pastry with egg white. Distribute salmon over bottom of pastry and sprinkle with cheese. Beat all remaining ingredients together except garnish and pour over cheese. Bake 15 minutes. Reduce oven temperature to 350° and continue baking until top is golden, about 15 minutes. Garnish with caviar.

Serve with a salad of icy cold greens and chilled white grapes with an oil and lemon dressing, a rich chocolate dessert and champagne.

SALMON IN PASTRY

6 servings

1	pound salmon, cooked and flaked or
1	15-ounce can salmon
1	teaspoon basil
1	tablespoon chopped parsley
3	green onions, chopped
¼	cup mayonnaise
	Salt and pepper to taste
1	package frozen patty shells, thawed (6 shells)
6	tablespoons Parmesan cheese
1	egg
1	tablespoon cream

Preheat oven to 400°. Combine salmon, basil, parsley, green onion, salt, pepper and mayonnaise. Taste and correct seasoning. Roll out each patty shell into a rectangle. Sprinkle 1 tablespoon grated Parmesan cheese on each rectangle. Divide salmon mixture evenly among the 6 shells. Bring sides together to make a rectangular package, tucking in ends. Brush each package with an egg wash made by combining the egg and cream. Bake 20 minutes or until pastry is golden brown.

A dill sauce would be very nice served with this.

SALMON EN CROUSTADE

6 servings

1	small loaf bread, unsliced
2	tablespoons melted butter
1½	cups soft bread crumbs
	Liquid from 15½-ounce can salmon
⅓	cup evaporated milk
1	teaspoon dry mustard
½	teaspoon salt
¼	teaspoon pepper
2	cups canned salmon drained, skinned and boned
2	hard-boiled eggs
3	tablespoons chopped parsley

Slice crusts from sides and ends of loaf. Slice off top. Take out center of loaf leaving ½" on sides and bottom. Bake at 350° 15 minutes. Remove loaf from oven and brush sides and bottom with butter. Bake again at 425° until lightly browned. Remove and cool. Combine crumbs, juice, milk and seasonings. Fill crust with alternating layers of salmon, chopped eggs, parsley and milk mixture. Place on cookie sheet and bake 30 minutes at 425°.

POACHED SOLE IN AVOCADO POCKETS 4 servings

1	cup white wine
½	cup water
2	teaspoons lemon juice
1	pound sole fillets
2	very soft avocados, pitted, peeled and mashed
2	egg yolks
1	tablespoon wine vinegar
1	tablespoon lemon juice
½	teaspoon dry dill
2	teaspoons parsley
1	teaspoon Dijon style mustard
	Salt
	Freshly ground pepper
2	avocados, cut lengthwise, pitted

Combine wine, water and lemon juice and heat to a boil; reduce heat to low. Roll up sole and secure with toothpicks. Poach fish in wine mixture, covered, for 5-7 minutes until opaque. Drain fillets; keep warm or refrigerate, covered. Puree remaining ingredients except avocado halves in a blender. Place fillets in each avocado pocket; serve with sauce.

Wonderful on warm summer's day, especially when served cold.

SOLE IN CRANBERRY-SHERRY SAUCE 6 servings

1	cup fresh cranberries
½	cup water
1	tablespoon sugar
4	tablespoons butter
½	pound fresh mushrooms, chopped
2	green onions, chopped
1	tablespoon parsley
1½	pounds fillet of sole
	Salt
	Freshly ground pepper
1	cup sweet light sherry
¼	cup clam broth
¼	cup water
¼	teaspoon tarragon
1	cup heavy cream
3	tablespoons pistachios, chopped

Combine cranberries, water and sugar and heat to boiling. Reduce heat and simmer 10 minutes. Cool and puree in blender. Melt 2 tablespoons butter, add mushrooms and green onions and cook about 3 minutes. Add parsley and saute 3 more minutes. Cool. Sprinkle sole with salt and pepper. Mix cranberry puree with mushroom mixture; spread evenly over fillets. Roll up and secure with toothpicks. Melt remaining butter and arrange fillets in skillet. Add wine, clam broth and water. Heat to simmer. Poach fish, covered, about 10 minutes. Remove to a warm serving plate. Heat poaching liquid to a boil; add tarragon. Cook until liquid is reduced by half, about 5 minutes. Add cream. Cook again 5 minutes to reduce sauce further. Spoon sauce over fish rolls. Sprinkle with nuts.

Serve with a red cabbage slaw, crisp green vegetable and rice.

CHINESE STEAMED TROUT

2-4 servings

About 1 pound trout
1 clove garlic, sliced
2 slices fresh ginger, slivered
2 green onions, cut into 2" strips
2 tablespoons salted black beans
1 tablespoon pale dry sherry
1 teaspoon oil
1 teaspoon corn starch

DIPPING SAUCE:

2 tablespoons soy sauce
¼ teaspoon sugar
1 teaspoon sesame oil

Clean fish, leaving head and tail on, and dry with paper towels. Cut 3-4 slashes diagonally on each side of the fish's body. Place some of the garlic, ginger and onions in each of the slashes on the fish. Distribute the black beans evenly inside the body cavity of the fish. Stir together sherry, oil and corn starch. Rub outside of fish with this mixture. Place fish on a damp cloth, put in steamer and steam for 20 minutes. While fish is steaming, combine sauce ingredients. Serve fish immediately with dipping sauce.

ROCKY MOUNTAIN FRIED TROUT

4 servings

4 10-ounce trout, cleaned but with heads and tails left on
2 teaspoons salt
Freshly ground black pepper
1 cup unsifted flour
1 cup yellow cornmeal
2 eggs
1 cup salad oil
8 tablespoons butter, cut into bits
¼ cup fresh lime juice
2 tablespoons finely chopped fresh chives
2 tablespoons finely chopped fresh parsley

Wash the trout under cold running water; pat them dry and season inside and out with salt and pepper. Spread the flour on one piece of wax paper and the cornmeal on a separate piece; break the eggs into a shallow bowl and beat them with a fork. In a 12" skillet, heat the oil over moderate heat until a light haze forms above it. Roll each trout in the flour, immerse it in the egg and then turn it in the cornmeal to coat it evenly. Fry the trout in the hot oil, two at a time, 4-5 minutes on each side, or until they are golden brown. Drain the trout on paper towels, then place them on a heated platter. Melt the butter in a separate skillet. Remove the pan from the heat, stir in remaining ingredients and taste for seasoning. Pour over the trout and serve at once.

BACON STUFFED TROUT

8 servings

2 eggs
1 tablespoon milk
1 teaspoon dried parsley
flakes
1 clove garlic, crushed
½ teaspoon allspice
8 cleaned trout
16 strips bacon, cooked
Lemon wedges

Beat together eggs, milk, parsley, garlic and allspice. Coat fish inside and out with mixture. Put 2 slices of bacon in each trout and place in a greased wire broil basket or on a greased grill. Cook over hot coals 15-20 minutes, turning once. Serve with lemon wedges.

QUICK AND EASY CIOPPINO

6 servings

2 tablespoons salad oil
1 large onion, chopped
1 16-ounce can spaghetti sauce
1½ cups white wine
1 16-ounce package frozen perch, sole or flounder, cubed
1 teaspoon salt
16 ounces shrimp, shelled and deveined
2 8-ounce cans whole baby clams, undrained
1 teaspoon parsley
1 teaspoon dill weed

Heat oil in Dutch oven and cook onion until soft. Stir in spaghetti sauce and wine. Add cubed fish and salt; cover and cook 20 minutes. Add shrimp and clams with broth. Bring soup up to a boil; reduce heat to a simmer and cook 5 minutes longer. Add parsley and dill weed and serve hot.

SCALLOP CEVICHE

6-8 servings

1½ pounds raw scallops, cut into bite-size pieces
⅔ cup fresh lime juice
2 ripe tomatoes, finely chopped
½ cup chopped onion
¼ cup olive oil
1 tablespoon chopped parsley
2 teaspoons finely chopped jalapeno peppers
1 teaspoon salt
¼ teaspoon oregano
⅛ teaspoon pepper

Put scallops in a glass bowl and add lime juice. Be sure all scallops are immersed; cover. Refrigerate at least 6 hours or overnight, stirring occasionally. Up to 3 hours before serving, add remaining ingredients. Cover and refrigerate until serving. Drain off and discard excess liquid before serving.

A surpassingly refreshing first course.

SCALLOPS À LA AVOCADO

4 servings

12	ounces fresh or frozen scallops
2	medium avocados
	Lemon juice
¼	cup onion, chopped
2	tablespoons butter or margarine
2	tablespoons all-purpose flour
1	cup half-and-half
2	tablespoons parsley
¼	teaspoon salt
	Dash white pepper
	Dash garlic powder
1	slightly beaten egg
2-3	cups hot cooked rice

Thaw scallops, if frozen. Halve avocados lengthwise; remove seeds and peel halves. Brush avocados with lemon juice; set aside. Poach scallops in enough water to cover till tender, about 5 minutes; drain. In 1-quart saucepan, cook onion in butter or margarine till tender but not brown, about 5 minutes. Blend in flour. Stir in half-and-half. Cook and stir till mixture thickens and bubbles; about 5 minutes. Add scallops, parsley, salt, white pepper and garlic powder. Gradually stir about half of the hot mixture into the egg. Return all to hot mixture. Cook and stir till mixture bubbles again. Cook and stir 1-2 minutes more. Spoon rice onto serving platter. Place avocado halves, hollow side up, atop hot cooked rice; spoon scallop sauce over avocados.

SPICY SUCCULENT SHRIMP

6-8 servings

2	pounds large uncooked, unpeeled shrimp, slit down the back
½	cup butter
3	tablespoons oil
2	tablespoons chili sauce
1	tablespoon Worcestershire sauce
1	tablespoon lemon juice
½	lemon, thinly sliced
1	teaspoon parsley
½-¾	teaspoon ground red pepper
¾	teaspoon liquid smoke
½	teaspoon paprika
½	teaspoon dried oregano
¼	teaspoon hot pepper sauce
	French bread cut in cubes

Wash shrimp. Dry well and spread in shallow pan. Combine remaining ingredients except bread in a small pot and simmer 10 minutes. Pour over shrimp and mix thoroughly. Cover and refrigerate 2-3 hours, stirring every 30 minutes. Preheat oven to 300°. Bake shrimp in shallow baking dish until they turn pink, about 15 minutes. Adjust seasonings to taste. Serve in soup bowls with chunks of French bread.

SHRIMP ARIOSTO WITH CHICKEN

6-8 servings

3 cups cooked chicken
½ cup butter
1 pound shrimp, cooked
½ head cabbage, shredded
1 onion, sliced and separated into rings
2 10¾ ounce cans condensed cream of chicken soup
1 2-ounce jar pimiento, diced and undrained
1 teaspoon soy sauce
¼ teaspoon garlic powder
2 drops liquid smoke
Salt and pepper
¼ cup dry white wine
Lettuce
Tomatoes, chopped
½ cup salted peanuts, chopped

Flake chicken with a fork. Melt butter in a Dutch oven and add chicken, shrimp, cabbage and onion. Cook until onion is tender. Stir soup, pimiento, soy sauce, garlic and liquid smoke into meat mixture. Season to taste with salt and pepper. Simmer 15 minutes, then stir in wine and cook 2 more minutes over low heat. Remove from heat. Serve chicken mixture on lettuce leaves and garnish with chopped tomatoes and peanuts.

A modern version of a traditional dish.

SHRIMP AND ARTICHOKE HEARTS CASSEROLE

4 servings

1 10-ounce package frozen artichoke hearts, thawed
1 pound shrimp, cooked
½ pound fresh mushrooms, sliced and sauteed in 2 tablespoons butter
4 tablespoons butter
2½ tablespoons flour
½ teaspoon salt
¼ teaspoon pepper
⅛ teaspoon cayenne pepper
1½ cups half-and-half
1 tablespoon Worcestershire sauce
¼ cup dry sherry
½ cup Parmesan cheese
1 teaspoon paprika

Preheat oven to 375°. Arrange artichoke hearts in buttered 11" x 7" casserole. Cover with shrimp. Top with sliced sauteed mushrooms. Make cream sauce: melt butter in saucepan; stir in flour, salt, pepper and cayenne. Remove from heat and gradually stir in half-and-half. Return to low heat and cook until thick. Add sherry and Worcestershire sauce. Pour over shrimp. Sprinkle with Parmesan, then with paprika. Bake 20-30 minutes at 375° until hot and bubbling.

Good with saffron rice (white rice cooked with ¼ teaspoon saffron) and a salad.

INDONESIAN SHRIMP

4 servings

2   cloves garlic, minced
1   cup onion, chopped
1   tablespoon oil
2/3   cup peanut butter
1   cup water
1   teaspoon coriander
      seeds, crushed
1/8   teaspoon crushed red
      chili
1   teaspoon salt
1½   pounds shrimp
      Hot cooked rice

In a large skillet, saute' garlic and onion in oil until tender. Stir in peanut butter and gradually blend in water, coriander seeds, chilies and salt. Heat to boiling, stirring constantly. Add shrimp and cook 6-8 minutes or until shrimp is done. Stir occasionally. Serve hot over rice.

SHRIMP IN GREEN CHEESE SAUCE

6 servings

1   pound cooked medium
      shrimp, peeled and
      chilled
1   small avocado
1   3-ounce package
      softened cream
      cheese
      Dash of tequila
      Salt and pepper to
      taste
1   teaspoon lime juice
1   tablespoon minced
      parsley

Arrange shrimp on serving dish. Peel and mash avocado and blend with cream cheese, tequila, salt, pepper and lime juice. Serve sauce over shrimp or on the side. Garnish with parsley. May substitute crabmeat or scallops.

LAND-LOCKED SEAFOOD CASSEROLE

8 servings

1½   cups chopped celery
1   chopped green pepper
1   chopped medium
      white onion
¼   cup butter
¼   cup chopped pimiento
2   10½-ounce cans con-
      densed cream of
      mushroom soup
1   cup shrimp
1   cup flaked crabmeat
1   6-ounce package long
      grain and wild rice,
      prepared as label
      directs

Saute' celery, pepper and onion in butter. Add all other ingredients. Place mixture in buttered 9" x 13" baking dish. Bake at 350° for 1 hour.

🐦 SOUTHWESTERN CLAM STROGANOFF   4-6 servings

½   cup butter
1   tablespoon cooking oil
4   cloves garlic, crushed
1   tablespoon Wor-
     cestershire sauce
2   teaspoons seasoned
     salt
     Pepper to taste
2   tablespoons instant
     minced onion
2   cups chopped parsley
1   pound mushrooms,
     sliced
6-7 tablespoons canned
     diced green chilies
3   6½-ounce cans chop-
     ped clams, drained
1   cup sour cream
     Hot cooked rice or
     spaghetti

Heat butter and oil in skillet. Add garlic, Worcestershire sauce, seasoned salt, pepper and onion. Saute about 3 minutes. Stir in parsley, mushrooms and chilies. Saute 20 minutes longer. Add clams and mix well. Cover and simmer 30 minutes; stir in sour cream. Remove from heat and let stand, covered, for 5 minutes. Serve over hot cooked rice or spaghetti.

An intriguing combination of ingredients!

STIR-FRY LOBSTER IN OYSTER SAUCE   4 servings

4   large dried mushrooms
2   tablespoons peanut oil
2   garlic cloves
3   small zucchini, sliced
     very thin
1   pound lobster meat,
     cooked and cut in
     chunks
1   8-ounce can water
     chestnuts, drained and
     chopped
3   tablespoons oyster
     sauce
1   teaspoon sesame
     sauce

Place mushrooms in bowl; cover with hot water. Let stand until softened, about 25 minutes. Drain well. Cut mushrooms into quarters. Heat oil in wok; add garlic. Stir-fry until golden. Add zucchini and cook until crisp, about 2 minutes. Add lobster, water chestnuts and mushrooms and cook 2 more minutes. Add oyster sauce and sesame oil. Stir. Transfer to platter and serve with rice.

BAKED DOVE

15   doves
1   10½-ounce can con-
     densed cream of
     mushroom soup
1   envelope dry onion
     soup mix
¼   cup chopped celery
1   cup dry vermouth
1   cup water
     Pinch Italian season-
     ing

Preheat oven to 350°. Place doves in 2 quart casserole. Combine remaining ingredients and pour over the doves. Cover and bake for 2 to 3 hours, turning and basting the birds frequently.

BRANDIED DUCK BREASTS

½   cup butter
⅓   cup brandy
⅓   cup white wine
4   tablespoons current
     jelly
1   tablespoon Worcester-
     shire sauce
4   wild duck breasts,
     halved
3   cups cooked wild rice
     (1 cup uncooked)
2   teaspoons cornstarch
2   tablespoons water

In skillet with a lid, melt butter; stir in brandy, wine, jelly and Worcestershire. Bring mixture to a boil, stirring to dissolve jelly. Add duck breasts. Cover and reduce heat to low. Simmer breasts 20-30 minutes or until fork tender, turning once. Place wild rice on serving platter, top with duck breasts; cover and keep warm. Blend cornstarch and water until smooth. Combine with brandy liquid in skillet. Stir and cook over low heat until sauce thickens. Spoon sauce over duck and rice.

QUAIL IN WINE SAUCE

12   quails
     Salt
     Pepper
     Pinch of garlic salt
     Italian seasoning
     Flour
     Bacon drippings and/or
     shortening
2   10½-ounce cans con-
     densed cream of
     mushroom soup
2   soup cans sherry

Clean quails, season with salt, pepper, garlic salt and Italian seasoning. Roll quails in flour and quickly brown in bacon drippings. Place 6 quails in each of 2 2-quart casseroles and add mixture of 1 can cream of mushroom soup and 1 soup can sherry to each casserole. Cover each casserole and bake at 325° for 1 hour or until quail are tender. Serve with rice or potatoes.

BARBECUE VENISON

15-20 servings

1	3-pound venison roast
1	large onion, chopped
1½	cups celery, chopped
2	tablespoons vinegar
2	tablespoons brown sugar
1	cup catsup
3	tablespoons Worcestershire sauce
1	teaspoon chili powder
1½	cups water
4	tablespoons lemon juice
1	teaspoon liquid smoke (optional)
	Salt and pepper to taste
2	pinches oregano
2	bay leaves
2	garlic cloves, crushed

Place meat in roaster. Mix remaining ingredients and pour over meat. Bake, tightly covered, at 275° for 5-6 hours or until meat will shred. Serve on toasted, buttered buns.

Freezes well.

VENISON PARMIGIANA

5-6 servings

1½	pounds venison steak, sliced 3/8″ thick
1	egg, beaten
⅓	cup grated Parmesan cheese
⅓	cup fine dry bread crumbs
⅓	cup cooking oil
⅓	medium onion, minced
1	teaspoon salt
¼	teaspoon pepper
½	teaspoon sugar
½	teaspoon marjoram
1	6-ounce can tomato paste
2	cups hot water
½	pound mozzarella cheese

Place meat between pieces of wax paper larger than the meat and lay on a board. Pound meat thin with a mallet. Trim off gristle and excess fat; cut into 6-8 pieces. Dip meat in egg; roll in mixture of Parmesan cheese and crumbs. Heat cooking oil in larger skillet. Brown steak on both sides until golden brown. Lay meat in shallow baking dish. In same skillet cook onion over low heat until soft. Stir in salt, pepper, sugar, marjoram, tomato paste, and gradually add hot water, stirring constantly. Boil 5 minutes, scraping browned bits from pan. Pour all but 1 cup sauce over meat. Top with mozzarella cheese slices and remaining sauce. Bake in 350° oven about 1 hour or until tender.

The Main Attraction.....

Albuquerque's "heart" dates back to 1706 when Cuervo y Valdes, territorial governor, established a colony called Villa de Albuquerque near the present Old Town Plaza. Made up of 30 families, the colony was centered about the thick adobe walls of San Felipe de Neri Church. Built almost three centuries ago, it still stands on the north side of the Plaza, an enduring reminder of Albuquerque's proud past. The color and excitement of Old Town are perpetuated by the mariachi bands that often play in the small bandstand, by gay fiestas and by the tourists that come from all over the world to enjoy the area's native restaurants, art galleries and intriguing little shops. The four flags that flew over Old Town -- the Spanish, Mexican, Confederate and United States -- lend drama and meaning to the atmosphere of Old Town Plaza and its surroundings ⁕

Meats

ZIA STORAGE JAR

MANDARIN BEEF FILLET

6-8 servings

4   pounds beef fillet, tied
¾   cup dry sherry
½   cup soy sauce
5   cloves crushed garlic
4   minced green onions
½   cup hoisin sauce
½   teaspoon sesame oil
⅛   teaspoon five spice
     powder
     Snow peas

Place meat in shallow glass dish. In a bowl mix remaining ingredients except peas. Pour over meat; let beef marinate, loosely covered, at least 8 hours or overnight. Turn often. Place beef on rack in roasting pan, reserving marinade. Roast in a 425° oven basting with marinade every 5 minutes for 30 minutes for rare meat or longer for more well done. Transfer meat to platter and let stand, covered, 10 minutes. Garnish with crisp-cooked snow peas.

STEAK CARAVELLE

4-6 servings

3   pounds sirloin steak,
     1½-2 inches thick
¼   teaspoon garlic
     powder
½   cup red wine
½   cup vegetable oil
⅓   cup frozen orange
     juice concentrate,
     thawed
¼   teaspoon ground
     ginger
⅓   cup soy sauce

Rub steak with garlic powder. Generously pierce steak with a fork. Combine wine, oil, soy sauce, orange juice and ground ginger. Pour over steak in a shallow dish. Cover and marinate overnight in refrigerator, turning occasionally. Broil about 6 inches from broiler unit or hot coals 10 to 12 minutes per side for rare doneness. Thinly slice across grain to serve.

VENEZUELAN STEAK

4-6 servings

3   pounds top round
     steak, cut 1½ inches
     thick
1½   teaspoons unseasoned
     meat tenderizer
1   large bell pepper
     Boiling salted water
4   slices bacon, cut in
     half
¼   cup butter
½   cup brown sugar
⅓   cup vinegar
1   teaspoon salt
2   bay leaves
2   8-ounce cans tomato
     sauce

Have pocket cut in steak. Sprinkle with tenderizer. Trim and seed bell pepper, cut in strips and cook 5 minutes in boiling salted water; reserve. Cook bacon until limp; drain off drippings and reserve. Stuff steak with bacon and peppers; skewer pocket shut. Brown steak in reserved bacon drippings. In another pan melt butter; add brown sugar and stir until it bubbles. Add vinegar, salt, bay leaves and tomato sauce and mix well. Preheat oven to 325°. Place steak in a 9" x 13" baking dish and pour sauce over meat. Bake for 1¾ hours or until meat is tender. Slice across grain to serve.

POT ROAST CARIBE

3	pound beef chuck roast
2	tablespoons cooking oil
2	cloves garlic, crushed
1	cup chopped onion
1	teaspoon salt
1	15-ounce can tomato sauce
1	4-ounce can chopped green chilies
2	tablespoons sugar
1	tablespoon chili powder
1	tablespoon cocoa
1	teaspoon ground cumin
1	teaspoon ground coriander
¼	teaspoon cinnamon
1	teaspoon dried oregano
1	tablespoon flour
1	teaspoon grated orange rind
½	cup ground almonds
8	small onions, peeled
3	medium yellow crookneck squash, cut into 1½" chunks
¼	cup slivered almonds, lightly toasted
	Parsley and cherry tomatoes for garnish

In a large Dutch oven brown chuck roast in hot cooking oil on all sides. Remove roast and in same oil cook garlic and chopped onions about 5 minutes or until onions are lightly browned. Stir in salt, tomato sauce and chilies. In a small bowl combine sugar, cocoa, chili powder, cumin, coriander, cinnamon, oregano and flour. Stir into the tomato mixture in the pan along with the orange rind and ground almonds. Mix well. Return roast to pan and cook, tightly covered, over low heat for 2 hours or until meat is tender. Add vegetables to sauce around meat; cover and continue to cook about ½ hour or until vegetables are fork tender. To serve, place meat in center of platter; spoon sauce over. Arrange vegetables around the roast and sprinkle with toasted almonds. Garnish with parsley and cherry tomatoes.

A prize-winning recipe that's a take-off on traditional Mexican mole sauces.

MARINATED FLANK STEAK

2	tablespoons soy sauce
1	tablespoon tomato paste
1	tablespoon vegetable oil
1	clove garlic, minced
1	teaspoon salt
½	teaspoon pepper
½	teaspoon oregano
1	1-1½ pound flank steak

Combine the soy sauce, tomato paste, oil, garlic, salt, pepper and oregano and spread on both sides of steak which has been placed in shallow glass bowl. Marinate in refrigerater overnight, turning occasionally. Broil 5 minutes on each side or to desired degree of doneness. Slice thin, cutting diagonally.

BAKED STUFFED FLANK STEAK

4-6 servings

2 pounds flank
steak
¼ cup vinegar
¼ cup oil
1 tablespoon Worcester-
shire sauce
½ teaspoon salt
¼ teaspoon pepper
¼ pound ground ham
½ cup whole wheat
bread crumbs
1 small egg
1 tablespoon oats or
wheat germ (optional)
¼ cup chopped dill
pickles
1 cup chopped green
olives
1 tablespoon raisins
½ teaspoon dill weed,
basil or oregano
Dash salt
1 beef bouillon cube
dissolved in 1 cup hot
water
½ cup red wine
Dash salt and pepper
½ small onion, chopped

Pound flank steak, marinate in vinegar, oil, Worcestershire sauce, ½ teaspoon salt and ¼ teaspoon pepper overnight or all day, turning occasionally. Combine stuffing ingredients: ground ham, crumbs, egg, pickles, olives, raisins and seasonings. Spread on drained steak. Roll steak as for jelly roll, tie with string or fasten with toothpicks. Place in a small roaster. Add bouillon, wine, dash salt and pepper and chopped onion. Bake at 400° for 30 minutes, covered. Slice and serve with sauce from pan.

STUFFED FLANK STEAKS

6-8 servings

2 flank steaks, with
pockets cut in them
¼ cup salad oil
¼ cup soy sauce
½ cup red wine
¼ teaspoon nutmeg
6 tablespoons butter
1½ cups chopped green
pepper
1 cup chopped celery
2 onions, chopped
2 cups bread crumbs
3 tablespoons sweet
pickle relish
½ cup slivered almonds
1 teaspoon salt
½ teaspoon pepper

Marinate steaks for several hours in a marinade made with salad oil, soy sauce, wine and nutmeg. In butter saute' green pepper, celery and onions until tender. Add bread crumbs, relish, almonds, salt and pepper. Mix stuffing well together. Spoon into steak pockets. Secure with skewers. Grill over hot coals 25 minutes. To serve cut on a slant.

FRICO: A MEAT STEW

6-8 servings

1	pound boneless chuck roast cut into 1" cubes
1	pound pork cut into 1" cubes
½	cup oil
	Salt and pepper to taste
1	teaspoon paprika
1	cup hot beef bouillon
1	bay leaf
3	onions, thinly sliced
6	large potatoes, thinly sliced
1	cup sour cream
1	tablespoon butter

Preheat oven to 375°. Brown meat in ¼ cup oil. Season with salt, pepper and paprika and stir until browned. Add bouillon and bay leaf and simmer covered for 20 minutes. Saute onion slices in remaining oil until golden. In a buttered casserole layer the meat cubes and onion and potato slices. End with layer of potato slices. Pour ¾ cup sour cream on top, dot with butter, cover and bake 1 hour. Uncover and bake 10-15 minutes. Mix remaining sour cream and pour over frico.

Serve with pickled beet salad, garlic bread and beer.

SANGRE DE CRISTO STEWPOT

8 servings

2	pounds beef stew meat, cut in 1½" cubes
4	cups water
2	beef bouillon cubes
½	cup celery, coarsely chopped
½	cup onion, coarsely chopped
2	cloves garlic, minced
1	tablespoon oregano
2	teaspoons ground cumin
1	bay leaf
1½	teaspoons salt
5	carrots, cut in chunks
4	ears of corn, cut in 2" pieces
1	15-ounce can garbanzo beans, undrained
8	cabbage wedges
1	16-ounce can tomatoes
½	cup onion, finely chopped
1	4-ounce can chopped green chilies
1	clove garlic, minced
½	cup parsley, minced
½	teaspoon salt

Combine first 9 ingredients in a large Dutch oven and simmer, covered, 2 hours or until meat is tender. Stir in salt, carrots, corn, garbanzo beans and gently lay the cabbage on top. Cover and simmer 30 minutes. To make salsa, combine the last 6 ingredients and mix well. Serve stew in bowls and pass salsa with it.

BEEF WITH CAULIFLOWER AND BROCCOLI

3-4 servings

1 tablespoon soy sauce
1 tablespoon sake or dry vermouth
1 teaspoon sugar
2 slices fresh ginger
⅓ pound beef, cut in bite-size strips
  Cooking oil
½ teaspoon salt
½ pound cauliflower, cut in bite-size pieces
½ pound broccoli, cut in bite-size pieces

Make a sauce of soy sauce, sake, sugar and ginger; stir and set aside. Saute' beef in 1½ tablespoons oil until done in wok or large skillet. Remove beef and add enough oil to make 1½ tablespoons. Add salt and vegetables; cook 3-5 minutes. Add meat and sauce, stir and warm 1-2 minutes. Serve immediately.

BEEF CURRY BARON OF BEEF

4-6 servings

2 pounds top round beef, cut into ¾" cubes
  Water
  Dash cinnamon
¼ cup cooking oil
3 cloves garlic, minced
¾" square piece of fresh ginger, minced
2 medium onions, cut in ¾" discs
2-3 heaping tablespoons curry powder
  Ground red chili to taste
  Dash cinnamon
¼ teaspoon sugar
1 grinding of pepper
½ cup white wine or ¾ bottle of beer
1 green pepper, cut in ¾" squares
2 carrots, thinly sliced
  Raisins
  Salt
6 tablespoons coconut milk
  Cooked rice
  Condiments

Cover beef with water, add a dash of cinnamon and bring to a boil. Skim off foam as it forms and boil gently 5 minutes. Drain, reserving 1½ cups of the liquid. In a large frying pan heat ¼ cup cooking oil. When quite hot add cloves of garlic and ginger. Saute briefly then add meat. As meat begins to brown add onions. When onions become soft add curry powder, chili, cinnamon, sugar and pepper. Mix until all meat is well coated with the spices. DO NOT BURN! Add white wine or beer and enough of the reserved liquid to almost cover meat. Simmer slowly until meat is tender. More liquid may be added if necessary. Then add green pepper, carrots, a small handful of raisins and salt to taste. Continue to simmer until vegetables are cooked. Just before serving add coconut milk. Serve with rice and side dishes of chopped nuts, onions, yogurt, small chilies, chutney and the like.

🐦 STEW VAQUERO

3	pounds beef stew meat, cut in ½" cubes
2	tablespoons olive oil
4	bay leaves
3	teaspoons salt
2	teaspoons pepper
2	teaspoons garlic salt
2	tablespoons sugar
2	tablespoons dried parsley flakes
1	10-ounce can beef bouillon
1	medium onion, chopped
10	small green onions, chopped
1	celery stalk, chopped
1	14½-ounce can tomatoes, chopped and undrained
3	medium potatoes, peeled and cubed
3	large carrots, sliced
5	tablespoons Worcestershire sauce
8	cloves garlic, peeled and minced
1	15-ounce can pinto beans with chili sauce
8	mushrooms, sliced Chili powder to taste (2-4 teaspoons)

Place all ingredients in a 5-quart crockery slow-cooker and pour water over all to fill the container. Cover and cook 8-10 hours on medium heat. (If cooked on top of the stove, use covered stew pot and cook 6-8 hours on low heat, then 1-2 hours on medium heat before serving.)

BEEF TERIYAKI

4 servings

1½	pounds sirloin cut into ½" x 1" strips
1	cup cooking oil
½	cup honey
½	cup soy sauce
1	tablespoon Worcestershire sauce
1	teaspoon ginger
½	teaspoon monsodium glutamate

Combine all ingredients except meat and mix in blender or processer. Pour over meat and refrigerate for 24 hours, stirring once or twice. Place meat on skewers and cook over charcoal or a portable broiler to desired doneness.

BEEF JARDINIERE CREPES

4 servings

½ cup onion, chopped
½ cup celery, chopped
2 tablespoons vegetable oil
2 10-ounce cans condensed beef broth
¾ cup carrots, chopped
½ teaspoon basil leaves
½ teaspoon sage
½ teaspoon salt
Pepper to taste
8 crepes
2 tablespoons flour
¼ cup water
1 pound cooked beef, cut in strips
Wine sauce (below)

Cook onion and celery in vegetable oil in large skillet. Add broth, carrots, basil, sage, salt and pepper, stirring to combine. Cover and cook 15 minutes. Prepare crepes. Pour off 1½ cups cooking liquid; reserve. Combine flour and water; add to remaining cooking liquid and vegetables; stir constantly until thickened. Add beef strips and heat through. Place ½ cup hot filling across center of each crepe, overlap opposite sides to enclose filling and place in 13" X 9" baking dish. Bake at 375° 15-20 minutes. Serve with wine sauce.

WINE SAUCE:

2 tablespoons flour
1 tablespoon catsup
1 tablespoon Burgundy wine
⅛ teaspoon garlic salt
Dash pepper
2 teaspoons minced parsley

To make wine sauce, combine flour with catsup in small saucepan. Add reserved 1½ cups broth, wine, garlic salt and pepper. Cook, stirring constantly 6-8 minutes. Stir in parsley. Serve with crepes.

CURRIED BEEF STEW WITH NECTARINES

6 servings

2½ pounds lean stewing beef cubes
½ cup bottled or canned taco sauce
1 cup water
½ cup red dinner wine
2 tablespoons chili sauce
1 tablespoon chili powder
2 tablespoons beef stock base
½ teaspoon salt
2 teaspoons curry powder
½ pound fresh mushrooms, sliced
3-5 fresh nectarines
Hot cooked rice

Trim off any excess fat from beef cubes. Combine beef with taco sauce, water, wine, chili sauce, chili powder, beef stock base, salt and curry powder in Dutch oven. Bring to boil and simmer, tightly covered for 2½ hours or until meat is tender. Meanwhile, slice enough nectarines to measure 3 cups. When beef is tender, stir in sliced mushrooms and nectarines; heat 5 minutes. If you prefer a thicker sauce, blend 1 tablespoon flour with 3 tablespoons water; stir into sauce and cook until it thickens. Other fresh fruit or drained canned fruit may be substituted for the nectarines. Serve over hot cooked rice.

ANTOINETTE'S STROGANOFF

6-8 servings

2 pounds boneless beef chuck, cut in 1" cubes
¼ cup flour
¼ cup oil
½ pound mushrooms, sliced
2 medium onions, thinly sliced
1 cup water
2 teaspoons salt
1 teaspoon pepper
¼ teaspoon marjoram
2 teaspoons dry mustard
1 teaspoon liquid gravy base
⅓ cup catsup
1 cup sour cream

Roll meat in flour and brown well in oil. Add all ingredients except sour cream, cover tightly and cook slowly at a simmer for 1½-2 hours. Just before serving add sour cream.

Wonderfully easy on the budget.

CHILI VERDE ROBERTO

6-8 servings

Salad oil
1½ pounds beef stew meat
1½ pounds cubed lean pork
3 cloves garlic, crushed
1 green bell pepper, seeded and chopped
2 29-ounce cans tomatoes
2 4-ounce cans chopped green chilies
½ cup chopped parsley
¼ teaspoon ground cloves
2 teaspoons ground cumin seed
¼ cup lemon juice
¾ cup beef broth
Salt to taste

In a large Dutch oven heat oil and brown beef and pork. Add garlic and green pepper and saute' until pepper is soft. Add tomatoes, breaking up with a spoon, and their liquid. Stir in remaining ingredients and cook, covered, over low heat for at least 2 hours, stirring occasionally. Remove cover and simmer for about 45 minutes or until mixture is thick. Serve as a thick soup with warm tortillas or use to smother burritos.

BEEF SATÉ

2	pounds beef sirloin
1	teaspoon caraway seeds
1	teaspoon ground coriander
1	teaspoon garlic powder
1	tablespoon brown sugar
	Salt to taste
¼	teaspoon pepper
2	tablespoons soy sauce
1	tablespoon lemon juice
2	tablespoons dehydrated onion flakes
1	tablespoon vegetable oil
¾	cup water
2	tablespoons lemon juice
¼	cup peanut butter
	Chili powder to taste
	Salt to taste

Cut steak into ¾ inch cubes. Marinate in a mixture of caraway seeds, ground coriander, garlic powder, brown sugar, salt and pepper, soy sauce and lemon juice. Refrigerate overnight. Drain and thread on skewers. Grill or broil 10 minutes, turning several times. Serve with peanut sauce. To make sauce, brown onion flakes in 350° oven until crisp and golden. Blend in vegetable oil, water, lemon juice, peanut butter, chili powder and salt and bring to a boil. Simmer 5 minutes. Sauce can be prepared in advance and reheated.

RANCHERS POT ROAST

1	3-4 pound brisket or bottom round beef
2	cloves garlic, cut into slivers
1	onion, thinly sliced
1	cup vinegar
3	tablespoons bacon drippings or oil
2	cups strong black coffee
2	cups water
1	pound carrots, peeled and quartered
12	small white onions
	Salt and freshly ground pepper

With a sharp knife make slits in the meat and insert the garlic. Place onion on top of meat. Place meat in bowl and pour vinegar over. Refrigerate 24 hours, turning meat several times. Drain and discard vinegar. Pat roast dry. Heat bacon drippings and brown meat well. Pour off excess oil and add coffee and water. Bring to a boil, cover and simmer 3 hours until very tender. One hour before the end of cooking add the carrots and small onions and season to taste with salt and pepper. If desired, the gravy may be thickened with 2 tablespoons flour mixed with ¼ cup cold water. Serve with rice or noodles.

MOM'S CORNED BEEF

4-6 servings

1   **4-5 pound corned beef brisket**
1   **medium onion, sliced**
1   **tablespoon mixed pickling spices**
4   **tablespoons prepared mustard**
2   **tablespoons brown sugar**
¼   **teaspoon nutmeg**
⅛   **teaspoon pepper**

In a kettle place corned beef brisket with onion and pickling spices. Cover with water and cook over low heat for 3 hours. Let stand until cool. Glaze meat with 2 tablespoons mustard. Mix together the other 2 tablespoons mustard, brown sugar, nutmeg and pepper; brush over corned beef. Bake at 350° for 1 hour, brushing with mustard and brown sugar mixture and turning every 15 minutes. Slice very thin against the grain.

BARBEQUE BRISKET

6-8 servings

4   **pound beef brisket, trimmed of all fat**
3   **tablespoons liquid smoke**
¾   **teaspoon garlic salt**
¾   **teaspoon onion salt**
1   **tablespoon celery seed**
3   **tablespoons Worcestershire sauce**
1   **cup bottled barbeque sauce**

Place brisket on heavy-duty foil and cover with liquid smoke, garlic salt, onion salt, celery seed and Worcestershire sauce. Seal and refrigerate overnight. Preheat oven to 300°. Open foil and add ¾ teaspoon salt and ¼ teaspoon pepper. Reseal and cook 3½ hours. Slice open foil and add 1 cup barbeque sauce and cook another hour; baste occasionally but do not reseal. Slice across grain to serve.

The leftovers are great, too!

ZIPPY BEEF BRISKET

6-8 servings

1   **5-pound brisket**
    Salt and pepper to taste
2   **onions, sliced thin**
1   **5-ounce jar prepared horseradish**
1   **10½-ounce can beef consomme**
1   **cup red wine**

Season meat with salt and pepper. Brown in a 350° oven for 30 minutes. Cover meat with onions. On top spread horseradish. Pour ½ can undiluted consomme over brisket. Cook, covered, at 300° for 4-5 hours. Add remaining consomme as needed. One-half hour before serving, add the wine. Skim grease off pan juices and serve meat sliced thin.

🐦 BEEF WITH SMOKY CHILI SAUCE   10-12 servings

4   pounds boneless beef chuck roast or brisket of beef
1   large onion, sliced
3   bay leaves
    Salt
¼   cup fresh coriander (cilantro or Chinese parsley), finely chopped
1   cup Monterey Jack cheese, cut in ½" cubes
2   cups tomatoes, cut in ½" cubes
1   8-ounce can garbanzos, drained and rinsed
2   limes, cut in wedges
    About 4 dozen butter lettuce cups or 1 dozen Arab pocket bread (halved) or warm flour tortillas
    About 2 cups guacamole (See Index)
1   cup sour cream

SMOKY CHILI SAUCE:

1   6½-7-ounce can pickled chipotle peppers, retain liquid
⅓   cup salad oil

ALTERNATE SAUCE:

1½ tablespoons brown sugar, packed
¼   cup vinegar
3   tablespoons chili powder
1   tablespoon catsup
1   teaspoon hickory-flavored salt
1   teaspoon sesame oil (optional)
½   teaspoon liquid smoke
½-¾ teaspoon cayenne

Trim off excess fat from meat. Place meat in a large piece of foil, cover with onion and bay leaves. Wrap in foil and place in a pan. Bake in a 350° oven until very tender, 2½-3 hours. Let cool; chill, if desired. Remove onions and bay leaves. Scrape off any fat. Tear meat with grain into match stick-size pieces, about 2" long. Drizzle ⅓ cup of the chili sauce over meat and toss with forks until all meat is coated. Cover and chill at least 2 hours or overnight. Taste meat; add salt and more chili sauce if desired. Sprinkle coriander and cheese over meat and toss with forks to mix. Arrange meat on platter. Sprinkle tomatoes and garbanzos over meat; garnish with lime wedges. To eat, spoon some of the meat mixture into lettuce cups, pocket bread or tortillas; top with guacamole, sour cream, extra chili sauce if desired and a squeeze of lime; then roll up lettuce or tortillas. To make Smoky Chili Sauce remove and discard stems from the chilies. Place chilies, including liquid, in blender or food processor along with salad oil; whirl until smooth. To make Alternate Chili Sauce combine all ingredients and mix well.

BAVARIAN MEAT LOAF

8-9 servings

1½ pounds lean ground
beef
½ pound ground pork
1 medium onion, finely
chopped
½ cup pumpernickel
bread crumbs
½ cup crushed
gingersnaps
2 eggs
3 tablespoons cider
vinegar
1½ teaspoons prepared
mustard
2 teaspoons salt

GLAZE:

¼ cup brown sugar
3 tablespoons cider
vinegar
3 tablespoons catsup
1 tablespoon prepared
mustard

Preheat oven to 375°. In a large bowl combine all ingredients except those for glaze; mix well. Pack mixture into a 9" x 5" loaf pan. Combine all of the glaze ingredients into a small bowl. Spoon glaze over the top of the meat loaf. Bake for 1 hour. Transfer to platter and serve.

DUTCH MEATLOAF

6-8 servings

1½ pounds ground beef
1 chopped onion
1 egg, beaten
1 cup fresh bread
crumbs
½ of 8-ounce can tomato
sauce
1½ teaspoons salt

TOPPING:

½ of 8-ounce can tomato
sauce
2 tablespoons mustard
2 tablespoons brown
sugar
1 cup water
2 tablespoons vinegar

Preheat oven to 350°. Lightly mix meatloaf ingredients, place in a 2-3 quart casserole and form into a loaf. Bake 15 minutes. To make topping, mix ingredients and pour over meatloaf. Bake an additional 1¼ hours, basting occasionally. Serve over a bed of noodles.

This is guaranteed to please meatloaf lovers and haters alike. It is extra juicy and also is delicious spooned over rice or potato dumplings.

🦃 MEATBALLS MOLE

6 servings

1	pound ground beef
1	egg, slightly beaten
¾	cup crushed corn chips
½	cup milk
2	teaspoons salt
2½	tablespoons flour
2	tablespoons butter
2	cups sliced onion
1	clove garlic, crushed
2	tablespoons sugar
1	tablespoon chili powder
1	teaspoon ground cumin
1	teaspoon ground coriander
1	teaspoon dried oregano leaves
1	19-ounce can tomatoes, undrained
1	square unsweetened chocolate
3	cups cooked white rice

In a large bowl, combine beef, egg, corn chips, milk and 1 teaspoon salt. Refrigerate, covered, 1 hour. Shape into 15 meatballs, using 2 tablespoons meat mixture for each. Roll meatballs lightly in 2 tablespoons flour, coating completely. Melt butter in large, heavy skillet and saute' meatballs, half at a time, until nicely browned all over. Remove meatballs from skillet as they are browned. In the same skillet saute' onion and garlic, stirring occasionally, about five minutes. Remove from heat. In a small bowl, combine sugar, chili powder, cumin, coriander, oregano and remaining salt and flour. Stir into skillet along with tomatoes, chocolate and 1 cup water, mixing well. Bring to boiling, stirring constantly. Reduce heat; simmer, covered and stirring occasionally, for 30 minutes. Add meatballs to skillet; simmer, covered, 20 minutes. Uncover; simmer 10 minutes more. Turn meatballs and sauce into warm serving dish. Serve over hot rice.

These meatballs are also excellent as an appetizer.

🦃 SOUR CREAM ENCHILADAS

4 servings

1	pound lean ground beef
½	cup chopped onion
½	teaspoon salt
8	corn tortillas
½	cup cooking oil
½	cup canned or bottled taco sauce
1	cup shredded Monterey Jack cheese
¼	cup butter
6	tablespoons all-purpose flour
2	teaspoons instant chicken bouillon granules
2	cups water
1	cup sour cream
¼	cup chopped green chilies

Cook meat and onions until meat is brown; drain off any excess fat. Add salt. Dip tortillas in hot oil; fry quickly until limp. Drain on paper towels. Spoon equal portions of the meat mixture onto tortillas. Top each with 1 tablespoon taco sauce and cheese. Roll up; place seam-side down in a lightly greased 10" x 6" baking dish. In medium saucepan melt butter; add flour and bouillon granules, stirring until smooth. Gradually add water. Cook, stirring often, until thick. Remove from heat and stir in sour cream and chilies. Pour mixture over rolled tortillas. Top with remaining cheese. Bake at 400° 15 minutes.

CASSEROLE MOUSSAKA

4-6 servings

1   **pound ground beef or lamb**
1   **large onion, chopped**
1   **medium eggplant, chopped and peeled**
1   **large potato, peeled and chopped**
½-¾ **cup tomato sauce**
1   **teaspoon chili powder**
¾   **teaspoon ground nutmeg**
      Salt to taste
1   **clove garlic, minced**
½   **cup Parmesan cheese**
2   **eggs**
1   **cup plain yogurt**

Cook beef or lamb and onion until brown. Drain excess fat. Stir in eggplant, potato, tomato sauce, chili powder, nutmeg, salt and garlic. Simmer, covered, until potato and eggplant are tender, 25-35 minutes. Stir in cheese. Spoon into 1½ quart casserole. Beat eggs and yogurt. Spoon over eggplant mixture. Bake uncovered 350° for 30-35 minutes.

SPANISH BEEF AND BARLEY

4-6 servings

1   **pound lean ground beef**
1   **large onion, coarsely chopped**
1   **cup seeded and chopped green pepper**
1   **clove garlic, minced or pressed**
1   **16-ounce can tomatoes**
2   **tablespoons chili powder**
1   **teaspoon ground cumin**
1   **teaspoon oregano leaves**
1   **cup pearl barley**
1½   **cups water**
1   **cup raisins**
      Salt and pepper

Heat frying pan over medium heat; add beef and cook until crumbly. Stir in onion, green pepper, and garlic and cook until onion is limp. Drain excess fat. Stir in tomatoes and their liquid, breaking up tomatoes with a spoon. Add chili powder, cumin, oregano, barley, and water; bring to a boil. Reduce heat, cover, and simmer 35 to 40 minutes or until barley is tender to bite. Add raisins and season to taste with salt and pepper. To cook in microwave oven: crumble ground beef into a 2½ quart casserole and stir in onion, green pepper, and garlic; cover and set aside. Drain liquid from tomatoes into another 2½ quart casserole and set tomatoes aside. Add chili powder, cumin, oregano, barley, and water to the tomato liquid, stirring to mix. Cover and cook in the microwave oven for 15 minutes. Remove from oven, do not uncover, and set aside to absorb liquid. Cook ground beef mixture 8 minutes or until ground beef is no longer pink; stir in tomatoes (break up with a spoon). Test barley for tenderness (if not yet tender to bite, return to oven for 2 to 3 minutes). Add barley mixture to ground beef. Stir in raisins and season to taste with salt and pepper. Cover and let stand about 10 minutes.

PICADILLO (BRAZILIAN SAVORY BEEF)

4 servings

½   cup raisins
¼   cup hot beef broth
1   clove garlic
1   small onion, chopped
1   pound ground beef
    Salt to taste
    Pepper to taste
1½ cups canned tomatoes
2   tablespoons vinegar
    Dash of liquid hot pep-
    per sauce
¼   teaspoon cumin
⅛   teaspoon cloves
1   green pepper,
    chopped
4   tablespoons green
    olives, chopped
2   tablespoons capers
    Dash of cinnamon
½   cup slivered almonds
    (optional)

Soak raisins in beef broth for 10 minutes. Saute' garlic, onion and ground beef for 5 minutes. Add salt, pepper, tomatoes, vinegar, hot pepper sauce, cumin, cloves, green pepper, olives, capers and cinnamon. Bring to a boil and simmer, uncovered, for 15-20 minutes. Stir in almonds. Serve with rice.

ZUCCHINI PIZZA

6-8 servings

4   ounces mozzarella
    cheese, grated
4   ounces Cheddar
    cheese, grated
4   cups zucchini, grated
2   eggs, slightly beaten
2   tablespoons flour
¼   teaspoon baking
    powder
¼   teaspoon salt
1   pound ground beef
1   onion, chopped
1   clove garlic, minced
1   cup tomato sauce
2   ounces mozzarella
    cheese, grated
2   ounces Cheddar
    cheese, grated

Combine first seven ingredients and press into a 10" x 15" jelly roll pan. Bake at 400° for 15 minutes. While crust is baking, saute' ground beef with onion and garlic. Drain fat. Add 1 cup tomato sauce to meat mixture and cook 5 minutes. Spoon sauce over baked crust. Top with cheese. Bake at 400° for 20 minutes.

🦃 PICADILLO TACOS

12	corn tortillas
1	onion, chopped
2	tablespoons cooking oil
½	cup chopped green pepper
3	large garlic cloves, minced
1	pound lean ground beef
1	16-ounce can plum tomatoes, chopped and undrained
⅔	cup chopped pimiento-stuffed green olives
½	cup corn
⅓	cup raisins
2	tablespoons brown sugar
1½	tablespoons white vinegar
⅛	teaspoon cinnamon
⅛	teaspoon ground cloves
	Salt and pepper to taste
4	cups shredded iceberg lettuce
½	pound grated Monterey Jack cheese

Prepare corn tortillas according to package directions and shape into taco shells. Keep warm. In a large skillet cook onion in hot oil until softened; add green pepper and minced garlic and cook the mixture, stirring, for 3 minutes. Add the ground beef and cook the mixture, stirring until meat is no longer pink. Add tomatoes, including the juice; olives, corn, raisins, brown sugar, vinegar and spices. Cook the picadillo, stirring, for 10 minutes or until excess liquid is evaporated. Spoon ⅓ cup of the picadillo into each taco shell and top it with some of the lettuce and cheese.

The spicy ground beef filling of these tacos makes for a taste treat that is delightfully different. Picadillo also is delicious spooned inside warm pita pockets.

RANCH-STYLE RIBS

6-8	country-style pork ribs
1	16-ounce bottle catsup
1	envelope dry onion soup mix
¼	cup red wine vinegar
¼	cup dark corn syrup
2	tablespoons peanut oil
1	teaspoon dry mustard

Slightly brown ribs over grill or under broiler. Put in slow-cooker with sauce and cook on low heat for about 8 hours or until meat is done. (Can also be done in a 275° oven). To make sauce, combine catsup, onion soup mix, vinegar, corn syrup, peanut oil and dry mustard in small saucepan. Heat 3 minutes on medium high heat, stirring constantly.

🦢 RENO RED CHILI

3	pounds coarsely ground round steak
3	pounds coarsely ground chuck
6	dried red chili pods, stemmed and seeded
3	tablespoons cumin seed, crushed
6	medium cloves garlic, minced
1	tablespoon oregano brewed in ½ cup beer (like tea)
8	tablespoons monosodium glutamate (optional)
3	medium onions, chopped
2	tablespoons paprika
2	tablespoons cider vinegar
2	10½-ounce cans beef broth
1	cup pureed, stewed tomatoes
2	tablespoons masa flour

Brown meat and drain off excess fat. Boil red chili pods in 4 cups of water for 30 minutes. Remove skins from boiled chilies, mash pulp and add to browned meat along with remaining ingredients except for one can of beef broth and masa flour. Simmer, covered, for 45 minutes. Dissolve masa flour in remaining can of beef broth, stir into chili mixture and simmer 30 minutes. Taste and add salt if needed. Simmer 15 minutes longer and serve piping hot.

This hearty chili recipe won the $15,000 "world title" in competition sponsored by the International Chili Society in Reno, Nevada.

🦢 SAN ANTONIO TOSTADA MIX

2	pounds ground beef
1	large onion, chopped
1	bell pepper, seeded and chopped
1	15-ounce can tomato sauce
1	8-ounce can tomato sauce
2	tablespoons Worcestershire sauce
¼	cup chili powder (or to taste)
1	tablespoon hot pepper sauce
1	7-ounce can chopped green chilies
	Dash ground cumin
1	clove garlic, crushed
	Salt and pepper to taste

Brown beef, onion and chopped pepper until onion is soft and beef is done. Add both cans tomato sauce and remaining ingredients and simmer, tightly covered, for 3 hours. Remove lid and continue to cook at low heat until mixture thickens (about 45 minutes). Serve mixture over corn tortillas that have been sauteed in hot oil and drained. In separate bowls offer chopped tomatoes, chopped green onions, shredded Cheddar cheese, sour cream, avocado slices and shredded lettuce. Offer additional hot sauce for those who want it hotter.

🐦 MAIN DISH MEXICAN PIE

4-6 servings

1	pound lean ground beef
1	cup chopped onion
1	envelope taco seasoning mix
1	4-ounce can chopped green chilies
1	cup shredded Monterey Jack cheese
1¼	cups milk
¾	cup prepared biscuit mix
3	eggs
¼	teaspoon hot pepper sauce

Preheat oven to 400°. Lightly grease a 10" pie plate. In a skillet over medium heat, cook beef and onion stirring occasionally, until beef is browned; drain off excess fat. Stir in seasoning mix and spread mixture in pie plate. Sprinkle chilies and cheese over beef. Beat remaining ingredients until smooth about 20 seconds in blender or 90 seconds with a hand beater. Pour egg mixture gently over mixture in pie plate. Bake about 25-30 minutes or until golden brown and until a knife inserted in center comes out clean. Let stand 5 minutes before cutting. Garnish, if desired, with additional red or green chilies or shredded cheese.

Easy and inexpensive! And leftovers can be frozen with great success.

🐦 CHIMICHANGAS SAN CARLOS

6 servings

3	tablespoons salad oil
3	onions, chopped
1	clove garlic, crushed
2	pounds lean ground beef
4	ripe tomatoes, peeled, seeded and chopped
½	teaspoon chili powder
½	teaspoon ground cumin
¼	teaspoon oregano
1	teaspoon salt
12	flour tortillas, warmed in oven
½	cup salad oil
1	cup Cheddar cheese, grated
	Sour cream
2	large ripe avocados, peeled and sliced lengthwise

In a skillet heat salad oil and cook onions and garlic until translucent. Add meat and brown well. Add tomatoes and seasonings, blending well. Cook mixture, stirring often, for five minutes or until it is fairly dry. Drain off any excess fat. On each tortilla arrange some of the meat mixture; sprinkle with cheese and top with slices of avocado. (Reserve 12 avocado slices for garnish.) Fold tortillas over the meat like an envelope. In a skillet, heat the ½ cup oil and fry tortillas until golden, taking care not to open the "envelopes." Drain them on absorbent paper. Serve the tortillas garnished with sour cream and the reserved avocado slices.

This recipe doubles easily and can be prepared up to the frying step and refrigerated. One tortilla per serving is adequate for lunch; two will make a hearty supper serving.

MACHO CASSEROLE

6-8 servings

½ pound Mexican chorizo
  sausage
½ pound lean ground
  beef
1 large onion, chopped
2 16-ounce cans refried
  beans
1½ pounds shredded
  Cheddar cheese
1 4-ounce can green
  chilies
2 7-ounce cans taco
  sauce
¼ cup chopped green
  onion
1 3½-ounce can sliced
  black olives

Guacamole
(See Index)

1 cup sour cream

Pierce chorizo skin with fork. Boil in water for 10 minutes to remove fat from chorizo. Drain chorizo and slice. Brown meat with onion. Drain off excess grease and set aside. In a large, shallow baking dish, layer in the following order: beans, half the green chilies, half the cheese, half the taco sauce, the meats, remaining taco sauce, remaining chilies, remaining cheese, green onions and olives. Heat in a 350° oven for 30 minutes or until cheese is melted and casserole is bubbly. To serve, spoon portions onto serving dishes, top with guacamole and dollups of sour cream. If desired, surround with shredded lettuce and chopped tomatoes and a generous supply of tortilla chips. For variety, use hot mixture as filling for warm flour tortillas or serve as a hot appetizer straight from the baking dish with lots of crisp tortilla chips for dipping.

A spicy dish that's versatile and nutritious.

LAMB CHOPS WITH SPINACH

6 servings

1 medium onion, minced
2 tablespoons butter
6 lamb chops
2 teaspoons salt
4½ cups fresh spinach or
  2 10-ounce packages
  frozen chopped
  spinach, thawed &
  squeezed dry
3½ cups fine soft bread
  crumbs
¼ cup melted butter
2 eggs, well-beaten
  Celery salt to taste

In a large skillet, saute the onion in the butter until onion is soft; remove onion from skillet and set aside. Season lamb chops with ½ teaspoon salt and brown on both sides in the same skillet. Combine spinach, bread crumbs, melted butter, onions, eggs, celery salt and the remaining 1½ teaspoons salt. Place in a shallow baking dish and top with the lamb chops. Cover and bake in a 350° oven for 1 hour or until the lamb is tender.

GRILLED BUTTERFLY LAMB

6-8 servings

1   **leg of lamb, boned**
1   **cup dairy sour cream**
2   **teaspoons monosodium glutamate**
1   **teaspoon salt**
¼   **teaspoon pepper**
¼   **teaspoon oregano**
¼   **teaspoon parsley flakes**
¼   **teaspoon ground cloves**
¼   **teaspoon garlic powder**
    Fresh mint

Leave lamb flat. Combine sour cream and seasonings, except mint. Cover both sides of lamb thickly with mixture. Marinate at least 4 hours. Grill over hot coals until done, 1 to 1½ hours. Garnish with fresh mint.

Serve with an artichoke, orange and almond salad.

ARTICHOKE STUFFED LEG OF LAMB

6-8 servings

1   **leg of lamb, boned**
1   **clove garlic**
    Salt and pepper to taste
⅓   **cup chopped onion**
3   **tablespoons butter**
½   **cup coarsely chopped canned or frozen artichoke hearts**
1   **cup fresh bread crumbs**
2   **teaspoons chopped parsley**
¼   **teaspoon salt**
⅛   **teaspoon each thyme, marjoram, dill weed and pepper**
1½   **cups beef consomme**
2   **tablespoons flour**

Rub inside and outside of lamb with garlic clove, salt and pepper. To prepare stuffing; saute' onion in butter until onions are golden. Add artichoke hearts; cook 1 minute. Add bread crumbs, parsley, salt, thyme, marjoram, dill weed and pepper. Mix thoroughly. Place stuffing inside lamb, secure with skewers and string. Place on rack in open roasting pan. Roast at 325° for 35 minutes per pound or until meat thermometer registers 170° for rare or 180° for medium done. Baste lamb with ½ cup consomme 20 minutes before meat is done. Remove lamb to hot platter. To make gravy; skim all but 2 tablespoons fat from pan drippings. Blend in 2 tablespoons fat from pan drippings. Blend in flour; mix until smooth. Add 1 cup consomme, stirring constantly until gravy is smooth and thick. Season to taste with salt and pepper.

HERBED LEG OF LAMB

6-8 Servings

1   teaspoon dry mustard
1   teaspoon sweet basil
1   teaspoon rosemary
2   tablespoons dried mint leaves
    Lemon pepper to taste
1   tablespoon paprika
1   tablespoon olive oil
1   leg of lamb

Sprinkle the herbs and spices on the leg of lamb. Roast at 350° for 3½ to 4 hours. Serve with rice.

ITALIAN VEAL ROAST

8-12 servings

4-5   pounds boned veal, tied
1   8-ounce package pepperoni
2   teaspoons seasoned salt
1   green pepper, cut in squares
1   sweet red pepper, cut in squares
    Bottled Italian-style dressing

TUNA SAUCE:

1   7-ounce can tuna
½   cup chicken broth
¼   cup heavy cream
2   anchovy fillets, chopped
2   tablespoons capers, well drained
1   tablespoon pimiento, chopped

Cut pepperoni into 4 or 5 pieces; insert one piece into each hole where bone was removed. Cut several more holes straight through roast, then fill with remaining pieces of pepperoni. Rub meat all over with seasoned salt. Place on a rack in roasting pan. Roast at 325° 35 minutes per pound or 2½ to 3 hours, or until meat thermometer registers 170°. Remove from oven; cool, then chill until serving time. Pour boiling water over pepper squares in a bowl. Let stand 5 minutes; drain then drizzle lightly with salad dressing. When ready to serve, slice and garnish with seasoned pepper squares. Serve with Tuna Sauce. Combine tuna and broth in blender; cover; blend till thick and smooth. Add cream; blend 1 minute longer. Stir in anchovies, capers and pimiento. Pour into a serving bowl. (Make sauce no longer than 1 hour ahead of serving time.)

VEAL PICCATA

4 servings

1	pound veal, sliced thin
2	tablespoons flour
½	teaspoon salt
¼	teaspoon pepper
¼	cup white wine
1	lemon, sliced paper-thin
¼	cup chopped parsley
1	tablespoon butter
1	egg yolk
¼	cup white wine

Coat veal with flour, salt and pepper. In 2 tablespoons hot butter, saute' veal until well-browned on both sides. Add wine, lemon slices and parsley; simmer, covered, for 10 minutes. Remove veal to serving platter; keep warm. Discard lemon slices. To make sauce, slowly heat 1 tablespoon butter in same skillet. Beat 1 egg yolk with ¼ cup white wine and slowly add to butter in skillet, stirring constantly. Cook over low heat until sauce is thickened. Pour over veal.

STUFFED VEAL STEAKS

4-6 servings

2½	pounds veal steak, boneless
	Flour
	Salt and pepper
4	tablespoons chopped parsley
1	medium onion, chopped
½	cup cooked ham, chopped
3	eggs
½	cup Parmesan cheese
½	cup bread crumbs
½	teaspoon salt
¼	teaspoon pepper
½	cup white wine
1	teaspoon sage
1	teaspoon rosemary
1	teaspoon oregano
½	cup sliced green olives

Cut meat into 8 pieces; pound thin with flour, salt and pepper. Saute' parsley, onion and ham in butter until onion is tender. Mix eggs, cheese, crumbs, salt and pepper with ham mixture. Spread each piece of meat with this mixture. Roll up and tie securely with string. Brown on all sides in oil and butter. Cover with wine, sage, rosemary and oregano. Cover and simmer over low heat 1 hour. May add more wine if needed. Add olives during the last 15 minutes. Serve with pasta.

Utterly elegant!

VEAL CUTLETS WITH WALNUT SAUCE

6 servings

1½	pounds veal cutlets, pounded thin
½	cup flour
	Salt, pepper and paprika to taste
⅓	cup butter
⅓	cup Marsala or dry sherry
¾	cup chopped walnuts
¾	cup heavy cream

Dredge veal with flour. Sprinkle with salt, pepper and paprika. Heat butter in pan and saute veal. Cook about 5 minutes on each side. Remove to a plate and keep warm. Stir in Marsala to pan and add walnuts and cream. Increase heat and boil sauce, stirring, for 1 minute. Correct seasoning, return veal to pan and heat.

Serve with an apple and endive salad and dry white wine.

ITALIAN VEAL CUTLETS

6-8 servings

1½ pounds thin cut veal
cutlets
Salt and pepper to
taste
1 egg, beaten
Cracker meal
Vegetable oil
1 16-ounce can tomatoes
½ teaspoon salt
½ teaspoon oregano
½ cup diced green pep-
pers
1 large onion, chopped
1 clove garlic, crushed
½ cup sliced mushrooms
¼ cup butter
Grated Romano
cheese
Mozzarella cheese,
sliced

Preheat oven to 350°. Season cutlets with salt and pepper. Dip into egg, coat with cracker meal and brown in hot oil. Cook tomatoes with ½ teaspoon salt and oregano for 10 minutes. Saute' green peppers, onion, garlic and mushrooms in butter until soft, not browned. Add to tomatoes and pour over cutlets. Sprinkle layers of veal with grated Romano cheese and slices of mozzarella cheese before adding tomato sauce. Bake 45 minutes.

VEAL IN SOUR CREAM

6 servings

1½ pounds boneless veal,
cubed
1-2 tablespoons butter
1 medium onion, sliced
½ pound sliced
mushrooms
1 tablespoon chopped
parsley
1 tablespoon flour
3 tablespoons water
¼ cup white wine
¾ cup sour cream
½ teaspoon salt
⅛ teaspoon freshly
ground pepper

Brown veal in butter in a medium sized skillet. Remove meat to oven-proof dish. Add onion and mushrooms to skillet, stir and saute lightly. Remove skillet from heat and slowly stir in the remaining ingredients. Pour sauce over meat in baking dish. Cover and bake at 250° for 1 hour or until done. Serve with noodles.

Try this with green spinach noodles.

TOURTIÈRE

5-6 servings

6   slices bacon
1   pound lean pork, minced
½   pound veal, minced
1   small onion, finely chopped
½   cup boiling water
1   clove garlic, minced
1½   teaspoons salt
¼   teaspoon pepper
¼   teaspoon celery salt
¼   teaspoon sage
      Pinch ground cloves
1   cup mashed potatoes
      Pastry for 9" double crust pie

Cut bacon into small pieces and fry until cooked, but not crisp. Add pork, veal and onion; cook until meat is lightly browned. Drain meats. Add water and spices; reduce heat to simmer; cover pan and cook 45 minutes more. Combine meat with mashed potatoes; cool slightly. Meanwhile, line a 9" pie plate with half the pastry; fill with meat mixture. Place top crust in position; seal and flute edges. Cut several slashes in top. Bake at 450° 10-12 minutes. Reduce heat to 350° and bake 30 minutes longer.

A French-Canadian recipe served especially during the Christmas holiday season.

BARBECUED COUNTRY RIBS

4-6 servings

12   country-style ribs
1   large onion, chopped
¼   cup butter or margarine
2   cups ketchup
2   cups water
4   tablespoons vinegar or lemon juice
5   tablespoons Worcestershire sauce
¼   cup brown sugar
½   cup bourbon (optional)

Fry ribs 20-30 minutes until done. Drain. Saute' onion in butter until transparent. Add remaining ingredients. Cover bottom of large pan with coating of sauce. Add ribs in one layer. Cover with remaining sauce. Bake at 350° for 1½-2 hours. Do not turn.

MARMALADE-GLAZED BAKED HAM

16 servings

1   5-pound canned ham
½   12-ounce jar orange marmalade
2   tablespoons brown sugar
1   tablespoon catsup
1   tablespoon soy sauce
½   teaspoon garlic powder
⅛   teaspoon pepper

Place ham in a 9" x 13" baking dish; bake at 325° for 1 hour. In small bowl, mix well marmalade and remaining ingredients. With a pastry brush, brush marmalade mixture over ham, and continue baking ham 15-20 minutes longer, basting often.

HAM-CAULIFLOWER CASSEROLE
4-6 servings

1 medium head
   cauliflower
   Dash salt
1¼ cups diced cooked
   ham
   Butter
3 tablespoons chopped
   chives
1¼ cups sour cream
   Dash white pepper
½ teaspoon paprika
   Dash nutmeg
¼ teaspoon salt
2 egg yolks, lightly
   beaten
1 cup grated sharp
   Cheddar cheese

Cook cauliflower in salted water just until crisp. Drain, cool and break into flowerettes. Butter a 1½-quart casserole and make alternate layers of cauliflower and ham. Dot each layer with butter. Mix remaining ingredients, except cheese, and pour over casserole. Bake, covered, in a 375° oven for 30 minutes or until bubbly. Remove cover, top with sharp Cheddar cheese and bake until browned, about 15 minutes.

PORK WITH CRANBERRY DRESSING
12 servings

12 rib crown roast
   of pork
   Salt and pepper

CRANBERRY DRESSING:

1 medium celery rib,
   diced
2 medium onions, diced
6 tart apples, diced
2 tablespoons margarine
2 1-pound loaves stale
   raisin bread
1½ cups orange juice
1 pound fresh cranber-
   ries
   Pinch of cinnamon

Place crown roast in shallow pan, bone ends up; wrap tips of ribs in foil to prevent excess browning. Roast, uncovered, in a 325° oven about 55 minutes per pound. An hour before meat is done, fill center with cranberry dressing. Dressing: Fry the celery, onion and apples in 2 tablespoons margarine until just soft. Break raisin bread into small pieces and mix into cooled apple mixture. Moisten with orange juice. Add cranberries, salt, pepper and cinnamon. Put dressing in center of roast and cover with foil. Baste with pan drippings once or twice. Remove foil the last 15 minutes of cooking. To carve, slice between ribs.

This elegant entree earns its reputation as a timeless classic.

STIR-FRIED PORK WITH PEPPERS

6 servings

1   **pound boneless pork cutlets**
3   **teaspoons cornstarch**
1   **teaspoon sugar**
3   **tablespoons soy sauce**
1   **tablespoon water**
5   **tablespoons peanut or corn oil**
6   **large peppers, cut in 1″ pieces**
1½   **teaspoons salt**
¼   **teaspoon ground ginger**
1   **clove garlic, crushed**
2   **tablespoons dry sherry**
2   **tablespoons water**

Slice pork into 2″ X ½″ X 1/8″ strips. Combine 1½ teaspoons cornstarch, ½ teaspoon sugar, soy sauce and 1 tablespoon water in a bowl. Add pork; mix well; set aside. Heat a large wok or skillet until very hot. Add 2 tablespoons oil; add peppers and stir-fry 4-5 minutes. Add salt and remaining sugar; mix well and transfer to a warm platter. Clean out wok, then reheat until hot. Add remaining oil. Add pork and the marinade to wok. Add ginger and garlic; stir-fry until pork begins to separate into slices and the color of all the meat has changed (about 10 minutes). Sprinkle in sherry and peppers; stir and cook to heat through. Mix remaining 1½ teaspoons cornstarch with 2 tablespoons water and slowly pour into wok; stir until sauce thickens and the clear glaze coats meat and peppers. Serve at once. (Note: almost any combination of fresh vegetables can be used instead of green peppers. Beef or chicken can be substituted for pork.)

PORK-CIDER STEW

4-6 servings

3   **pounds lean pork, cubed**
¾   **cup flour**
½   **cup cooking oil**
3   **cups apple cider**
6   **small carrots, sliced**
1   **medium onion, chopped**
¾   **teaspoon rosemary**
2   **teaspoons salt**
1   **teaspoon freshly ground pepper**

Dredge pork in flour. Heat oil in a large frying pan. Add pork and cook until browned, stirring occasionally. Remove pork with a slotted spoon and place in a 2-quart casserole. Drain excess oil from pan; then pour the cider into the pan. Heat cider, stirring to remove browned particles from the bottom of the pan. Add carrots, onions and rosemary to the pork, then stir in the hot cider. Season with salt and pepper. Cover and bake in a preheated 325° oven for 2 hours or until the pork is tender.

There's a natural affinity between the blandness of pork and the tartness of apple cider.

MA McGUIRE'S PORK CHOP SUPPER   4-5 servings

4	thick pork chops
	Salt and pepper
1	tablespoon butter
2	tablespoons oil
¾	cup long grain rice
1	cup ham, thinly sliced
1	clove garlic, diced
¼	teaspoon thyme
½	teaspoon oregano
½	cup white wine
1	cup chicken bouillon
1	cup thinly sliced onions
½	cup thinly sliced green pepper
½	cup thinly sliced mushrooms

Season chops with salt and pepper. Heat butter and oil in skillet and brown chops slowly on both sides. Remove. Stir in rice in skillet for 2 minutes. Return chops to pan, cover with ham and herbs. Add wine, simmer 3 minutes; add chicken broth, cover tightly and simmer 30 minutes until meat is thoroughly cooked. Add vegetables and simmer another 8 minutes until vegetables are cooked but still are crunchy. Serve in the skillet.

POSOLE MI CASA   8-10 servings

1	pound posole, washed well
6	cups cold water
5	medium onions, coarsely chopped
4	large garlic cloves, peeled and crushed
4	tablespoons cooking oil
3	pounds boned pork shoulder, cut in ¾″ cubes
1	teaspoon crumbled leaf oregano
½	teaspoon thyme
2	teaspoons salt (or more as needed to taste)
¼	teaspoon black pepper
1⅔	cups chicken broth
1	10-ounce can whole green chilies, drained and cut in long strips
1-3	jalapeno peppers, minced (1 pepper makes a mild posole; 3, a torrid one)

Place the posole and water in a large, heavy pot; bring to a simmer, cover and cook slowly until kernels burst and are almost tender (about 3½ hours). When posole is almost done, lightly brown onions and garlic in 2 tablespoons cooking oil; drain on paper towels. Add another 2 tablespoons of oil to the skillet and brown pork cubes, a few at a time. Drain on paper towels. Add onion, garlic, pork; add all remaining ingredients to the posole; mix in well and simmer covered for 3 more hours. Taste for salt and adjust as needed. Serve in large soup plates and pass a rich red chili sauce for topping if desired.

Posole is a feast day favorite among the Pueblo Indians who live in the Rio Grande Valley. Its special flavor and character, however, have made it a year-around favorite of all New Mexicans.

PORK CHOPS WITH MUSHROOMS

4 servings

2 tablespoons Parmesan cheese
2 tablespoons cornmeal
3 tablespoons fine dry bread crumbs
½ teaspoon garlic salt
½ teaspoon oregano
6 tablespoons butter or margarine
4 lean pork chops, cut ½" thick
½ pound mushrooms, sliced
1 clove garlic, crushed
¼ teaspoon rosemary
½ cup whipping cream
¼ cup thinly sliced green onions
Salt and pepper to taste

In a paper bag combine Parmesan, cornmeal, bread crumbs, garlic salt and oregano. Melt butter in a skillet; dip each chop into butter, drain briefly, then shake each chop in the bag. Shake off excess coating and arrange chops on rack of a broiler pan. Bake, uncovered, in 400° oven about 40-50 minutes. Meanwhile heat the butter remaining in skillet over medium heat; add mushrooms and garlic and saute' 5 minutes. Stir in rosemary and cream and cook over high heat until liquid is reduced to about ¼ cup. Stir in green onions and salt and pepper to taste. Pour into a bowl and pass at the table with the pork chops.

PORK CHOPS WITH OLIVES

6 servings

6 ¾-inch butterflied pork chops
¾ teaspoon salt, divided
2 tablespoons salad oil
1 cup chopped onion
¾ cup beef broth
¾ cup orange juice
½ teaspoon oregano
1 cup canned pitted ripe olives
1½ tablespoons cornstarch
2 tablespoons cold water
1 cup orange sections

Sprinkle chops with ¼ teaspoon of the salt. Heat oil in skillet and brown chops on both sides. Remove chops; add onion to skillet and brown lightly. Add broth, orange juice, oregano and remaining ½ teaspoon salt and heat to boiling. Return chops to skillet, add ripe olives. Cover tightly and cook over low heat until tender, about 1 hour. May add water if needed. Stir cornstarch into cold water. Remove chops to heated serving dish. Stir cornstarch mixture into liquid remaining in skillet. Cook, stirring constantly until sauce boils and thickens. Add orange sections and heat one minute. Spoon sauce over chops.

Excellent with buttered caraway noodles.

HUNGARIAN PORK GOULASH
8 servings

2 onions, chopped
2 tablespoons oil
1 tablespoon Hungarian paprika
2 pounds boneless pork, cut in 2" cubes
1½ pounds pork spareribs cut into 2" lengths
1 teaspoon salt
½ cup water
2 pounds sauerkraut, rinsed and drained
1 tablespoon caraway seeds
1 cup sour cream

Saute' onions in oil until softened. Stir in paprika. Add cubed pork, spareribs and salt. Cook 10 minutes; add water. Bring to a boil, reduce heat to simmer and cook covered 20 minutes. Stir in sauerkraut and cook covered 1½ hours. Add caraway seeds and, adding water as needed, simmer 30 minutes more. Top goulash with sour cream.

SAUSAGE STROGANOFF
4-6 servings

1½ pounds smoked or German sausage, cut on diagonal in ¼" pieces
2 tablespoons butter
¼ cup chopped onion
½ pound sliced mushrooms
3 tablespoons flour
1¼ cups beef broth
2 tablespoons catsup
¼ teaspoon pepper
2 tablespoons dry sherry
1 cup dairy sour cream

In a 10" skillet cook sausage in butter 3-4 minutes over medium heat. Remove from skillet, reserve and keep warm. Add onions and mushrooms to skillet and saute' until tender and most of the liquid has evaporated. Sprinkle flour over vegetable mixture. Cook, stirring constantly for 2 minutes. Add beef broth, catsup and pepper; stir until smooth and cook until mixture begins to boil. Reduce heat and simmer 5 minutes. Stir in sherry, sour cream and sausage. Serve immediately over cooked noodles or rice.

OLD-FASHIONED COUNTRY CASSEROLE
6 servings

1 cup brown rice
2½ cups boiling water
2 chicken bouillon cubes
½ pound bulk sausage
3 tablespoons butter or margarine
2 tablespoons minced onion
½ pound fresh mushrooms, sliced
½ pound chicken livers, quartered
¼ teaspoon salt
Pinch of pepper

Cook the rice in the boiling water to which the bouillon cubes have been added; cover the pot and simmer for about 30 minutes or until water is almost all absorbed. Fry the sausage until nearly done, breaking the meat apart with a fork. Drain off excess fat and add butter, onion, mushrooms and livers. Cover and cook about 10 minutes, stirring frequently, until livers have lost any red color. Add salt and pepper. Combine the rice and the meat mixture and place in a buttered 2-quart baking dish. Cover and bake in a 400° oven for 20 minutes.

SAUSAGE CASSEROLE ALA ITALIENNE   6 servings

2   pounds Italian sausage, cut into 12 pieces
½   cup water
2   onions, thinly sliced
1   clove garlic, crushed
1   teaspoon raisins, chopped
1   28-ounce can tomatoes, chopped
¼   cup bourbon
    Pinch rosemary
2½   pounds potatoes, peeled and cut into wedges
    Salt
¼   cup grated Romano or Parmesan cheese
2   teaspoons minced parsley, preferably Italian

Put sausage in pot, add water and cook until water evaporates and sausage browns. Discard excess fat. Add onions and garlic; cook 2 minutes, stirring. Add raisins, tomatoes, bourbon and rosemary. Bring to a boil, cover and simmer slowly 30 minutes. Add potatoes and salt to taste. Simmer until potatoes are tender. If sauce is too thick, add a little water. Stir in cheese and parsley.

Hearty and wholesome!

CREOLE HOUSE JAMBALAYA   8 servings

12   link breakfast sausages
1   cup uncooked rice
2   tablespoons butter
2   garlic cloves, crushed
1   cup chopped green pepper
1   cup chopped onion
1   cup diced ham
1   cup diced cooked chicken
2½   cups chicken stock
½   teaspoon leaf thyme
1   tablespoon chopped parsley
1½   teaspoons salt
¼   teaspoon pepper
¼   teaspoon chili powder
1   cup grated sharp Cheddar cheese
    Paprika

Fry sausages; drain and cut in small pieces. Set aside. Cook rice according to package directions and set aside. Melt butter in large Dutch oven. Add garlic, green pepper, onion, ham, chicken, stock, thyme, chopped parsley, salt, pepper, chili powder and sausage pieces. Simmer 30 minutes. Remove from heat and allow to cool; then add rice. Pour mixture into buttered 2½-quart casserole. Sprinkle with cheese. Bake at 400° 20-30 minutes. Place a dot of butter in center; then top with paprika.

Tradition!

In accordance with years of Spanish tradition, many communities in New Mexico hold annual fiestas to honor patron saints and pay homage to the state's Hispanic heritage. Mayordomos (councillors) are appointed to plan a religious procession, celebration of the Mass, feasting, coronation of a queen, dancing and other lively festivities. The best-known New Mexican fiesta in the Spanish tradition is Fiesta de Santa Fé, a four-day celebration held in early September to commemorate the Spanish reconquest of the city in 1692. The burning of Zozobra (Old Man Gloom), an enormous papier maché giant, heralds the opening of the fiesta and the ensuing pageantry, parades and parties. Albuquerque's oldest fiesta is the Fiesta of San Felipe de Neri which takes place around the historic church in the city's Old Town Plaza. A newer celebration, Fiesta Encantada, takes place in December to spotlight the many sports, arts and special events of the Christmas season ❖

Poultry

ÁCOMA BIRD POT

SUSAN'S ELEGANT CHICKEN PUFFS

6 servings

¼ cup oil
3 chicken breasts, halved, boned and skinned
½ teaspoon garlic salt
¼ teaspoon dried rosemary
1 10-ounce package (six) frozen patty shells, thawed
1 3-ounce package cream cheese with chives, cut into 6 pieces

Heat oil and lightly saute' chicken breasts. Do not brown as all you want to do is start cooking process. Sprinkle each breast with rosemary and garlic salt. Roll each pastry shell into a circle about 7-9 inches in diameter. Place a chicken breast on half of each pastry. Spread each piece of chicken with one piece of chive cheese. Fold pastry over chicken and seal edges. Place on baking sheet. Place in 450° preheated oven and immediately reduce heat to 400°. Bake uncovered about 30 minutes or until golden brown.

CHICKEN TAHITIAN

6-8 servings

6-8 chicken breasts
1 6-ounce can frozen orange juice, thawed
⅛ cup oil
1 teaspoon ground ginger
2 teaspoons curry powder
1 teaspoon dry mustard
¼ cup soy sauce
⅓ cup sliced almonds
Pineapple chunks
Avocado slices

Marinate chicken breasts overnight in a mixture of the orange juice, oil, ginger, curry powder, dry mustard and soy sauce. Bake in the marinade uncovered at 350° for 1 hour. Sprinkle almonds over chicken during the last 10 minutes of cooking. Serve chicken on rice garnished with pineapple chunks and avocado slices.

CHICKEN TOSCANINI

3-4 servings

2 chicken breasts, halved, boned and skinned
2 tablespoons sherry
Juice of 1 lemon
2 eggs
2 tablespoons heavy cream
1 teaspoon salt
1 teaspoon onion juice
½ teaspoon white pepper
½ cup cracker or bread crumbs
¼ cup butter
Lemon slices

Soak chicken breast halves in sherry and juice of lemon for 2 hours. Wipe dry, flatten out each piece to ½" thickness with a wooden mallet. Prepare batter by beating eggs, cream, salt, onion juice and white pepper. Dip chicken in egg mixture; roll in fine cracker crumbs. Saute' in butter until golden brown on both sides. Serve with slices of lemon.

ITALIAN CHICKEN ROLLS

6 servings

2 tablespoons butter or margarine
3 tablespoons olive oil
2 cloves garlic, minced or pressed
¼-½ teaspoon crushed red pepper
¼ cup chopped parsley
6-8 anchovies, chopped (optional)
2½-3 pounds chicken breasts, skinned, boned, and cut in 1-inch chunks
1 3½-ounce jar capers, rinsed and drained
2 2¼-ounce cans sliced pitted ripe olives, drained
¾ cup dry white wine
¼ teaspoon pepper
Salt
6 crusty sandwich rolls
Garlic butter

In a wide frying pan, place butter and oil over medium heat. When hot, add garlic, red pepper, parsley, anchovies (if used), and chicken. Cook, stirring, until lightly browned, about 5 minutes. Add capers, olives, white wine, and pepper. Simmer, uncovered, stirring occasionally, until most of the juices evaporate, about 5 minutes. Add salt to taste. Split rolls and tear out soft portions (save for other uses). Brush insides with garlic butter. Fill tops equally with chicken mixture; cover with bottoms. Bake, uncovered, in a 350° oven until warm, about 5 minutes. (If made ahead, wrap in foil and refrigerate. Heat in a 350° oven until warm, about 15 minutes. Unwrap and bake 5 minutes more — until rolls are crisp.) Garlic Butter: Combine ⅓ cup melted butter or margarine with 1 clove garlic, minced or pressed.

BAKED CHICKEN BREASTS SUPREME

6-8 servings

6 whole fryer breasts
2 cups dairy sour cream
¼ cup lemon juice
4 teaspoons Worcestershire sauce
4 teaspoons celery salt
2 teaspoons paprika
½ teaspoon garlic powder
4 teaspoons salt
½ teaspoon pepper
1¾ cups packaged bread crumbs
½ cup butter or margarine

Cut chicken breasts in half, remove skin if desired and wipe well with damp paper towels. In a bowl, combine sour cream with lemon juice, Worcestershire sauce, celery salt, paprika, garlic, salt and pepper. Dip each piece of chicken in mixture, coating well. Place in a large bowl and let stand, covered, in refrigerator overnight. Preheat oven to 350°. Remove chicken from refrigerator. Roll in crumbs, coating evenly. Arrange in a single layer in large, shallow baking pan, skin side up. This can be done early in the day, covered and refrigerated again until ready to bake. Melt butter in a saucepan. Spoon half over chicken. Bake uncovered for 45 minutes. Spoon rest of butter over chicken and bake 10-15 minutes more until chicken is tender and nicely browned.

🦃 BAKED CHICKEN, MEXICAN-STYLE   5-6 servings.

4   eggs
         Bottled green chili
         salsa or taco sauce
¼   teaspoon salt
2   cups fine dry bread
         crumbs
2   teaspoons chili powder
2   teaspoons ground
         cumin
1½   teaspoons garlic salt
½   teaspoon ground
         oregano
3   large chicken breasts
         (about 1¼ lbs. each)
         split, skinned, and
         boned
         About ¼ cup butter or
         margarine
4-6   cups shredded
         iceberg lettuce
         About 1 cup sour
         cream
         About 6 tablespoons
         thinly sliced green
         onion
1-1½dozen cherry
         tomatoes
1-2   limes, cut in wedges
1   ripe avocado, peeled,
         pitted and sliced

In a pan beat together the eggs, 4 to 5 tablespoons of the salsa, and salt. In another pan, combine the bread crumbs, chili powder, cumin, garlic salt, and oregano. Dip each chicken piece in egg mixture to coat, then dip in crumb mixture; repeat and set aside. Place the butter in a large shallow roasting or broiler pan in an oven while it is preheating to 375°. As soon as the butter is melted, remove pan from oven. Put in chicken pieces, turning to coat with butter. Bake, uncovered, in a 375° oven until chicken is done, about 35 minutes. To serve, place chicken on a bed of shredded lettuce. Garnish with a dollop of sour cream, green onion, cherry tomatoes, lime wedges and avocado. Pass extra sour cream and salsa.

CHICKEN BREASTS IN HERB SAUCE   10-12 servings

½   cup margarine, melted
         Juice of 2 lemons
½   teaspoon pepper
1   teaspoon salt
1   teaspoon garlic salt
1   teaspoon celery salt
1   teaspoon dry mustard
1   teaspoon paprika
2   tablespoons Parmesan
         cheese
9   chicken breasts,
         halved and skinned
         Salt and pepper

In saucepan melt margarine and add lemon juice, pepper, salt, garlic salt, celery salt, dry mustard, paprika, and Parmesan cheese. Mix completely and heat 1 minute. Lay chicken breasts, which have been lightly salted and peppered, in shallow roasting pan so pieces do not overlap. Pour warm herb sauce over chicken and cook uncovered for 2 hours at 300°.

CHICKEN-WILD RICE CASSEROLE

8-10 servings

1   package dry onion soup mix
1   10½-ounce can condensed cream of mushroom soup
1   10½-ounce can condensed cream of celery soup
1   cup sour cream
1   soup can of milk
¼   cup dry sherry
½   pound fresh mushrooms, sliced and sauteed
1   6-ounce box long grain and wild rice
1½   cups uncooked instant rice
4-5   chicken breasts, boned and skinned
     Salt, pepper and paprika

Combine soup mix, soups, sour cream, milk, sherry and mushrooms. Add two-thirds of this mixture to the 2 uncooked rices in a bowl and mix well. Pour into a 3-quart greased casserole. Place chicken breasts on rice. Add salt and pepper to taste. Pour remaining one-third of soup mixture over top. Sprinkle with paprika. Bake at 350° covered for 1 hour and 15 minutes. Remove cover and bake ½ hour longer.

CHICKEN-SOUTHWESTERN STYLE

8 servings

4   tablespoons butter, softened
3   tablespoons Old English-style process cheese spread
2   tablespoons onion, minced
¾   teaspoon salt
2   tablespoons green chilies, chopped
4   chicken breasts, split, boned and skinned
¼   cup melted butter
1   cup cheese crackers, crushed
1½   tablespoons dry taco seasoning mix

Mix together the softened butter, cheese spread, onion, salt, and chopped green chilies. Flatten each chicken breast between sheets of waxed paper. Divide butter mixture into 8 equal portions and place in the middle of each breast. Roll to close and secure with 2 toothpicks. Dip each breast in melted butter and roll in mixture of cracker crumbs and taco mix. Place in 9" x 13" baking dish and bake covered for 1 hour at 350°. May be made ahead and refrigerated before baking, if desired, increasing baking time 5 minutes.

CHICKEN WELLINGTON

12 servings

12 chicken breasts, halved and boned
Seasoned salt and pepper
1 6-ounce package long grain and wild rice mix
2 tablespoons orange peel, grated
2 eggs, separated
3 8-ounce cans refrigerated crescent dinner rolls
1 tablespoon water
Salt and white pepper
1 20-ounce jar orange marmalade
1 tablespoon Dijon-style mustard
4 tablespoons port wine
¼ cup orange juice

Preheat oven to 375°. Sprinkle chicken breasts with seasoned salt and pepper. Cook rice according to package directions; add orange peel. Cool. Beat egg whites until slightly firm and fold into rice mixture. On floured surface, roll 2 triangular pieces of dinner roll dough into a rectangle large enough to accommodate chicken. Repeat with remaining rolls until you have 12 rectangles. Place a chicken breast on each rectangle and spoon about ¼ cup of rice mixture on top of chicken; roll up chicken jelly roll fashion. Trim off excess dough and seal seams with water. Place seamside down on baking sheet. Slightly beat egg yolks with water, a little salt and a little white pepper. Brush over dough. (Excess dough from trimmings may be rolled out and used for decorating, if desired.) Bake, covered with foil, for 30 minutes; uncover and continue baking for an additional 20 minutes or until chicken is tender and dough is nicely brown. Combine marmalade, mustard, wine and orange juice and heat through. Serve warm with the chicken.

CHICKEN ANGELINA

6 servings

3 whole chicken breasts, split and skinned
3 tablespoons butter or margarine
Salt and pepper
1 cup chicken broth
1 onion, chopped
1 4-ounce can green chilies (preferably hot)
1 small clove garlic, chopped
1 tablespoon flour
½ cup cream
½ cup shredded Cheddar cheese

In a skillet brown chicken in half the butter and season with salt and pepper. Lay chicken in single layer in greased shallow baking dish. Splash with about ¼ cup chicken broth. Cover tightly and bake in preheated 350° oven 20 minutes. While chicken bakes, heat onion gently in remaining butter until soft and golden. Rinse, dry and seed chilies. Dice the chilies and add with garlic and flour to the onions. Stir and cook a minute or so. Stir in broth (add broth from chicken to measure 1 cup). Stir over low heat until smooth and slightly thickened. Pour into blender and whirl until pureed. Put back in skillet and stir in cream. Heat just to simmering and pour over chicken. Sprinkle with cheese. Bake in 350° oven 25-30 minutes, or until chicken is heated through and cheese is melted.

LA DOÑA LUZ'S CHICKEN

6 servings

6   boneless chicken
     breasts
     Seasoned salt
     Pepper
6   slices Swiss cheese
6   teaspoons finely
     chopped parsley
6   thin slices ham
     Bread crumbs
½   pound butter, melted
1   15-ounce can whole
     tomatoes, slightly
     drained
¾   cup heavy cream
1   teaspoon salt
1   teaspoon sugar
1   tablespoon white wine
     Dash white pepper
     Dash garlic powder
     White rice

Lay chicken breasts, skin side down and season with seasoned salt and pepper. Lay 1 slice Swiss cheese, 1 teaspoon parsley and 1 slice ham on each breast. Roll the combination with ham and cheese on the inside and the chicken skin side up. Put into a 6" x 6" pan very tightly together so that the melted cheese cannot run out. Cover the breasts with a generous amount of bread crumbs and pour melted butter over the top. Season again with seasoned salt. Cover with foil. Bake 1 hour at 325°. Remove foil and bake for another ½ hour. Remove from oven. In a blender put the tomatoes, cream, salt, sugar, white wine, white pepper and garlic powder. Blend gently so as to leave the tomatoes in small chunks. Heat to a boil. Remove chicken breasts from pan and place on a bed of white rice. Spoon the hot tomato bisque over the breasts.

CRAB-STUFFED CHICKEN

8 servings

4   large chicken breasts,
     halved, skinned, boned
     and pounded
3   tablespoons butter
¼   cup flour
¾   cup milk
¾   cup chicken broth
⅓   cup dry white wine
¼   cup onion, chopped
1   tablespoon butter
1   7½-ounce can
     crabmeat, drained and
     flaked
1   4-ounce can
     mushrooms
½   cup crumbled saltine
     crackers (about 10)
2   tablespoons parsley,
     chopped
½   teaspoon salt
     Dash pepper
1   cup shredded Swiss
     cheese
½   teaspoon paprika

In saucepan melt 3 tablespoons butter; blend in flour, milk, broth and wine. Cook and stir until mixture thickens and bubbles. Set aside. In skillet cook onion in 1 tablespoon butter until transparent but not browned. Stir in crabmeat, mushrooms, crackers, parsley, salt and pepper. Add 2 tablespoons white sauce. Take 1 piece of chicken and put ¼ cup crab mixture in center. Fold in sides and roll up. Place seam side down in 11" X 13" baking dish. Repeat procedure for remaining chicken. Pour remaining sauce over all chicken rolls. Bake covered in 350° oven for 45 minutes-1 hour. Sprinkle with cheese and paprika and return to oven for 2-5 minutes uncovered until cheese melts.

CHICKEN BREASTS IN ORANGE SAUCE   6-8 servings

½   cup flour
½   teaspoon salt
½   teaspoon paprika
    Dash of pepper
    Dash of garlic powder
6   chicken breasts, halved
6   tablespoons salad oil
1   4-ounce can mushrooms, whole or sliced, reserve liquid
1   10½-ounce can condensed cream of mushroom soup
½   cup chicken broth
½   cup orange juice
½   cup dry white wine or dry sherry
¼   teaspoon nutmeg or mace
2   teaspoons brown sugar
2   cups carrots, sliced diagonally about ½" thick

Blend flour, salt, paprika, pepper and garlic powder. Coat chicken breasts with flour mixture. Heat oil and brown chicken well on both sides in the hot oil. Drain the mushrooms, reserving liquid; scatter mushrooms over chicken. Blend soup, reserved mushroom liquid, chicken broth, orange juice, wine, nutmeg or mace and brown sugar until smooth; pour soup mixture over chicken. Cover and cook at 225° in electric skillet or simmer in a regular frying pan over low heat about 30 minutes or until tender. Add carrots about 15 minutes before done. Serve with rice, buttered or plain.

PROVENCALE CHICKEN   4 servings

2   chicken breasts, split
2   tablespoons flour
3   tablespoons Parmesan cheese
½   teaspoon salt
⅛   teaspoon pepper
1   tablespoon butter
1   tablespoon vegetable oil
¼   cup chopped onion
1   clove minced garlic
2   tablespoons chopped green pepper
2   medium tomatoes, chopped
½   cup dry white wine or dry sherry
2   tablespoons chopped parsley

Skin and bone chicken. Flatten slightly between sheets of wax paper with flat side of meat mallet. Combine flour, cheese, salt and pepper on one piece of wax paper. Turn chicken in mixture to coat on all sides. Heat butter and oil in large skillet. Saute' chicken 4 minutes on each side; remove to warm plate. Saute' onion, garlic and green pepper for 3 minutes. Stir in tomatoes and wine. Return chicken to skillet and spoon sauce over chicken. Lower heat and simmer for 5 minutes. Garnish with parsley.

Delicious served with noodles or spaghetti, French bread and lettuce salad.

CURRIED ORANGE CHICKEN

6-8 servings

8	chicken breast halves
8	tablespoons butter or margarine
2	cups orange juice
2	tablespoons curry powder
8	tablespoons honey
1	cup prepared mustard
1	cup raisins (optional)

Saute' the chicken in the butter or margarine over medium heat until lightly browned. Combine the orange juice, curry, honey and mustard and pour it over the chicken in a pan. Cover and cook over low heat about 45 minutes or until tender. (More orange juice may be added if needed.)

FIESTA CHICKEN

6-8 servings

4	large chicken breasts, split and skinned
1½	teaspoons salt
1	teaspoon paprika
¼	cup flour
¼	cup shortening or salad oil
¼	cup finely chopped onion
⅓	cup catsup
3	tablespoons white wine vinegar
3	tablespoons Worcestershire sauce
¾	cup Sauterne or other dry white wine
4	cups hot cooked rice
1	4-ounce can chopped green chilies
1	large avocado, peeled and sliced

Dust chicken with mixture of salt, paprika and flour. Brown chicken in shortening or oil. Combine onion, catsup, vinegar, Worcestershire sauce and wine and pour over chicken. Cover and simmer about 45 minutes or until chicken is tender. Place hot rice on a hot platter and arrange chicken breasts around it. Stir green chilies into sauce and spoon over chicken. Arrange avocado slices between chicken breasts, pinwheel style.

Spectacular to look at as well as a treat to eat! It's perfect party fare.

CHICKEN DIJON

4 servings

4	chicken breasts, split, skinned and boned
3	tablespoons butter or margarine
2	tablespoons flour
1	cup chicken broth
½	cup half-and-half
2	tablespoons Dijon-style mustard
	Tomato wedges
	Parsley

In a large skillet cook chicken breasts in butter or margarine until tender, about 20 minutes. Remove chicken to warm serving platter. Stir flour into skillet drippings. Add chicken broth and half-and-half. Cook and stir until mixture thickens and bubbles. Stir in mustard. Add chicken breasts. Cover and heat 10 minutes. Garnish with tomato wedges and parsley. (If serving for guests, brown chicken and make the sauce ahead; heat them together when guests arrive.)

CHICKEN SALTIMBOCA

6 servings

6   chicken breast halves, skinned and boned
6   thin ham slices
6   thin slices mozzarella cheese
    Italian herb seasoning
4   tablespoons butter, melted
⅓   cup bread crumbs
2   tablespoons Parmesan cheese
2   tablespoons parsley, chopped

Pound chicken breasts between 2 pieces of waxed paper, until about ¼" thickness. On boned side of each breast, place 1 slice of ham, 1 slice of mozzarella cheese and a dash of Italian herb seasoning. Roll up. Dip each piece in melted butter. Then roll in mixture of bread crumbs Parmesan cheese and parsley. Place in shallow pan and bake at 350° for 40-45 minutes or until brown and tender. These can be made early in the day and cooked just before guests arrive. (A light cream sauce may be spooned over each breast, if desired.)

PECAN BREADED CHICKEN

4 servings

2   whole chicken breasts, skinned, boned and cut in half
10   tablespoons butter
3   tablespoons Dijon mustard
5-6   ounces ground pecans
2   tablespoons vegetable oil
⅔   cup sour cream
    Salt
    Freshly ground pepper

Flatten chicken breasts, season with salt and pepper. Melt 6 tablespoons butter. Remove from heat and stir in 2 tablespoons mustard. Dip each piece of chicken into butter and mustard mixture and coat each one with ground pecans by patting them on with your hands. Preheat oven to 200°. Melt 4 tablespoons butter in large skillet. Add oil and saute' chicken pieces 3 minutes on each side. Remove to baking dish and place in oven to keep warm. In small saucepan add sour cream and remaining mustard, 1 teaspoon salt and ¼ teaspoon pepper. Remove from heat. Place a dollop of sour cream sauce in the middle of warmed dinner plates and cover it completely with a portion of chicken. Sauce should not be visible on the plate and thus will be a surprise to the diner.

So luxurious, a plain steamed vegetable provides excellent contrast!

CHICKEN ST. JOHN

8 servings

2   broiler-fryers,
     quartered
1   quart hot water
1   stalk celery
1   small onion
1   sprig of parsley
1   whole carrot
1   tablespoon salt
4   peppercorns
1   bay leaf

SAUCE:

2   tablespoons butter
3   tablespoons flour
1   cup chicken broth
1   cup whipping cream
½   cup grated Longhorn
     cheese
½   teaspoon salt
     Generous pinch each
     rosemary and basil
     Dash Tabasco
½   pound fresh
     mushrooms, sliced and
     lightly sauteed in but-
     ter
2   avocados, sliced
1½   cups toasted almonds,
     sauteed in butter

Place chicken quarters in heavy kettle; add hot water, celery, onion, parsley, carrot, salt, peppercorns and bay leaf. Bring to boiling point; cover tightly and let simmer over low heat 1 hour. Let chicken cool in the liquid. Strain and reserve 1 cup of broth for sauce. Melt butter in saucepan, blend in flour and cook 1 minute. Stir in broth and cream. Stir until thick but do not boil. Add cheese, salt, rosemary, basil and Tabasco. Preheat oven to 350°. Place sauteed mushrooms in bottom of a 9" X 13" baking pan, add chicken quarters and pour sauce over all. Bake covered for 30 minutes. During the last 10 minutes, remove cover, top with sliced avocados and toasted almonds.

TANDOORI CHICKEN

4 servings

1   cup plain yogurt
2   teaspoons ground cor-
     iander
1   teaspoon ground
     cumin
1½   inch fresh ginger,
     scraped and chopped
3   cloves garlic, minced
¼   teaspoon ground chili
     powder
½   teaspoon paprika
1   teaspoon salt
2   tablespoons vegetable
     oil
2-2½ pounds chicken
     pieces, skinned

In the blender combine ½ cup yogurt, coriander, cumin, ginger, garlic, chili powder, paprika and salt. Remove from blender and add remaining yogurt and oil. Mix. Place the chicken pieces in a large deep casserole. Pour the yogurt sauce evenly over the chicken and cover with a lid or foil and marinate for 12 hours at room temperature or for at least 24 hours in the refrigerator. Before cooking, arrange the chicken side by side on a rack in a shallow pan and broil in the middle of the oven for 15-20 minutes per side or barbeque over the grill. Serve with cut lemons, onions, tomatoes and radishes.

HUNGARIAN CHICKEN

8 servings

8   slices bacon
½   cup chopped onion
2   3-4 pound chickens, cut up or 8 chicken breasts, halved
1   cup flour
2   teaspoons salt
1   tablespoon paprika
8   tablespoons chicken broth

Chop bacon and cook in large skillet until crisp. Remove bacon from skillet. Add onion to fat and cook until soft but not brown. Remove and set aside. Combine flour, salt and paprika in paper bag. Shake chicken pieces in mixture to coat. Brown chicken in bacon fat, adding more fat if necessary. Spoon 8 tablespoons of chicken broth over browned chicken, cover and cook over low heat until tender, about 25 minutes.

GRAVY:

3   tablespoons flour
1   cup chicken broth
⅔   cup milk
1½   teaspoons paprika
½   teaspoon salt
1½   cups sour cream

Remove chicken from skillet. Stir flour into the fat to make a smooth paste. Add broth, milk and cook stirring constantly until thick. Add paprika, salt and reserved onion and bacon. Add sour cream and heat, stirring until blended. DO NOT BOIL. Return chicken to sour cream mixture, coat, cover and let stand, off heat for 1 hour to blend flavors. Reheat gently and serve with noodles, if desired.

CHICKEN ALMOND

4-6 servings

1   3-pound fryer, cut up
¼   cup butter or oil
¼   cup onion, chopped
½   cup celery, chopped
1   10½-ounce can condensed cream of mushroom soup
1   tablespoon cornstarch
1   tablespoon lemon juice
1   tablespoon soy sauce
1   4-ounce package blanched, slivered almonds
½   of 8-ounce can water chestnuts, thinly-sliced
1   cup fresh bean sprouts
   Chow mein noodles

Brown chicken in butter or oil. Remove chicken and saute' onions and celery until golden. Put chicken back in pan. Combine soup, cornstarch, lemon juice and soy sauce and pour over chicken. Cover tightly and cook 30-40 minutes over medium low heat or until chicken is done. Add almonds, water chestnuts and bean sprouts just before serving. Serve over crisp chow mein noodles.

COUNTRY CAPTAIN CHICKEN

4-6 servings

3   pounds chicken
    pieces, skinned
⅓   cup flour
1   tablespoon salt
    Pepper
¼   cup shortening
1   cup onion, chopped
1   cup green pepper,
    chopped
1   clove garlic, crushed
1½ cups water
1   12-ounce bottle catsup
2   teaspoons curry
    powder
½   teaspoon ground
    thyme
3   cups hot cooked rice
⅓   cup currants or raisins
½   cup almonds, chopped
    or sliced

Preheat oven to 350°. Coat chicken with mixture of flour, salt and pepper. Brown chicken in shortening in skillet. Remove chicken after it has browned and place in 9" X 13" pan. Add onions, green pepper and garlic to drippings in skillet and saute' lightly. Stir in water, catsup, curry powder and thyme and mix well. Pour sauce over chicken and bake uncovered for 1 hour. Serve by placing a serving of rice on each plate; top rice with sauce from the chicken and sprinkle currants or raisins and nuts on top. Place a piece of chicken on each plate with a green vegetable of your choice.

An excellent company recipe. The chicken may be prepared early in the day and baked before serving.

POLLO PEPITORIA

6-8 servings

2   2½-3-pound chickens,
    cut into serving pieces
    Salt and freshly
    ground pepper
4   thick slices French
    bread, about two
    ounces
1   tablespoon red-wine
    vinegar
6   tablespoons olive oil
45 unblanched almonds
    or ⅓ cup pumpkin
    seeds
6   whole cloves garlic,
    peeled
1   bay leaf
2   cups hot chicken broth
¼   cup mayonnaise
1   tablespoon lemon
    juice

Sprinkle the chicken pieces with salt and pepper to taste and set aside. Trim the crusts from the bread and sprinkle each slice with equal amounts of vinegar. Heat four tablespoons of oil in a heavy skillet and add the bread, almonds, garlic and bay leaf. Cook, turning the bread and shaking the skillet, until all the elements are golden brown. Remove the bread, garlic, almonds and bay leaf and add them to the container of a food processor or electric blender. Leave the oil in the skillet. Blend the bread and garlic mixture. Scrape the mixture into a bowl and add the hot chicken broth. Blend well. Add two more tablespoons of oil to the skillet and add the chicken, skinside down. Cook until golden and turn. Cook for a total of 25 minutes. Pour off the fat. Pour the bread and broth mixture over the chicken and stir. Cover and cook about 15 minutes longer. Blend the mayonnaise and lemon juice and stir this mixture, little by little, into the sauce. Serve piping hot. Do not boil after the mayonnaise is added.

🦃 NEW MEXICAN HOT POT

8 servings

2	tablespoons vegetable oil
1	cup finely chopped onion
1	cup dark seedless raisins
1	teaspoon minced garlic
¼	teaspoon ground cloves
1	28-ounce can plus 1 8-ounce can peeled whole tomatoes, un-drained
1	cup chicken broth
1	4-ounce can chopped green chilies
¾	cup sliced pimiento-stuffed green olives
4	pounds chicken drum-sticks, thighs and breasts, skin removed
2	pounds potatoes, peeled and cut in 1″ chunks (about 6 cups)

In large Dutch oven heat oil over moderate heat. Stir in onion and cook 5 minutes, stirring occasionally. Stir in raisins, garlic and cloves and cook 1 minute. Stir in tomatoes, chicken broth, chilies and olives and bring to a boil over moderate heat. Add chicken and potatoes. When simmering, reduce heat; cover and simmer 45 minutes, or until done. Uncover pot; stir gently and cook 10 minutes longer. Add salt if needed.

CAPERED CHICKEN

4 servings

1	3-pound chicken, cut into pieces
	Salt
	Pepper
3	tablespoons olive oil
1	onion, minced
2	garlic cloves, minced
3	tomatoes, seeded and chopped
¼	cup white wine
¼	teaspoon cumin
¼	teaspoon oregano
10	blanched almonds, lightly toasted
1¼	cups chicken broth
4	tablespoons raisins
4	tablespoons green olives, sliced
2	tablespoons drained capers

Sprinkle chicken with salt and pepper and brown in oil. Transfer chicken to another dish. Saute' onion and garlic in remaining oil. Add tomatoes and simmer 5 minutes until most of the moisture has evaporated. Add wine, cumin and oregano. Simmer 5 more minutes. In a blender grind the almonds. Add chicken broth to the tomato mixture along with the ground almonds, raisins, olives and capers. Add chicken, turning it to coat with sauce. Cook, covered, for 25-30 minutes. Add traditional salt and pepper to taste. Serve with rice.

KAPAMA - STEWED GREEK CHICKEN   4-5 servings

1   4-pound chicken
     Juice of ½ lemon
2   teaspoons cinnamon
     Salt and pepper
¼   pound butter
½   cup tomato paste
1½   cups boiling water
¼   cup red wine

Cut chicken into serving-size pieces and sprinkle with lemon juice, cinnamon, salt and pepper. Brown chicken in butter. Mix tomato paste with water in a large saucepan and bring to a boil. Reduce heat and carefully place browned chicken into sauce. Pour the browning butter through a strainer over the chicken and sauce. Add wine and cook 1 hour or until chicken is tender. Serve chicken and sauce over noodles.

OVEN LEMON CHICKEN   4 servings

1   3-pound fryer, cut up
½   cup flour
1   teaspoon salt
1   teaspoon paprika
4   tablespoons margarine
     or butter

LEMON BASTE:

¼   cup lemon juice
1   tablespoon oil
2   tablespoons minced
     onion
1   clove garlic, minced
½   teaspoon salt
½   teaspoon white pepper
½   teaspoon thyme

Coat chicken in mixture of flour, salt and paprika. Melt butter or margarine in baking dish. Add chicken pieces and coat with margarine. Arrange skin side down in a 9" X 13" pan. Bake at 375° for 30 minutes. While chicken bakes, prepare the lemon baste by mixing together the remaining ingredients. Turn the chicken pieces and spoon lemon baste evenly over them. Bake 30 minutes longer.

CHICKEN NORMANDIE   6-8 servings

2   3-pound fryer-broilers,
     cut up
     Salt and pepper
¼   pound butter
4   tablespoons Calvados,
     warmed (or Apple Jack
     or apple brandy)
5-6 shallots, finely chop-
     ped
1   tablespoon parsley,
     chopped
1   sprig thyme or ¼ teas-
     poon dried thyme
½   cup cider or white
     wine
½   cup whipping cream

Wash and dry chicken pieces thoroughly. Salt and pepper each piece. Lightly brown the pieces on all sides in butter in heavy skillet with a cover. Lower heat and cook 15 minutes, turning the pieces often. Slowly pour in the warmed Calvados, light it and shake until the flame dies. (BEWARE! This is 100 proof brandy and will make a very high flame.) Add the shallots, parsley, thyme and cider or white wine. Blend well. Cover and cook about 45 minutes or until chicken is tender. Remove chicken to heated platter and add ½ cup whipping cream to juices in skillet. Heat thoroughly and pour sauce over chicken just before serving. Serve with hot cooked rice.

HERB-BUTTER GLAZED CHICKEN

4 servings

¼ cup melted butter or margarine
½ teaspoon marjoram
½ teaspoon salt
¼ teaspoon tarragon
1 small clove garlic, minced
Juice of half a lemon
2 pounds chicken pieces

Melt butter or margarine. Add marjoram, salt, tarragon and garlic. Sprinkle lemon juice over chicken pieces and then brush with herb butter. Place chicken skin side down on preheated charcoal grill. Turn chicken frequently brushing with remaining herb butter throughout the cooking period. Cook 45 minutes, or until done.

CHICKEN ARTICHOKE CASSEROLE

3-4 servings

1 3-pound chicken cut into serving pieces
1½ teaspoons salt
¼ teaspoon pepper
½ teaspoon paprika
6 tablespoons butter
1 14-ounce can artichoke hearts, drained
¼ pound fresh mushrooms, sliced
2 tablespoons flour
⅔ cup chicken broth
3 tablespoons sherry
¼ teaspoon rosemary

Sprinkle chicken with salt, pepper, and paprika. In skillet brown chicken in 4 tablespoons of the butter and transfer to a 2-quart casserole. Arrange artichoke hearts between chicken pieces. Melt remaining butter in the skillet and in it saute' mushrooms until barely tender. Sprinkle flour over mushrooms and stir in broth, sherry and rosemary. Cook, stirring, until slightly thickened, then pour over chicken and artichoke hearts. Cover and bake in 375° oven for 40 minutes or until tender.

VIENNESE CHICKEN

4 servings

1 3-4 pound chicken, cut up
Flour seasoned with salt and pepper
1 cup chopped onions
1 cup fresh mushrooms
⅔ cup chopped fresh parsley
¾ cup dry white wine
4 slices bacon cut in 1" squares
Juice of ½ lemon
1 cup sour cream

Dust chicken with seasoned flour. Brown on all sides with butter. Put ½ of the onions, mushrooms and parsley in a medium sized casserole with a tight fitting lid. Arrange chicken over them and top with rest of the onions, mushrooms and parsley. Pour in white wine. Sprinkle with salt and pepper. Cook bacon briefly, just long enough to remove a little fat; drain well and crumble over chicken. Cover and bake at 350° for 1 hour. Just before serving, remove chicken from casserole. Mix a ladle full of juices with lemon juice and sour cream; and stir into remaining casserole.

A superb blend of Old World flavors!

CHICKEN MARINADE

4-6 servings

1   8-ounce can tomato
     sauce
½   cup oil
½   cup orange juice
¼   cup vinegar
1½   teaspoons oregano
1   teaspoon salt
6   peppercorns
½   teaspoon dry mustard
1   clove garlic, minced
¼   cup honey
1   broiler-fryer, cut up

Combine first 10 ingredients and pour over chicken. Marinate 3-4 hours. Grill over hot coals or under heated broiler unit until tender, basting often with marinade.

CANTONESE CHICKEN

3-4 servings

1   2½ pound chicken, cut
     into pieces
     Seasoned flour
     Peanut oil
2   tablespoons dry ver-
     mouth or sake
4   tablespoons soy sauce
⅓   cup water
3   slices fresh ginger,
     peeled and chopped
2   green onions, sliced
     diagonally
1   teaspoon sugar

Coat chicken in seasoned flour and fry in peanut oil until golden. Drain most of the oil and add the remaining ingredients. Cover and cook 15-30 minutes, or until done. Turn often while cooking; add water if needed.

An easy and delicious Chinese dish which also is excellent as an appetizer.

DYNASTY CHICKEN

4 servings

1   large chicken, cut up
½   cup catsup
3   tablespoons honey
3   tablespoons soy sauce
1   clove minced garlic
2   tablespoons lemon
     juice
1   tablespoon cornstarch
2   tablespoons water
1   papaya or pineapple,
     cut into spears
1   lime (optional)

Arrange chicken pieces skin side up in 9″ X 13″ pan. Mix together catsup, honey, soy sauce, garlic and lemon juice and pour over chicken pieces. Let marinate at least 2 hours or longer. Cover and bake at 375° for 30 minutes. Uncover pan, baste with sauce and continue baking 30 minutes longer. Pour off juices into a sauce pan and bring to a boil. Mix together cornstarch and water, add to juices in pan and cook until sauce thickens. Arrange chicken on serving dish and spoon sauce over. Slice papaya or pineapple and arrange around chicken. Garnish with lime slices, if desired.

SPECIAL SESAME CHICKEN

4-6 servings

½   **cup flour**
¼   **teaspoon chili powder**
¼   **teaspoon paprika**
½   **teaspoon onion salt**
½   **teaspoon lemon-pepper seasoning**
1½ **teaspoons garlic salt, divided**
1   **broiler-fryer, cut up**
4   **tablespoons butter, melted**
1   **tablespoon vegetable oil**
¼   **teaspoon pepper**
1   **cup sesame seeds, lightly toasted**

Preheat oven to 350°. Thoroughly mix flour, chili powder, paprika, onion salt, lemon-pepper seasoning and ½ teaspoon garlic salt. Roll chicken pieces in seasoned flour. Combine melted butter, oil, 1 teaspoon garlic salt and pepper. Dip floured chicken pieces in seasoned butter and then roll in sesame seeds. Place pieces in shallow greased 9″ X 13″ baking pan and bake at 350° for 1 hour, turning after 30 minutes.

BAKED GINGERED CHICKEN

4 servings

1   **3-pound fryer, cut up**
1   **cup soy sauce**
1   **garlic clove, minced**
1   **tablespoon vinegar**
2   **tablespoons lemon juice**
6   **ounces ginger marmalade**

Marinate chicken several hours in soy sauce, garlic, vinegar and lemon juice, turning often. Remove from sauce and place chicken pieces in shallow baking pan. Cover pan tightly with foil and cook in 300° oven 30 minutes. Remove from oven, turn pieces and baste with marmalade that has been thinned with a little water. Return to oven and bake another 30 minutes, basting frequently. Serve with rice.

CHINESE CHICKEN-IN-A-BAG

4-6 servings

24 **peeled cloves of garlic**
1   **whole chicken or 3-4 pounds chicken pieces**
2-4 **tablespoons soy sauce**
½   **cup honey**
1   **slice fresh ginger, diced**
4   **tablespoons frozen orange juice concentrate**
2   **tablespoons sesame oil**

Place garlic inside whole chicken or if using chicken pieces, place garlic on the bottom of roasting pan then put pieces on top. Mix soy with honey; add diced fresh ginger, orange concentrate and sesame oil. Brush chicken with soy mixture. If using whole chicken, place chicken inside a paper bag; tie bag closed and place in roasting pan. If using chicken pieces, cover roasting pan with a paper bag and secure. Bake in 375° oven 1¼ to 1½ hours.

🐦 MEXICAN CHICKEN

5-6 servings

4	pounds chicken breasts
1	tablespoon salt
3	cups water
1	tablespoon margarine, melted
1	medium onion, chopped
2	green peppers, finely chopped
1	clove garlic, minced
1	16-ounce can tomatoes
2	4-ounce cans button mushrooms, drained
4	tablespoons parsley, chopped
1	teaspoon sugar
1	teaspoon black pepper
1	teaspoon chili powder
½	teaspoon oregano
1	10½-ounce can condensed cream of tomato soup
1	10½-ounce can condensed cream of mushroom soup

Place chicken breasts, salt and water in large pot and simmer until chicken is tender. Cool chicken in broth. Remove bones. Reduce broth to 2 cups; strain and reserve broth. In the margarine saute' the onion, green peppers and garlic until the onion is transparent. Add tomatoes, mushrooms, parsley, sugar, black pepper, chili powder, oregano and reserved 2 cups broth. Cook uncovered for 15 minutes. Add soups and mix well. Preheat oven to 400°. Place chicken in 8" x 12" baking pan. Add tomato mixture and cover. Bake for 30 minutes. Serve over hot cooked rice.

NIGERIAN CHICKEN PEANUT STEW

4 servings

4	cups chicken broth
¾	cup creamy peanut butter
3	tablespoons butter
4	tablespoons flour
1	3-4 pound chicken, cooked and cubed
	Salt and pepper to taste
3	tablespoons vermouth

In a bowl combine chicken broth and peanut butter. In a pan melt butter; stir in flour and cook stirring constantly for 3 minutes. Remove from heat and stir in peanut butter mixture and cubed chicken. Heat stew over moderately low heat stirring until hot. Season with salt and pepper. Stir in vermouth. Serve with halved hard-boiled eggs, rice, orange sections, sliced banana, chutney or chopped peanuts.

Wonderful as a party buffet item.

🦆 MOLE CON ARROZ
(Mole with Rice)

4 servings

2	tablespoons vegetable oil
1	cup slivered almonds
1	cup chopped onion
1	medium clove garlic, minced
⅛	teaspoon cinnamon
⅛	teaspoon cloves
¼	teaspoon pepper
1	ounce unsweetened chocolate, coarsely chopped
2	7-ounce cans green chile salsa
1	15-ounce can tomato sauce
2	cups cooked turkey or chicken, cut in bite-size pieces
4	portions hot cooked rice
1	avocado, peeled and sliced
1	orange, sliced
	Dairy sour cream

Heat oil in skillet over medium heat and saute' almonds, onion and garlic for 10 minutes, stirring often. Stir in next 6 ingredients; heat, stirring, until chocolate melts. Puree mixture in blender or food processor. Return mixture to skillet, stir in turkey; simmer 5 minutes. Serve over hot rice and garnish with slices of avocado, orange, dollops of sour cream.

This is an easy version, with authentic flavor, of one of Mexico's favorite dishes. Served with crisp green salad, warm tortillas and beer, it makes a festive and delicious meal.

DELHI CHICKEN

4-6 servings

½	cup chopped onion
½	cup chopped celery
2-3	tablespoons curry powder
¼	cup oil
⅓	cup cornstarch
2	cups chicken stock or chicken bouillon
1	cup tomato juice
½	teaspoon Worcestershire sauce
	Salt and pepper to taste
4-5	cups cooked diced chicken
½	pound fresh mushrooms, sliced and sauteed in butter

Lightly brown onions, celery and curry powder in oil. Add cornstarch and blend. Add stock and cook until thick, stirring constantly. Add tomato juice, Worcestershire sauce, salt, pepper, chicken and mushrooms. Heat thoroughly. Serve over rice. Also serve with chutney, cucumbers in yogurt, raisins marinated in white wine, diced tomatoes in mint sauce, chopped bacon, chopped green pepper and chopped onions.

🦃FAMILY-STYLE CHICKEN CASSEROLE   6-8 servings

1   10½-ounce can con-
    densed cream of
    mushroom soup
1   10½-ounce can con-
    densed cream of
    chicken soup
1   cup milk
1   medium onion,
    chopped
1   4-ounce can chopped
    green chilies
2   cups cooked chicken
    or turkey, diced
12 corn tortillas
    Cooking oil
12 ounces Cheddar
    cheese, grated

Combine the soups, milk, onion, chilies and chicken in a large saucepan and heat through. Fry tortillas in hot oil to soften, about 1 minute; drain well on paper towels. In a 3-quart buttered casserole, place a layer of tortillas, a layer of soup mixture and a layer of grated cheese. Repeat layers, ending with cheese. Bake in 350° oven for 30 minutes.

A perennial family favorite.

🦃CHICKEN EMPANADA   6 servings

1   cup butter
1   8-ounce package
      cream cheese,
      softened
½   teaspoon salt
2⅓   cups unsifted all pur-
      pose flour
4   green onions, finely
      minced
¼   cup celery, finely
      chopped
2   tablespoons butter
6   ounces pasteurized
      processed garlic
      cheese
1   10½-ounce can con-
      densed cream of
      mushroom soup
2   tablespoons finely
      chopped green chili
1   whole chicken, cooked
      and diced
1   egg yolk
2   teaspoons milk

Beat butter, cream cheese and salt together until completly soft and smooth. Work in flour gradually to form a smooth dough. Flatten dough to an 8" x 6" rectangle. Chill overnight in plastic wrap. Saute' onions and celery in butter until soft. Add garlic cheese, soup, green chili and chicken. Cool. Ten minutes before making empanadas, remove dough from refrigerator. Divide in 3 pieces. Using 2 sheets of wax paper, roll each piece until 1/8" thick. Cut into 7" circles. Drop filling onto lower half of circle. Fold top of dough over and pinch edges together well. Place each completed empanada on a cookie sheet and place in refrigerator until all are made. Beat egg yolk with milk and brush tops of each empanada well with mixture. At this point they may be frozen. Bake at 350° until light brown, 25-30 minutes. If frozen defrost only 10 minutes before baking. If allowed to come to room temperature pastry tends to get very soft and fall apart.

🦃 SAGEBRUSH INN'S CHIMICHANGAS   6 servings

1   3-4 pound chicken, boiled, boned and shredded
½   cup green chilies, peeled and chopped
½   cup fresh tomatoes, chopped
¼   cup onion, chopped
6   large flour tortillas
     Shredded Cheddar or Monterey Jack cheese
     Cooking oil
     Chili sauce

Combine chicken, chili, tomatoes and onion; mix well. Divide mixture into 6 portions and place one on each tortillas. Top with desired amount of cheese. Roll and secure with toothpicks. Deep fry to golden brown. Top with chili sauce.

CORNISH HENS IN WINE   6 servings

6   Cornish game hens
6   cloves garlic, peeled
6   teaspoons dried tarragon
     Salt and pepper
     Garlic salt
¾   cup butter, melted
¾   cup dry white wine
1   tablespoon tarragon

In cavity of each hen place 1 clove garlic, 1 teaspoon tarragonn ¼ teaspoon salt and 1/8 teaspoon pepper. Sprinkle outsides liberally with garlic salt. Chill. Roast hens for 45 minutes, or until done, in large shallow pan at 450°. Baste frequently with sauce made from melted butter, white wine and tarragon.

🦃 TURKEY ENCHILADAS   6 servings

2   14-ounce cans enchilada sauce
12   fresh corn tortillas
½   cup cooking oil
3   cups cooked turkey, diced
½   cup green onions, chopped
½   pound Longhorn cheese, grated
½   pound Monterey Jack cheese, grated
½   cup sliced black olives

Warm enchilada sauce in a saucepan and set aside. Dip corn tortillas in hot cooking oil only until limp; dip into warmed enchilada sauce and then fill each tortilla with small amounts of turkey, onions, cheeses and olives. Carefully roll each enchilada and place seamside down in a 9" x 13" pan. Pour enchilada sauce over the top and sprinkle with remaining cheese. Garnish with extra sliced olives if desired. Bake in 325° oven for 25 minutes or until cheese is melted and sauce is bubbly.

New Mexicans serve this dish with a generous sprinkling of shredded crisp lettuce, an accompaniment of hot sopaipillas and a side dish of pineapple sherbert to clear and cool the palate. These enchiladas are perfect for leftover holiday turkey!

🦃 TURKEY WITH TAMALE STUFFING

2½   10-ounce cans mild enchilada sauce
2   10-ounce cans water
2   13¾-ounce cans chicken broth
2   teaspoons chili powder
½   teaspoon poultry seasoning
1   teaspoon salt
1   medium onion, quartered
1   clove garlic, sliced
     Turkey liver, gizzard and neck
8   ounces hot sausage
1   large onion, chopped
¼   cup butter
24   tamales, broken into pieces
1   recipe day-old corn bread to fill a 9″ x 9″ pan
2   eggs, beaten
1¼   cup chicken broth
½   teaspoon ground cumin
     Salt to taste
     Pepper to taste
1   16-20 pound turkey

Combine enchilada sauce, water, chicken broth, chili powder, poultry seasoning, salt, onion, garlic, turkey liver, gizzard and neck and simmer 3-4 hours, adding more water if necessary. Set aside to use as basting sauce and gravy. Strain before using. Brown sausage and drain if necessary. Sauté onions in butter. Crumble tamales and corn bread into a large bowl. Add sausage, onions, eggs, broth, cumin, salt and pepper and mix gently. Loosely stuff turkey and truss before baking. Roast stuffed turkey as usual, basting frequently with gravy until done. Serve with remaining gravy.

New Mexicans continue a tradition begun by the Pilgrims!

TURKEY PAPRIKA

4-5 Servings

1   medium onion, sliced
3   tablespoons butter
2   tablespoons flour
2   teaspoons paprika
½   teaspoon salt
1   cup turkey or chicken broth
2   slightly beaten egg yolks
1   cup sour cream
2   cups diced, cooked turkey
1   4-ounce can sliced mushrooms, drained

In medium saucepan cook onion in butter until tender but not brown. Blend in flour, paprika and salt. Add broth; cook and stir until mixture thickens and bubbles. Cook 1 minute more. Stir a small amount of sauce into beaten egg yolks; return to saucepan. Cook over low heat for 1 minute more. Stir in sour cream until well-blended. Add turkey and mushrooms. Heat slowly just until sauce is hot. Serve with poppy seed noodles.

Baked by the Sun.....

Up and down the enchanting Rio Grande Valley, pueblo-style buildings dominate the architectural scene. Evolved from the pueblos of centuries ago, this simple style is exquisitely adapted to a dry, timberless land where the most readily available building material is clay. Clay and straw are mixed with water and formed into adobe blocks to be baked in the sun. Walls are thick and have blunt angles. Flat roofs are supported by vigas (log beams) that project through the wall. To protect the soluble adobe from the elements, exterior surfaces are plastered and drain spouts are shaped to direct the runoff well beyond the wall line. Many homes in New Mexico employ this simple, sturdy indigenous style as does the University of New Mexico which sometimes is called a "gigantic academic pueblo." The home of the Junior League of Albuquerque, formerly Albuquerque's first aviation terminal, is a charming example of pueblo revival architecture.

Cakes and Cookies

NAVAJO WEDDING BASKET

HAPPINESS CAKE

1   cup sugar
1   cup butter or
      margarine
1   teaspoon vanilla
4   eggs
1   pint can chocolate
      syrup
1   cup flour

Preheat oven to 350°. Cream sugar, margarine and vanilla. Add eggs one at a time, beating thoroughly after each addition. Add chocolate syrup and flour and mix well. Pour into a greased and floured fluted tube pan. Bake for one hour or until cake tests done with a toothpick or cake tester.

Kids love this cake and it is very easy!

HOT FUDGE SUNDAE CAKE

6-8 servings

1   cup flour
¾   cup sugar
2   tablespoons cocoa
2   teaspoons baking
      powder
¼   teaspoon salt
½   cup milk
2   tablespoons oil
1   teaspoon vanilla
1   cup chopped nuts
1   cup brown sugar,
      packed
¼   cup cocoa
1¾   cups hottest tap water

Preheat oven to 350°. In ungreased pan, 9" x 13", stir together flour, sugar, 2 tablespoons cocoa, baking powder and salt. Mix in milk, oil and vanilla with fork until smooth. Stir in nuts. Spread evenly in pan. Sprinkle with brown sugar and ¼ cup cocoa. Pour hot water over batter. Bake 25 minutes. Let stand 15 minutes. Cut into squares and invert each square into a dessert dish. Top with ice cream.

MILKY WAY CAKE

16-20 servings

8   1-7/8 ounce Milky Way
      candy bars
½   cup melted butter
2   cups sugar
½   cup butter, softened
4   eggs
1   teaspoon vanilla
1¼   cups buttermilk
½   teaspoon soda
3   cups flour
1   cup pecans, chopped

Preheat oven to 350°. Combine candy bars and ½ cup melted butter in saucepan and place over low heat until candy is melted, stirring constantly. Cool. Cream sugar and ½ cup softened butter. Add eggs, one at a time, beating well after each addition. Add vanilla. Combine buttermilk and soda and add alternately with flour, beating well. Stir in candy mixture and pecans. Pour into greased and floured tube pan and bake 1 hour and 20 minutes or until cake tests done.

A very rich cake. A tube pan with a removable bottom is advisable.

TRIPLE CHOCOLATE CAKE

1   dark chocolate cake mix
1   4-ounce box instant chocolate pudding mix
¾   cup sour cream
½   cup vegetable oil
½   cup water
¼   cup mayonnaise
4   eggs
3   tablespoons almond liqueur
1   teaspoon almond extract
1   cup chocolate chips
½   cup toasted chopped almonds

GLAZE:

1   cup powdered sugar
2   tablespoons milk
¼   teaspoon almond extract

Preheat oven to 350°. Place all ingredients except chocolate chips and almonds in large bowl and beat 2 minutes with an electric mixer at medium speed. Fold in almonds and chocolate chips. Pour into a 10" bundt pan that has been greased and dusted with cocoa. Bake 50-55 minutes. Cool 15 minutes and remove from pan. Mix glaze ingredients and drizzle over warm cake.

MOCHA CAKE

8-10 servings

1   12-ounce package semisweet chocolate chips
2   tablespoons instant coffee granules
2   tablespoons sugar
    Pinch salt
4   tablespoons water
7   eggs, separated
1   teaspoon vanilla
1   8½-ounce package chocolate wafers, crushed
    Sweetened whipped cream for topping
2   tablespoons coffee-flavored liqueur (optional)

In a small saucepan, combine chocolate chips, coffee, sugar, salt and water. Heat over low heat until chocolate is melted. Cool. Add egg yolks and vanilla and blend with an electric mixer. Beat egg whites until stiff and fold into chocolate mixture. Arrange a thin layer of chocolate wafer crumbs in a 8" x 8" pan. Cover with half of the chocolate mixture. Sprinkle another layer of crumbs over mixture. Chill one hour in freezer. Repeat the second layer of chocolate mixture and crumbs. Chill again in freezer for one hour. Place dessert in refrigerator as this is not intended to be a frozen dessert. To serve, top with sweetened whipped cream. Add coffee liqueur to whipped cream, if desired.

APRICOT BRANDY POUND CAKE   16-20 servings

3   cups sugar
1   cup butter
6   eggs
3   cups flour
¼   teaspoon baking soda
½   teaspoon salt
1   cup sour cream
½   teaspoon rum flavoring
1   teaspoon orange
     flavoring
¼   teaspoon almond ex-
     tract
½   teaspoon lemon flavor-
     ing
1   teaspoon vanilla ex-
     tract
½   cup apricot brandy

Preheat oven to 325°. Cream sugar and butter. Add eggs one at a time beating thoroughly after each addition. Sift dry ingredients together. Combine sour cream with flavorings, extracts and brandy. Add dry ingredients alternately with sour cream mixture. Mix just until blended. Pour into greased bundt pan and bake 70-80 minutes. Cool 15 minutes and turn out of pan.

MARZIPAN CAKE   12-16 servings

1   cup butter
1½   cups sugar
1   teaspoon vanilla ex-
     tract
½   teaspoon almond ex-
     tract
2   eggs
1   cup sour cream
2   cups flour
1   teaspoon baking
     powder
½   teaspoon soda

ALMOND STREUSEL:

½   cup chopped almonds
½   teaspoon cinnamon
¼   cup sugar
8   ounces almond paste

MARZIPAN CAKE TOPPING:

1   cup sour cream
2   tablespoons sugar
½   teaspoon vanilla

Preheat oven to 350°. Cream butter and sugar. Add vanilla extract, almond extract and eggs, beating well. Stir in sour cream. Sift flour, measure and sift again with baking powder and soda. Add flour mixture, beating just until blended. Spoon half of batter into a well greased and floured bundt pan and spread to cover. Add a layer of Almond Streusel, cover with remaining batter and top with remaining Almond Streusel. Bake for 1 hour or until a toothpick inserted comes out clean. Cool on rack for 10 minutes and then turn out of pan. Cover with topping. To make Almond Streusel mix all ingredients in a food processor. To make Marzipan topping mix ingredients and pour over top of cake. Return to oven for 5 minutes. Thoroughly cool, wrap tightly and let sit 3-5 days before cutting.

BAVARIAN SPICE CAKE

2½	cups flour
1	cup sugar
1	cup brown sugar
1	cup oil
2	eggs
1	cup buttermilk
1	teaspoon baking soda
1	teaspoon salt
1	teaspoon cinammon
1	teaspoon nutmeg
1	teaspoon vanilla
1	cup chopped pecans
1	cup coconut

Mix all ingredients together thoroughly. Bake in a greased and floured bundt pan at 350° for 45 minutes - 1 hour. Frost when completely cooled. Cream the cheese and margarine. Add sugar and vanilla and mix well.

FROSTING:

6	ounces cream cheese
¼	cup margarine or butter
2	cups powdered sugar
1	teaspoon vanilla

WHOLE WHEAT CARROT CAKE

1	cup cooking oil
1	cup granulated sugar
1	cup packed brown sugar
1	teaspoon vanilla
4	eggs
2	cups whole wheat flour
⅓	cup nonfat dry milk powder
1	teaspoon baking soda
1	teaspoon baking powder
1	teaspoon salt
2	teaspoons ground cinnamon
3	cups finely shredded carrots
1	cup chopped walnuts
	Powdered sugar

In a large mixer bowl blend oil, granulated sugar and brown sugar on low speed of electric mixer until mixed. Add vanilla; beat in eggs, one at a time, beating well after each addition. In another bowl stir together flour, milk powder, baking soda, baking powder, 1 teaspoon salt and cinnamon. Add to egg mixture until well blended. By hand, stir in carrots and walnuts. Pour batter into a greased and floured 12-cup fluted tube pan. Bake in a 350° oven for 50 minutes or until cake tests done. Cool in pan; invert onto serving plate. Sprinkle sifted powdered sugar atop.

A moist and wholesome cake with a down-home flavor.

PUTTIN' ON THE PEACH CAKE

16-20 servings

1 cup sugar
½ cup margarine
3 eggs
2 cups unsifted flour
1 teaspoon baking powder
1 teaspoon soda
½ teaspoon salt
½ teaspoon cinnamon
2 cups fresh peach puree (made in blender)
1 teapoon vanilla
½ cup chopped pecans or walnuts

Preheat oven to 350°. Cream sugar and margarine. Add eggs and mix thoroughly. Sift together flour, baking powder, soda, salt and cinnamon. Add peach puree and dry ingredients alternately to egg mixture, beating well after each addition. Add vanilla and nuts. Mix well. Spoon batter into a well-greased and floured fluted tube pan. Bake 30-40 minutes. Do not over-bake. Invert pan on serving plate and let stand to cool. Remove and serve with Peach Sauce. To make sauce, combine sugar, cornstarch and salt in a saucepan. Add peaches and water. Cook, stirring, until thick. Add butter and liqueur. Chill.

PEACH SAUCE:

¾ cup sugar
3 tablespoons cornstarch
3 cups sliced peaches
1½ cups water
3 tablespoons butter
6 tablespoons orange-flavored liqueur

BLUEBERRY APRICOT BUNDT CAKE

16-20 servings

1 2-layer size package yellow cake mix
½ cup cooking oil
1 3½-ounce package instant lemon pudding mix
⅔ cup sour cream
1 cup cold water
4 eggs
1 15-ounce can blueberries
½ cup dried apricots, cut up
¼ cup flour
1 tablespoon cinnamon
⅓ cup sugar
½ cup chopped nuts
Powdered sugar

Combine cake mix, oil, dry pudding, sour cream, water and eggs. Beat at medium speed for a full ten minutes. Drain the blueberries, rinse with cold water and drain again thoroughly. Combine berries, apricots and flour. Mix lightly, but thoroughly. Fold berry mixture into batter. Mix cinnamon, sugar and nuts. Spoon half the batter into a well greased and floured bundt pan. Sprinkle half the cinnamon mixture over batter. Add the remaining batter and sprinkle remaining cinnamon on top. Swirl a rubber spatula or knife several times about an inch down through batter so the cinnamon mixture will sink. Bake at 375° for 1 hour. Let cool in pan at least 1 hour. Dust with powdered sugar before serving.

PATIO OATMEAL CAKE

12-16 servings

1½	cup boiling water
1	cup quick-cooking oats
1	stick margarine
1	cup sugar
2	eggs
1	teaspoon vanilla
1⅓	cup flour
1	teaspoon soda
¼	teaspoon salt
1	cup brown sugar
1	teaspoon cinnamon

Preheat oven to 350°. Pour boiling water over oats, margarine and sugar. Let stand 20 minutes. Stir in eggs and vanilla. Then stir in flour, soda, salt, brown sugar and cinnamon. Stir only to blend — do not beat. Pour into a greased 9" x 13" pan. Bake for 35 minutes. Top with icing. Combine all icing ingredients. Spread over warm cake and put under heated broiler unit to brown.

ICING:

1	stick margarine, melted
¾	cup brown sugar
¼	cup evaporated milk
1	cup coconut, shredded
1	cup chopped nuts
1	teaspoon vanilla

POPPY SEED CAKE

16-20 servings

1	cup shortening
3	cups sugar
6	eggs, separated
3	cups flour
¼	teaspoon soda
¼	teaspoon salt
1	cup buttermilk
1	teaspoon vanilla
1	teaspoon almond extract
1	teaspoon lemon extract
1	tablespoon butter flavoring
1	tablespoon poppy seeds

Preheat oven to 350°. Cream sugar and shortening. Add egg yolks, one at a time, and beat with each addition. Beat until creamy. Mix dry ingredients and add to egg yolks and shortening alternately with buttermilk. Add extracts and fold in stiffly beaten egg whites and poppy seeds. Pour into well-greased fluted tube pan and bake 1 hour. Cake is done when firm to touch. Mix glaze ingredients and brush over hot cake with a pastry brush; keep brushing as long as it will soak in.

GLAZE:

1	cup powdered sugar
½	cup lemon juice
1	teaspoon vanilla
1	teaspoon almond extract
1	teaspoon butter flavoring

PUMPKIN CAKE

2 cups sugar
½ cup oil
1 16-ounce can pumpkin
4 eggs
2 cups prepared biscuit mix
2 teaspoons cinnamon
½ teaspoon nutmeg

Preheat oven to 350°. In a large bowl, with mixer at medium speed, beat sugar and oil. Add pumpkin and eggs and beat 1 minute. Stir in biscuit mix, cinnamon and nutmeg. Pour into greased and floured 9" x 13" pan. Bake 25-30 minutes. Cool and top with cream cheese frosting.

CREAM CHEESE FROSTING:

3 ounces cream cheese, softened
⅓ cup margarine, softened
1 tablespoon milk
1 teaspoon vanilla
2 cups powdered sugar

Cream together cream cheese, margarine, milk and vanilla until smooth. Blend in powdered sugar and stir until creamy and of spreading consistency. Spread on cool cake.

CARROT SQUARES

½ cup butter
1½ cups firmly packed light brown sugar
2 cups unsifted all-purpose flour
1 teaspoon nutmeg
1 teaspoon cinnamon
2 teaspoons baking powder
½ teaspoon salt
2 eggs
2 cups finely grated carrots
½ cup chopped walnuts

Melt butter in large saucepan. Add brown sugar; stir until blended. Remove from heat; cool slightly. Sift flour, nutmeg, cinnamon, baking powder and salt in a separate bowl. Beat eggs into cooled butter mixture one at a time. Stir in flour mixture, blending well. Add carrots and chopped walnuts, mixing well. Pour into two greased 8" square pans. Bake in a 350° oven for 30 minutes or until centers spring back when lightly pressed with fingertip. Cool 10 minutes in pans on wire rack; remove from pans; cool completely. To make cream cheese frosting, combine cream cheese and butter in a small bowl; beat until smooth. Stir in vanilla and powdered sugar and beat until fluffy and smooth. Frost squares and top with a walnut half if desired.

CREAM CHEESE FROSTING:

3 ounces softened cream cheese
⅓ cup butter, softened
1 teaspoon vanilla
1½ cups powdered sugar
Walnut halves (optional)

ADOBE BARS

¼ cup shortening
¼ cup butter
1 cup sugar
1 whole egg
2 eggs, separated
1½ cups flour
1 teaspoon baking powder
¼ teaspoon salt
1 cup nuts, chopped
½ cup semisweet chocolate pieces
1 cup miniature marshmallows
1 cup light brown sugar, packed

Preheat oven to 350°. Cream shortening, butter and sugar. Beat in the whole egg and two egg yolks. Sift flour, baking powder and salt together; combine the two mixtures and blend thoroughly. Spread batter in a greased 9" x 13" pan. Sprinkle nuts, chocolate pieces and marshmallows over the batter. Beat 2 egg whites stiff; fold in brown sugar. Spread over top of cake. Bake 35 minutes. Cool and then cut into bars.

Delicious warm or cold, these chewy bars have a rich brown topping that looks like New Mexico adobe.

APRICOT SQUARES

3 dozen cookies

1 stick unsalted butter
1 cup flour
¼ cup powdered sugar
Pinch of salt
20 dried apricot halves, soaked in water and drained
Juice of 1 lemon
1 cup sugar
2 eggs
¼ cup lemon juice
½ teaspoon baking powder
⅛ teaspoon salt

Cut butter in 6 pieces and place in food processor with flour, sugar and salt. Press into the bottom of ungreased 9x9 pan. Bake at 350° for 15 minutes. Place apricots, juice of 1 lemon and sugar in processor bowl. Mince finely and set aside. Using the plastic processor knife, mix eggs for 10 seconds. Add lemon juice, baking powder, salt and apricots. Mix with 3 on-off turns. Pour over baked crust and return to oven for 25-30 minutes. Cut into 1" squares.

CREAM CHEESE SQUARES

16-25 cookies

⅓ cup butter
⅓ cup brown sugar
1 cup flour
½ cup chopped nuts
¼ cup sugar
8 ounces cream cheese, softened
1 egg
2 tablespoons milk
1 tablespoon lemon juice
1 teaspoon vanilla

Cream butter and sugar. Add flour and nuts and mix until crumbly. Reserve 1 cup of the mixture for topping. Press the remainder of the mixture in an 8" square pan. Bake at 350° for 12-15 minutes. Blend sugar with cream cheese. Add egg, milk, lemon juice, and vanilla. Beat well. Spread over baked crust. Sprinkle remaining crumbs on top. Bake at 350° for 25 minutes. Store in refrigerator.

DAKOTA LAYER COOKIES

36 cookies

CRUST:

½ cup butter
1 tablespoon sugar
1 cup flour

FILLING:

2 eggs
1 cup brown sugar
1 cup coconut
½ cup finely chopped nuts
1 teaspoon vanilla
2 tablespoons flour
½ teaspoon baking powder

FROSTING:

½ cup soft butter
1 cup confectioners sugar
2 tablespoons orange juice

For crust cream first three ingredients together; mix well. Press into 8" x 8" greased pan. Bake at 350° for 20-25 minutes. To make filling, beat eggs until light. Add next 6 ingredients; mix well. Spread over baked crust. Bake for 15-20 additional minutes or until dry. Frost with a mixture of soft butter, confectioners sugar and orange juice. Spread over cooled cookies. Chill in refrigerator before cutting. Cut into 1" squares. Store cookies in refrigerator.

Freezes well.

GINGER BARS

30-40 cookies

½ cup shortening
1 cup sugar
1 egg
¼ cup molasses
½ teaspoon salt
¼ teaspoon cloves
½ teaspoon ginger
1 teaspoon cinnamon
1 teaspoon vanilla
1⅓ cups boiling water
2 cups flour
1 teaspoon baking soda

FROSTING:

½ cup butter
1 cup brown sugar
¼ cup milk
2 cups confectioners sugar

Cream together shortening and sugar. Blend in egg, molasses, salt, spices, vanilla and water. Stir in flour and baking soda and mix thoroughly. Pour batter into greased 10" x 15" baking pan. Bake at 350° for 15-20 minutes. Cool. To make frosting, melt butter and brown sugar in saucepan. Boil 2 minutes. Remove from heat and add milk. Return to heat and boil 1 minute. Stir in confectioners sugar. Spread on cooled bars. Cut into rectangles.

BROWN SUGAR-ALMOND BARS

2 dozen

½   cup butter or
     margarine, softened
½   cup sifted confec-
     tioners sugar
1   cup flour
3   tablespoons butter or
     margarine
½   cup packed brown
     sugar
1   tablespoon water
¾   teaspoon lemon juice
¾   cup sliced almonds
¾   teaspoon vanilla

Cream ½ cup butter with confectioners sugar. Add flour; mix well. Pat into ungreased 8" x 8" x 2" pan. Bake at 350° for 12-15 minutes. Melt remaining butter. Add brown sugar, water and lemon juice; bring mixture to a boil, stirring constantly. Remove from heat; stir in almonds and vanilla. Spread mixture over warm crust. Bake 15-20 minutes more. Cut into bars while warm. Cool before removing bars from pan.

WONDERFUL NUT BARS

36 cookies

¼   cup butter
⅔   cup flour
¼   teaspoon baking soda
¼   teaspoon salt
2   cups brown sugar
2   cups pecans, finely
     chopped
4   eggs, beaten
2   teaspoons vanilla
     Confectioners sugar

Line bottoms and sides of a 9" x 13" baking pan with foil. Melt the butter in the baking pan. Sift together flour, baking soda and salt. Stir in brown sugar and nuts. Blend in eggs and vanilla. Carefully spoon batter over butter in pan. Don't stir. Bake at 350° about 25 minutes. Don't overbake. Immediately invert pan onto wire racks to remove cookies; peel off foil. Dust with confectioners sugar. Cool thoroughly before cutting.

Rich and chewy, these bar cookies have a taste reminiscent of old-fashioned pecan pie. They store well in the pantry or can be frozen with good results.

MILK CHOCOLATE CARAMEL BARS

about 2 dozen cookies

1¼   cups flour
½   cup firmly packed
     brown sugar
½   cup butter or
     margarine, melted
¾   cup caramel ice cream
     topping
3   ounces cream cheese
1   teaspoon vanilla
1   egg
1   cup chopped nuts
1   cup milk chocolate
     chips

Preheat oven to 375° (350° for glass pan). Mix flour, sugar and butter until crumbly. Reserve ⅔ cup of this mixture. Press remainder in ungreased 9" x 9" pan. Using the same bowl, combine the reserved crumb mixture, caramel topping, cream cheese, vanilla and egg. Mix until blended. Stir in nuts. Pour over crust. Bake 30-35 minutes or until firm. Immediately sprinkle with chocolate chips; when softened spread to make frosting. Cool before cutting.

MINT-GLAZED BROWNIES

16-24 cookies

½   cup butter, softened
1   cup sugar
1   teaspoon vanilla
2   eggs
2   ounces unsweetened chocolate, melted and cooled
½   cup chopped nuts
½   cup flour

FROSTING:

1   cup confectioners sugar
2   tablespoons butter, softened
2   tablespoons milk
½   teaspoon peppermint extract
2   drops green food coloring (optional)

CHOCOLATE GLAZE:

2   tablespoons butter
2   ounces unsweetened chocolate

In a large mixing bowl beat first 5 ingredients until well-blended. Stir in nuts and flour. Spread batter in a greased 8″ x 8″ baking pan. Bake in 350° oven 25-35 minutes, or until top is firm; do not overbake. Remove from oven and cool. To make frosting, beat all frosting ingredients together until smooth. Spread frosting over cooled brownies; let stand until set. To make glaze, melt butter and chocolate in small saucepan over low heat. Stir until smooth. Pour glaze over frosting and spread in thin, even layer. Chill until firm. Bring brownies to room temperature before cutting.

INCREDIBLE CHOCOLATE BARS

75 cookies

1   cup butter or margarine
2   cups brown sugar
2   eggs
2   teaspoons vanilla
2½ cups flour
1   teaspoon baking soda
1   teaspoon salt
3   cups quick-cooking rolled oats
1   14-ounce can sweetened condensed milk
1   12-ounce package semi-sweet chocolate chips
2   tablespoons butter or margarine
½   teaspoon salt
2   teaspoons vanilla

In large mixer bowl cream together 1 cup butter and brown sugar. Beat in eggs and 2 teaspoons vanilla. Sift together flour, baking soda and 1 teaspoon salt; stir in oats. Stir dry ingredients into creamed mixture until blended, set aside. In heavy saucepan, over low heat, melt together condensed milk, chocolate chips and the remaining butter and salt; stir until smooth. Stir in vanilla. Pat ⅔ of oat mixture into bottom of 10″ x 15″ pan. Spread chocolate mixture over dough. Dot with the remaining oat mixture. Bake at 350° for 20-25 minutes. Cool. Cut into 2″ x 1″ bars.

QUEEN ELIZABETH SQUARES

9-12 servings

1 cup dates, chopped
1 cup boiling water
1 teaspoon baking soda
¼ cup butter or margarine
1 cup sugar
1 egg, beaten
1½ cups flour
1 teaspoon baking powder
Pinch of salt

TOPPING:

½ cup brown sugar
5 teaspoons butter
3 tablespoons half-and-half
½ cup chopped nuts
½ cup coconut
Sweetened whipped cream

Over medium heat cook dates, boiling water and baking soda for 10-15 minutes until dates are soft; cool. Cream together butter and sugar. Add egg, flour, baking powder and salt; mix well. Add cooled date mixture. Spoon into 8" x 8" greased pan and bake at 350° for 30 minutes. To make toppping, boil together brown sugar, 5 teaspoons butter and half-and-half for 3 minutes. Stir in nuts and coconut. Spread topping mixture on baked cake. Place under broiler until topping is brown and bubbly. Serve warm with sweetened whipped cream.

IRISH CRUNCHIES

4½ dozen cookies

½ cup butter, softened
⅔ cup sugar
2 tablespoons Irish whiskey
2 teaspoons strong coffee
2 cups quick cooking oats
1 cup flour
1 teaspoon baking powder

FROSTING:

2 tablespoons Irish whiskey
2 teaspoons coffee
1 cup butter, softened
1 cup confectioners sugar

Beat butter with sugar until fluffy. Add whiskey and coffee. Stir in oats, flour and baking powder. Between two pieces of wax paper, roll out dough into an 11" x 16" rectangle. Transfer dough to a buttered 15½" x 10½" jelly roll pan and press into place. Bake at 325° for 20-25 minutes. Let dough cool before frosting.

To make frosting: Combine whiskey and coffee in bowl. Beat butter and sugar until well blended; add liquid.

PEANUT BUTTER CUPS   36 cookies

½   cup butter
½   cup peanut butter
1   cup crushed graham
    crackers
1¼ cup powdered sugar
1   cup milk chocolate
    chips

Melt butter. Add peanut butter, graham crackers, and sugar; mix well. Press into bottom of 9″ square cake pan. Sprinkle chocolate chips on top and set in warm (200°) oven for a few minutes to soften. Spread chocolate on top. Cool to room temperature. Cut in squares.

Easy for children to make.

THE BEST OATMEAL COOKIES EVER   7-8 dozen cookies

1¼ cups raisins
1   cup water
1   teaspoon baking soda
1   cup margarine
1¼ cups sugar
2   eggs
1   teaspoon salt
3   cups flour
4   teaspoons cinnamon
2   teaspoons ground
    cloves
2   teaspoons nutmeg
1   teaspoon vanilla
2   cups quick-cooking
    rolled oats
1   cup walnuts, coarsely
    chopped
1   12-ounce package
    semi-sweet chocolate
    chips (use real
    chocolate)

Combine raisins and water in small saucepan. Bring to a boil. Add baking soda; stir well. Let cool. Drain and reserve liquid. In large mixing bowl, cream margarine and sugar with electric mixer. Add eggs. Combine flour, salt and spices. Add flour mixture and raisin liquid alternately to mixture in bowl, mixing well after each addition. Add vanilla and quick oats, mixing well. Remove from mixer. Using a large spoon, thoroughly mix in raisins, nuts and chocolate chips. Drop by teaspoonful onto ungreased cookie sheet. Do not flatten; cookies should be irregular in shape. Bake for 8-10 minutes at 350°. Do not brown; cookies should not change color too much in baking and should be soft.

MELT-IN-YOUR-MOUTH COOKIES   4 dozen cookies

1   cup confectioners
    sugar
1   cup butter, cubed
1   egg
1   teaspoon vanilla
½   teaspoon almond ex-
    tract
2½ cups flour, sifted
1   teaspoon baking
    powder
1   teaspoon cream of tar-
    tar
¼   cup granulated sugar

Insert steel blade into food processor. Cream butter and confectioners sugar with on/off bursts until light and fluffy. With motor on, add the egg and flavorings and the dry ingredients except granulated sugar. Process only until the dry ingredients are completely incorporated. Drop by teaspoonfuls on a greased cookie sheet. Flatten each cookie with the bottom of a glass which has been dipped in the granulated sugar. Bake at 350° 10 to 15 minutes, or until lightly browned on the edges.

BLACK BOTTOM MINIATURES

24 cookies

1½   cups flour
1   cup sugar
¼   cup cocoa
½   teaspoon salt
1   cup water
⅓   cup vegetable oil
1   tablespoon vinegar
1   teaspoon vanilla

CREAM CHEESE MIXTURE:

1   8-ounce package
     cream cheese, soften-
     ed
1   egg
½   cup sugar
⅛   teaspoon salt

Sift together flour, sugar, cocoa and salt. Stir in water, oil, vinegar and vanilla; mix well. Set aside. To make cream cheese mixture, combine cream cheese, egg, sugar and salt and mix well. Line miniature muffin tin with 24 paper cups. Fill cups ⅔ full with cocoa batter. Top each with 1 heaping tablespoon cream cheese mixture. Bake at 350° for 30-35 minutes.

These little cakes freeze very well.

RUGELACH

48 cookies

1   cup butter, softened
1   8-ounce package
     cream cheese, soften-
     ed
2   cups unsifted flour,
     stir to aerate before
     measuring
½   cup sugar
1   teaspoon cinnamon
½   cup finely chopped
     walnuts
½   cup raisins

In a mixing bowl, with a wooden spoon, blend butter and cheese; gradually blend in flour. Divide into 4 equal portions and shape each into a ball; flatten each ball. Tightly cover each portion with plastic wrap and refrigerate until firm enough to roll out — overnight if you like. Work with 1 portion of the dough at a time keeping the remainder refrigerated. On a floured pastry cloth with a floured stockinet-covered rolling pin, roll out 1 portion of dough to an 8" round. Mix 2 tablespoons sugar with ¼ teaspoon cinnamon and 2 tablespoons nuts; sprinkle over round of dough, then cover with 2 tablespoons raisins. Cut into 12 wedges; roll each wedge from wide end and curve to form a crescent. Treat remaining portions of dough the same way. Place slightly apart, pointed side down, on a greased cookie sheet and bake in a preheated 375° oven until lightly browned, 20 to 25 minutes. Remove to wire racks to cool.

HUNGARIAN BUTTERHORNS

64 cookies

4   cups flour
½   teaspoon salt
1   cake yeast
1½   cups butter
3   egg yolks (reserve
      whites for filling)
½   cup sour cream
1   teaspoon vanilla
      Confectioners sugar

FILLING:

3   egg whites
1   cup sugar
1   cup finely ground nuts
1   teaspoon vanilla

Sift flour and salt, add crumbled yeast, cut in butter, add beaten egg yolks, sour cream and vanilla. Mix well. Wrap in waxed paper and chill until filling is made. To make filling: Beat egg whites until stiff; gradually add sugar. Fold in nuts and vanilla. Set aside. Dredge working surface with confectioners sugar. Divide chilled dough into 8 parts. Roll out each part in a circle about the size of a pie plate and cut into eight wedges. Spread 1 teaspoon of filling on each wedge and roll from wide end of triangle to the tip. Line a baking sheet with greased brown paper. Arrange the horns on the paper and bake in a preheated 400° oven for 15-18 minutes. Any remaining filling may be baked as meringues.

Stored in air-tight tins, these keep well for weeks.

MEXICAN SWIZZLE STICKS

5½-6½ dozen

1   cup butter or
      margarine
1½   cups confectioners
      sugar
1   egg
1   teaspoon vanilla
2½   cups flour
2   ounces unsweetened
      chocolate, melted
1   teaspoon cinnamon

GLAZE:

1   cup confectioners
      sugar
1   ounce unsweetened
      chocolate, melted
4-6   teaspoons milk
      Colored sugar or cin-
      namon sugar

Mix butter, sugar, egg and vanilla thoroughly. Blend in flour. Add melted chocolate and cinnamon; mix well. With star plate in cookie press, form 4" fingers on ungreased baking sheet. Bake at 375° for 5-7 minutes or until set. Cool. To make glaze: Thoroughly combine sugar, chocolate and milk. Drizzle cookies with glaze. Sprinkle with colored sugar or cinnamon sugar.

DANISH CHERRY BONBON COOKIES

36 cookies

½ cup butter, softened
¼ cup sifted confec-
tioners sugar
1 teaspoon vanilla
1½ cups flour, sifted
Pinch of salt
36 Maraschino cherries,
well-drained

FROSTING:

1 cup sifted confec-
tioners sugar
1 tablespoon evaporated
milk
1 tablespoon maraschino
cherry juice
1 teaspoon vanilla

Mix butter and sugar to creamy consistency. Add vanilla. Add flour and salt gradually, mixing with fingers. Take a maraschino cherry and fold a piece of dough around it, making it a small ball — the smaller the better, but the cherry should be completely enclosed in the dough. Place on ungreased cookie sheet and bake 12-15 minutes at 350°. Cool cookies. To make frosting: Thoroughly blend together frosting ingredients. Dip tops of cookies into the frosting; allow to dry on a rack.

ORANGE BALLS OLÉ

about 6 dozen cookies

2¾ cups vanilla wafer
crumbs
2½ cups confectioners
sugar
1 cup finely chopped
nuts
¼ cup orange juice con-
centrate
½ cup melted butter
Confectioners sugar or
coconut

Mix together vanilla wafer crumbs, 2½ cups confectioners sugar, and nuts. Add orange juice concentrate and butter. Mix thoroughly. Shape into 1" balls and roll in confectioners sugar or coconut.

PECAN TARTS

24 cookies

½ cup margarine, soften-
ed
3 ounces cream cheese,
softened
1 cup flour
Pinch of salt
¾ cup brown sugar
1 teaspoon vanilla
1 egg
½ cup chopped pecans

Blend together margarine and cream cheese. Add flour and salt. Divide dough into 24 balls. With fingers, shape each ball into a small-size muffin tin. For filling mix together remaining ingredients. Fill each crust ¾ full with filling. Bake 15 minutes at 350° then 10 minutes at 250°.

These tarts freeze well.

FENIKIA

½ cup butter
2 cups salad oil
6 tablespoons powdered sugar
4 teaspoons baking powder
1 teaspoon cinnamon
¼ teaspoon allspice
¼ teaspoon cloves
1 cup orange juice
7 cups flour (or more if needed)
2 cups honey
1 cup water
1 cup sugar
Chopped nuts

Melt butter; add oil and sugar and blend well. Add baking powder, spices, and orange juice. Blend well again. Add flour gradually until a smooth dough is formed. Knead with hands. Pinch off small portions of dough and form into little oblong rolls. Bake on ungreased cookie sheet in 350° oven for 30 minutes or until light brown. To make syrup, boil honey, water and sugar for five minutes over low flame. When cookies are cool, dip them into syrup but do not allow them to become soggy. Keep syrup warm during dipping process. Sprinkle with chopped nuts.

A wonderful Greek cookie!

SPICED NUTS

4 cups

2 sticks butter or margarine
4 cups halved pecans or walnuts
3 cups confectioners sugar
2 tablespoons each cinnamon, ground cloves and nutmeg

In a heavy skillet, melt butter. Stir in nuts. Cook over low heat, stirring frequently for 20 minutes or until nuts are lightly browned. In a paper bag sift together sugar and spices. Remove nuts from skillet and drain on a paper towel. Add nuts to spiced sugar in bag and toss until generously coated. Then turn them into a colander and shake gently to remove the excess sugar. Spread spiced nuts on paper towels to dry.

Makes an excellent Christmas gift.

ORANGE CANDIED NUTS

3 cups

3 cups walnut or pecan halves
2 tablespoons butter or margarine
3 tablespoons orange juice
½ cup sugar
¼ cup grated orange rind
1 teaspoon grated lemon rind
½ cup light corn syrup

Place nuts in a 9" x 13" baking pan. Heat in a slow oven (250°) for 5 minutes. Melt butter in a medium-sized saucepan. Stir in orange juice, ¼ cup sugar, orange and lemon rinds and corn syrup, sirring constantly. Bring to a boil over medium heat. Boil without stirring for 5 minutes. Pour syrup over nuts, stirring constantly, to coat evenly. Bake in a 250° oven for 1 hour, stirring several times. Sprinkle with remaining ¼ cup sugar; do not stir. Immediately spread out onto greased cookie sheets and separate into individual nuts with 2 forks; cool. Store in a tightly covered container for up to 3 weeks.

TURKISH HONEY-SESAME CANDY

2 logs

1	pound (about 3-1/8 cups) sesame seeds
1	cup chopped almonds, pistachios or flaked coconut
¾	cup honey
⅓	cup sugar
¼	cup water
¼	teaspoon salt
	Optional: ½ cup coarsely chopped almonds, walnuts, or coconut; or additional whole sesame seed
1	teaspoon vanilla

Spread the sesame seed evenly over two 10" x 15" rimmed baking pans. Bake in a 350° oven for about 15 minutes, stirring often, until very lightly toasted. Cool. In a covered blender, whirl the seeds, 1 cup at a time, until they are the texture of cornmeal. Turn into a 5-quart bowl and stir well to break up large lumps. Mix in the 1 cup chopped nuts or coconut. In a 2-quart pan, combine the honey, sugar, water, and salt. Place over high heat and bring to a boil, stirring, until sugar is dissolved. Reduce heat to medium and continue to cook, without stirring, until a candy thermometer registers 250° (the hard ball stage). Remove from heat, and immediately start pouring this mixture into the 5 quart bowl mixture until the dry ingredients are thoroughly moistened. Divide mixture in half; squeeze and press each half into a ball. On a board, roll one portion at a time to make a log about 1½ inches in diameter. If desired, evenly spread the ½ cup chopped nuts (or coconut or seed) on a board, and roll each log over to coat evenly. Wrap in clear plastic wrap and cool. Store in the refrigerator; the flavor is best if eaten within 2 weeks. To serve, let warm slightly, then slice into ½-inch thick rounds. Make 2 logs, each about 14 inches long.

For chocolate lovers add 3 tablespoons cocoa to the sugar-honey mixture before bringing it to a boil.

OVEN BAKED CARAMEL CORN

5 quarts

2	cups brown sugar
1	cup butter or margarine
½	cup dark corn syrup
1	teaspoon salt
½	teaspoon baking soda
5	quarts popped corn

Combine sugar, butter, syrup and salt. Boil 5 minutes. Remove from heat and stir in baking soda. Immediately pour over corn that has been placed in a large roasting pan. Toss corn and syrup mixture to coat. Bake at 250° for 1 hour, stirring every 15 minutes. Spread coated corn onto waxed paper-covered counters or cookie sheets and break up as it cools. Store in tightly covered container.

The Artists' Touch.....

Who can explain the special allure, the aura of romance, the rich cultural matrix that has made New Mexico known around the world as a mecca for creative and artistic minds and hands? Through the centuries distinctive art forms, unique to New Mexico, have developed at the hands of its native peoples. The Indians displayed excellence in weaving, sand painting, the carving of colorful Kachina dolls and in jewelry-making. Religious images such as bultos (carvings in the round) and retablos (flat panels or low relief) represent the artistic heritage of New Mexico's Hispanic culture as does the home-style weaving usually produced from a family's own flock on the horizontal loom. So-called Anglo art began to flourish in New Mexico in the early part of this century when "colonies" of famous artists were established in Taos and Santa Fé.

Pies and Desserts

WEDDING VASE

PERFECT PIECRUST

4½ cups all-purpose flour
1 tablespoon sugar
2 teaspoons salt
1¾ cup vegetable shortening (do not use oil, lard, butter or margarine)
½ cup water
1 tablespoon white or cider vinegar
1 large egg

With a fork, mix together flour, sugar and salt. Add shortening and mix with fork until ingredients are crumbly. In small bowl, beat together water, vinegar and egg. Combine the two mixtures, stirring with fork until all ingredients are moistened. Divide dough into 5 portions and, with hands, shape each portion into a flat round patty ready for rolling. Wrap each in plastic wrap and chill at least ½ hour. When ready to roll piecrust, lightly flour both sides of patty and place on lightly floured board or pastry cloth. Cover rolling pin with stockinet and rub in a little flour. Keeping pastry round, roll from center to 1/8" thickness and 2" larger than inverted pie pan. Fold in halves or quarters; transfer to pie pan, unfold and fit loosely in pan. Press with fingers to remove air pockets. Bake as desired. Dough can be left in refrigerator up to 3 days, or it can be frozen until ready to use. Also makes 20 tart shells.

No matter how much you handle this dough, it will always be flaky, tender and delicious.

PATE BRISEE SUCRE

2 cups flour
4 tablespoons sugar
¼ teaspoon salt
6 ounces butter or margarine
2-3 ounces sweet Vermouth

Combine flour, sugar and salt; cut in butter until dough is crumbly. Stir in sweet Vermouth to make a soft dough. Roll out to desired shape.

APPLE HONEY PIE

6-8 servings

Pastry for double crust pie
¾ **cup honey**
½ **cup sour cream**
3 **tablespoons flour**
¼ **teaspoon salt**
¼ **teaspoon ground cardamon**
2 **teaspoons grated lemon peel**
6 **cups tart cooking apples, peeled and thinly sliced**
½ **cup golden raisins**

Roll out half of pastry and fit into a 9" pie plate. Trim overhang to ½'. Combine honey, sour cream, flour, salt, cardamon and lemon peel in a large bowl. Add apples and raisins; toss to coat and turn into prepared shell. Roll out the remaining pastry to an 11" round; cut several slits near the center to allow steam to escape; cover pie. Trim overhang to ½". Turn edges under flush with rim and flute. Bake at 425° for 45 minutes, or until pastry is golden and juices bubble up. Cool at least 1 hour.

CROSTADA DI MIELE

8-10 servings

1 **recipe Pate Brisee Sucre (See Index)**
3 **tart apples, peeled and sliced**
12 **ounces apricot preserves**

Fit ⅔ Pate Brisee Sucre into a 10" tart pan. Arrange apple slices into the tart shell. Put preserves over apples. Make a lattice top with the remaining ⅓ pate and place over apples. Bake at 425° for 15 minutes. Reduce heat to 350° and bake about 30 minutes or until golden.

RICOTTA BERRY PIE

6-8 servings

Pastry for a 9-inch pie shell

2½ **cups fresh or unsweetened frozen blackberries or boysenberries**
¾ **cup sugar**
1½ **tablespoons quick-cooking tapioca**
½ **teaspoon ground cinnamon**
8 **ounces ricotta cheese**
1 **egg, separated**
¼ **teaspoon salt**
½ **cup heavy cream**
1 **tablespoon lemon juice**
¾ **teaspoon grated lemon peel**

Line a 9" pan with the pastry. Mix together the berries, ½ cup of the sugar, the tapioca, and cinnamon until blended; let stand 5 minutes. In a blender container or processor combine the ricotta, egg yolk, salt, cream, remaining ¼ cup of sugar, lemon juice, and peel; whirl until smoothly pureed. Beat the egg white until soft peaks form; fold in the cheese mixture just until blended. Spoon the berry mixture into the pastry; evenly spread over the cheese mixture. Bake in 425° oven for 10 minutes; reduce heat to 350° and continue baking 30 minutes or until topping appears firm when dish is gently shaken.

CURRANT TARTS

6-10 tarts

1 cup currants
  Hot water
2 eggs, lightly beaten
1 cup sugar
1 teaspoon cinnamon
  Unbaked 3″ tart shells

Place currants in a bowl and cover with hot water; let stand for 20 minutes. Drain currants and combine with eggs, sugar and cinnamon. Use Perfect Piecrust recipe (See Index) to make tart shells. Fill each tart shell with ¼-½ cup currant filling. Bake tarts in 350° oven for 30 minutes.

GOLDEN LEMON TART

6-8 servings

⅓ cup sugar
4 teaspoons cornstarch
1 teaspoon unflavored gelatin
5 egg yolks
1 cup water
⅓ cup fresh lemon juice
1 tablespoon butter or margarine
½ cup heavy cream, whipped
4 almond macaroons, coarsely crushed
1 baked 9″ pastry shell
½ cup apple jelly or apricot preserves
1-2 lemons, sliced paper thin

Combine sugar, cornstarch, and gelatin in a small saucepan. Add egg yolks and beat well until smooth; gradually stir in water and lemon juice. Bring to a boil over medium heat, stirring constantly, until mixture thickens and bubbles one minute. Remove from heat and stir in butter until melted. Place saucepan in a bowl of ice water to speed setting; chill, stirring often, until mixture mounds slightly on a spoon. Fold in whipped cream and macaroons; pour into baked pie shell. Chill 3-4 hours. If a tart pan was used, remove metal ring and transfer pie to a serving plate. Just before serving, melt apple jelly or apricot preserves in a small skillet to make a glaze. Dip lemon slices into glaze; arrange in overlapping circles on top of pie. Or, for easier serving, decorate top with poufs of whipped cream with a small twist of lemon on each.

FOUR-MINUTE BROWNIE PIE

6-8 servings

2 eggs
1 cup sugar
½ cup butter, softened
½ cup flour
4 tablespoons cocoa
1 teaspoon vanilla
  Pinch of salt
½ cup chopped walnuts (optional)
  Whipped cream or ice cream

In a small mixer bowl place the eggs, sugar, butter, flour, cocoa, vanilla and salt. Beat 4 minutes. Stir in nuts and pour into a greased 8″ pie pan. Bake at 325° for 35 minutes or until done. Pie will settle when cool. Cut in wedges and serve with whipped cream or ice cream.

GERMAN CHOCOLATE PIE

6-8 servings

2 ounces German sweet chocolate or semi-sweet chocolate
1 teaspoon instant coffee (optional)
½ cup butter
3 eggs
½ cup flour
1 cup sugar
1 teaspoon vanilla
½ cup chopped pecans or walnuts
Whipped cream

Melt chocolate, coffee and butter. Beat eggs until thick. Add flour, sugar and vanilla. Add cooled chocolate to egg mixture. Stir in nuts. Grease and flour a 9" pie pan. Bake at 350° for 25 minutes. Serve with whipped cream.

CHOCOLATE RASPBERRY PIE

6-8 servings

CRUST:

1¼ cups graham cracker crumbs
¼ cup softened butter
¼ cup chopped walnuts or pecans
1 tablespoon sugar

FILLING:

1 10-ounce package frozen raspberries
1 cup whipping cream
½ cup butter softened
⅓ cup sugar
2 ounces unsweetened chocolate, melted and cooled
2 eggs
½ cup raspberry jam

SAUCE:

⅓ cup currant jelly
Reserved raspberry juice
1½ tablespoons cornstarch
2 tablespoons water
2 tablespoons Cream de Cassis

Combine all of the crust ingredients and press mixture firmly onto bottom and sides of a lightly buttered 9" pie plate. Bake at 375° for 8 minutes. Cool on rack. To make filling: In a colander or sieve set over a bowl thaw the raspberries, reserving the juice. Whip the cream until it holds soft peaks. In an electric mixer bowl cream together the butter and sugar until mixture is light and fluffy. Stir in chocolate. Add eggs, one at a time, and beat mixture for 3 minutes after each addition. Fold in the whipped cream, berries and jam. Spoon mixture into the crust, making a slightly raised edge. Chill for 2 hours. To make sauce: In a small saucepan heat jelly and juice over low heat, stirring frequently. Dissolve cornstarch in water and add to the jelly mixture; bring mixture to a boil, stirring constantly, and simmer until thickened. Remove from heat and stir in the Cream de Cassis. Cool to room temperature and then chill. Pour the sauce into the center of the pie and garnish with walnut or pecan halves and a frill of whipped cream, if desired.

An elegant dessert for special company.

MOCHA CHIFFON PIE

6-8 servings

CRUST:

2   egg whites
½   cup sugar
¼   teaspoon salt
½   cup pecans, chopped
     fine

FILLING:

2   tablespoons instant
     coffee
½   cup boiling water
½   pound marshmallows,
     halved
2   egg yolks, beaten
2   cups whipping cream
½   teaspoon almond extract
     Shaved chocolate (optional)

Beat egg whites until soft peaks form. Gradually add sugar and salt, continuing to beat until whites are stiff. Fold in pecans. To form the crust, press meringue mixture into a well-buttered 9″ pie plate. Prick with a fork. Bake at 250° for 1 hour. Cool. To make filling, mix together coffee, water and marshmallows. Add egg yolks. Cook mixture for 3 minutes, stirring constantly. Cool. Whip cream, flavoring with almond extract. Fold into cooled marshmallow mixture. Reserve a cup of the mixture and pour the rest into the meringue pie shell. As filling congeals add reserved mixture to the center of the pie to make it higher. Refrigerate overnight. If desired, cover with shaved chocolate before serving.

BLUE RIBBON COCONUT CREAM PIE

6-8 servings

1   cup sugar
⅓   cup flour
⅓   teaspoon salt
2   cups milk
3   egg yolks, slightly
     beaten
1   tablespoon butter
1   teaspoon vanilla
¾   cup chopped dates
½   cup shredded coconut
1   9″ baked pie crust

MERINGUE:

3   egg whites
¼   teaspoon cream of tartar
½   teaspoon vanilla
6   tablespoons sugar

Combine sugar, flour and salt. Gradually stir in milk. Cook and stir over medium heat until mixture thickens. Stir small amount of hot mixture into egg yolks; return to hot mixture; cook two minutes longer. Remove from heat. Add butter, vanilla, dates and coconut. Stir until well blended. Pour into baked pie crust. Top with meringue. To make meringue, beat egg whites with cream of tartar and vanilla until soft peaks form. Gradually add sugar, beating until stiff peaks form and sugar is dissolved. Spread on top of pie, taking care to seal edges. Bake about 12-15 minutes in a 350° oven or until meringue is golden brown.

This pie was the sweepstakes winner in the 1979 cookbook contest sponsored by the Farmington Daily Times.

LEMON ICE CREAM PIE

6-8 servings

6   tablespoons butter, melted
1   cup flour
¼   cup powdered sugar
2   eggs, beaten
¾   cup sugar
2   tablespoons flour
3   tablespoons lemon juice
1   teaspoon fresh grated lemon rind
1   quart lemon ice cream
1   cup whipping cream
2   tablespoons sugar
1   teaspoon vanilla
    Lemon slices for garnish

Combine the butter, flour and powdered sugar and press into a 9″ pie pan. Bake at 325° for 15 minutes. Combine the eggs, sugar, flour, lemon juice and lemon rind and mix. Pour the mixture over the hot crust and bake 20 minutes longer. Remove from oven and cool completely. Fill the cooled crust with slightly softened ice cream. Freeze. Beat the cream with sugar and vanilla until stiff peaks form. Swirl over top of pie. Freeze at least 3 hours. Remove from freezer about 10 minutes before serving. Garnish with lemon slices.

LUNA MANSION MUD PIE

8-10 servings

38   (14 ounces) cream-filled chocolate cookies
½   cup butter, melted
1½   quarts coffee ice cream
1   cup thick fudge sauce
     Sweetened whipped cream
     Slivered almonds

Crush cookies and mix with melted butter. Press into bottom and sides of 9″ spring-form pan. Crust should be approximately ¼″ thick. Freeze until firm. Soften ice cream. Spoon into crust and freeze until hardened. Cover with fudge sauce and freeze until firm. Top each serving of pie with sweetened whipped cream and almonds.

PEACH ICE CREAM PIE

6-8 servings

¾   cup ginger snap cookies, finely crushed
¼   cup butter, melted
¼   cup sugar
¼   teaspoon cinnamon
1   quart peach ice cream, softened
1   pint vanilla ice cream, softened
1   10-ounce package frozen red raspberries, thawed
½   cup sugar
1   tablespoon cornstarch

Combine cookies, butter, sugar and cinnamon. Press on bottom and sides of a 9″ pie plate. Bake at 325° for 5-10 minutes, or until lightly browned. Cool. Spoon peach ice cream on top of crust. Freeze. Spoon softened vanilla ice cream on crust. Freeze. Drain raspberries, reserving syrup. Combine sugar, cornstarch and reserved syrup. Cook over medium heat, stirring constantly, until thickened. Boil 2 minutes longer. Stir in raspberries and cool. Cut pie into wedges and top with the raspberry sauce.

FROZEN LIME PIE

CRUST:

¾   cup rolled oats
⅓   cup firmly packed
    brown sugar
¼   cup butter, melted

FILLING:

3   eggs, separated
¼   cup lime juice
⅔   cup sugar
¼   teaspoon salt
½   teaspoon grated lime
    rind
1   teaspoon vanilla
5   drops green food col-
    oring
1   cup whipping cream

To make crust, combine oats, brown sugar and melted butter. Spread mixture on a cookie sheet. Toast at 350° for 6-8 minutes. Stir mixture frequently and watch carefully as it will burn easily. Cool mixture by tossing with a fork. To make filling: combine slightly beaten egg yolks, lime juice, sugar and salt in a saucepan. Cook over low heat, stirring constantly, until mixture comes to a boil. Remove from heat and cool. Stir in lime rind, vanilla and food coloring. Beat egg whites to soft peaks. Fold into lime mixture. Whip cream and fold it into lime mixture. Reserve ¼ cup of crust; spread remainder in the bottom of a 9" pie plate. Pour in filling and sprinkle reserved crumbs on top. Freeze pie until firm. (The crust and filling will make 12 servings if frozen in individual paper-lined muffin tins.) Pie may be made several days ahead. Cover with plastic wrap or foil.

BUTTERSCOTCH WALNUT PIE

1   envelope unflavored
    gelatin
¼   cup cold water
1   6-ounce package
    butterscotch chips
3   ounces cream cheese
½   cup milk
3   egg yolks
½   cup + 2 tablespoons
    chopped walnuts
½   teaspoon rum flavoring
4   egg whites
¼   cup sugar

CRUST:

⅓   cup butter or
    margarine
3   tablespoons sugar
1   egg yolk
1   cup flour

Soften gelatin in cold water. Dissolve in a pan over boiling water. Stir in butterscotch chips and cream cheese. Stir until melted and smooth. Remove from heat and add milk, egg yolks, ½ cup walnuts, and rum flavoring. Beat well. Chill until very thick, but not set (about ½ hour or less in freezer). Meanwhile beat egg whites until soft mounds form. Add sugar gradually and beat until stiff. Fold into chilled butterscotch mixture. Spoon into baked crust. Mix reserved crumbs and nuts and sprinkle over top of pie. Chill at least 2 hours. To make crust, blend butter, sugar and egg yolk. Add flour. Stir until mixture forms a ball. Press all except ¼ cup of dough into a 9" or 10" pie pan. Crumble up reserved ¼ cup dough into a small oven-proof pan. Bake crust at 350° for 12-15 minutes, crumbs for 10-12 minutes, watching that crumbs do not brown too much.

ORANGE PIE VALENCIANA

6-8 servings

2   8-ounce packages
     cream cheese, soften-
     ed
     Grated rind of two
     oranges
¼   cup freshly squeezed
     orange juice
1¼   cups confectioners
     sugar
½   teaspoon orange ex-
     tract
3   teaspoons lemon juice
1   cup whipping cream,
     whipped
1   11-ounce can man-
     darin oranges, well
     drained
9"   prepared graham
     cracker pie shell

In large bowl blend cream cheese, orange rind, orange juice, sugar, orange extract and lemon juice. Gently fold in whipped cream. Measure ½ cup mandarin orange sections and chop coarsely; reserve remaining orange sections for garnish. Fold chopped oranges into cheese mixture and pour mixture into prepared pie shell. Arrange reserved orange sections decoratively on top of filling. Chill several hours before serving.

CASSATELLE ALLA SICILIANA

6 servings

1   recipe Pate Brisee
      Sucre (See Index)
1½   pounds ricotta cheese
¼   pound toasted
      almonds, chopped
2   tablespoons citron
2   tablespoons orange
      peel, chopped
4   eggs
1   teaspoon vanilla
⅓   cup sugar

Fit ⅔ Pate Brisee Sucre into a 9" or 10" tart pan. Combine cheese, almonds, citron, orange peel, eggs, vanilla and sugar; place in tart shell. Make a lattice top with the remaining ⅓ pate. Bake 45 minutes at 350°. Filling must be firm but not dry. Serve warm sprinkled with powdered sugar if desired.

RUM RAISIN FESTIVAL PIE

6-10 servings

¼   cup rum
1½   cup raisins
¼   cup butter
¾   cup sugar
3   eggs
1   teaspoon vanilla
½   cup chopped almonds
      or walnuts
1   5½-ounce stick pie
      crust mix
      Whipped cream

Marinate raisins in rum for 10 minutes. Beat butter and sugar until creamy. Beat in eggs and vanilla. Add nuts and marinated raisins. Crumble in pie crust stick, stirring until well distributed (may look curdled). Turn mixture into greased 9" pie plate. Bake at 325° for 35-45 minutes or until set. Cool before cutting. Top with whipped cream.

This pie is great for a last minute dessert since all the ingredients are usually on the pantry shelf!

MINCEMEAT CHEESE PIE

6-8 servings

4 3-ounce packages cream cheese, softened
½ cup sugar
2 eggs
1 tablespoon grated lemon peel
1 tablespoon lemon juice
¾ teaspoon vanilla
1½ cups prepared mincemeat
1 9″ baked pie crust

Preheat oven to 375°. In medium bowl with electric mixer at medium speed, beat cream cheese until smooth. Beat in sugar, eggs, lemon peel, lemon juice and vanilla until well blended. Spread mincemeat into pie crust. Top with cheese mixture and bake about 35 minutes until cheese is firm when lightly touched in center. Keep leftovers refrigerated.

Rich and delicious!

ROCKY MOUNTAIN PIE

6-8 servings

2 eggs
½ cup unsifted flour
½ cup sugar
½ cup firmly packed brown sugar
1 cup butter, melted and cooled to room temperature
1 6-ounce package (1 cup) semi-sweet chocolate morsels
1 cup chopped walnuts
1 9″ unbaked pie shell
   Whipped cream or ice cream (optional)

Preheat oven to 325°. In large bowl, beat eggs until foamy; beat in flour, sugar and brown sugar until well blended. Blend in melted butter. Stir in semi-sweet chocolate morsels and walnuts. Pour into pie shell. Bake at 325° one hour. Remove from oven. Serve warm with whipped cream or ice cream.

OATMEAL PIE

6-8 servings

¼ cup softened butter
½ cup sugar
¼ teaspoon salt
½ teaspoon cinnamon
½ teaspoon ground cloves
1 cup maple syrup
3 eggs
1 cup quick-cooking oatmeal
1 unbaked 9″ pie shell

Cream butter with the sugar, then blend in salt and spices. Stir in the syrup, then beat in the eggs, one at a time, beating well after each. Stir in oatmeal and pour into pie shell. Bake 1 hour at 350°. Cool before serving.

The oatmeal gives the effect of fine-ground nuts. Tasty and nutritious.

RUM FLAVORED WALNUT PUMPKIN PIE   6-8 servings

1	unbaked 9" pie shell
4	eggs, separated
1	cup light brown sugar, firmly packed
½	teaspoon cinnamon
½	teaspoon nutmeg
½	teaspoon allspice
2	cups canned pumpkin
4	tablespoon rum
1	cup whipping cream
¼	cup melted butter
1	tablespoon cornstarch
½	cup honey
½	cup chopped walnuts
¼	teaspoon vanilla extract

Preheat oven to 450°. In large bowl beat egg yolks until thick and lemon colored. At low speed, beat in sugar, cinnamon, nutmeg, allspice, pumpkin, rum, ⅓ cup whipping cream, and butter. Beat egg whites until frothy. Gradually add cornstarch, beating until stiff but not dry. Fold into pumpkin mixture. Turn into pie shell. Bake 15 minutes, then reduce heat to 350° and bake 30 to 40 minutes or until knife inserted in center comes out clean. Cool and refrigerate. Before serving, mix honey and nuts. Spread on pie. Whip remaining ⅔ cup cream and flavor with vanilla. Spread over honey and nut mixture. The pie may be made a day ahead and the topping put on a few hours before serving.

This pie is worth the effort involved.

NO-BAKE DAIQUIRI CHEESECAKE   10-12 servings

1	cup graham cracker crumbs
¼	cup sugar
6	tablespoons butter or margarine, melted
1	envelope unflavored gelatin
½	cup sugar
½	cup rum
2	teaspoons grated lime peel
1	teaspoon grated lemon peel
½	cup lime juice
4	beaten egg yolks
2	8-ounce packages cream cheese, cubed and softened
4	egg whites
½	cup sugar
1	cup whipping cream

Combine the graham cracker crumbs, the ¼ cup sugar, and butter or margarine. Remove 2 tablespoons crumbs; set aside. Press remaining crumbs in bottom and 1¾ inches up sides of a 9" springform pan. Chill 45 minutes. Meanwhile, in medium saucepan, combine gelatin and the first ½ cup sugar. Stir in rum, citrus peels, lime juice, and egg yolks. Cook over medium heat, stirring constantly, till slightly thickened, 8 to 10 minutes. Remove from heat. Beat in cream cheese till smooth. Beat egg whites on medium speed of electric mixer till soft peaks form (tips curl over). Gradually add remaining sugar, beating to stiff peaks (tips stand straight). Whip cream to soft peaks. Fold egg whites and whipped cream into gelatin mixture. Turn into crumb-lined pan. Sprinkle reserved crumbs around edge. Cover; chill till firm.

CHOCOLATE ALMOND CHEESECAKE

12 servings

1½ cups chocolate wafer crumbs
1 cup blanched almonds, lightly toasted and chopped
⅓ cup sugar
6 tablespoons butter, softened
1½ pounds cream cheese, softened
1 cup sugar
4 eggs
⅓ cup heavy cream
¼ cup almond-flavored liqueur (such as Amaretto)
1 teaspoon almond extract
1 teaspoon vanilla
2 cups sour cream
1 tablespoon sugar
1 teaspoon vanilla
½ cup slivered almonds, lightly toasted

For crust, combine first four ingredients in a bowl. When well combined, pat mixture onto the bottom and sides of a buttered 9½" springform pan. To make filling: in a large bowl cream together the cream cheese, 1 cup sugar and 4 eggs; beat well. Add the cream, liqueur, 1 teaspoon vanilla and almond extract. Beat the mixture until it is light. Pour batter into the shell and bake for 35 minutes in a 375° oven. Transfer the cake to a rack and let it stand for 5 minutes. (The filling will not be set.) To make topping, combine sour cream with 1 tablespoon sugar and 1 teaspoon vanilla; spread the mixture evenly on the cake and bake the cake for 6 minutes more. Transfer the cake to the rack and let it cool completely. Chill it, lightly covered, overnight. Before serving, remove the sides of the pan, transfer the cake to a cake stand and press slivered almonds around the top edge.

Rich and elegant, this spectacular cheesecake has a rich, nutty crust and a filling that is smooth and creamy and laced with the subtle flavor of almonds. Your guests will rave!

AUTUMN APPLE CRISP

6-8 servings

4 medium cooking apples, pared and thinly sliced
½ cup dark corn syrup
¼ cup hot water
¼ cup margarine
¾ cup quick oats
½ cup firmly packed brown sugar
¼ cup unsifted flour
½ teaspoon salt
1 cup finely chopped pecans

Grease an 8" x 8" baking pan. Place apples in pan. Mix corn syrup and hot water; pour over apples. Mix together margarine, oats, brown sugar, flour and salt until crumbs form; stir in pecans. Sprinkle mixture evenly over apples. Bake in a 350° oven 45 minutes.

Autumn in New Mexico is apple-eating time!

APPLE CUSTARD CAKE

12 servings

CRUST:

2¼   cups graham cracker crumbs
2   tablespoons sugar
½   teaspoon cinnamon
¼   cup lightly salted butter, softened

FILLING:

2   tablespoons butter or margarine
9   medium-size tart apples (3 pounds), pared, cored and sliced thin
2   tablespoons sugar
½   teaspoon grated lemon peel
½   teaspoon lemon juice
6   large eggs
2   cups sour cream
1   cup sugar
1   teaspoon vanilla
   Pinch of salt

To make the crust: Generously butter a 9" springform pan. Mix crumbs, sugar and cinnamon in a bowl and stir in butter. When well-mixed, set aside 1 tablespoon. Press remaining crumb mixture evenly on bottom and sides of prepared pan up to 1 inch from top of pan. For the filling: In a large skillet melt butter over moderately low heat. Add apple slices, sprinkle with the 2 tablespoons sugar, the lemon peel and juice. Cover pan and cook 10-15 minutes, until apples are tender. Remove from heat and let cool. Heat oven to 350°. Beat eggs in the top of a double boiler; add the sour cream, the 1 cup of sugar, the vanilla and salt and beat again until well blended. Put pan over simmering water and cook, stirring constantly, until mixture thickens. Remove from heat. Put cooked apple slices into prepared crust and pour the egg mixture over. Sprinkle with reserved tablespoon of crumbs. Bake for 1 hour, until custard is set. Remove from oven and place on wire rack to cool for at least 2 hours before removing sides. Serve warm or cold. Keeps 1 or 2 days in the refrigerator.

BANANA SPLIT DESSERT

16-24 servings

3   sticks butter or margarine
2   cups graham cracker crumbs
2   eggs
1½   cups confectioners sugar
3-4   bananas, sliced
1   16-ounce can crushed pineapple, drained
1   cup whipping cream, whipped
¼   cup maraschino cherries, drained and chopped
   Chopped pecans

Melt 1 stick butter or margarine in a 9" x 13" pan; toss in graham cracker crumbs and press on bottom of pan. Beat 10 full minutes at high speed 2 sticks butter or margarine, eggs and confectioners sugar. Pour over graham cracker crust. Layer sliced bananas, crushed pineapple, whipped cream, maraschino cherries and chopped pecans over crust. Refrigerate until well-chilled. Cut in squares to serve.

CHERRY CRISP

4-6 servings

4	cups pitted sweet black cherries
3	tablespoons sugar
2	tablespoons lemon juice
1	teaspoon grated lemon rind
½	teaspoon almond extract
¾	cup flour
6	tablespoons butter, cut into bits
3	tablespoons sugar
½	teaspoon cinnamon
½	cup chopped pecans
	Vanilla ice cream

In a bowl combine cherries, 3 tablespoons sugar, lemon juice, lemon rind and almond extract; transfer mixture to a buttered shallow 1-quart baking dish. In another bowl combine flour, butter, 3 tablespoons sugar and cinnamon until mixture resembles meal; add pecans and sprinkle the streusel over the cherries. Bake mixture in a preheated 375° oven for 45 minutes or until top is browned. Serve the crisp warm with vanilla ice cream.

Sweetly sensational!

POACHED PEARS WITH ELEGANT SAUCES

8 servings

4	cups water
1	cup sugar
1	vanilla bean
	Rind of 1 lemon, cut into strips
8	small pears
	Juice of 1 lemon
4	cups water

RASPBERRY SAUCE:

1½	cups fresh raspberries or 1 10-ounce carton frozen raspberries, thawed and drained
2	tablespoons superfine sugar
2	tablespoons raspberry-flavored liqueur or Kirsch

CHAMPAGNE SAUCE:

4	large egg yolks
½	cup sugar
⅔	cup champagne

Combine water, sugar, vanilla and lemon rind and cook over low heat until sugar is dissolved, stirring constantly. Bring the syrup to a boil and simmer for 5 minutes. Peel pears, leaving the stems intact. Combine the juice and water and drop the peeled pears in it while peeling the remaining pears. Drain pears and drop into the syrup. Simmer until just tender, about 30-60 minutes. Transfer pears with liquid to a bowl; cover and chill. To make the raspberry sauce, puree raspberries through a fine sieve into a bowl. Add the sugar and liqueur. Chill. To make champagne sauce, combine egg yolks and sugar in the top of a double boiler set over simmering water. Beat until mixture is thick and lemon colored. Add champagne in a stream, beating constantly. Heat the mixture until light and foamy and until it holds soft peaks. Use immediately. Top the pears with the raspberry sauce and cover with the champagne sauce.

RASPBERRY-PEAR COBBLER

6-8 servings

1	10-ounce package frozen raspberries, thawed
⅓	cup sugar
2	teaspoons cornstarch
¼	teaspoon ground cinnamon
3	medium fresh or canned pears, sliced (2½ cups)
½	cup sugar
1	cup flour
1	teaspoon baking powder
¼	teaspoon salt
1	beaten egg
¾	cup sour cream
2	tablespoons butter, melted

Drain raspberries, reserving syrup. Add enough water to syrup to make 1 cup. In saucepan, combine the ⅓ cup sugar, cornstarch, and cinnamon. Add syrup. Cook and stir until bubbly. Add fruits; heat through. Pour into 10" x 6" baking dish. Combine dry ingredients. Combine the egg, sour cream and butter and add to flour mixture; blend well. Drop by spoonfuls onto fruit. Bake 30 minutes at 350°.

LEMON PEACHES IN WHITE WINE SYRUP

5 pints

6	pounds firm, ripe peaches
3	cups dry white wine
1½	cups sugar
3	tablespoons lemon juice
½	teaspoon grated lemon peel

Peel and pit peaches; cut into ¾ inch thick slices. In a 5 or 6 quart kettle combine wine, sugar, lemon juice and lemon peel. Add peaches as you slice them to prevent browning. Over high heat, bring peach-syrup mixture to a simmer; continue simmering for 2 minutes. With a slotted spoon, transfer peach slices to 5 clean, hot pint-sized canning jars. Arrange so that few spaces in jar remain unfilled and allow ½ inch head space. Over high heat, bring syrup mixture to a boil and cook until syrup is reduced to 2 cups. Pour the boiling syrup over peaches in jars leaving ¼ inch head space. Run a table knife around inside of each jar to release bubbles between fruit, then add more syrup if necessary. Wipe jar rims with a clean, damp cloth; put on hot, scalded lids, and screw on ring bands. Process pints for 15 minutes. Serve with ice cream or whipped cream.

STRAWBERRIES WITH ALMOND CREAM   6-8 servings

1   **4-serving package
vanilla instant pudding
mix**
2   **cups whipping cream**
1   **cup milk**
½   **teaspoon almond ex-
tract**
2   **pints strawberries,
hulled**

In large bowl with mixer at low speed, beat instant pudding, cream, milk and almond extract until blended. Increase speed to high and beat until soft peaks form. Spoon mixture in center of a chilled bowl; arrange strawberries around mixture.

So simple! So delicious!

WHIPPED STRAWBERRY DESSERT   8-10 servings

1   **cup sifted flour**
¼   **cup brown sugar**
½   **cup chopped walnuts**
½   **cup melted butter**
2   **egg whites**
2/3 **cup sugar**
1   **10 ounce can frozen
strawberries, thawed**
2   **tablespoons lemon
juice**
1   **cup whipping cream**

Mix first 4 ingredients and spread in 9" square pan and bake at 350° for 20 minutes. Sprinkle crumbs in pan. Combine egg whites, sugar, strawberries, and lemon juice and beat at high speed for 10 minutes. Then whip the cream and fold into strawberry mixture. Spoon over crumbs. Freeze for at least 6 hours.

PLUM CLAFOUTI   4-5 servings

     Butter
5   **tablespoons sugar**
¾   **pound small purple
plums**
¼   **teaspoon cinnamon**
1¼ **cups milk**
3   **large eggs**
⅓   **cup flour**
⅛   **teaspoon salt**
1   **teaspoon vanilla**
     Powdered sugar

Butter a 10" glass pie plate and sprinkle it with ½ tablespoon sugar. Cut plums in half and remove pits; place them skin side down in the pie plate. Combine 1½ tablespoons sugar with the cinnamon and sprinkle over the plums. In a food processor with the steel blade, combine the milk, eggs, flour, remaining sugar and salt. Blend until batter is smooth. Add the vanilla and blend for a few seconds more. Pour the batter over the plums and bake the clafouti at 375° for 40-45 minutes, or until puffed and golden. Sprinkle with powdered sugar and serve warm.

CANDY APPLE PUDDING

6 servings

6   **medium apples, peeled and sliced**
1⅓   **cups brown sugar, firmly packed**
½   **teaspoon cinnamon**
1   **tablespoon lemon juice**
1   **cup sifted flour**
½   **cup softened butter**
   Pinch of salt
½   **cup ground nuts**

Spread apple slices evenly in buttered 9″ pie plate. Sprinkle with ⅓ cup of the brown sugar, the cinnamon and the lemon juice. Mix the remaining cup of brown sugar with the flour and blend in the butter. Add salt and ground nuts. When the mixture is crumbly, spread in a thick layer over the apples, pressing down firmly to make the crust. Bake in 350° oven for 1 hour or until apples are tender and top is brown. Serve warm.

Deliciously sweet, this pudding is good served with cream or just by itself.

DELMONICO PUDDING

6-8 servings

3   **cups cold milk**
2   **tablespoons unflavored gelatin**
4   **egg yolks**
1   **cup sugar**
3   **ounces whiskey**
1   **teaspoon vanilla**
12   **crushed macaroons**
4   **egg whites, beaten stiff**
   Whipped cream

Soak gelatin in milk for 10 minutes. Put the milk and gelatin on the stove and scald for 2 minutes, stirring constantly. Beat egg yolks with sugar and add to the milk and gelatin mixture. Put on the stove and stir until it thickens. Cool. Add whiskey, vanilla, macaroons, and egg whites. Chill until set. Serve with whipped cream.

🐎 FLAN CAFÉ

6-8 servings

3   **eggs, slightly beaten**
6   **tablespoons sugar**
¼   **teaspoon salt**
3   **tablespoons instant coffee granules**
1   **teaspoon vanilla extract**
3   **cups milk, scalded**
6   **tablespoons coffee-flavored liqueur**
½   **cup whipped cream**

In a mixing bowl, combine eggs, sugar, salt, coffee and vanilla. Mix thoroughly. Gradually add scalded milk, stirring vigorously. Pour mixture into 6 custard cups. Place in pan of hot water and bake at 375° for 25 minutes or until firm. Chill thoroughly. To serve, spoon liqueur over flan and top with whipped cream.

FANTASTIC TRIFLE

ORANGE CAKE:

2	cups flour
1	teaspoon baking soda
1	teaspoon salt
3	ounces orange juice concentrate, thawed
1	cup sugar
¾	cup softened butter
½	cup milk
2	large eggs
1	cup seedless raisins
½	cup chopped walnuts

Sift flour, soda and salt together. Combine with the orange juice concentrate, sugar, butter, milk and eggs. Mix at low speed of electric mixer for 35 seconds. Beat at medium speed for 3 minutes. Fold in raisins and nuts. Pour into a well greased 13" x 9" pan. Bake at 350° for 40-45 minutes or until cake comes away from the sides of the pan. Cool and then tear into bite size pieces.

PUDDING:

1	3½-ounce package regular vanilla pudding mix
1½	cups milk
⅓	cup plus 3 tablespoons cream sherry
1	cup strawberry jam
2	16-ounce cans pear halves
1	cup whipping cream, whipped and sweetened

Cook pudding as label directs using 1½ cups milk and ⅓ cup sherry. Spread bottom of a serving bowl with ½ of the cake pieces. Cover the cake with 1½ tablespoons of cream sherry, ½ of the pears, and ½ of the jam. Make another layer with the remaining cake and cover with another 1½ tablespoons of cream sherry, pears and jam. Spread with warm pudding. Set several hours. Before serving, cover with whipped cream.

Beautiful served in an over-sized brandy snifter or a large glass bowl.

ZUPPA INGLESE

3	4-serving packages regular vanilla pudding mix
6	cups milk
6	ounces brandy
4	ounces vermouth
1	ounce maraschino cherry juice
1½	dozen ladyfingers Maraschino cherries for garnish

Combine pudding and milk in a saucepan. Cook, stirring constantly, over medium heat. When the pudding starts to coat the spoon, remove from heat. Put wax paper on top of the pudding and let cool to room temperature. Then peel the paper off top. Combine the brandy, vermouth, and cherry juice. In a bowl, put a thin layer of pudding. Quickly dip the ladyfingers in the juice mixture and place in a layer on top of the pudding. Continue layering the pudding and the ladyfingers, ending with the pudding. Garnish with cherries. Chill overnight.

A modern-day version of an Old World classic.

PUMPKIN ICE CREAM SQUARES

9 servings

1½   cups graham cracker
     crumbs
¼   cup sugar
¼   cup melted butter
2   cups canned pumpkin
½   cup brown sugar
½   teaspoon salt
1   teaspoon cinnamon
¼   teaspoon ginger
⅛   teaspoon cloves
1   quart vanilla ice
     cream, softened
     Whipped cream
     Pecan halves

Mix crumbs with sugar and butter. Press into bottom of 9″ square pan. Combine pumpkin with salt and spices. Fold in ice cream. Pour into crumb-lined pan. Cover; freeze until firm. Remove from freezer to room temperature about 10 minutes before serving. Cut into 3″ squares and top each square with whipped cream and a pecan half.

CARAMEL ICE CREAM DESSERT

12-15 servings

½   cup butter or
     margarine
1   cup flour
¼   cup brown sugar
½   cup chopped pecans
½   gallon vanilla ice
     cream, slightly
     softened
8   ounces caramel ice
     cream topping

Melt butter. Mix together butter, flour, brown sugar and chopped nuts. Spread on a greased cookie sheet. Bake 15 minutes at 325°. Chop mixture into small pieces. Spread half of the mixture on the bottom of a 9″ x 13″ pan; spread ice cream on top of mixture. Sprinkle remaining mixture on top of ice cream. Drizzle caramel topping over top. Place in freezer until ready to serve.

TORTONI SQUARES

6-9 servings

⅓   cup chopped toasted
     almonds
3   tablespoons melted
     butter
1⅓ cups crushed
     vanilla wafers
1   teaspoon almond ex-
     tract
3   pints vanilla ice cream,
     softened
12   ounces apricot
     preserves
     Whipped cream

Mix almonds, butter, wafers and almond extract. Pour one-third of the crumb mixture in a buttered 9″ square pan. Top with half the ice cream and half the apricots. Repeat layers ending with crumbs on top. Freeze until firm. Cut in squares and top with whipped cream.

SWEDISH CREAM

1   cup sugar
1   envelope unflavored
      gelatin
2   cups heavy cream
1   pint sour cream
2   teaspoons vanilla
2   teaspoons almond
      extract
2   pints strawberries

Combine sugar and gelatin in saucepan; add cream and mix well. Heat gently. Stir over low heat until gelatin dissolves. (Do not boil.) Cool until mixture thickens. When cool, fold in sour cream. Flavor with vanilla and almond extract. Chill in refrigerator and add strawberries before serving. Also good with raspberries.

CHOCOLATE MOUSSE CREPES

6   ounces semi-sweet
      chocolate
3   tablespoons sugar
3   tablespoons water
3   egg yolks, well beaten
2½   cups heavy cream,
      whipped
12   dessert crepes
½   teaspoon nutmeg

In a heavy saucepan, melt, over a low heat, chocolate, sugar and water until smooth. Remove from heat and cool a few minutes. Add beaten yolks a little at a time. Let mixture cool to room temperature. Stir frequently as mixture cools. When cool, whip 1½ cups heavy cream until stiff and fold it into the chocolate mixture. Put a spoonful or two of filling down the center of each cooled crepe. Roll and place seam side down on large plate. Cover and refrigerate until ready to serve. Whip 1 cup heavy cream until thick, not stiff. Place crepes on dessert plates and spoon cream over top. Sprinkle with nutmeg and serve.

CREPES FRANGIPANE

1   cup sugar
¼   cup flour
1   cup milk
2   eggs
2   egg yolks
3   tablespoons butter
2   teaspoons vanilla
½   teaspoon almond
      extract
½   cup ground toasted
      almonds
20-24 crepes
¼   cup melted butter
      Powdered sugar for
      garnish
      Grated chocolate for
      garnish

Mix sugar and flour. Add milk. Cook and stir until thick. Cook and stir 1-2 minutes longer. Beat eggs and egg yolks slightly. Stir some of hot mixture into eggs and return to hot mixture while stirring. Bring just to boiling. Remove from heat and add butter, vanilla, almond extract and almonds; cool. Spoon 2 tablespoons into each crepe. Fold crepes. Place in buttered dish, brush with melted butter and bake in 350° oven for 20-25 minutes. Garnish with powdered sugar and grated chocolate.

WALNUT AND SUGAR CREPES

6-8 crepes

1½	cups walnuts, chopped
¾	cup sugar
6-8	6" dessert crepes
2	tablespoons butter, melted
1	cup whipping cream, whipped
1	tablespoon brandy

Mix together walnuts and sugar. Lightly grease 9" x 12" baking dish. Brush crepes with butter and sprinkle nut mixture evenly over them. Roll up each crepe and place seamside down in baking dish. Cover and place in a preheated 250° oven and bake until hot, about 15 minutes. Whip cream until thick, not stiff. Fold in brandy. Place crepes on dessert plates, spoon cream over crepes and serve immediately.

LEMON SOUFFLÉ CREPES

12-18 servings

1	envelope unflavored gelatin
¼	cup cold water
4	eggs, separated
½	cup lemon juice
1¼	cup sugar
½	teaspoon salt
1	teaspoon grated lemon peel
1	cup heavy cream, whipped
12-18	dessert crepes
2½	cups strawberries, crushed

Soften gelatin in cold water. In a double boiler, mix together yolks, lemon juice, ½ cup sugar and salt, stirring constantly until thick. Remove from heat, and stir in gelatin and lemon peel. Cool. Beat egg whites until soft peaks form. Add ½ cup sugar and beat until stiff. Fold whipped cream into whites and fold that mixture into gelatin mixture. Put ⅓ cup of the souffle mixture down the center of each cooled crepe. Roll and place seam side down on large plate. Cover and refrigerate until ready to serve. (These do not freeze well.) In a bowl, mix together strawberries and ¼ cup sugar. Cover and refrigerate until ready to use. To serve crepes, place on dessert plates, spoon strawberry mixture over the top and serve immediately.

PAVLOVA

6-8 servings

4	egg whites
1	cup superfine sugar
¼	teaspoon lemon juice
¼	teaspoon white vinegar
⅛	teaspoon salt
½	pint whipping cream
1	pint strawberries

Beat egg whites until stiff. Gradually add the sugar, lemon juice, vinegar and salt. Form the beaten egg whites into a circle on a cut out piece of brown paper bag. Bake at 250° for 1 hour and 15 minutes. Just before serving frost with whipped cream and top with strawberry halves. Fresh peaches, apricots or kiwi or frozen berries may be substituted for strawberries.

FRENCH MINT CREAMS

1 cup butter
2 cups sifted powdered sugar
4 squares unsweetened chocolate, melted
4 eggs
1 teaspoon peppermint extract
2 teaspoons vanilla
18 vanilla wafers
1 cup heavy cream, whipped
Maraschino cherries

Cream butter and sugar; blend in melted chocolate. Add eggs and beat well after each egg. Add flavorings. Using 18 cupcake liners, put a vanilla wafer in the bottom of each and then fill with chocolate mixture ¾ full. Place a dollop of whipped cream on each and top with a cherry. Freeze in muffin pans to retain shape. After the creams are frozen, they may be stored in plastic bags. Serve frozen.

Very rich!

ALMOND FUDGE TORTE

1 teaspoon instant coffee granules
2 tablespoons hot water
4 ounces semisweet chocolate, melted
3 eggs, separated
½ cup butter or margarine
¾ cup sugar
2 ounces almond paste, crumbled
½ cup unbleached flour
Cocoa
¼ cup Meyers Rum or Grand Marnier

Preheat oven to 375°. Dissolve coffee granules in hot water. Stir in melted chocolate. Beat egg whites just until stiff moist peaks form. In separate bowl, beat butter and sugar until creamy. Beat in almond paste. Mix in egg yolks, chocolate mixture and flour. Fold in beaten egg whites. Spread into a greased and cocoa dusted 8" pan. Bake 30 minutes or until lightly browned. Do not overbake. Cool 10 minutes, then turn out. Cool. Prick cake with cake tester and sprinkle rum or liqueur on top. When cool, glaze with Chocolate Glaze. In a small saucepan, over very low heat, melt chocolate and shortening. Add rum to taste. Pour over cooled cake.

CHOCOLATE GLAZE:

6 ounces semisweet chocolate
1 tablespoon solid shortening
Rum

Very rich — serve with a light dinner.

CREAMY BLUEBERRY TREAT

9 servings

2½ cups graham cracker crumbs
½ cup softened butter
1 cup confectioners sugar
2 eggs
1 21-ounce can blueberry pie filling
1 cup chopped pecans
1 cup whipping cream whipped

Generously butter a 9″ square cake pan. Pat 1½ cups of crumbs evenly over bottom of pan. In a small bowl beat butter until fluffy. Add sugar gradually, beating until light and fluffy. Add eggs and blend well. Pour mixture carefully over crumb layer. Spread the pie filling over the butter-sugar mixture. Sprinkle nuts evenly over pie filling and top with whipped cream, spreading evenly. Sprinkle remaining graham cracker crumbs over top; cover and chill overnight. Cut into squares to serve.

Festive but fast!

EASY BLUEBERRY LEMON SAUCE

4 cups

1 22-ounce can lemon pie filling
1 15-ounce can blueberries, undrained
¼ teaspoon grated lemon peel
2 tablespoons lemon juice

Combine pie filling, undrained blueberries, lemon peel and lemon juice in mixing bowl. Pour into storage container, cover and chill thoroughly. Serve chilled with parfaits, lemon sherbert, vanilla pudding, cheesecake or pound cake.

Colorful as it is delicious!

DOUBLE APRICOT SAUCE

2½ cups

2 tablespoons cornstarch
½ cup sugar
1½ cups apricot nectar
1 tablespoon lemon juice
¾ teaspoon almond extract
1 cup chopped, drained, canned apricots

Blend cornstarch with sugar in saucepan; add nectar and heat, stirring constantly, until thickened. Add remaining ingredients and mix well. Serve warm or chilled over ice cream, sherbert or on waffles.

A versatile sauce you'll love serving.

🦃 DESSERT CHIMICHANGAS

1 dozen fresh flour tor-
tillas
Choice of fillings
(below)
1 egg white beaten with
2 teaspoons water
Salad oil
Powdered sugar

CHEESE AND RAISIN
FILLING:

6 cups (1½ pounds)
shredded Monterey
Jack cheese
1½ cups raisins
½ cup firmly packed
brown sugar

FRUIT PIE FILLING:

2 23-ounce cans fruit pie
filling

Stack the tortillas, moistening the outside of the top and bottom tortillas with a few drops of water. Wrap securely in foil and heat in a 350° oven for 15 minutes or until warm and pliable. Meanwhile prepare the filling of your choice. To make Cheese and Raisin Filling, combine cheese, raisins and brown sugar and mix well. For fruit pie filling, spoon off some of the fruit sauce, reserving only the fruit for the chimichangas. To assemble, work with one tortilla at a time, keeping others warm in foil. Spoon about ¼ cup of filling in a strip at one side of tortilla. Brush surface of tortilla with egg white mixture and fold tortilla around filling envelope-style, tucking in sides securely. Moisten ends with egg white mixture and lay seam-side down; let stand several minutes to allow egg white to dry and seal. To cook, put 1½ inches of salad oil in a 3-quart pan and heat to 375° on a deep-fat thermometer. Add two filled tortillas at a time and cook, turning until golden brown on both sides, about 2 minutes. Drain on paper towels. Sprinkle with powdered sugar and serve warm.

A dessert version of that savory snack specialty from northern Mexico.

DESSERT CHEESE CENTERPIECE

2 cups cream-style
cottage cheese
1 3-ounce package
cream cheese,
softened
2 ounces crumbled
bleu cheese
1 cup whipping cream
Lemon or Mint
leaves
Assorted crackers
Apple wedges
Sliced fresh pears
Lemon juice

Beat together cottage cheese, cream cheese, and blue cheese till smooth and creamy. Gradually beat in whipping cream, beating till thickened. Stand a colander in a bowl. Line colander with several thicknesses of cheesecloth. Pour in cheese mixture. Tie cheesecloth at top. Let drain overnight in refrigerator. Untie cloth; turn out onto plate. Remove cheesecloth. Decorate top of cheese with lemon leaves or mint leaves. Surround cheese with assorted crackers, and apples and pears brushed lightly with lemon juice or ascorbic acid color keeper.

INDEX

INDEX

341

SIMPLY SIMPÁTICO

The Junior League of Albuquerque, Inc.
2920 Yale Boulevard SE
Albuquerque, New Mexico 87106

Please send_____ copies of SIMPLY SIMPÁTICO at $10.50 plus $1.50 postage and handling per book.
☐ Check if gift wrapping at $.50 per book is desired.
Enclosed is my check for $_____ , payable to SIMPLY SIMPÁTICO.
NAME _____
STREET_____
CITY_____ STATE_____ ZIP_____

All copies will be sent to the same address unless otherwise specified. All proceeds will be used for community service projects sponsored by The Junior League of Albuquerque, Inc.

SIMPLY SIMPÁTICO

The Junior League of Albuquerque, Inc.
2920 Yale Boulevard SE
Albuquerque, New Mexico 87106

Please send_____ copies of SIMPLY SIMPÁTICO at $10.50 plus $1.50 postage and handling per book.
☐ Check if gift wrapping at $.50 per book is desired.
Enclosed is my check for $_____ , payable to SIMPLY SIMPÁTICO.
NAME _____
STREET_____
CITY_____ STATE_____ ZIP_____

All copies will be sent to the same address unless otherwise specified. All proceeds will be used for community service projects sponsored by The Junior League of Albuquerque, Inc.

SIMPLY SIMPÁTICO

The Junior League of Albuquerque, Inc.
2920 Yale Boulevard SE
Albuquerque, New Mexico 87106

Please send_____ copies of SIMPLY SIMPÁTICO at $10.50 plus $1.50 postage and handling per book.
☐ Check if gift wrapping at $.50 per book is desired.
Enclosed is my check for $_____ , payable to SIMPLY SIMPÁTICO.
NAME _____
STREET_____
CITY_____ STATE_____ ZIP_____

All copies will be sent to the same address unless otherwise specified. All proceeds will be used for community service projects sponsored by The Junior League of Albuquerque, Inc.

SIMPLY SIMPÁTICO

The Junior League of Albuquerque, Inc.
2920 Yale Boulevard SE
Albuquerque, New Mexico 87106

Please send_____ copies of SIMPLY SIMPÁTICO at $10.50 plus $1.50 postage and handling per book.
☐ Check if gift wrapping at $.50 per book is desired.
Enclosed is my check for $_____ , payable to SIMPLY SIMPÁTICO.
NAME _____
STREET_____
CITY_____ STATE_____ ZIP_____

All copies will be sent to the same address unless otherwise specified. All proceeds will be used for community service projects sponsored by The Junior League of Albuquerque, Inc.